The Author

Damien Simonis

Years ago, in one cold, snowy winter, Damien found himself in Siena, the medieval archrival of Florence and an extraordinary Tuscan enclave in itself. Although he had already travelled to various parts of the country, on and off assignment, this was his first foray 'under the Tuscan sun'. And so he learned about Florence through impressions coloured by the ancient antipathy of the Sienese towards their splendid competitor to the north. Indeed, his first contact with Florence was on a bus trip from Siena, and he found it a magnificent way to be introduced to the riverside capital of the Italian Renaissance.

Florence began to leave its indelible mark on Damien with further visits over the years and, while on assignment, he moved to a centuries-old garret on Via di San Niccolò in Florence. He remained longer than intended, and explored the unending nooks and crannies of this extraordinary city, soon discovering why this place is on just about everyone's list of must-visit cities in Italy. The only thing Damien doesn't understand is why it took him so long to fully discover Florence in the first place. Having abandoned the garret some years ago he still returns regularly, in order to face his fears of coming down with another case of Stendhalismo.

LONELY PLANET AUTHORS

Why is our travel information the best in the world? It's simple: our authors are independent, dedicated travellers. They don't research using just the Internet or phone, and they don't take freebies in exchange for positive coverage. They travel widely, to all the popular spots and off the beaten track. They personally visit thousands of hotels, restaurants, cafés, bars, galleries, palaces, museums and more – and they take pride in getting all the details right, and telling it how it is. For more, see the authors section on www.lonelyplanet.com.

Damien's Top Florence Day

A leisurely coffee and read of the paper at Gilli on Piazza della Repubblica is the perfect way to start the day. I can't resist a stroll up Via Roma, stopping to window shop along the way, into Piazza di San Giovanni and the adjacent Piazza del Duomo. The physical beauty of the city seems concentrated here, from the Baptistery to the Campanile. I just need an occasional reminder that it's real. From there, I like to meander through the busy pedestrian streets at the heart of old Florence to Piazza della Signoria, where the Uffizi and Palazzo Vecchio beckon – I can only tackle one of these a day! Sightseeing always induces hunger, so a quick stroll leads to good food at Gustavino. The Oltrarno works a special magic, so I can't help wandering across the Ponte alle Grazie and on to Porta San Miniato to follow the bucolic lane along the city walls towards the Forte di Belvedere, where the views over Florence are wonderful. Then it's time to get down to La Dolce Vita on Piazza del Carmine for an *aperitivo* (how about a Negroni?) before repairing to Ristorante Beccofino for a delicious dinner.

PHOTOGRAPHER

Juliet Coombe

As a full-time freelance travel photojournalist, Juliet has taken pictures which have appeared in more than 200 Lonely Planet guidebooks. She has won the prestigious British Guild of Travel Writers award for Travel Photographer of the Year. Her images have also been published in the *New York Times* and *Geographical* magazine. Juliet has had her fair share of challenges in getting the ultimate photograph, including being put in prison after being mistaken as a spy and walking with man-eating tigers in the jungles of Northern Thailand. She finds that, in Florence, everything is art, even the way they make their ice cream.

Julia is represented by Lonely Planet Images. Many of the images in this guide are available for licensing: www.lonelyplanetimages.com.

Lonely Planet Publications
Melbourne | Oakland | London

D0011365

Damien Simonis

Florence

The Top Five

1 Palazzo Vecchio
Admire the traditional seat of the Florentine government (p76)
2 Galleria dell'Accademia
Pop in to visit David or explore the intriguing exhibitions (p94)
3 Galleria degli Uffizi
Book ahead to see the great collection of Renaissance art (p70)
4 Duomo
Ascend the 436 steps of Brunelleschi's dome (p65)
5 Fiesole
View Florence from the old town of Fiesole (p110)

Published by Lonely Planet Publications Pty Ltd
ABN 36 005 607 983

Australia Head Office, Locked Bag 1, Footscray, Victoria 3011, ☎ 03 8379 8000, fax 03 8379 8111, talk2us@lonelyplanet.com.au

USA 150 Linden St, Oakland, CA 94607, ☎ 510 893 8555, toll free 800 275 8555, fax 510 893 8572, info@lonelyplanet.com

UK 72–82 Rosebery Ave, Clerkenwell, London, EC1R 4RW, ☎ 020 7841 9000, fax 020 7841 9001, go@lonelyplanet.co.uk

Contents

Introducing Florence

So many lookers in such a good-looking city! Naked like Michelangelo's *David* or rugged up in the latest winter fashion by their own world-class designers, Florentines and their city never fail to impress. Already in need of oxygen after admiring their art, visitors are mesmerised by the vision of locals at *aperitivo* time, effortlessly strutting, flirting and evidently enjoying life. At times it seems nothing much has changed since the days of the Medici.

Of course much *has* changed. Florence's short-lived stint as capital of Italy in 1865 was like a shot of adrenaline. The city bulldozed, constructed, rearranged avenues, wiped out whole quarters and tore down the medieval walls. And so the scene was set for the modern regional capital of Tuscany. Along the broad *viali* (avenues) that encircle old Florence a confusion of endless traffic tears around in chaotic style. Horns honk and brakes squeal as Florentines dart in and out of lanes in search of a break in the traffic. Ignorant of fear, *motorini* (moped) riders dash in and around larger vehicles, as if protected by some divine force.

The jewel of Renaissance Italy remains essentially what it was – a busy business centre. Even before the Renaissance was over, the wily Florentines had to concede that their town was on the wane, increasingly ignored on the European stage. But they never forgot their proud heritage and it was rediscovered in earnest by the rest of Europe from the late 18th century. Curious and admiring travellers, particularly the English, descended on the city as part of their Grand Tour. Ever canny with currency (after all, Florentines invented the florin, one of the most successful currencies in history),

LOWDOWN

Population 367,260

Time zone Central European Time (GMT + 1 hour)

3-star double room €150-200

Coffee at the bar Around €0.90

Cappuccino on Piazza della Repubblica €4.50

Takeaway pizza slice €1.50-3

Lampredotto (veal tripe in a bread roll) €3

Gelato (one or two flavours) €1.50-2.50

Motorini Keep an eye out for scooters, which flit all over town, often disregarding road rules

Bus ticket (single ride) €1

Shopping hours Many shops are closed on Monday until about 3.30pm

the locals knew how to cash in, as they still do, with utter aplomb.

The fortunate few get their first glimpse of Florence from the south. The road from rival Siena leads you to the heights backing the south bank of the Arno. Suddenly, through the trees, the glories of Florence burst into view – Giotto's Campanile (bell tower), Brunelleschi's dome, the Basilica di Santa Croce. Only the hardest of hearts can remain unaffected.

The memory of the Medici, who for centuries commanded the city's fortunes and were, as generous patrons, instrumental in unleashing the Renaissance, lives on. To this day the family crest of six balls adorns many public buildings. The city's artists and sculptors, supported by the Medici and other powerful families, regaled the city with their finest creations. Michelangelo, Leonardo, Donatello, Giotto, the Lippis, Masaccio, Botticelli, Pontormo and a host of others left their mark, and formidable galleries such as the Uffizi, Pitti and Accademia today house many of their works.

Medieval and Renaissance Florence was a financial powerhouse but it was never a romantic place. Its great families built fine mansions and lavished money on churches, public buildings and the arts, but not out of a love of beauty. To *display* greatness was to be great. The majesty of the Romanesque Baptistery, the Gothic Duomo and Renaissance basilicas was an advertisement as much of the power and wealth of Florence's leading families as of the city's artistic prowess. The families have gone, but the advertisements live on!

Florentines are born into a world of extraordinary timeless beauty, so it is hardly surprising that they cultivate their appearance, and do it so effortlessly. Home to the likes of Gucci and Ferragamo, Florence means one thing: style, both past and present. Phalanxes of stylish boutiques line up alongside the galleries and *palazzi*.

When the shops close, it's time to eat. Sit down to a simple Tuscan meal of tomato stew followed by prime steak in a family-run trattoria or splash out on one of the city's classic gourmet restaurants or stylish designer eateries. Florence is known for its top-grade Chianti, but you should make the acquaintance of other exquisite tipples too: Montalcino's Brunello, the Vino Nobile di Montepulciano and the more daring Super Tuscans.

You can easily explore Tuscany using Florence as a base: enjoy the medieval splendours of Siena, Pisa, Lucca and San Gimignano, and wander the undulating Chianti countryside.

City Life

City Life

Being the birthplace of the Renaissance followed by long years of slow decline into flaccid provincial quietude have helped preserve the old city centre as it was, giving visitors the feeling that time has stood still for centuries. But Florence is a bustling and prosperous regional capital, grown far beyond the one-time city walls. The entrepreneurial spirit of the Florentines' forefathers lives on in the small businesses that dominate today, from hi-tech in the suburbs to tourism in the centre. Florentines, beautiful people born in a beautiful place, take immense pride in their town's treasures and profit from them too. But there's more to the city than *David* and the Duomo.

FLORENCE TODAY

Since at least the 1980s, the town fathers have been asking themselves: whither Florence? The exponential growth in tourism, the increase in immigration (clandestine and other-wise) and the growing perception that the old centre of the city is less and less livable colour the thoughts of Florentines.

And so many are leaving. Florentines are nothing if not practical. Those with property in the centre are renting out at high prices and moving elsewhere, if not out of the city altogether. Well-off professionals prefer to live in the hills around Florence anyway. Those without property frequently cannot afford to live in the centre, even if they want to, because of the exorbitant rents fellow citizens are asking for.

Waiting for the green light in Florence

Although it may seem ridiculous to visitors from bigger and more dangerous cities, one reason Florentines cite for moving is the conviction that they live in an increasingly dangerous city. Crime, which many link to uncontrolled immigration, is up (but by the standards of many other cities is pretty minor) and at least some locals are nervous.

Various long-standing urban projects are finally getting underway, but they under-score a split vision for Florence. By moving much of the university campus, the law courts and other offices (see p18) to areas in the city's west, the town hall hopes to create new poles of activity in the city. Sceptics say the end result is that the old city is being further sacrificed to the tourists, as fewer residents will need to come to the city to do business. The old city, they say, is rapidly becoming a Renaissance Disneyland.

One of the many grumbles from those who choose to live elsewhere is that the fabric of life in the city is being torn apart. Fashion stores, gelaterie and pizza stands are gradually replacing myriad other shops that long served the local community. When Spanish fashion chain Zara landed smack in the middle of the city in 2004, alarm bells rang. In 2005 rules were put in place to discourage big brands from swallowing up small (often historic) shops with yet more (usually fashion-oriented) megastores.

HOT CONVERSATION TOPICS

- To some, Michelangelo's *David* has a rather diminutive member...a solemn Dutch study on the subject confirms that David is no John Holmes, but quite 'normal' for someone stressed by an upcoming battle with the giant Goliath!
- Will Isozaki's planned hypermodern exit for the Nuovi Uffizi ever get the thumbs up? Local hostility, opposition from Rome and archaeological considerations suggest it won't.
- Shopping for some will never be the same now that you risk fines of up to €10,000 for buying all those tempting fashion fakes on the city streets.
- The time has come to build a proper mosque for the city's Muslim population, but where?
- Will the rent problems of the city's historic century-old cafés (including Gilli and Rivoire) force them to close?
- Florence needs a refuse incineration plant, but no-one wants it in their backyard!
- Get those tanks out of the centre! A municipal rule means 4WDs with wheels of a diameter greater than 70cm may not enter the city.
- An unnamed clothing company had 15 rabbits confiscated at the summer Pitti Immagine Uomo fashion fair and was charged with cruelty to animals – a rabbit features on the firm's logo, but the authorities were not amused.

That kind of intervention from on high reflects one of the city's odder characteristics. A city of middle-class small-business owners, Florence has since the end of WWII been ruled by the communists and their successors (albeit often in coalition with other left-wing forces). With such conspicuous wealth and a keen appetite for making euros, the Florentines make strange communists indeed! But, as they will proudly tell you, left-wing Florence has one of the best public health systems in the country.

CITY CALENDAR

Florence is at its best in spring. Optimal months are April and May, when the air is crisp and clear, and several unique festivities take place. Summer, especially July and August, is best avoided as the stifling heat can be insufferable – which explains why most Florentines leave and half the restaurants are shut (especially during the central fortnight in August). The only advantage of August is that many hotels put on generous deals. The quietest period is winter, especially early December and most of January and February. It can be chilly and wet, but at least the number of tourists drops considerably. National public holidays are noted in the Directory (p211).

JANUARY

ANNO NUOVO (NEW YEAR'S DAY)
A peculiarly Florentine touch to the first day of the year is the *tradizionale uscita del primo dell'anno dei canottieri,* when the Società Canottieri Firenze rowing club organises a parade of boats along the Arno near the Ponte Vecchio.

BEFANA (EPIPHANY)
In Italy this is traditionally the day when children receive the gifts that in Anglo circles are distributed at Christmas. The weight of commercialisation has brought the attention on Christmas to Italy, but the parade of the Re Magi (Three Wise Men) on 6 January still captivates hordes of people on the day of the Befana.

PITTI IMMAGINE UOMO
www.pittimmagine.com
Held over four days around the middle of the month (10 to 13 January 2007) in the Fortezza da Basso and other locations around town, this is the most prestigious men's fashion catwalk in Italy. A week later it is the children's turn in Pitti Immagine Bimbo.

MARCH

CAPODANNO FIORENTINO (FLORENTINE NEW YEAR)
What Westerners take for granted as the start of the New Year (ie 1 January) has only been a widely accepted date since Pope Gregory XIII ushered in the Gregorian

calendar in 1582. Most Christian states enthusiastically adopted the new 'universal' system but Florence had to be different. Since early republican days Florentines celebrated New Year with the coming of spring on 25 March. They only adopted the January date in 1749! To this day many Florentines, although they don't really think of it as New Year's Day, flock to the Chiesa di SS Annunziata to celebrate 25 March. On the same day market stalls set up in the square before the church and since 2001 the town hall has organised colourful historical processions.

APRIL/MAY
SCOPPIO DEL CARRO (EXPLOSION OF THE CART)

For centuries the Florentines have 'distributed Holy Fire' to the populace in this festival on Easter Saturday. An ox-drawn cart, known as the *brindellone* (which refers to its rather wobbly nature) and laden with fireworks, is dragged from its permanent home on Via del Prato to the Duomo for the ceremony. From the high altar the archbishop lights the *colombina* (little dove), virtually a small rocket, which he then launches along a wire into the cart outside. The subsequent explosions last for several minutes. They have been using the same cart since the 18th century, but the tradition goes back to at least the 15th century. The origins are unclear. Some say Pazzino de' Pazzi, a hero returned from the First Crusade, started the tradition on the day before Easter by lighting a fire with stone flints from the Holy Sepulchre in Jerusalem given to him for his courage in battle. Others say the original *carro* was a war cart captured in Fiesole and exploded in victory celebrations.

FESTA DEL GRILLO

The Cricket Festival happens on Ascension Day (40 days after Easter). The crickets that once featured in this fair held in May in the Cascine no longer suffer any pain as a result of environmentalists' protests. Since 2001 only simple terracotta figurines or toy crickets have been allowed. To families who remember picnic scenes in which Dad would accompany kids in the search for a cricket or two in the fields, or simply purchasing them already in small cages to

then take to the Cascine, the modern city rules must have robbed some of the colour. Anyone selling the real McCoy risks a fine. Traditionally in this welcome to spring, men placed a (live) cricket at the door of their lovers, rather like a hunter bringing home a trophy. The origins of the tradition are obscure. 'Hunting' the critters on this feast day was long seen as a symbolic act. In 1582 a veritable cricket massacre took place as citizens tried to protect their crops from a cricket plague.

CELEBRAZIONI PER LA MORTE DI SAVONAROLA

On 23 May the death of the radical theocrat in 1498 is celebrated by a mass in the Palazzo Vecchio and parades in Piazza della Signoria.

MAGGIO MUSICALE FIORENTINO
www.maggiofiorentino.com

Starting in late April and spilling over into June, Florence's Musical May was inaugurated in 1933. It is a high point on the musical calendar, with top names performing opera, ballet and classical music at the Teatro Comunale (p154) and other venues across the city.

MOSTRA INTERNAZIONALE DELL'ARTIGIANATO
www.mostraartigianato.it

This prestigious expo of handmade products, of every possible type and colour, is held in Fortezza da Basso. Unfortunately the exhibits aren't for sale!

JUNE
FESTA DI SAN GIOVANNI

The *fuochi artificiali* (spectacular fireworks) let off around 10pm on 24 June in Piazzale Michelangelo on this feast day of Florence's patron saint, St John (San Giovanni), is one of the high points of the city's festivities. In the week starting that day, teams from the city's four historical districts battle it out in the Gioco del Calcio Storico (Historical Soccer Match) – a somewhat lawless series of centuries-old football-style games (see www.globeit /caf). This 'game' was first played in 1530 as a display of nonchalance on the part of the Florentines before troops of Emperor

TOP FIVE QUIRKY EVENTS

- **Capodanno Fiorentino (Florentine New Year)** 25 March
- **Scoppio del Carro (Explosion of the Cart)** Easter Sunday
- **Festa del Grillo (Cricket Festival)** May (Ascension Day)
- **Gioco del Calcio Storico (Historical Soccer Match)** Around 24 June
- **Festa della Rificolona (Paper Lantern Festival)** 7 September

FESTA DELL'UNITÀ

A politically oriented festival held in mid-July in the Fortezza da Basso, with left-wing parties, world music concerts and a fairground feel.

FIRENZESTATE

Throughout the broiling months of summer, the city hosts a rich palette of cultural events, ranging from outdoor cinema to music concerts. Many Florentines flee the city, but those who remain behind and the city's many summertime visitors are regaled with activities. See the boxed text, p150.

Charles V, who had the city under siege. A cross between football (soccer), rugby and boxing, each team of 27(!) aims to launch the ball into the opponents' side. There are no holds barred, so it can get pretty nasty on the field. Each match is preceded by a procession of 1000 people in traditional costume across town and into Piazza di Santa Croce, which becomes the pitch for the matches. The winner is awarded...a live Chianina calf (the meat of this breed is prized in Florence). The Società San Giovanni (St John Society) has been organising the festivities and dedicating itself to good works since it was constituted in 1796. Tickets can be bought in advance at Box Office (see p153) or at booths erected on the day at vantage points around Piazza di Santa Croce (€15 for a standard spot in the grandstands). Bring water!

PITTI IMMAGINE UOMO

The second round of this key men's fashion show is held over four days towards the end of the month (20 to 23 June 2007). It is followed a week later by Pitti Immagine Bimbo. See also p9.

JULY/AUGUST

FLORENCE DANCE FESTIVAL

www.florencedance.org

Since the late 1980s Florence has hosted this annual celebration of dance. The location changes from year to year and there is usually something for every taste, from classical ballet to modern. The **Florence Dance Centre** (Map pp248–9; ☎ 055 28 92 76; Borgo della Stella 23/r) has information.

SEPTEMBER/OCTOBER

FESTA DELLA RIFICOLONA (PAPER LANTERN FESTIVAL)

A procession of drummers, *sbandieratori* (flag-throwers), musicians and others in medieval dress winds its way from Piazza di Santa Croce to Piazza della SS Annunziata to celebrate the eve of Our Lady's supposed birthday on 7 September. Children with *rificolone* (paper lanterns) accompany them. Smaller processions for kids and their families are organised in other quarters of the city too. On 8 September, for one day only, the walkway around the sides and façade of the Duomo is opened to the public.

CHIANTI WINE HARVEST FESTIVALS

Several Chianti towns have festivals at the time of the wine harvest. You need to ask at the Azienda di Promozione Turistica office (APT; p218) or check the local papers for details.

FRINGE FESTIVAL

The city stages a modest fringe theatre festival as Florentines get back into the swing of things after the summer holidays. Ask at the Azienda di Promozione Turistica office (APT; p218) for information.

RASSEGNA INTERNAZIONALE MUSICA DEI POPOLI

Local and international musicians come together to perform traditional and ethnic music from all over the world in this festival, which lasts for a month. Many of the performances are held in the Auditorium Flog (p151).

BIENNALE DELL'ANTIQUARIATO
www.mostraantiquariato.it
Every odd-numbered year this prestigious event is held in Palazzo Strozzi. It's an opportunity to search for high-quality antique furniture, paintings, jewellery and a host of other antique objects.

NOVEMBER
FIRENZE MARATHON
www.firenzemarathon.it
If you feel the urge to dash around Florence you can be part of the marathon towards the end of November. The finish line is in Piazza di Santa Croce where, the day after the race, prizes are awarded to the winners.

DECEMBER
FESTIVAL DEI POPOLI
www.festivaldeipopoli.org
An annual film and documentary event, the week-long Festival dei Popoli brings the world to the Florentines' doorstep. Prizes are awarded for national and international documentaries with a sociocultural content.

CULTURE
IDENTITY

The Florentines have an elusive slant to their character, which can be expected in a provincial capital inundated by a constant stream of tourists. In a city with a total population of 368,000, it is estimated about 20,000 new visitors stream into the old city every day. Outsiders are treated affably enough but Florentines take a certain haughty pride in their city, basking in the reflected glory of its splendid past and simply letting the hordes from outside wash by.

The spectacular rise of modern tourism in Florence and throughout Tuscany since the 1960s has helped inject unprecedented wealth into a city that had, since before the final fall of the Medici, sunk into decay and considerable poverty. That wealth has made Florence one of the most expensive cities in Italy.

A good-looking lot by birth and surrounded by natural and manmade beauty, Florentines like to look their best. They may vote communist, but Florence isn't a drab old Stalinist town! As long ago as the Middle Ages, Dante took his countrymen to task for their obsession with dressing well. Indeed, Florentines seem to oscillate between a certain flippancy and a deeply rooted sense of proportion and responsibility.

Local Florentines taking in the daily news

If Florentines are small 'c' communists, they are equally small 'c' conservatives. Enjoying the good life, they are attentive to business, money, family and lifelong friends. Wealth is passed down carefully from generation to generation. Few would allow themselves the frivolity of whittling away even modest family fortunes.

No-one would claim Florence was a multicultural place. But for decades it has attracted Italians from all over the peninsula to study and work, and not a few foreigners have been so bewitched by the city's beauty that they have elected to make Florence home.

Since the late 1980s, like the rest of Italy, Florence has also attracted its fair share of new migrants from Africa (Tunisia, Nigeria and Senegal), the Balkans, China and more recently South America. About a tenth of the city's legal residents are now foreigners, and indeed it is thanks to immigration that the city population remains stable. A report in mid-2005 estimated that the migrant population would continue to grow, reaching 12% of the Tuscan population in general by 2020, and considerably more in Florence and other cities.

The number of *clandestini* (illegal immigrants) is difficult to estimate and integration is not proving easy. People traffickers have lined the boulevards beyond the city with African and East European prostitutes. Dark claims are made about the growth of an Albanian mafia and floods of Chinese and Russian mafia money (in addition to that of home-grown Italian mafia groups) being laundered in the city.

Still, in a rare moment of cross-party unity, appeals in the town hall to allow the construction of a mosque for the city's growing Muslim community were supported by all in mid-2005. Given how long it usually takes to get things done here, it could be a while before the call to prayer wafts over the rooftops of Florence. Call to prayer or no, the Muslims are probably a good deal more attached to their religion than the average Florentine to his or hers. About 85% claim to be Catholics, but the city has for centuries had a diffident relationship with the Church, hardly surprising given its postwar political orientation.

For many years, Rom and Sinti families from Albania and Kosovo have lived in two precarious makeshift settlements on the west side of the city. After years of stand-off, the municipality has opted to (slowly) improve the housing and living conditions in the camps and incorporate them into the city.

LIFESTYLE

Voted Italy's most livable city in 2003 by Italy's prestige finance newspaper, *Il Sole 24 Ore*, Florence offers its inhabitants an enviable provincial lifestyle.

During the week, the city works. As many as 113,000 commuters enter the city centre each day from the suburbs and surrounding towns. Many others work in the industrial areas in the west of the city. Small businesses dominate the Florentine scene (see p16).

At the end of the working day, locals love to while away the early evening over an *aperitivo* (a drink or two with bar snacks), a great way to unwind after the stress of the day. This has become especially important as fewer and fewer Florentines have the time for a traditional long lunch – frequently replaced by a quick plate of pasta at bars dotted around the centre.

Florentines like to get out of the city. They think nothing of driving out of town to dine in trattorias in surrounding towns. Those who stay behind party in bars and clubs away from the centre (such as the clubs in the Le Cascine).

More affluent Florentines keep a country house, more often than not to the south of town, where they seek peace and quiet on weekends. Others are not averse to summer traffic jams to get to (and from) the Tuscan beaches around Viareggio, some 100km away. In winter they switch swimming costumes for ski gear and head for the moderate Abetone slopes north of Pistoia.

What local students know simply as *la facoltà* (the faculty) is an important element in Florentine life. The prestigious Università degli Studi di Firenze traces its history back to the Studium Generale established in 1321. Today the Florentine facilities are known above all for their fine-arts and architecture faculties. Many faculties have been drawn together in the Nuovo Polo Universitario campus at the ex-FIAT works in the Novoli district.

FASHION

Florentines have been dressing up and looking good for centuries. Wool, silk and textiles have been a pillar of the local economy since the 14th century. The nearby town of Prato indeed remains a centre of textile production. And although Florence has largely taken a back seat to Milan, it was the city on the Arno that launched Italy's postwar challenge to the fashion hegemony of Paris. In 1951 the city staged Italy's first modest international fashion show. Though by the 1970s women's *haute couture* and many big names had moved to Milan, Florence today remains host to the world's biggest men's fashion meet. Hundreds of Italian and foreign designers crowd into the city for Pitti Immagine Uomo, held in January and June (see p9 and p10 for dates). About a week after the prestigious men's event follows the three-day Pitto Immagine Bimbo expo for fashion-addicted kids.

The glittering capital of Italian fashion (Milan) may be where the money is, but some of the biggest names in the business remain resolutely Florentine. Salvatore Ferragamo (p165), which started off as king of the shoe business, is nowadays a multi-million-dollar business that spans signature suits and ties to watches. While Ferragamo had kept it all in the family, that other (in)famous label, Gucci (see the boxed text, below), is alive in name only; part of the much larger international conglomerate, it has somewhat lost its way since designer Tom Ford left the firm in 2003.

Both giants tend to produce classic fashion whereas other smaller local designers are more adventurous. Roberto Cavalli (p166) doesn't mind going out on a limb. From fur to sexy silk, from crocodile skin jackets to leopard skin themes, Cavalli exudes a youthful verve matched to some extent by relative newcomers like Ermanno Scervino (p164), who only emerged with his young fashions in the 1990s.

These and many other companies have their materials produced in the area around Florence. The bulk of textile production takes place in Prato, to the west, while half of the leather used in Florentine fashions is made south of Florence in the Valdarno area. Overall, some 15,000 firms are devoted to the fashion industry in the province of Florence, employing 100,000 people. The annual turnover is estimated at €200 million. About half of fashion and textile exports go to EU countries, and a quarter to Japan.

That Florence remains a force in fashion is demonstrated by the presence in the city of the Istituto Politecnico Internazionale della Moda (Map pp240–1; ☎ 055 73 99 61; www.polimoda .it; Via Pisana 77), a major fashion-design school founded in 1986. It has links with New York's Fashion Institute of Technology and for many is an obligatory stop on the route to education as a world-class designer.

Amid the furore over the big names, it is easy to forget that Florence is full of local artisans. When it comes to shoes and other leather goods, in particular, modest workshops still turn out first-class handmade products. Florentines are full of ideas. Catching on to a nascent trend, Giuditta Blandini has established the concept of organic fashion in her shop in Oltrarno (see Stile Biologico, p170).

FAMILY FEUD

The Gucci name is just that, a name. Taken over by the French Pinault Printemps Redoute distribution company in 2004 from the Bahrain Investcorp group, the brand has survived where its founding family has not.

Guccio Gucci founded a modest saddlery store in Florence in 1904 and soon involved his five sons. A difficult character, he tended to encourage rivalry among his sons, which would mark the history of the company. In 1938 Aldo founded Gucci's first Rome store and invented the company's double G logo. In the following decades, led by brothers Aldo and Rodolfo, and Aldo's son Paolo, the company expanded rapidly across Europe and the Middle East. But infighting saw all three depart from the scene, leaving the way open for Rodolfo's son, Maurizio, who gathered in the reins of the company and then sold the lot to Investcorp in 1993. He was gunned down two years later, a murder for which his angry ex-wife Patrizia, known affectionately as the Black Widow, was found guilty.

Texan fashion designer Tom Ford had been Gucci's fashion star since 1990. His departure in 2003 has ushered in a period of uncertainty for the company, whose identity has been watered down by the acquisition of other fashion houses, including Sergio Rossi, Yves Saint Laurent, Bottega Veneta, Stella McCartney, Balenciaga, Alexander McQueen and Boucheron.

SPORT

An earthquake shook the Florentine football world in the torrid summer of 2002. The AC Fiorentina club's owner, cinema impresario and former senator Vittorio Cecchi Gori, went into bankruptcy after a financial scandal that broke the previous year, leaving the *viola* (the 'purples') immersed in debt. The club disappeared from the face of Italian football, was reborn under the name Florentia Viola, and was obliged to start life in the lowly C2 division. When the going gets tough... In 2004–05 the side had recovered its original name and was back in the first division, albeit finishing the season fifth from the bottom.

Back in 1931, AC Fiorentina entered Serie A (the premier league). The side has won only two shields, in 1955–56 and 1968–69. On the other hand, it has taken the Coppa Italia (Italy Cup) six times, the last in 2001, just before the brown stuff hit the fan. For match information see p156.

North of the city, the Mugello race track hosts numerous car and motorcycle racing events throughout the year. See p156 for details.

Some Florentines like to profit from the Arno by heading out for a good row. Although rowing's a minority activity, two riverside clubs cater to this pursuit and one, the Società Canottieri Firenze, has a distinguished competition record.

In winter, Florentines who can't afford or can't be bothered heading north for the Alps get in their ski thrills at Abetone, north of Pistoia on the regional frontier with Emilia-Romagna. Surfing and windsurfing are increasingly popular on the Tuscan coast, such as at the nippy Golfo Baratti to the southwest.

See p155 for tips on sports activities in town.

A football match on the banks of the Arno

MEDIA

You can get all the national newspapers and many foreign ones at newsstands all over central Florence. The local media scene is decidedly small town. *La Nazione,* long a venerable right-wing broadsheet, is now a colour tabloid. Founded in 1859, it hired Alexandre Dumas as its war correspondent to follow Garibaldi's exploits in Sicily in 1860, but many would say those glory days are long past. Its main competition comes from the Florence insert in *La Repubblica,* closely identified with the left. Nastier tongues claim the insert is a mouthpiece for the town hall, although close reading would seem to contradict this. A racier tabloid competitor is *Il Corriere di Firenze.* For more on newspapers and magazines in Florence, see p214.

LANGUAGE

Florence may have sent Dante Alighieri into exile but it still likes to bask in his reflected glory. He is generally credited with breathing life into a serious, literary Italian language at a time when Latin still held sway in learned discourse. And so Florentine, or more generally Tuscan, is enthusiastically held up as the pre-eminent example of 'good' Italian. Whatever the merits of the claim, a modern standardised language only really started to gain ground in the 19th century. The Milanese novelist Alessandro Manzoni struggled with Tuscan to lend his writing a more broadly national appeal in his seminal work, *I Promessi Sposi* (The Betrothed). The modern media have, since the close of WWII, really taken a standardised Italian into the hearts and minds of Italians up and down the peninsula. And the Florentine variant? It has a rather husky, full flavour to it and a couple of quirks that set it apart from the standard language and

15

other regional accents and dialects. The most notable is the conversion of the hard 'c' into a heavily aspirated 'h'. *Voglio una Coca Cola con cannuccia* (I want a Coca Cola and a straw) in Florentine becomes *Voglio una Hoha Hola hon hannuccia*. See the Language chapter, p221.

ECONOMY & COSTS

In 1189 Florence gave the world the silver florin *(fiorino)*, and much later double-entry book-keeping and the cheque. From medieval times Florentines were considered the masters of international commerce.

Nowadays Florence and its province form a relatively prosperous part of Italy, albeit with some concerns about the future. Figures differ, but tourism accounts for about 30% of the city's wealth, and industry 27%. Florence is typical of Italy in that the bulk of activity is in the hands of small businesses. On a grander scale, the troubled US multinational General Electric (whose European base is in Florence) runs the Pignone machinery plants, which turn out turbines and related equipment. Chemicals and pharmaceuticals are also present, with Boehringer choosing Florence to set up a new plant in the early 2000s.

Textiles and fashion are important in Florence and adjacent Prato. Of the 105,000 people employed in industry in Florence, a third are in this sector, which is now under threat from tough competition from cheap Chinese imports.

Although still embryonic, as many as 4000 small firms, mostly in the city's west, are dedicated to hi-tech ventures. In Sesto Fiorentino, the Polo Scientifico is the city's research nerve centre. It includes the Centro Nazionale per le Ricerche (CNR, or National Research Centre) and several specialised research centres (including the European Magnetic Resonance Centre).

Although Italy's sluggish economy has created a sense of crisis in Florence, things are not so bad. Officially, unemployment is at 4.2%, well below the national average of 9.5% (and figures in excess of 20% for much of the country's south).

HOW MUCH?

Pizza €6-10

Good midrange meal (including wine) €30-45

Uffizi admission €6.50

Litre of mineral water €1-2

One day's bicycle hire €12

Dance club admission €10-20

Letter (20g) within Europe €0.62

Litre of petrol €1.10-1.15

Bus to Pisa airport €7.50

Cocktail €6-8

GOVERNMENT & POLITICS

Ever since the end of WWII, Tuscany, a hotbed of the Italian resistance, has remained loyal to the Partito Comunista Italiano (PCI). The party's 1990s name change to Democratici di Sinistra (DS; Democrats of the Left) did nothing to change Tuscan voting habits. The DS has also maintained uninterrupted control of Florence, often in coalition.

Florentines have kept the present *sindaco* (mayor), Leonardo Domenici, in power since 1999 (next elections due in 2009) but not because he inspires great sympathy. Considered distant and more interested in cultivating fellow politicians than chatting with citizens, he nevertheless has not been short on ideas. Under his mandate various urban projects are finally taking shape, ranging from the TAV high-speed train line and station and planned tram lines, through to imperfect urban development programmes and measures to shelter the historic centre from the excesses of city's traffic problems (see opposite).

The young, dapper and ambitious Domenici is quick to underline his busy devotion to the city, but he has his eye on bigger things. Head of the Associazione Nazionale dei Comuni d'Italia (ANCI), he already enjoys a high national profile. A protégé of the key national party boss Massimo D'Alema, Domenici is almost assured of a role in the national government if the left-wing coalition wins the next national elections in April–May 2006.

THE DIVISION OF POWER

Florence is the capital of Tuscany (Toscana to the Italians), one of the 20 regions into which the country is divided. It is bound to the west by the Ligurian Sea and to the north by the region of Emilia-Romagna, with which it shares a good chunk of the Apennines. To the east and south, Tuscany borders Le Marche, Umbria and Lazio.

The Tuscan region is divided into 10 provinces, each named after its respective capital: Florence (Firenze), Prato, Pistoia, Lucca, Massa, Pisa, Livorno, Siena, Grosseto and Arezzo. These are subdivided into local administrative *comuni* (districts).

The *comune* of Florence takes in a small area, falling short of Amerigo Vespucci airport in the west and extending about 4km east of Ponte Vecchio along the Arno. At its southernmost point it reaches only 2km south of Palazzo Pitti. To the northwest, and into the *comune* of Sesto Fiorentino especially, the city sprawl goes on and on. Heading clockwise from Sesto are the *comuni* of Fiesole, Bagno a Ripoli and Scandicci.

From medieval times the city (which until one and a half centuries ago was largely confined to the area within the last set of city walls) was subdivided in various ways. From 1343 the *comune* was a system of *quartieri* (quarters), three on the north bank (Santa Maria Novella, San Giovanni and Santa Croce) and one on the south (Oltrarno or Santo Spirito). Nowadays the *comune* is made up of five local councils *(quartieri)*. They are: Centro Storico, Campo di Marte, Gavinana-Galluzo, Isolotto-Legnaia and Rifredi-Le Piagge.

ENVIRONMENT

THE LAND

The Romans founded Florence at a strategic point on the Arno, approximately 85km inland from the Tuscan coast. Even this far from the Mediterranean, the river was still navigable but crossing was not arduous. Since the settlement was also perfectly placed to give access to three passes north across the Apennines, Roman Florentia was well positioned as a trade centre.

The Arno rises in the Tuscan Apennines near Monte Falterona, describes an arc south towards Arezzo and then heads northwest to Florence. From there it winds westwards, emptying out into the Mediterranean about 11km west of Pisa. In all it is about 240km long. On a quiet day it is hard to imagine it thundering down from the east, crashing into the city, sweeping away bridges and leaving countless dead. And yet it has done so repeatedly. In 1177 and 1333 floods swept away the Ponte Vecchio's predecessors, and some thought the same would happen in 1966.

The original Roman camp *(castrum)* lay on the north bank, and the bulk of the city has developed there for the simple reason that the valley is relatively wide and flat on that side of the river.

The foothills of the Apennines reach down to within 10km of the Arno and closer still on the eastern side of the city. As a consequence, the bulk of the suburban sprawl has been channelled west towards Prato.

South of the Arno, development is more limited. Historically the hills crowding up to the river allowed urban spread only within a rough triangle bounded by Porta Romana (Roman Gate), Ponte Amerigo Vespucci and Ponte alle Grazie.

In the past century the westward march of suburban expansion on the north bank has to some extent been mirrored to the south with the development of areas such as the factory zone of Pignone and Isolotto.

GREEN FLORENCE

Florence's biggest environmental problems are air pollution and garbage disposal. Intense traffic in the city remains the principal cause of the former, although a variety of measures means that people breathe a little easier in the old centre. The introduction of a growing number of buses using natural gas and others on types of diesel with reduced emissions has helped. Three regular electric minibus lines traverse the centre of the city. Plans to build three tramlines (see p18) may help reduce car traffic beyond the city centre.

A system of cameras was set up around the old city in 2004 (more are being installed) to control the flow of inward traffic. The cameras photograph all cars that enter and those unauthorised are automatically sent a €50 fine (some say these reach foreign visitors too). Traffic in the centre has dropped off noticeably. Small electric vehicles are exempt and more than 100 free recharging points have been set up across the city. Several companies renting out small electric vehicles have popped up as a result.

Still, the clatter and splutter of two-stroke engines on *motorini* (mopeds) goes on unchecked throughout the city! Indeed, it is estimated that the density of vehicles per capita in Florence is one of the highest in Europe. Some 200,000 *motorini* alone help clog Florence's roads.

The collection and elimination of refuse is a major problem. Although there are large bins for the separated collection of rubbish (paper, glass, plastic etc) around town, collection is uneven. In 2005 a decision was finally made to build an incinerator in northwest Florence, a project clearly not appreciated by the 40,000 inhabitants in the area. Until now the city has had to pay for refuse to be transported for destruction in other provinces – an expensive and inefficient business. Concerns over dioxin emissions from the incinerator have been dismissed by those who claim modern plants are low-risk.

Another problem is pesky animals. Although not as serious as Venice's pigeon plague, Florence has a fair-sized problem and the town authorities are forever trying to work out how to clip the pigeon population's wings. Of greater concern is the *norvegicus* rat, a beast the size of a small cat, weighing up to 3kg. These charmers live in the sewerage pipes and along riverbanks and streams.

URBAN PLANNING & DEVELOPMENT

The unchecked urban and suburban sprawl, fuelled by land speculation that seems to leave successive city governments helpless, has greatly depleted any sense of green in Florence. This is particularly so north of the river, although a few parks and patches remain, above all the Parco delle Cascine (p80). As if by a miracle, large parts of the Oltrarno are still a haven. Aside from the Giardino di Boboli and other gardens, south of the walls protecting Via di San Niccolò you can wander almost immediately into what to all intents and purposes is a stretch of countryside, dotted with villas and kept productive with the fruit of the vine.

It has been said that in Florence the last great public work carried out was the Santa Maria Novella train station in 1935! Not that people haven't been thinking about it. As far back as the 1980s, ambitious plans were on the table and largely shot down (see p48). Fifteen years later, the city seems to have finally started to wake up from its long urban sleep, although with uneven results. The former FIAT factories have been torn down and replaced with new university faculties (most of which have moved from central Florence), housing, offices and parkland. Much of it is still not completed. The biggest problem is the still unfinished Palazzo di Giustizia (law courts). The design was approved in the 1970s, and may be completed in 2007! The grand plans for the Castello area in the city's northwest have been resurrected in reduced form. The seats of the provincial and regional governments will probably be built there, along with a huge new national training school for *carabinieri* officers, 1500 houses and offices.

Public transport is also moving…slowly. In 1992 it was decided to build tramlines in Florence. The first might be finished in…2008. Two more lines linking the train station with the airport and Careggi hospital are on the drawing board. Another project that has been decades in coming is the high-speed train (TAV) link between Rome and Milan via Florence. The tunnel through the Mugello, north of Florence, was completed amid protests from environmentalists who predicted, rightly it appears, that the route would disrupt watercourses and so affect local wildlife. In the city, authorities planned to build new underground platforms at the Santa Maria Novella station, but this would have meant the tunnel to cross the city would have passed beneath the Duomo, a risk no-one wanted to take. Now Sir Norman Foster has won a competition for a brand-new station north of the Fortezza da Basso (see p26).

While many Florentines are abandoning the city centre, either because it is too expensive or simply because it is too complicated, others with a touch of luck are moving in. The conversion in 2004 of the former Alle Murate jails in Santa Croce into charming, though small, estate housing flats has allowed a lucky group of low-income earners to get low rent–controlled housing in the city's historic centre.

Arts & Architecture ∎

Arts & Architecture

In 1982 Unesco decided to make things easy on itself and simply declared the entire old city of Florence one big World Heritage site – since it was pointless trying to single out certain quarters or works! Most art-lovers think of Florence, quite rightly, as the launch-pad of the Rinascimento – better known in English by its French translation, the Renaissance (literally 'rebirth', which doesn't sound nearly so groovy). This extraordinary period of artistic, literary and scientific creativity sprouted roots in the 14th century and spanned much of the 15th and 16th centuries, but it's not the sum of Florentine beauty; much came before and a good deal after.

In the Renaissance, a rediscovery of classical writings (especially those of the Greek philosophers) and imperial Roman art and architecture awakened a curiosity in young thinkers and artists. Instead of attributing everything to God, people began to search for human explanations and to explore the natural world more scientifically, rather than with superstitious minds. The Church, anxious to maintain its tight social control in the Christian world through a monopoly of 'acceptable' knowledge and doctrine, rode uneasily with this; it embraced the artistic flourishes, while viewing warily the scientific developments, which were regarded as bordering on heresy.

Buontalenti's fountain, Piazza de' Frescobaldi

The blossoming of the Renaissance in Florence, earlier than elsewhere, coincided largely with its wealth. By the time Cosimo de' Medici returned from exile to Florence in 1434, the city was one of Europe's most prosperous trading and banking centres. The money was there to invest in art and the city's senior families were eager to splash out on improving their own and the city's image.

Indeed, those with dosh were considered honour-bound to lavish some of it on the prestige of the city. The mercantile dynasties had, in the past, subscribed to the building of the great churches – including the Duomo, Santa Maria Novella and Santa Croce – no doubt hoping to do their souls some good. Cosimo de' Medici once said: 'I shall never be able to give God enough to set him down in my books as a debtor.' This habit of patronage continued into the Renaissance.

Architects, painters and sculptors were often masters of more than one medium. Leonardo da Vinci is best known as a scientist and yet was a great painter; Michelangelo is revered as a sculptor but was just as deft with the brush, and some architects started out as goldsmiths.

Tuscany was rich in the raw materials for sculpture and building. The white marble of Carrara still attracts sculptors, while the green marble used mainly in the façades of great buildings was quarried in the hills around nearby Prato. Pink marble came from the Maremma district in southwest Tuscany. Various kinds of stone were quarried in and around Florence itself, including the dun-coloured *pietra forte* ('strong stone') that characterises the exterior of so many great Florentine buildings. From the 13th century

WHY FIX IT IF IT AIN'T BROKE?

In 2002 the Uffizi made a historic move by deciding *not* to restore Leonardo da Vinci's unfinished *Adorazione dei Magi* (Adoration of the Magi; see p70). International outcry in the art world led the gallery to reverse its restoration plans, although one feels it was rather half-heartedly. Gallery officials had maintained that the wood on which the painting is done was deteriorating, and paint was coming away. The back down came after a similar decision by the Paris Louvre, regarding da Vinci's *Mona Lisa*, and perhaps all were influenced by the hullabaloo that surrounded the 1999 restoration of Leonardo's *Cenacolo* (Last Supper) in Milan. The arguments are complex. In the case of Leonardo, his painting mixes and methods seem to be particularly prone to damage over time, and those in favour of the restorations say that his works will fade to nothing if nought is done to save them. Detractors say the restorers often destroy the nature of the works, creating something that bears no resemblance to the original – although, of course, no-one can know what the original of a 500-year-old painting looked like when just finished!

Much the same international outcry greeted plans to give Michelangelo's statue of *David* (p70), one of Florence's emblems, a cleansing bath after 10 years' painstaking study of the subject. A public spat in 2003 about how to go about it only whipped up further international displeasure. In that case, though, the work was done in 2004 and *David* got a nice bath in wet poultices; whether or not he needed it is another issue altogether.

To many, the argument may seem an esoteric storm in a teacup (and probably is), but what is most curious is the increasing wave of protest against restoration, after half a century in which it was all the rage. The seeds for the restoration frenzy were sown in the tragic events of 4 November 1966. As enormous high tides inundated Venice to the north, torrential rain swelled the banks of the Arno to create the worst flooding Florence had known in centuries. Both cities, two of the world's greatest treasure chests of human creativity, lay covered in grime and mud. The damage to art and buildings was incalculable. Many fine works were destroyed, countless more seriously damaged.

Something good had to come from so much misery and, as aid poured in from Rome and abroad in the following years, Florence and Venice became world leaders in the business of art restoration. A whole new science was created and methods were revolutionised. The fruits of the enormous labour in those two cities have since been applied to countless other works in need of repair elsewhere. Students from around the globe come to Florence to learn the trade, many to the Istituto Specializzato per il Restauro, established in 1975 in the premises of the centuries-old Opificio delle Pietre Dure (p97).

The niceties of modern restoration do provoke a chuckle. To think that in the 19th century *David* survived a good old-fashioned acid bath! Or that for several centuries earlier the statue had cheerfully withstood the elements and the occasional riot in Piazza della Signoria. Few (if any) visitors who have beheld the statue down the decades have been struck by *David's* dirtiness – they are too mesmerised by his beauty. And let's face it, his creator Michelangelo wasn't too keen on baths either!

this became the most commonly used material in civic and private construction and the Boboli quarry was one of its handiest sources. The stone par excellence of the Renaissance though, was the grey *pietra serena* ('tranquil stone') used mainly for interiors. Brunelleschi propelled the use of this easily worked stone to prominence.

Less remembered by those who do not read Italian is the literary flowering that preceded and accompanied the Renaissance. The use of Italian in literature, to replace Latin, can be attributed to Tuscan writers – above all, Florence's Dante Alighieri.

The Renaissance came to an end with mannerism, however, and by the time baroque was in vogue Florence was in decline. Reduced to a backwater in European politics and finance, the city seemed equally uninspired in the arts. Brief bursts, notably that of the French Impressionist–inspired Macchiaioli, attracted the spotlight back to the city in the 19th century, and the occasional great writer has emerged, but the arts never regained the pre-eminent position they held at the height of Florence's golden age.

ARCHITECTURE

Until the late Gothic period, and early into the Renaissance, little credit was given to the master builders behind the churches and bell towers, the palaces and castles that were raised in Italy and Europe. They were treated as tradesmen and not as creative stars. Even the masters behind the Duomo and its breathtaking bell tower, Arnolfo di Cambio and Giotto, barely got a passing mention.

One of the odd things about much Italian church architecture is that façades were often tacked onto the body as if in afterthought (and sometimes subsequently changed to meet new tastes). The Duomo and the Basilica di Santa Croce only got their façades in the 19th century and many other Florentine churches never received theirs. It appears money was frequently hard to come by for this final touch.

ROMANESQUE

As Florence recovered from the centuries of barbarian invasions, wars, devastation and confusion that ensued from the fall of the Roman Empire, its people could devote some energy to public building.

From the northern Lombard plains a modest building style, now known as Romanesque, began to spread across much of Europe from the 7th century.

The standard church ground plan – generally composed of a high nave and two aisles, no transept and between one and five apses, topped by a simple bowl-shaped cupola – followed that used in Roman-era basilicas. Initially, churches tended to be bereft of external decoration (inside, the walls and columns were frequently covered in murals or mosaics, mostly long since disappeared) except for the semicircular arches above doorways and windows. The apses tended to be semicircular too.

In Tuscany, the presence of invaluable marble quarries led to a more florid decorative style, the best examples of which can be seen in Pisa and Lucca. The key characteristics are the use of two-tone marble banding and complex rows of columns and loggias in the façade.

At the heart of old Florence emerged what remains one of the city's loveliest buildings – the Baptistery (p63) dedicated to St John (San Giovanni). Although its marble-banded façade dates to the 11th century, the building could have been preceded by others as far back as the 5th century and some see it as a direct link to Roman Florentia, as it is surmised a Roman temple once stood here. However, the finest example of Florentine Romanesque is the Chiesa di San Miniato al Monte (p103), high up on a hillside south across the Arno.

GOTHIC

The slow transition across Europe from Romanesque to soaring Gothic was uniformly spectacular but extraordinarily varied. In Florence it brought much destruction, as many preceding Romanesque structures were razed to make way for the new.

More daring building techniques, born of greater skill and a desire to more fully express human devotion to God, spurred the development of this new style. The first examples went up in the Île-de-France in the 12th century.

Examples of the north-European style of Gothic are rare in Italy, and nonexistent in Florence. The city's two great Gothic churches, aside from the Duomo, are Santa Croce and Santa Maria Novella, built for the dominant mendicant orders of the time, respectively the Franciscans and the Dominicans.

In terms of volume they are as impressive as their northern European counterparts and inside the Basilica di Santa Maria Novella (p78), which was designed by Dominican friars, you can admire the complex ribbed vaulting of the main ceiling above the nave. But there end the similarities. Decoration is minimal and the bicolour banding that edges arches and vaults is a Tuscan touch.

The Basilica di Santa Croce (p98) was designed by Siena-born Arnolfo di Cambio (c 1245–1302), the first great master builder in Florentine history. It shares with Santa Maria Novella the broad nave and simplicity of interior decoration but, in contrast to the Dominican church, an A-frame timber ceiling (a carena) obscures the roof vaulting. The privileged position given to uncovered stone is reminiscent of the Gothic of northern Europe.

> ## TOP FIVE BUILDINGS
>
> - **Duomo** (p65) The extraordinary Gothic cathedral.
> - **Palazzo Medici-Riccardi** (p92) The proud Renaissance home of Florence's most powerful family.
> - **Palazzo Vecchio** (p76) The centuries-old fortified seat of municipal power.
> - **Chiesa di San Miniato al Monte** (p103) The city's finest example of Romanesque architecture.
> - **Ponte Vecchio** (p107) Florence's emblematic medieval bridge

Florence was not a town of pious churchgoers. Just as the Gothic style took hold, the city was emerging as a vibrant republic. The land-holding nobles had ceded ground to increasingly wealthy burghers who came to exercise corporate power in Florence. Such a nascent governing municipal institution required a suitable home as much as the Church did, and so Arnolfo received the commission to design the Palazzo Vecchio (known when it was built as Palazzo dei Priori and later as Palazzo della Signoria; p76) in 1299. Built of *pietra forte*, with the rusticated surface typical of many grand buildings in Florence, it is one of the most imposing government buildings of the medieval Italian city-states.

Arnolfo also designed the Gothic Duomo (aka Santa Maria del Fiore – the flower being the red lily emblem of the city; p65), or cathedral, and it is believed that, when he died, construction of the nave had reached the transept. Giotto (see p28), although fundamentally a painter, was entrusted with designing the cathedral's bell tower and the result is quirkily unique, betraying his preference for a soft and graceful simplicity in structure and decoration. He only completed the base, however, and was succeeded by Andrea Pisano (c 1290–1348), killed by the plague, and Francesco Talenti (active 1325–69). Talenti amended Arnolfo's design for the Duomo and added polygonal apses, each with five chapels. Circular windows *(oculi)* were another novel element introduced in some Gothic churches. Talenti drew an octagonal dome between the apses, but had no grander ideas on how to build it than did Arnolfo.

BAD BOY BRUNELLESCHI

Enter Filippo Brunelleschi (1377–1446), complete with one of the hottest tempers in the history of Italian architecture. After failing to win the 1401 competition to design a set of bronze doors for the Baptistery (see p28), Brunelleschi left in a huff for Rome, where he focused on mathematics and architecture.

Brunelleschi would launch the architectural branch of the Renaissance in Florence.

TOP FIVE HIDDEN GEMS

- **Palazzo Davanzati** (p75) A rare example of a noble medieval house.
- **Cappella de' Pazzi** (p99) Brunelleschi's chapel in the Basilica di Santa Croce.
- **Chiesa Russa Ortodossa** (p110) A taste of Mother Russia in the Florentine suburbs.
- **Sinagoga** (p101) Florence's imposing, but little-visited, 19th-century synagogue.
- **Casa Galleria** (p79) One of the few Art Nouveau houses to survive in Florence.

It manifested itself in a rediscovery of simplicity and purity in classical building, with great attention paid to perspective and harmonious distribution of space and volume.

His most remarkable achievement was solving the Duomo dome conundrum. He proposed to raise the octagonal-based dome without the aid of scaffolding. Although incredulous, the Signoria agreed and Brunelleschi's double-skinned dome, raised in sections, was the greatest feat of its kind since ancient times. In later years Michelangelo, when commissioned to create the dome for St Peter's (San Pietro) in Rome, observed with undisguised admiration, 'io farò la sorella, già più gran ma non più bella' ('I'll make it the Brunelleschi dome's sister – bigger, yes, but no more beautiful').

That feat alone was tremendous but Brunelleschi's importance goes beyond the splendid dome. He 'created' the role of architect. Rather than act as a foreman, guiding construction as it progressed and to some extent making it up as he went along, Brunelleschi devised formulae of perspective and balance that allowed him to create a completed concept at the drawing board. Inspired by Roman engineering and Tuscan aesthetics, he launched a new era in construction. In essence, the architectural Renaissance, based on the rational tackling of human and mathematical problems, took flight with him. Other examples of Brunelleschi's keen sense of human proportion are: the portico of the Spedale degli Innocenti (1421; p98), considered the earliest work of the Florentine Renaissance; the Sagrestia Vecchia (Old Sacristy) in Basilica di San Lorenzo (1428; p82); and the Cappella de' Pazzi in the Basilica di Santa Croce (1430; p98). If Gothic sought to exalt God, with impossibly lofty construction dwarfing its admirers, Renaissance building aimed as much to exalt human reason, pleasing with its geometrical harmony and more earthly proportions.

Brunelleschi also designed the Basilica di San Lorenzo (1425; p82) and the Basilica di Santo Spirito (1436; p102). San Lorenzo had Medici money behind it, allowing the architect some latitude in design and choice of materials. He died long before either project reached completion and the supervisors who came after him were not completely faithful to his plans, particularly in the case of the latter church.

BEYOND BRUNELLESCHI

It is generally accepted that Cosimo de' Medici commissioned Michelozzo di Bartolommeo Michelozzi (1396–1472) to build his new residence. Brunelleschi had proposed something altogether too grand for Cosimo, whose policy was to keep his head down while effectively ruling the city. Brunelleschi, predictably, flew into a rage and smashed the model.

Michelozzo's building, now known as Palazzo Medici-Riccardi (p92), was nevertheless no dwarf. Three hefty storeys with the air of a fortress are topped by a solid roof, whose eaves jut far out over the streets below – a typical trait of Florentine *palazzi* (mansions). The lowest storey features rustication – the rough-hewn, protruding blocks of stone used to build it, as opposed to the smoothed stone of the upper storeys, something which you can also see on the

The ornate façade of Santa Maria Novella (p78)

Palazzo Vecchio. The mansion ushered in an era of grand patrician building and other influential families would soon follow suit.

It was thought that the initial 15th-century core of the Palazzo Pitti (begun in 1458; p106) was built for the powerful, if rather mouthy, Luca Pitti by Settignano-born Luca Fancelli (1430–95), but experts are increasingly convinced that Brunelleschi provided the design.

Benedetto da Maiano (1442–97), meanwhile, was chosen by Filippo Strozzi to build the Strozzi family mansion (p82). In terms of size alone it outstrips any other *palazzo* raised during the Medici era. The courtyard, attributed to Simone del Pollaiuolo (1457–1508), better known as Il Cronaca, is considered one of Florence's finest.

The acclaimed theorist of Renaissance architecture and art was Leon Battista Alberti (1404–72). Born in Genoa into an exiled Florentine family, he was a true Renaissance figure, learned and multitalented, but to his native city he contributed only the striking façade of the Basilica di Santa Maria Novella. His influence on artists, sculptors and architects in Florence and beyond came mostly through his theoretical writings.

MICHELANGELO

Michelangelo Buonarroti (1475–1564) was foremost a sculptor and painter (see p30) but in later years he also turned his attention to building design. In 1516, after stints in Rome, he was called back to Florence to design a façade for the Basilica di San Lorenzo, but the project was dropped and he ended up working on the Sagrestia Nuova (New Sacristy; p91) for the same church, intended as part of the funerary chapels for the Medici family. This was as close as Michelangelo got to finishing one of his architectural-sculptural whims in Florence.

Another of Michelangelo's tasks is the grand staircase and entrance hall for the Biblioteca Medicea Laurenziana (Laurentian Library; p91), which Michelangelo never saw completed, as he returned to Rome beforehand. It is a startling late-Renaissance creation, with columns recessed into the walls (and thus deprived of their natural supporting function) and other architectural oddities, precursors of mannerism.

MIND YOUR MANNERISM

Most scholars date the end of the later, or High, Renaissance to around 1520. Certainly by 1527, with the sacking of Rome (a real bonfire of the vanities) led by Charles de Bourbon, it was all over; not least because war and suffering had snuffed out the funds and desire to continue creating.

What followed is generally called mannerism, although this intermediate phase between the Renaissance and baroque is not easily defined. For many, Michelangelo's work in San Lorenzo is clearly mannerist, breaking with the more austere classical lines of the Renaissance. For others, the mannerists were a fairly unimaginative lot, fiddling around the edges of what had been the core of Renaissance thinking.

In Florence, little of note was built in the hangover period after the sacking of Rome. The menacing Fortezza da Basso (p111), aimed more at controlling disgruntled Florentines under the miserable reign of Alessandro de' Medici than protecting the city, was among the few exceptions.

Giorgio Vasari (1511–74), born in Arezzo and better known to us for his biography of the great artists who preceded him, became a big wheel in Florence and created the Uffizi (p70).

TOP FIVE BOOKS ON FLORENTINE ARCHITECTURE

- **Brunelleschi's Dome** (Ross King) A novelised account of this extraordinary construction feat.
- **La Cupola di Santa Maria del Fiore** (Lamberto Ippolito & Chiara Peroni) A drier and more technical explanation of the making of the Duomo's dome.
- **Florence – The City and Its Architecture** (Richard Goy) An overview of the city through its outstanding monuments, in words and beautiful photography.
- **Palaces of Florence** (Francesco Gurrieri and Patrizia Fabbri) A richly illustrated coffee table book that takes you through a phalanx of Florence's grand mansions, many of which can't normally by visited.
- **The Cathedral, The Baptistery, The Campanile** (Gabriella di Cagno) A simple introduction to the religious heart of Florence

Arts & Architecture

ARCHITECTURE

DON'T BAROQUE THE BOAT

The 17th century brought little new construction of note in Florence, although many projects were undertaken to restructure, expand or finish existing sites. This was the baroque era, which often had more impact on décor than design. At its most extreme, as in Rome, such decoration was sumptuous to the point of giddiness, all curvaceous statuary, twisting pillars and assorted baubles. In Florence, a long-established tradition of architectural sobriety excluded such excesses, and clear cases of baroque architecture are rare.

A couple of notable examples include the Chiesa di SS Michele e Gaetano (p80) and the façade for the Chiesa di Ognissanti (p79). The former, finished by Gherardo Silvani (1579–1675), is considered the finest piece of baroque work in Florence, and a demonstration of the restraint typical of the city – in stark contrast to the flimflam buoyant baroque of Rome.

URBAN RENEWAL

After Napoleon's French rulers retired in 1814, a process of urban renewal already begun before the arrival of the French continued. The space around the southern flank of the Duomo was cleared and fronted by neoclassical buildings. The architect behind that project was Gaetano Baccani (1792–1867), who also built the singular Palazzo Borghese (p114) in distinctive imperial style on Via Ghibellina. It was around this time that the former Stinche prison, also on Via Ghibellina, was converted into a neoclassical theatre (now the Teatro Verdi; p101).

Between the 1840s and 1870s – from the unstable years prior to the Europe-wide uprisings of 1848, through to Florence's limited days as capital of the newly united Italy – a programme of street-widening gathered pace. It may have improved traffic flow and hygiene, but it meant tearing away centuries of history. Neoclassical façades replaced medieval leftovers. In the 1890s engineers carved out Piazza della Repubblica (p68), for the sake of which much of the heart of old Florence and its timeless Mercato Vecchio (Old Market) were mercilessly ripped out.

THE TRAIN OF MODERNITY ARRIVES IN FLORENCE...TWICE

The long-awaited Treno ad Alta Velocità (High Speed Train, or TAV) due to link Rome with Milan, via Florence and Bologna, will eventually roll into a very 21st-century station north of the Fortezza da Basso. Work on Sir Norman Foster's design will start in 2007, and the station will be a revolutionary addition to the cityscape. Partly buried underground, the station will boast a dazzling glass canopy and be linked to the city centre by a new tram line.

Oddly enough, the last major modernising public work undertaken in Florence, back in the Fascist Italy of the 1930s, under Mussolini, was...a train station. The Stazione di Santa Maria Novella may look like an average train station nowadays, but at the time it caused quite a tempest. The winning project presented in Rome was a then revolutionary design by a young group of Florentine architecture students under the watchful eye of Giovanni Michelucci (1891–1991).

It unleashed a storm of conservative protest in Florence – how could you plant such a modern monstrosity in the midst of this historic city? But young intellectuals, such as the writer Pratolini, were just as vehemently behind the project. Mussolini no doubt liked the clean rational lines, reflecting the Fascist go-ahead self-image, although it lacked the monumental pomposity of other Fascist-era buildings. He probably also saw an opportunity to get the intelligentsia, generally not well disposed to his rule, on side for once. Frank Lloyd Wright, for one, was in full agreement!

Between 1865 and 1869 the city walls north of the Arno were pulled down and replaced by the boulevards you see today. The *lungarni,* the roads that follow the course of the river, were also laid out in this period.

The Mercato Centrale (p92), finished in 1874, is a rare Florentine example of the late-19th-century passion for iron and glass structures. It was designed by Giuseppe Mengoni (1829–77), the Bologna-born architect responsible for Milan's Galleria Vittorio Emanuele II.

THE 20TH CENTURY

One of the few early-20th-century residences to survive is the Casa Galleria (p79) by Giovanni Michelazzi (1879–1920). Its Art Nouveau façade contrasts with a city without much whimsical architecture.

Mussolini was not averse to controversy, and gave the go-ahead to the design for the city's main train station, Stazione di Santa Maria Novella (see the boxed text, above), completed in 1935. Sport was also important to the Fascists and so the city was graced with the Stadio Franchi (p156) in Campo di Marte.

INTO THE FUTURE

After so many decades of virtual inactivity, Florence finally seems to be waking up architecturally. Well, at least it has opened one eye. Aside from transport projects such as the long-awaited new tramway and high-speed train line, urban improvement plans (see p18) have brought some building sparkle to the city, at least in theory. The most exciting project is Sir Norman Foster's planned high-speed railway station, on which it is hoped work will begin in 2007 (see the boxed text, above).

Another startling plan is, or perhaps was, the planned exit for the new expanded Uffizi (see the boxed text, p73) by Arata Isozaki. An imaginative portico design, full of glass, would have revolutionised the heart of medieval Florence and for that very reason may never be built. Some rumours suggest the decision will ultimately be political. If the centre-left Unione coalition win government from the present right-wing government in the April 2006 elections, it will go ahead, insiders claim; if not, it won't.

The name architects don't stop with Foster. Spain's Santiago Calatrava is behind expansion work at the Museo dell'Opera del Duomo (p67), while Jean Nouvel has been elected to make a bold contribution to the urban renewal project at the former FIAT works in the west of the city. On the dark side, the 'new' Palazzo di Giustizia, being built in the former FIAT works, is a design chosen in the 1970s, almost universally considered a disaster in the early 21st century but made unavoidable by binding contracts. In the suburb of Scandicci, Richard Rogers is working on a civic centre project. He may also have some ideas on what to do with the nearby 'palazzaccio' (roughly translated as 'horrible big building'), an enormous concrete horror raised in the 1990s to house the Tuscan branch of the finance ministry and never actually used – an incredible example of wasted public funds.

PAINTING & SCULPTURE

In the chaos of invasions, pillage and general dissolution of the Roman Empire that ushered in the fearful centuries of the early Middle Ages in Italy, the whole classical heritage of Greco-Roman art, exemplified in its sculptures and mosaics, was seemingly lost forever.

The reawakening of Christian Romanesque architecture had its corollary in art – the churches were quickly filled with lively frescoes and, to a lesser extent in Tuscany, mosaics.

Romanesque art has to modern eyes a naive, two-dimensional feel. And yet it is full of bright and bold colour, shimmering gold, deep reds and daring black. It is almost exclusively religious, and served a didactic purpose in an age when even kings and emperors were often illiterate. The crucifixion, the Virgin and Child, Christ Pantocrator (enthroned Christ), the saints and numerous Old and New Testament scenes jostle alongside deeply symbolic images that conveyed the essence of Christian teaching to the masses.

It is also full of extraordinary detail: images of saints undergoing grisly martyrdoms with almost divine indifference to pain, scenes influenced more by medieval Europe than any imagined New Testament Israel. Were Romanesque artists incapable of capturing human features in a realistic fashion? To the people of the time, their images had to exude a strangely detached other-worldliness to differentiate them from life on earth. This basic precondition remained at the heart of European Christian art until the Renaissance.

Gothic art is marked by an increasing sophistication and more lifelike rendering of figures compared with the stiff Romanesque, but the real revolution came later. Giotto made some early steps and was ahead of his time, yet even while later Renaissance artists were sweeping Florence with a new broom, artists in other cities (as close as Siena) remained self-confidently faithful to Gothic precepts. In Florence itself 'old style' artists still got plenty of commissions.

Much of this was down to the tastes or daring of the patron. It so happened that the trendsetters in Florence were the Medici and they liked the daring avant-garde that inspired so many new artists. These artists were considered tradesmen, the mostly anonymous interior decorators of their day, but the Florentine Renaissance finally brought fame and recognition to individual painters and sculptors.

Wealthy laypeople began to commission art for public places or their homes. This promoted a broadening of themes, and so, alongside the still-dominant religious strain, emerged portraits, busts and sculptures of (self-)important people, scenes from battles and classical mythology.

Florence as a centre of art began to decline noticeably as the Renaissance was succeeded by mannerist, baroque and subsequent periods. As Florence stagnated, the great revolutions in Western art took place on other stages. That remains the case to this day.

EMERGING FROM THE MIDDLE AGES

Before the 13th century, little of artistic note was happening in Florence. In Tuscany, Pisa was on the rise. Master of Sardinia and supporting a busy sea trade, Pisa was more open than Florence to external influences and artistic interchange. This was perhaps most evident in building and sculpture. Nicola Pisano (c 1215–78) is best known for his work on Pisa's Baptistery (p197) and influenced fellow sculptors all over Tuscany.

Arnolfo di Cambio (see p21) was a student of Pisano and not only designed the Duomo and Palazzo Vecchio, but also decorated the former's façade. Some of this sculpture remains in the Museo dell'Opera del Duomo (p67) but most was destroyed in the 16th century.

Andrea Pisano (c 1290–1348) moved from Pisa to Florence for a while and left behind the bronze doors of the south façade of the Baptistery (p63), which he finished in 1336. The realism of the characters combines with the fine linear detail of a Gothic imprint, revealing that already in the 14th century a transition was in process.

GIOTTO & CO

If any proof were needed that things were on the boil in 14th-century Florence, one need look no further than the work of Giotto di Bondone (c 1266–1337). Born in the Mugello, northeast of Florence, he is one of the pivotal names in the Italian artistic pantheon. In Giotto the move away from the symbolic, other-worldly representations of Gothic religious art is clear. His figures are essentially human and express feeling, alien to earlier phases of art in Christian Europe.

Better known for his work in other towns, in particular Padua (Cappella degli Scrovegni), he left behind several works in Florence. Among the most important are the frescoes in the Peruzzi and Bardi chapels in the Basilica di Santa Croce (p98).

Confirmation of Giotto's influence comes in the work of several other painters active at the same time. Maso di Banco, of whom little is known except that he was at work in the eight or so years prior to the plague of 1348, was a student of Giotto. His *Storie di San Silvestro* (Stories of St Sylvester) series in the Basilica di Santa Croce reflects in its luminosity and simplicity the hand of his master.

Andrea di Cione Orcagna (active 1343–68), though, stuck to the old canons. His most important remaining works are the very Gothic tabernacle and statuary inside the Chiesa di Orsanmichele (p69). Indeed, Gothic lived on side by side with Renaissance for many years.

THE DAWN OF THE RENAISSANCE

In 1401 Lorenzo Ghiberti (1378–1455) beat the irascible Brunelleschi in a competition to create a second set of bronze doors for the venerable Baptistery (now on the northern flank). Ghiberti's was an exquisite solution in the International Gothic style, a loose description for the final wave of enthusiasm for Gothic to wash across Europe.

But Ghiberti saw which way the wind was blowing. Called upon to do another set of doors on the eastern side, he dedicated 17 years to what an admiring Michelangelo (and it was not Michelangelo's wont to admire anything much) would dub the 'Porta del Paradiso' (Gate of Paradise), a Renaissance masterpiece.

Ghiberti's workshop was a prestige address and Donatello (c 1386–1466) was apprenticed there. As the Renaissance gathered momentum in the 1420s and '30s, Donatello produced forceful and dynamic sculpture. The results swing from his rather camp, bronze *David,* the first nude sculpture since classical times (now in the Museo Nazionale del Bargello; p74) to the racy *Cantoria* (Choir), a marble and mosaic tribune where small choirs could gather, done for the Duomo (now in the Museo dell'Opera del Duomo; p67).

Meanwhile, the young Masaccio (1401–28) can probably be given a good deal of the credit for the definitive break with the Gothic style in Florentine painting. Born in an Arno village at the dawn of the 15th century (what the Italians call the Quattrocento, or the 'Four Hundreds'), his brief but dynamic career (he died in Rome at the age of 27) makes him to painting what Brunelleschi and Donatello were to architecture and sculpture.

You don't need to look long and hard at his Florentine masterpieces, such as the Cappella Brancacci frescoes (Basilica di Santa Maria del Carmine; p102), to see what sets Masaccio apart. The relatively new game of perspective dominates his pictorial solution. Colours are subtle and characters are brought into relief by the use of light and shadow. His best-known image, the *Cacciata dei Progenitori* (Expulsion of Adam and Eve) in the Cappella Brancacci, depicts all the anguish and shame of Adam and, especially, Eve; never before had such raw and believable human emotion been depicted.

TOP FIVE MUSEUMS

- **Museo Archeologico** (p95) Especially strong on Egyptian and Etruscan finds.
- **Museo di Storia della Scienza** (p75) All sorts of instruments and inventions from down the centuries.
- **Museo dell'Opera del Duomo** (p67) Housing Michelangelo's *Pietà* and Ghiberti's *Porta del Paradiso.*
- **Museo Horne** (p100) An eclectic collection of art and artefacts in a medieval house.
- **Museo Nazionale del Bargello** (p74) With sculptures by Donatello, Giambologna, Cellini, Michelangelo and the della Robbia family.

THE FRIARS OF ART

Following in Masaccio's footsteps were two masters who, in temperament, could not have been more different from one another.

Fra Angelico (c 1395–1455), a Dominican monk later known as Beato (Blessed) Angelico for his piety, for a while dominated the Florentine art world. His work, much of it done for the Museo di San Marco (p96), is suffused with a diaphanous light, aimed at emphasising the good in humankind.

Although also a friar, Fra Filippo Lippi (c 1406–69) had an appetite for sex, drink and general carousing that left him the father of two by a nun. Some of his finest work can still be seen in Florence: A *Madonna col Bambino* (Madonna with Child) in the Uffizi (p70) and another in Palazzo Pitti (in the Sala di Prometeo; p106) demonstrate his mastery of light and shadow, a weighty reality about the characters and an eye for detail.

TOP FIVE GALLERIES

- **The Uffizi** (p70) The best round-up of Tuscan art in the world.
- **Museo di San Marco** (p96) A virtual temple to the art of Beato Angelico and Fra Bartolommeo.
- **Galleria dell'Accademia** (p94) Best known for Michelangelo's *David*.
- **Galleria Palatina** (Palazzo Pitti; (p106) Containing a smattering of works by Botticelli, Fra Filippo Lippi, and Andrea del Sarto, along with Venetian and Flemish masters.
- **Museo Marino Marini** (p80) A monothematic display of this modern Tuscan's sculptures.

FROM UCCELLO TO BOTTICELLI

A strange bird was Paolo Uccello (1397–1475). More preoccupied with perspective studies than making a living, he did manage to crank out a few masterpieces, including the *Diluvio* (Deluge) fresco in the Basilica di Santa Maria Novella (p78) and the *Battaglia di San Romano* (Battle of San Romano) done for the Medici family and now (in part) in the Uffizi (p70).

Benozzo Gozzoli (c 1421–97) introduced a cheerfully naive touch to painting, an element notable by its absence in the brooding works of some of his confrères. One of the last painters of the International Gothic style, Gozzoli's big break came when the Medici commissioned his sumptuous *Corteo dei Magi* (Procession of the Magi) in 1459 for the Palazzo Medici-Riccardi (p92).

Mythologised in the 19th century, Sandro Botticelli (1445–1510) has, as a result, probably been the least understood painter of the period. By most he is remembered for the milky dreaminess of *Nascita di Venere* (Birth of Venus) and *Primavera* (Spring), in the Uffizi, but his later works were of greater intensity, fired by religious fervour. Botticelli fell out of step with his time, however, and in his last 10 years received few commissions. He died an unhappy man.

Filippino Lippi (1457–1504), Fra Filippo's son, worked in Botticelli's workshop but was more directly influenced by Leonardo da Vinci and Flemish artists. Lippi's frescoes of the *Storie di San Giovanni Evangelista e San Filippo* (Stories of St John and St Phillip) in the Cappella Strozzi (Basilica di Santa Maria Novella) reveal a move away from the humanist ideals of Quattrocento painting. In one of the frescoes, depicting St Philip exorcising the devil in the temple of Mars, perspective has been flattened and the subject has a disturbing quality absent from other works of the time. The architectural busyness and attention to detail in people's faces presage mannerism.

Leonardo da Vinci stands in the Uffizi (p70)

29

Although he would subsequently be best known for his crowd-pleasing decorative, glazed terracotta, Luca della Robbia (c 1400–82) for a while showed promise as a sculptor, as the examination of his exquisite *Cantoria* (Choir), now in the Museo dell'Opera del Duomo (p67), will reveal. His nephew Andrea (1435–1525) and the latter's son Giovanni (1469–1529) continued the successful family ceramics business.

THE GENIUS FROM VINCI

Leonardo da Vinci (1452–1519), born in a small town west of Florence (his name means 'Leonard from Vinci'), stands apart. Painter, sculptor, architect, scientist and engineer, Leonardo brought to all fields of knowledge and art an original touch, often opening up whole new branches of thought. In the thousands of pages of notes that he left behind, he repeatedly extols the virtue of sight and observation. Paying little heed to received wisdoms, whether Christian or classical, Leonardo barrelled along with unquenchable curiosity. His learning was all-embracing and in da Vinci we have the model of the 'Renaissance man'.

To Leonardo, painting was the noblest art, and much of it he did far from home (he spent 20 years in Milan alone).

Still, a few of the grand master's works can be seen in Florence. His *Annunciazione* (Annunciation), in the Uffizi (p70), reveals his concern with light and shadow. His techniques were quite different from those of his contemporaries. His unfinished *Adorazione dei Magi* (Adoration of the Magi), also in the Uffizi, reveals how he first applied a dark wash to the surface, from which he could then extract his figures and shed light upon them. Among his most beguiling portraits are the *Mona Lisa* and *Madonna col Bambino e Sant'Anna* (Madonna with Child and St Anna), both now in the Louvre in Paris.

TOP FIVE BOOKS ON FLORENTINE ART

- **The Renaissance** (Paul Johnson) An easy-to-follow general history of the explosion and waning of Renaissance art in Italy, with special emphasis on Florence.
- **Leonardo da Vinci – The First Scientist** (Michael White) An intriguing look at one of Florence's most gifted sons, a truly universal man.
- **Michelangelo Una Vita Inquieta** (Antonio Forcellini) A fascinating account of the life and times of *David*'s creator.
- **Fra Angelico at San Marco** (William Hood) A close study of the some of the finest but least noticed painting in Florence.
- **Donatello and his World: Italian Renaissance Sculpture** (Joachim Poeschke) Concentrating on the works of the great master Donatello, the author looks at the dawn of Renaissance sculpture in Florence.

THE FIERY FLORENTINE

While Leonardo was in Milan, Michelangelo Buonarroti (1475–1564) was asserting himself as a rival painter, albeit of a very different ilk, and first and foremost as a sculptor. It was in this capacity that he left his greatest gifts to the city. As a young lad he got the luckiest break in his life when he came to the attention of Lorenzo de' Medici, who had a keen eye for talent and the patience to deal with artistic temperaments.

Michelangelo was a testy individual and, early on in life, got what was coming to him when he made some acid remarks about a drawing by the sculptor Pietro Torrigiani one day in the Cappella Brancacci. Torrigiani thumped the smart-alecky Michelangelo, and left him with a *very* broken nose. After a stint in Rome, where he carved the remarkable *Pietà*, Michelangelo returned to Florence in 1501 to carry out one of his most striking commissions ever, the colossal statue of *David* (see p94). By now Michelangelo had long established himself as the champion of full nudity. The body, he argued, was a divine creation and its beauty without peer. Only three years before, under the greatest prude of recent Florentine history, the monk-dictator Savonarola, such a work would have been unthinkable.

Among Michelangelo's last great works, not quite completed, are the statues in the Medicis' Sagrestia Nuova (New Sacristy) of San Lorenzo (p91). That so many of his works were left unfinished is indicative perhaps of the temperament of an artist incapable of satisfaction with his own work. The *Pietà* he began to work on for his own tomb so disappointed him that, in a fit of temper, he took to it with a hammer. It was later cobbled back together and stands in the Museo dell'Opera del Duomo (p67).

In contrast to Leonardo's smoky, veiled images, Michelangelo demonstrated a searing clarity of line in painting. His greatest project was the ceiling of the Sistine Chapel in Rome. In Florence, the *Tondo Doni* (depicting the Holy Family), in the Uffizi provides stunning insight into his craft.

Always a difficult character in life, this lover of the human (especially male) body was, by all accounts, little fussed by personal hygiene. They say he rarely bothered to wash and that, when he died, his clothes had to be prised from his crud-encrusted corpse.

FROM HIGH RENAISSANCE TO MANNERISM

Lesser artists were at work around the turn of the century in Florence, not to mention outsiders, like Raphael, who stopped in Florence for a while before heading off to pursue their careers elsewhere.

Among the Florentines, Fra Bartolommeo (1472–1517) stands out for such paintings as the *Apparizione della Vergine a San Bernardo* (called 'Vision of St Bernard' in English), now in the Galleria dell'Accademia (p94). A follower of Savonarola and convinced by his rantings, Fra Bartolommeo demonstrated his commitment to the cause and burned all his studies of the nude in a bonfire of the vanities. His art is clearly devotional, with incidental detail eliminated in favour of the central subject.

Andrea del Sarto (1486–1530) remained essentially true to the values of High Renaissance painting, turning out works with grace and dignity but none of the tumultuous conflict that would be associated with the likes of Jacopo Pontormo (1494–1556), his student. With Pontormo, the move to mannerism, already explored by Michelangelo, is clear. An initial comparison of frescoes by the two artists in the atrium of the Chiesa della SS Annunziata (p93) is enough to identify the differences. In Pontormo's *Visitazione* (Visitation) his figures seem on the verge of taking flight, or turning about with preoccupation, as indeed they do in his frescoes in the Chiesa di Santa Felicita (p104). It is this sense of nervous movement that marks the break with the classical bounds set by the Renaissance.

Il Rosso Fiorentino ('the Florentine Redhead'; 1495–1540) also worked on the SS An-nunziata frescoes before heading to Rome. In his works one detects a similarly fretful note, although his style is different from Pontormo's. The flashes of light and dark create an unreal effect in his characters.

A student of Pontormo, Il Bronzino (1503–72) began the move away from mannerism. He was employed by the Medici family, and his approach lacked the disquiet evident in his tutor's work. Rather he fixes images in a static fashion, reflecting perhaps his patrons' desire to convey the sureness of their sovereignty, however spurious. His greatest achievement was Eleonora de Toledo's chapel in the Palazzo Vecchio (p76).

The works of Giorgio Vasari (1511–74) and his students litter Florence, with some better than others. His particular boast was speed – with an army of helpers he was able to plough through commissions for frescoes and paintings with great alacrity, if not always with equal aplomb. He is most important in the history of Italian art as the author of *Lives of the Artists,* a rich compendium of fact and fiction about Italian artists until his own day. Vasari and company were largely responsible for the decoration of the Palazzo Vecchio.

Not only Vasari and his minions were at work for Duke Cosimo I de' Medici. Sculptors were increasingly called on to decorate ducal Florence's public places. The master goldsmith, Benvenuto Cellini (1500–71), was also a dab hand at sculpture, turning out the bronze *Perseo e Medusa* (Perseus and Medusa), which stands in the Loggia della Signoria (p73). Bartolom-meo Ammannati (1511–92) is best known for the *Fontana del Nettuno* (Neptune Fountain) in Piazza della Signoria, which has met more often than not with disapproval; Michelangelo, for one, thought Ammannati had ruined a perfectly good block of marble.

Giambologna (Jean de Boulogne; 1529–1608), a Flemish sculptor who arrived in Flor-ence around 1550, dominated the city's scene in the latter half of the 16th century. In 1594, some 20 years after the autocratic Cosimo's death, his successors had Giambologna raise the grand equestrian statue of Cosimo in Piazza della Signoria, where it still stands triumphant today. His is considered an early herald of the turbulent baroque style, all curves and movement, which is best expressed in his *Il Ratto della Sabina* (Rape of the Sabine Women) in the Loggia della Signoria.

BAROQUE

Cosimo's autocratic dynasty proved a lasting affair and ushered in a long period of relative tranquility in Florence. With it came artistic mediocrity, at least compared with the previous two centuries. As the 17th century wore on, flocks of artists continued to work in Florence, but few of great note. Giovanni da San Giovanni (1592–1636) was the leading light of the first half of the century, and some of his frescoes remain in the Palazzo Pitti.

The arrival of artists from out of town, such as Pietro da Cortona (1596–1669) and the Neapolitan Luca Giordano (1632–1705), brought with them the winds of baroque taste. Baroque artists used a riot of colour and movement, leaving any semblance of reality behind. Angels and chariots charge at you from the heavens in a whirlwind of exaggerated movement. One of Florence's senior court sculptors, Giovanni Battista Foggini (1652–1725), immersed himself in the baroque circles of Rome, where the style became particularly florid, and when he returned put his new-found knowledge to use in reliefs and other decoration in several churches, notably the Basilica di Santa Maria del Carmine (p102).

THE MACCHIAIOLI

By the middle of the 19th century, Florentine art was stuck in a rut, and the slumbering capital of the Grand Duchy of Tuscany had long ceased to be a centre of any great importance. Painters produced soulless, academic pieces that, after the excitement of the 1848 Europe-wide revolts, seemed inadequate. In 1855 several Florentines visited Paris for the Universal Exposition. They came back with news of the developments that were taking place in French naturalist painting that proved a precursor to impressionism.

In Florence anti-academic artists congregated in the Caffè Michelangelo and declared that painting real-life scenes was the only way forward. This movement, which lasted until the late 1860s, was known as the Macchiaioli (the 'stainers' or 'blotchers') because of a disparaging newspaper article written in 1862 about their technique of splotching various colours onto the canvas to explore effects of tone before proceeding. They abandoned the religious and historical themes to which painting, no matter how innovative in style, had largely been bound for centuries. Then they dropped *chiaroscuro* (strong contrast between light and shadow) effects in favour of the playful use of colour plus light, or colour plus shade, or both.

> ## TOP FIVE SCULPTURES
>
> - **David** (Michelangelo) Galleria dell'Accademia (p94) .
> - **David** (Donatello) Museo Nazionale del Bargello (p74).
> - **Perseo e Medusa** (Benvenuto Cellini) Loggia della Signoria (p73).
> - **La Pietà** (Michelangelo) Museo dell'Opera del Duomo (p67).
> - **Mercurio Volante** (Giambologna) Museo Nazionale del Bargello (p74).

Telemaco Signorini (1835–1901), born in Via de' Macci, moved around Europe and dabbled in such things as journalism, poetry and painting. Despite his restlessness, he remained true to his hometown. His work followed two thematic lines: Florentine life and warm Tuscan landscapes, although he painted wherever he travelled.

Although the hub of their activity was Florence, the Macchiaioli came from all over Italy. They included Livorno-born Giovanni Fattori (1825–1908), Neapolitan Giuseppe Abbati (1836–68) and the Emilian painter Silvestro Lega (1826–95). Many (including Signorini) fought in the conflicts leading to the unification of Italy. You can see works by a variety of these artists in the Galleria d'Arte Moderna in Palazzo Pitti (p106).

THE PRESENT DAY

Florence's next decline as a centre of artistic ferment was during the 20th century. Futurism, which preached an all-embracing faith in science, technology and the future, did not have the impact here that it did elsewhere. At their most extreme, Futurists declared that museums, libraries, and all repositories of past splendour, should be destroyed to make way for the brave new world.

In retrospect, flowering as it did before WWI, the movement was touchingly innocent. Although some of the big names of the movement, like Giacomo Balla, exhibited in Florence, Futurism failed to really ignite the Florentine scene. The Novecento ('20th Century') movement, which preached a return to order in the wake of various avantgarde tendencies, also bore precious little fruit in Florence.

Painter Primo Conti (1900–88) experimented with all sorts of styles and wound up in a sprawling studio-cum-house in Fiesole. The house is now open as a gallery of his art (see Fiesole, p110). Ottone Rosai (1895–1957), a controversial figure and enthusiastic Fascist, was one of the senior figures in experimental art in the 1920s.

After WWII, the Arte Oggi (Art Today) movement of so-called dissident artists in

Statues in the Museo Nazionale del Bargello (p74)

Florence championed a 'classical abstractism', but by and large the 20th-century art scene overlooked Florence.

Although born in Paris, Silvio Loffredo (b 1920) adopted Florence after WWII and is the Accademia di Belle Arti's professor of painting, as well as one of the most interesting of Florence's postwar artists. A student of Oskar Kokoschka, he can be loosely categorised as an Expressionist.

The awe-inspiring legacy of the great masters has largely proved too great a burden for modern sculptors to shake off. Pescia-born Libero Andreotti (1875–1933) and the tormented Florentine Evaristo Boncinelli (1883–1946) were among the prominent figures in the first half of the century, while Pistoia-born Marino Marini (1901–80) was doubtless the torchbearer of 20th-century Tuscan sculpture. You can admire his work in the museum dedicated to him in Florence (p80).

LITERATURE

THE MASTER

Long after the fall of Rome, Latin remained the language of learned discourse and writing throughout much of Europe. The elevation of local tongues to literary status was a long and weary process, and the case of Italian was no exception.

In the mid-13th century, Tuscan poets began experimenting with verse and song in the local tongue, inspired by the troubadours of Provence. But all the poetry, song, didactic and religious literature of 13th-century writers couldn't compare to the genius of the Florentine Dante Alighieri (1265–1321) and his inspired *La Divina Commedia* (The Divine

Comedy). The work is split into three parts – Hell, Purgatory and Heaven – and the first is the most gripping.

The gloomy circles of Dante's hell do not serve merely to remind his readers of the wages of sin; far more interestingly, they become an uneasy resting place for a parade of characters, many of them his contemporaries, whom he judged worthy of an uncomfortable time in the next life. No doubt he was at least partly inspired by sour grapes, after being exiled from his home town.

Dante's decision to write in his Tuscan dialect was a literary coup. In doing so he catapulted Italian, or at least a version of it, to the literary stage. Scholars have been enthusing ever since that Italian was 'born' with Dante's *La Divina Commedia*.

Dante died in exile in Ravenna. As keen as Florence's rulers had been to see him ago, they have ever since wanted to have his ashes back. The city that took him in has rightly stood fast and refused.

PETRARCH & BOCCACCIO

Dante does not stand alone, and two Tuscan successors form with him the literary triumvirate that laid down the course for the development of a rich vein of Italian literature.

Petrarch (Francesco Petrarca; 1304–74), born in Arezzo to Florentine exiles, wrote more in Latin than in Italian. *Il Canzoniere* (The Canzoniere) is the result of his finest poetry. Although the core subject is the unrequited love for a girl called Laura, the breadth of human grief and joy is treated with a lyrical quality. So striking was his clear, passionate verse, filtered through his knowledge of the classics, that a phenomenon emerged known as *petrarchismo* – the desire of writers within and beyond Italy to emulate him.

> ### TOP FIVE BOOKS
>
> - **Buio** (*Darkness*; Dacia Maraini)
> - **Il Principe** (*The Prince*; Niccolò Machiavelli)
> - **La Divina Commedia** (*The Divine Comedy*; Dante Alighieri)
> - **Le Avventure di Pinocchio** (*The Adventures of Pinocchio*; Carlo Lorenzini)
> - **Una Storia Italiana** (*An Italian Story*; Vasco Pratolini)

A contemporary and friend of Petrarch was the Florentine (possibly born in Certaldo) Giovanni Boccaccio (1313–75). His masterpiece was *Il Decameron* (The Decameron), written in the years following the plague of 1348, which he survived. His 10 lusty characters, seven women and three men who have fled to a country retreat to avoid the plague in Florence, each recount a symbolic story in which various personalities, events and meanings are explored. It is akin to Chaucer's *The Canterbury Tales*.

THE RENAISSANCE

These three would have made a hard act for anyone to follow, and while the visual arts experienced a seemingly boundless creative explosion in the Renaissance, Florence could not continue to produce writers of the same stature. That said, it was writers and thinkers who provided the intellectual roots for the artistic rebirth.

Nurtured by such open-minded rulers as Lorenzo de' Medici the so-called humanists, spurred on by their rediscovery of the classics, thirsted for knowledge and new realms of learning. Their goal was the attainment of *humanitas*, combining knowledge and wisdom with action. The ideal humanist was compassionate and merciful, but also strong, eloquent and honourable. Action without knowledge and wisdom was barbaric, but the sedentary accumulation of knowledge barren.

The best known literary figure to emerge from this environment was Niccolò Machiavelli (1469–1527). He is celebrated for his treatise on the nature of power and politics, *Il Principe* (The Prince; see the boxed text, opposite) but was a prolific writer in many fields. His *Mandragola* is a lively piece of comic theatre and a virtuoso example of Italian literature, considered by many the best of the 16th century.

PINOCCHIO

It was not until the 19th century that a local writer would become a household name. Carlo Lorenzini (1826–90), better known to Italians by his pseudonym of Carlo Collodi, created *Le Avventure di Pinocchio* (The Adventures of Pinocchio). Outside Italy, Pinocchio is better known in his saccharine Walt Disney guise, but in Italy this bestseller has been a bedrock source of amusement and instruction for children and adults for generations. Try and get hold of the bilingual edition translated by Nicholas J Perella and published by the University of California Press.

THE MUSSOLINI YEARS

In the 1920s and '30s Florence bubbled with activity as a series of literary magazines flourished, at least for a while, in spite of the Fascist regime. Publications such as *Solaria*, which lasted from 1926 to 1934, its successor *Letteratura* (which began circulating in 1937) and *Il Frontespizio* (from 1929 to 1940) gave writers from across Italy a platform from which to launch and discuss their work. Most of the magazines, including Vasco Pratolini's short-lived *Campo di Marte*, fell prey sooner or later to censorship. That some lasted as long as they did is remarkable.

MACHIAVELLI'S MANOEUVRES

A handy little book of about 100 pages that went largely unnoticed in its writer's lifetime, *Il Principe* (The Prince) later came to be considered one of the most astute handbooks on the art of leadership and statecraft in Renaissance Europe. That it was written at all was largely the result of bad luck. Niccolò Machiavelli, a man who had devoted his working life to the state of Florence, found himself down on his luck and inactive. And so he chose to write, as much as a distraction as for any literary ambition.

Born in 1469 into a poor branch of what had been one of Florence's leading families, Machiavelli got off to a bad start. But he managed to swing a post in the city's second chancery at the age of 29, and so embarked on a colourful career as a Florentine public servant. Our man must have shown early promise, as by 1500 he was in France on his first diplomatic mission.

Impressed by the martial success of Italian-born Cesare Borgia and the centralised state of France, Machiavelli came to the conclusion that Florence needed a standing army. The city, like many others in Italy, had a habit of employing mercenaries to fight its wars. But mercenaries had few reasons to fight and die for anyone. They took their pay and as often as not did their level best to avoid mortal combat. They were, he wrote later in *Il Principe*, the root cause of the 'ruin of Italy'.

Machiavelli convinced his rulers of the advantages of an army raised to defend hearth and home and in 1506 formed a conscript militia. In 1509 he got to try it out on the rebellious city of Pisa, whose fall was largely attributed to the troops led by the wily statesman.

Florence, however, was not Rome's flavour of the month and troops from the Holy See and its allies marched on the city. Machiavelli was now defending not only his hearth but his future – to no avail.

The return of the Medici family to power was a blow for Machiavelli, who was promptly removed from all posts. Suspected of plotting against the Medici, he was even thrown into the dungeon in 1513 and tortured. He maintained his innocence and was freed, but reduced to penury as he retired to his little property outside Florence.

It was in these years that he produced his greatest writing. In *Il Principe* he developed his theories not only on politics and power but on history and human behaviour (Voltaire later said that the rational telling of history began with Machiavelli).

The term Machiavellian has a tone of conspiratorial sneakiness. But in his book he advocated realism, common sense and decisiveness. If honesty and sincerity were likely to endanger a prince and his state, then the prince had an obligation to be street-smart and flexible with the truth. A ruler owed it to himself and his subjects to be firm in war, cunning in diplomacy and just to his people. He exemplifies Cesare Borgia, son of Pope Alexander VI and scourge of central Italy. Machiavelli didn't like Borgia or even agree with his aims, but he recognised that when a leader had ambitions he had to have the conviction to pursue them.

Published after his death, his manual came to be read in the halls of power throughout Europe. They say Richelieu, among others, wholly concurred with Machiavelli's conclusions.

Machiavelli regained office but never as solidly as before. After the fall of the Medici he again fell from grace and died in 1527, frustrated and on the brink of poverty.

MODERN TIMES

Standing tall among a handful of notable Florentine writers since WWI is Vasco Pratolini (1913–91), son of a manual labourer and a self-taught writer who dabbled successfully in the mediums of theatre and cinema, as well as in prose and poetry.

Among his most enduring works is the trilogy *Una Storia Italiana* (An Italian Story), whose first part, *Metello,* set off a heated debate in Italian literary circles. Those who liked it saw in the novel a mature departure from neorealism to a more robust realism. Pratolini's detractors regarded him as caught in a rigid ideological trap. The trilogy follows the lives of working- and middle-class Florentines, through whom Pratolini analyses political, social and emotional issues. The narrative is interlaced with stories of people's lives told with verve and colour.

One of the most prolific and respected women writing in Italy today is the Rome-based Florentine Dacia Maraini (b 1936), a columnist and feminist novelist, poet and playwright. Author of 10 novels and several collections of stories, she confronts some tough subjects. *Buio* (Darkness; 1999) is a collection of 12 stories about children neglected or abused. Drawing from crime reports, she has created hard-hitting narrative held together by the central character, a woman detective by the name of Adele Sòfia, who also appeared in an earlier novel, *Voci* (Voices; 1994). Her *La Nave per Kobe* (2001), based on her mother's diaries, recounts her family's time in a concentration camp for antifascists in Japan (she was an infant at the time).

One of the last great 20th century Italian poets, Florentine Mario Luzi (1914–2005), was made a life Senator in 2004 in honour of his work, which spanned a good 50 years from his first collection of verse, *La Barca* (The Boat) in 1935. A collection of all his poetry, *Tutte Le Poesie* (1998), was published in the Meridiani series by Mondadori.

On an altogether lighter note are the pop detective novels set in Florence by Magdalen Nabb, such as *The Marshall and The Murderer* and *Death in Autumn.* Nabb is to Florence what Donna Leon is to Venice. UK radio journalist and novelist Sarah Dunant, who spends much time in Florence, set her historical novel *The Birth of Venus* (2004) in the city. It recounts the (fictional) story of an adolescent girl's artistic and sexual awakening, brought about largely by her wealthy merchant father's decision to bring a painter in to lavish decoration on their house. It is a large tale, weaving in Renaissance Florentine politics and life with art and love.

MUSIC
OPERA & CLASSICAL MOMENTS

Possibly the most colourful musical figure to have emerged from Florence is Giovanni Battista Lulli (1632–87). The name may not ring too many bells, until we add that he moved to France, where he would dominate the musical life of the court of Louis XIV as Jean-Baptiste Lully. With Molière he created new dramatic forms such as the comedy-ballet. Among his operatic works are *Alceste* and *Armide* and he also gave instrumental suites their definitive form.

Earlier, the Rome-born composer Jacopo Peri (1561–1633) and Florentine writer Ottavio Rinuccini (1562–1621) are credited with having created the first opera in the modern sense, *Dafne,* in 1598. They and Giulio Caccini (1550–1618) also wrote *Euridice* a couple of years later. It is the oldest opera for which the complete score still exists.

One of the most powerful instruments in western music, the pianoforte, was invented in Florence in 1711 by Paduan musician Bartolomeo Cristofori (1655–1731).

Another Florentine export to Paris was the composer Luigi Cherubini (1760–1842), who managed the tricky feat of keeping his head attached to his torso through the French Revolution, the Napoleonic era and the Restoration.

CONTEMPORARY SOUNDS

The undisputed king of Tuscan folk music (yes, there is such a thing) is Riccardo Marasco, who, since the 1960s, has tracked down traditional material, written his own and kept a witty and wide-ranging repertory of Tuscan music alive.

On a quite different note, one of Italy's leading rock bands, Litfiba, was originally a Florentine product, although since they started in the early 1980s they have seen a procession of changing band members – only one, Ghigo Renzulli, has remained throughout. Among their classic albums is *Mondi Sommersi* (1997), with the original lead singer, Piero Pelù, who has since embarked on a solo career. They still play live and in recent years seem to have recovered some of the original rocky oomph of the 1990s.

Florence-born Marco Masini emerged on the scene in the late 1980s with a classic of Italian pop, "Si Può Dare di Più", actually sung by bigger stars at the time, and "Perchè lo Fai?", which won him third place at the 1991 San Remo Song Festival.

Irene Grandi came to the fore in the early 1990s and her first solo album, *Irene Grandi* (1994), with songs by Eros Ramazzotti and rap icon Jovanotti, was a turning point. She has since toured and been associated with some of the big names of the Italian music world, such as Pino Daniele and evergreen rocker Vasco Rossi, who has written several of her songs. Her 2005 album (the seventh), *Indelebile,* consists of original songs with a strong rock flavour, but her previous effort, *Prima di Partire,* is better.

Lorenzo Cherubini 'Jovanotti', born in Rome of Tuscan parents (from Arezzo),

TOP FIVE CDS

- **Lorenzo 1990-1995 Raccolta** (1996; Jovanotti)
- **Prima di Partire** (2003; Irene Grandi)
- **Lully: Les Divertissements de Versailles** (Grandes Scènes Lyriques ; 2002; Giovanni Battista Lulli/Jean-Baptiste Lully)
- **Mondi Sommersi** (1997) Litfiba
- **Vecchia Toscana** (1985) Riccardo Marasco

started his career as a DJ in Cortona and then Rome. By the early 1990s his socially critical lyrics had made him the country's rap sensation. With 14 albums under his belt, he has become one of the icons of contemporary Italian music. For a live listen, you could try *Jova Live 2002,* although there are better studio albums.

Florence itself has all sorts of bands playing various pubs and bars around town. They include the Paolo Amulfi band, which covers classic rock, heavy metal groups like Holy Sinner and such oddities as Sir Randha, a Jamaican-style ska band. One of the big local names of ragamuffin and reggae since the late 1980s is Il Generale. His fourth album, *Toh, Più Che Mai,* is one of his bounciest and most eclectic yet. Tracks are done with other local musicians, such as the emerging band I Cerchioni and Senegalese rapper Young G.

See the Entertainment chapter (p144) for tips on bars and venues for plugging into the local live scene.

CINEMA

Italian cinema has known periods of enormous productivity and contributed some proud gems to Europe's film archives. Most people think of the postwar period of neorealism as the apogee of Italian film-making, and there is no doubting the richness of the output at that time. It didn't end there though, and Italy has continued to produce good directors ever since. The particular role of Florence and Tuscany has been to produce some of Italy's top comic actors. For decades they found their patron in the Cecchi Gori film business. Mario Cecchi Gori and his son Vittorio ran this Florence-based production company successfully until Vittorio made a series of investment mistakes that sent him bankrupt in 2003.

An early Florentine film-maker of note was Gianni Franciolini (1910–60). After spending 10 years in France studying journalism and then film, Franciolini returned to Italy in 1940, from which time he turned out a film almost every year until his death. An early flick, *Fari Nella Nebbia* (Headlights in the Mist; 1941) shows the French influence on his ideas, but also presages the fecund period of Italian film-making that lay just around the corner – neorealism.

The biggest name to come out of Florence is Franco Zeffirelli (b 1923). His varied career took him from radio and theatre to opera productions and occasional stints as an aide to Luchino Visconti on several films. His film-directing days began in earnest in the late 1970s and some may remember his TV blockbuster *Jesus of Nazareth* (1977). Many of his productions have been non-Italian. A couple of his more interesting works are *Young Toscanini*

(1988) and *Hamlet* (1990), a British-US co-production, and he visited his hometown to film *Tea with Mussolini*, starring Maggie Smith, in 1999.

Neri Parenti (b 1950) started directing in 1979. Since 1980 he has been kept busy directing the comedian Paolo Villaggio in a seemingly endless stream of films featuring Fantozzi, Villaggio's best-known comic character, a sort of thinking-man's cross between Mr Bean and Benny Hill.

Two of Italy's success stories at the mo-

TOP FIVE FILMS SET IN FLORENCE

- **Hannibal** (2001; Ridley Scott)
- **Paisà** (1946; Roberto Rossellini)
- **A Room With a View** (1985; James Ivory)
- **Tea With Mussolini** (1999; Franco Zeffirelli)
- **Portrait of a Lady** (1996; Jane Campion)

---

ment are Tuscan, if not Florentine. Light-hearted comedy is a forte of Leonardo Pieraccioni (b 1965), who directs and acts in his productions. *Il Ciclone* (The Cyclone; 1996), about the effects of the arrival of a small flamenco troupe on the lads of a small Tuscan town, was one of the biggest ever box-office hits in Italian cinema history and marked the high point of the Cecchi Gori film company that produced it. *Il Principe e Il Pirata* (The Prince and the Pirate; 2001) has Pieraccioni starring as a timid Florentine school teacher who discovers at his father's funeral that his dad isn't dead, he's just trying to avoid debts, opening up a whole can of worms in the protagonist's hitherto tranquil life.

Long established as one of Italy's favourite comedy actors, Roberto Benigni (b 1952) won three Oscars in 1999, including Best Actor – an honour rarely bestowed by Hollywood upon anyone but its own – for his *La Vita è Bella* (Life is Beautiful; 1998). The film, which he directed and starred in, is the story of an Italian Jewish family that ends up in a concentration camp, where the father tries to hide its horrors from his son by pretending it's all a game.

Florence has starred in many local and foreign films, from Roberto Rossellini's neorealist *Paisà* (1946), which deals with the Allied entry into Florence in WWII, to James Ivory's mellifluous *A Room With a View* (1985), starring Helena Bonham-Carter in a pre-WWI story of romance and coming of age based on a novel by E M Forster, and Jane Campion's rendition of Henry James's *Portrait of a Lady* (1996), starring Nicole Kidman and John Malkovich.

From the sublime to the plain scary, *Hannibal* (2001) moves the spine-tingling story of the cannibal to Florence where, since *Silence of the Lambs*, Dr Lecter has been in reclusive retirement…up to a point. Ridley Scott directed this blood-curdling sequel which, perhaps predictably, isn't quite up to the original. It's not short on horror and gore however, as the terrifying murder scenes in the Palazzo Vecchio attest. For a little more on Florence as a movie set, see the last walking itinerary in the Walking Tours chapter (p122).

THEATRE & DANCE

Florence attracts plenty of theatre and dance performances, ranging from the classics at the Teatro Verdi to more avant-garde and experimental work. But the city has not had a starring role in the history of Italian theatre. True, the Florentine Giovanni Battista Fagiuoli (1660–1742) was among those who made the first tentative steps away from the *commedia dell'arte* (popular comedy), which had become something of a fixture in the Italian repertoire since the early 16th century, but it would fall to the Venetian Carlo Goldoni to work a true revolution in the theatre.

Nowadays local companies are thin on the ground. The busiest is Teatro della Limonaia (p154), which performs a lively mix of international contemporary pieces and original home-grown productions.

The Florence Dance Festival (p11) attracts hundreds of modern dance companies from around the world to the Arno. Local dance groups, such as the Florence Dance Cultural Center and the Centro Danza Company Blu, occasionally stage contemporary pieces around town, financed by year-round courses and workshops (sometimes run by international figures) for the city's aspiring dancers.

Food

Food

As with many Mediterranean cuisines, the cooking of Florence and Tuscany is essentially the result of poverty. Making the best of a bad thing, Florentines of centuries ago set store by fresh products thrown together as best as possible to provide tasty, simple meals. In some ways, little has changed, except that the range of products available is greater than the average Florentine might have imagined back in the Middle Ages.

Florentines, now as then, rely heavily on the quality of ingredients and the liberal use of herbs such as basil, thyme, parsley and rosemary. Walk into a grocery shop and marvel at all the different types of tomato – small wonder some staple dishes are tomato-based (see Primi Piatti, p42). Being inland, Florence is a city of carnivores. Aside from the huge *bistecca alla fiorentina,* a massive T-bone steak, the lo-

Dolci *(p43), the sweet and light fourth course*

cals have a penchant for pork, game (especially boar and rabbit) and several other cuts of beef. Many Florentines, following a tradition dating from a time when most could often not afford meat, gorge themselves on bovine tripe. Pasta, as we shall see, is not a quintessential Tuscan element, but olive oil winds up in just about everything. It hardly requires mentioning that all is washed down with the wonderful (and predominantly red) wines produced across Tuscany.

Pasta is not the only import from elsewhere in Italy. A handful of Florentine restaurants specialise in seafood, importing in part some rich traditions from the Tuscan coast – some are very good, others less so.

Although less impressed by the fusion fashions that have so inundated cities across much of the West, Florence is no slouch on style – whether in preparing its own great dishes or presenting an innovative interpretation on local, national or international recipes.

HISTORY & CULTURE

We may read about the legendary culinary excesses of medieval barons and, later, the Medici and their pals, but these table habits were not passed down through the ages.

While the bulk of the population could rarely afford meat, and in times of bad harvests were reduced to cooking up dishes using anything that came to hand (including tree bark), Florence's movers and shakers gorged themselves on delicacies such as beef, pheasant, peacock, pike and eel, dressed in all sorts of weird and wonderful sauces – sometimes to disguise a rancidity hard to avoid in the days without refrigerators. These ranged from such red sauces as *savore sanguino* (which contained wine, raisins, meat, cinnamon, sandal and sumac) to spicy concoctions of ground almonds, cinnamon, ginger and cloves. Huge pies were often cooked up, with all but the kitchen utensils thrown into what today might appear a strange mix: pork, dates, fruit, cured meats, eggs – you name it, they chucked it in.

Still, even without such medieval extravagance, the modern diner in Florence has a rich choice, from simple hearty local dishes through to Tuscan and Italian regional specialities.

In Tuscany, tradition influences much of the cook's work. She or he may tweak and fiddle (as exemplified in the growing boldness in the preparation of pasta sauces), but generally

CHOOSING YOUR DINING LOCATION

Florentines don't just go to *ristorantes* (restaurants) to eat – although they may well do so if looking for a fine gourmet experience or to sample one of the handful of trendy new designer spots in town. An earthier, frequently cheaper and often family-run alternative is the trattoria, and another similar option is the *osteria*. The distinctions between such places have become blurred, as many *ristorante* owners use the name trattoria or *osteria* to convey a homely, down-to-earth style that may not always reflect what you find inside.

Wine lovers should look out for the local *enoteca*. These establishments offer snacks and sometimes full meals to accompany a selection of wines, but their main business is the latter – food is viewed as an accompaniment to your chosen tipple(s). Generally the idea is to try different wines by the glass as you nibble.

At lunchtime you have further options. Some wine bars, known as *vinai*, are good places to snack or put together a full meal from a range of enticing options on display. A *fiaschetteria* may serve up snacks and sandwiches, usually at the bar while you down a glass of wine or two. A *tavola calda* (literally 'hot table') usually offers cheap, pre-prepared meat, pasta and vegetable dishes in a self-service style.

The traditional Florentine answer to fast food is the *trippaio* or *tripperia* – the tripe stand. These are dotted around town and Le Cascine park, and serve various simple *trippa* dishes or *lampredotto* rolls with spicy sauce. The raw material is basically cow stomach (the *lampredotto* is a particular cut of the gut). *Trippa alla fiorentina* (Florentine-style tripe) is prepared with a carrot, celery, tomato and onion mix. *Lampredotto* is boiled and liberally sprinkled in black pepper or a vaguely hot sauce. For more on this, see p133.

must remain faithful to the old ways. There are those who can solemnly state exactly what sauce will go with which kind of pasta – any deviation from the rules is met with scorn. Undoubtedly many of these rules are sound, but at times they are merely oppressive.

Pasta does not occupy a place of honour in traditional Tuscan menus. Some believe it was the Arabs who introduced pasta to Sicily in the early Middle Ages, from where it was later exported to the rest of Italy. Even today pasta dishes are not considered, strictly speaking, a local product.

One of the city's best-known chefs, Fabio Picchi, refuses to serve pasta at his Ristorante Cibrèo (p136), where, since he started business in 1979, he has stood by a rigidly Tuscan menu. As in other good restaurants, the menu is heavily influenced by the seasonal availability of fresh produce and deep freeze is largely sidestepped. It's a formula that works, attracting VIPs from around Italy and beyond; Picchi once told the Queen of Holland that she should eat her pigeon with her hands – and she took his advice. Indeed, he's quite a success. In addition to his restaurant and next-door trattoria, he runs a café across the road and a theatre-restaurant across the other road, and has lent Cibrèo's name to a couple of franchise restaurants in Tokyo! Picchi has become such an iconic figure in Florence that the mayor, Leonardo Domenici, awarded him the city's highest honour, the Fiorino d'Oro, in 2005 for his services to the city.

ETIQUETTE

Breakfast in Florence, and throughout Italy, is no more than a cappuccino and pastry taken on the hop at a bar on the way to work. Lunch was, and for some still is, the main meal of the day, while dinner used to be a relatively light affair. Modern work habits are obliging many people to devote less time to lunch and have a bigger meal at night.

In the early evening, the *aperitivo* has always been a traditional marker to separate the working day from dinner. For many this means a cocktail and perhaps a few bar nibbles, but a growing number of bars and restaurants are now staging more elaborate buffets. In the past few years the *aperitivo* hour has become a major social gathering for Florentines, who often manage to dine out on the buffet offerings alone – try to be discreet if you are aiming to satiate yourself on bar snacks! See p146 for some tips on where to indulge this habit.

A full Italian meal can seem a little overwhelming, with *antipasto* (starter), *primo* (first course, often pasta), *secondo* (main course, frequently with optional vegetable side order) and *dolce* (dessert). Don't feel embarrassed if you can't face such an onslaught; even many locals, perhaps with an eye on the waistline, now tend to skip one or more courses.

The first one to ditch is the *antipasto,* which kills your appetite and distracts attention from the main. It is of course much more fun to have a first and a main dish, as traditionally everyone once did, but you can opt for one over the other. Some have an *antipasto* instead of a *primo*.

If ordering house wine, it will generally come in carafes of a quarter, half or full litre. The same goes for the water. When you're ready to order, seek out a waiter and ask *Posso/ possiamo ordinare?* (May I/we order?).

Smokers beware. Since early 2005 smoking has been banned in all closed public areas, and few restaurants have created special smoking areas. If you eat outside, no problem.

And, before you dig in, remember to wish your fellow diners *buon appetito!*

STAPLES & SPECIALITIES

In the dark years of the barbarian invasions in to what was left of the Roman Empire, times became difficult for many Tuscans. Salt was scarce and *pane sciocco* (unsalted bread) became the basis of nutrition; this has remained a feature of local cooking ever since.

Locals have been cultivating the green olive since Etruscan times. Harvest time is around late November, and certainly not later than the Festa di Santa Lucia (13 December). In Tuscany olives are still largely harvested by hand and sent to presses. After an initial crushing, the resulting mass is squeezed. Some of the best extra-virgin olive oil, with its alluring emerald tones, looks good enough to drink. To obtain it, olives are collected early and crushed within 24 hours. One of the better oils is Laudemio, produced in several areas across Tuscany. It is deep green in colour, with a slightly tangy, even lightly bitter taste. It retains much of the flavour of the fruit itself, unlike so many olive oils whose most noticeable quality is merely a bland oiliness.

The main Tuscan cheese is *pecorino,* made with ewe's milk. It can be eaten fresh *(fresco),* after light maturing of a couple of months *(semi-stagionato)* or after up to a year's maturing *(stagionato),* when it has more tang.

ANTIPASTI

You have the option of starting a meal with a 'pre-meal'. The classic *antipasto* in Tuscany are *crostini,* lightly grilled slices of unsalted bread, traditionally covered in a chicken-liver pâté. Other toppings have become equally widespread – diced tomato with herbs, onion and garlic is a popular version, indistinguishable from the Pugliese bruschetta.

The other classic is *fettunta,* basically a slab of toasted bread rubbed with garlic and dipped in olive oil.

Another favourite, *prosciutto e melone* (cured ham and melon), is known well beyond the confines of Tuscany. Other cured meats and sausages are also popular.

PRIMI PIATTI

By the 14th century the use of pasta had spread to Florence, but without displacing local favourites. A light summer dish is *panzanella,* a cold mixed salad with breadcrumbs. Tomato, cucumber, red onions and lettuce are tossed into a bowl with stale bread that has been soaked and broken up. This mixture is then combined with oil, vinegar and basil and refrigerated.

The winter equivalent is *ribollita.* Another example of making use of every last scrap, this is a vegetable stew with bread mixed in – a hearty dish for cold winter nights. *Pappa di pomodoro* is bread and tomato paste served hot.

Tuscan pasta specialities include *pappardelle sulla lepre* (ribbon pasta with hare), *pasta e ceci* (a pasta and bean broth) and *spaghetti allo scoglio* (spaghetti with seafood – basically a national dish). Ravioli and *tortelli,* both kinds of filled pasta, are also popular. The most Tuscan sauce to accompany them is *burro e salvia* (butter and sage).

SECONDI PIATTI

In keeping with the simplicity for which local cuisine is known, meat and fish tend to be grilled. Meat eaters will want to try *bistecca alla fiorentina*, a generous slab of Florentine T-bone steak. Traditionally the meat used for this dish was only from bovines that were raised in the Val di Chiana, but nowadays the number of people wanting to enjoy the meal far outweighs supply. The true T-bone (with bone) only made its way back to tables in late 2005 after years in the doghouse over mad-cow *(mucca pazza)* fears. It is best eaten *al sangue* (rare) and seared on the grill to seal in the juice. You can ask for it to be cooked through *(ben cotta)* but you will get strange looks and the result will be tough on the teeth.

Cuisines born of poverty find a use for everything. Animal innards become an integral part of the local diet. *Rognone*, a large plate of kidneys, is one favourite, although you might find it a little too rich. Tripe is particularly prized by some (see p41).

Tuscany is hunting territory and *cinghiale* (wild boar), along with other game meats, are served at many restaurants. Favourites include *coniglio* (rabbit), *piccione* (pigeon) and *fagiano* (pheasant).

Main meals are accompanied by *contorni* (side dishes). Possible choices include *fagiolini alla fiorentina*, little beans prepared with tomatoes, fennel seeds, onion and garlic.

TOP FIVE TUSCAN FOODIE READS

- **The Complete Illustrated Book of Tuscan Cookery** (Elisabetta Piazzesi; 2002) A prettily illustrated book filled with specifically Tuscan cuisine, which has been translated into several languages.
- **Ricette di Osterie di Firenze** (Slow Food Editore publications; 1999) If you read Italian, this is a wonderful source of traditional Florentine recipes.
- **Tuscan Cookbook** (Stephanie Alexander and Maggie Beer; 2001) A beautifully illustrated coffee-table tome.
- **Traditional Recipes from Florence** (Carla Geri Camporesi; 1999) A handy pocket book with a good array of traditional home-cooking recipes.
- **Around the Tuscan Table; Food, Family and Gender in Twentieth Century Florence** (Carole Counihan; 2004) A rather learned approach to food and Florentine society, this is not a recipe book!

DOLCI

Tuscan menus are a little poor in after-dinner sweets. Almond-based biscuits, such as Siena's *cantucci* or *biscottini di Prato*, are traditional and best chomped while sipping sweet *vin santo*. Lighter, but also using almonds, are *brutti ma buoni* (literally 'ugly but good') pastries. *Schiacciata con l'uva* is a flat pastry covered in crushed red grapes and is available in the late autumn months after the grape harvest.

When trawling speciality food shops, search out *cassata fiorenza*, a light wafer biscuit stuffed with almond cream and covered in a thick layer of chocolate.

If it's a gelato you want, head for a *gelateria* rather than taking whatever ice cream the restaurant offers.

VEGETARIANS & VEGANS

Vegans will only feel at home in a couple of places in Florence (noted in the Eating chapter) but less strict vegetarians will have little trouble. In most restaurants you will find at least one or two pasta dishes prepared with vegetables. You can then follow up with salads or vegetable side dishes.

CHILDREN

As a rule children are welcome in typical Florentine restaurants, although active infants may not be well received in some of the classier dining options. A few places offer a children's menu or half portions but it's just as easy to improvise with a tasty pasta dish. Few restaurants are equipped with highchairs for infants, although it never hurts to ask.

DRINKS

You are bound to hear the call of the wine in Florence, capital of one of the world's greatest wine-making regions. Those who prefer a beer or something stronger are catered for, but the thought of passing up the luscious fruit of the vine is almost too painful to contemplate.

NONALCOHOLIC DRINKS

The first-time visitor is likely to be confused by the many ways in which the locals consume their caffeine. As in other Latin countries, Italians take their coffee seriously. Consequently they also make it complicated – see the boxed text, p126.

Italians don't drink a lot of *tè* (tea) and, if they do, it's generally only in the late afternoon, when they might take a cup with a few *pasticcini* (small cakes). You can order tea in bars, although it will usually arrive in the form of a cup of warm water with an accompanying tea bag. If this doesn't suit your taste, ask for the water *molto caldo* or *bollente* (boiling).

Granita, a drink made of crushed ice with fresh lemon or other fruit juices – or with coffee topped with fresh whipped cream – is a Sicilian speciality, but you'll see it in Florence in the summer months too.

Tap water is safe but Italians prefer *acqua minerale* (mineral water). You will be asked in restaurants and bars whether you would prefer *frizzante/gasata* (sparkling water) or *naturale/ferma* (still). If you just want a glass of tap water, ask for *acqua del rubinetto*.

ALCOHOLIC DRINKS

Vino (wine) is an essential accompaniment to any meal, and *digestivi* (liqueurs) are a popular way to end one. Florentines are justifiably proud of the myriad wines produced throughout Tuscany and it would be surprising for dinnertime conversation not to touch on the subject at least for a moment. If you happen to be in Tuscany around the end of May (check precise dates with the tourist office), keep your eyes open for wine-makers and cellars who open their doors to visitors, and for tasting tours (often at a price) in the annual Cantine Aperte (Open Cellars) event. For dates and information (in Italian only) you can check the Movimento del Turismo del Vino website (www.movimento turismovino.it).

Wine prices are reasonable and you will rarely pay more than €15 for a decent bottle. To be sure of top quality, you need to look around the €25 mark. A ruby-red Brunello will be yours from about €35 to €45. An exceptional *riserva* (reserve) or Super Tuscan can cost €80 to €100.

In Florence you will often see wines from other Italian regions on sale, but only rarely from outside of Italy. The average trattoria will generally stock only a limited range of bottled wines, but better restaurants should present a carefully chosen selection from around Tuscany and beyond. Wine shops, *enoteche* and some *osterie* concentrate on presenting a range of fine wines rather than on the food, which is almost seen as an accompaniment to the drink.

Tuscan Wines

Tuscany, perhaps surprisingly to some, actually ranks third (behind the Veneto and Piedmont regions) in Italy's production of

A PRE-DAWN CALL

The best alarm clock is a hungry cockerel! Legend has it that in misty medieval times Florence and Siena decided to settle their dispute over control of the Chianti region by each sending a knight into the territory. Where they met would mark the boundary line. The knights were to leave upon being woken at dawn by the cock's cry. In Florence the citizens half-starved a black cockerel so that it would sing early, but in Siena they decided to stuff a white cockerel with food so that it would have the strength to cry out loudly. In the end, the Florentine chook, awoken by hunger pangs, had the knight awake and saddled up before dawn. The Sienese knight snoozed through, along with the white cockerel, until late in the morning. And so the point where they met was so far south that Florence annexed practically the entire Chianti region (the deal was sealed by treaty in 1208). They later set up the Chianti League, which adopted the Black Cockerel as its standard, and it has remained a symbol of the region ever since.

THE NOBLEST NAMES

In 1385 Giovanni di Piero Antinori joined the Florentine winemakers' guild (Arte dei Vinattieri) and so began one of the longest family business traditions in the world. Today, the **Marchesi Antinori** (www.antinori.it) represent one of the great established and noble wine-making families that still call some of the shots on the Tuscan scene. They have vineyards in Tuscany and Umbria and as far off as California and Chile.

The Antinori family produces all sorts of wines, from the prize-winning Badia a Passignano Riserva (a Chianti Classico) to a little known rosé, Cipresseto. They also have holdings that produce Brunello di Montalcino and Vino Nobile di Montepulciano.

Barone Ricasoli (www.ricasoli.it) is another of the grand names in the business. The Ricasoli clan have been based at the Castello di Brolio in Gaiole del Chianti since 1141. The Chianti Classico produced under that label is a constant winner with the judges, and their *riserva*, Rocca Guicciarda, is also excellent. They produce many wines, as well as grappa, Vin Santo and olive oil.

The **Marchesi de' Frescobaldi** (www.frescobaldi.it) is another family with centuries of wine history. Like the others, they are not shy about combining tradition with adventure. In the 1990s they were the first to produce wine (their Luce line) in Montalcino that combined the classic Sangiovese with Merlot.

Other names of similar ilk include **Folonari** (www.tenutefolonari.com) and **Mazzei** (www.fonterutoli.it). The former's Il Pareto (2001) has received wide acclaim. The Mazzei family is based in the Castello di Fonterutoli, south of Castellina in Chianti, where Florence and Siena signed a treaty in 1208 assigning the Chianti area to Florence.

classified wines. In total volume it comes eighth out of the country's 20 regions, largely because the lie of the land is restrictive.

Six of Italy's 26 top-ranked DOCG (see the boxed text, p46, for an explanation of the terminology) wines come from Tuscany: Brunello, Carmignano, Chianti, Chianti Classico, Vernaccia di San Gimignano and Vino Nobile di Montepulciano.

There was a time when the majority of wine coming out of Tuscany was the rough and ready, if highly palatable, Chianti in flasks. The Chianti region remains the heartland of Tuscan wine production, but since the 1970s and '80s vintners have been concentrating on quality rather than quantity.

The best, Chianti Classico (red wine), comes from seven zones and under many different guises. The base for all is the Sangiovese grape, although other grape types are added in varying modest quantities to produce different styles of wine. Chianti Classico wines share the Gallo Nero (Black Cockerel) emblem (see the boxed text, opposite).

But the choice doesn't stop at Chianti. Among Italy's most esteemed and priciest drops is the Brunello di Montalcino (in Siena province). Until not so long ago only a handful of established estates produced this grand old red, but now everyone seems to be at it. One reckoning counts some 60 producers turning out a good product, which as usual varies a great deal in style depending on soil, microclimate and so on. Like the Chianti reds, the Sangiovese grape is at the heart of the Brunello. It is aged in oak casks for four years and then for another two years in bottles. A particularly good one is the Prime Donne (1999).

Another Sangiovese-based winner is Vino Nobile di Montepulciano, named after a hill-top town in Siena province. The grape blend and conditions here make this a quite distinctive wine too, but it is not aged for as long as the Brunello.

An important development since the end of the 1980s has been the rise of Super Tuscans. Departing from the norms imposed

Relaxing at table, Via del Pronconsolo

WHAT'S IN A LABEL?

Since the 1960s, Italian wine has been graded according to four main classifications, which appear on their labels. *Vino da tavola* (table wine) indicates no specific classification; IGT *(indicazione geografica tipica)* means that the wine is typical of a certain area; DOC *(denominazione di origine controllata)* declares that the wines are produced subject to certain specifications regarding grape types and method; and DOCG *(denominazione di origine controllata e garantita)* shows the wine is subject to the same requirements as normal DOC, but that it is also tested by government inspectors.

Superiore can denote DOC wines above the general standard (perhaps with greater alcohol content or longer ageing). *Riserva* is applied only to DOC or DOCG wines that have aged for a specified time.

Tuscany has 13 DOC wine areas and six DOCGs. Several producers in the same area can boast the same label. The Chianti Classico label, for instance, covers a long list of producers who respect the wine-type rules and are present in the geographical area concerned.

In general, the presence or absence of such labels guarantees nothing. Many a *vino da tavola* and IGT wine is so denominated simply because its producers have chosen not to adhere to the regulations governing production. These sometimes include prestige wines.

by DOC and DOCG requirements, a growing number of vineyards are diversifying their use of grape types and methods to produce exciting new wines. The ball started rolling a long time ago with the Sassicaia wine, produced by a branch of the Antinori family using cabernet cuttings brought from Bordeaux and planted as early as 1944 at the now well-respected Bolgheri estate in the coastal south of Tuscany. The wine won the attention of an international audience in the late 1970s and a trend was born. Not long after, the Antinori clan produced Tignanello, combining Sangiovese with cabernet sauvignon. Now vintners are growing, with increasing enthusiasm, Cabernet, Cabernet Sauvignon, Merlot, Syrah, Pinot Noir and other foreign grape varieties, and mixing them with the Sangiovese.

The results are some first-class wines that continue to shake the wine establishment as the public is weaned off DOC-dependence. Some have been classed among the best wines in all Italy. By all means try the classics, but then experiment with these emerging wines.

Tuscany is not all about reds. Easily the most widely known white is the Vernaccia di San Gimignano. Increasingly they are aged in modern oak *barriques* (small barrels). Another important white is the Bianco di Pitigliano, from southern Tuscany. It is not so well known and appears less frequently on Florentine wine lists.

Less well known still are the Tuscan *rosati* (rosés), of which there is a growing variety. The region even produces a handful of champagne-style bubbly whites.

A regional speciality that will appeal to the sweet tooth is *vin santo* (literally 'holy wine'), a dessert wine also used in Mass. Malvasia and Trebbiano grape varieties are generally used to produce a strong, aromatic and amber-coloured wine, ranging from dry (good for a pre-dinner *aperitivo*) to very sweet (perfect for dessert with traditional almond-based *cantucci* biscuits). It is produced by wine-makers across much of Tuscany. Grapes are left to dry out until deep into winter, leading to a wine with around 16% alcohol. A good one will last years.

Liqueurs

After dinner try a shot of grappa, a strong, clear brew made from grapes. It originally comes from the Grappa area in the Veneto region of northeast Italy, although plenty is also produced locally. Or you could go with an *amaro,* a dark liqueur prepared from herbs. If you prefer a sweeter liqueur, try an almond-flavoured amaretto or the sweet aniseed *sambuca*. The black version of the latter is truly heavenly.

Beer

The main Italian labels are Peroni, Dreher and Moretti; all very drinkable and cheaper than the imported varieties. If you want a local beer, ask for a *birra nazionale*. Italy also imports beers from throughout Europe and the rest of the world. You can find anything from Guinness to Australia's XXXX *alla spina* (on tap) in *birrerie* (bars specialising in beer).

History

History

From a garrison town built for Roman war veterans, Florence rose to become the hotbed of Renaissance creativity and one of the nerve centres from which modern Western Europe transformed itself after the Middle Ages. The city's visual splendour stands as testimony to its momentous and colourful past. Since then it has largely languished as a second-tier regional capital – with the exception of a brief stint as Italy's national capital – living it large on the wealth of its historic and artistic heritage.

THE RECENT PAST

There are times when, in terms of elections, there just doesn't seem to be any choice. When Sindaco (Mayor) Leonardo Domenici stood for a second five-year term in 2004 he managed to get in, but only in the second round of voting. A local chieftain of the Democratici di Sinistra (DS) party – the former Communist Party of Italy – and protégé of DS national party boss Massimo d'Alema, Domenici encountered only half-hearted opposition from within the left-wing coalition he heads, and the right-wing opposition has rarely taken power in Florence since free elections were first held in post-WWII Italy. Tuscany, as they say, has always been red.

Politics aside, a national report in 2003 showed that Italy's main crime organisations, the Sicilian Mafia, the Neapolitan Camorra and 'ndrangheta from Calabria, are increasing their presence in Tuscany. They dedicate themselves to drugs and arms trafficking, extortion, protection rackets and gaining control of construction contracts. That said, criminal activity in Florence seems limited to laundering ill-gotten gains. Other reports suggest dirty cash from the Russian and Chinese mafias is also filtering in to the city.

The Sicilians have been around for a while. In 1993 a massive car bomb exploded in Via de' Georgofili, killing five people and injuring 37. The blast hit the Uffizi (where the city's most important gallery is housed), destroying several works. A mere seven years later, the renowned Mafia boss Totò Riina, long in prison for other crimes, was sentenced to still more time for his involvement. Only in 2005 did relatives of the victims finally get civil proceedings against Riina under way.

The Mafia have not been the only bombers in Florence. Terrorists of the left-wing Red Brigades, infamous for the 1978 assassination of the former Italian prime minister Aldo Moro, brought misery to Florence when they killed Lando Conti, the city's then mayor, in 1986.

Less dramatic than acts of terror, but with an infinitely greater influence on the city's life, was a party political decision taken in 1989. After a decade of debate on what direction the city needed to take, the Communist-led government approved an ambitious plan to create a new urban centre, with trade centres, thousands of houses and vast amounts of office space, in empty land in the northwest Castello part of town, owned by the Fondiaria-SAI insurance giant. It was reasoned that a new economic pole would be created close to the airport.

At the same time, plans were also in motion to transform the former FIAT works, closer to the city centre, into another key district of the modern city, destined to house a new university campus (the Nuovo Polo Universitario), Palazzo di Giustizia (courts), housing, offices and parkland.

The Castello project provoked fierce opposition from environmentalists, who soon found allies within the Communist Party. As the debate heated up, stresses on the party grew. Just three days before a definitive vote on the project was due to go before a full session of the

59 BC	AD 476
Julius Caesar becomes consul and founds the barracks town of Florentia	German Odovacar proclaims himself king in Rome, ending the Roman Empire

municipality, in a move reminiscent of the Cold War days in the Eastern Bloc, national party secretary Achille Ochetto called the Florentine branch and ordered the vote be called off and the project shelved. Only since 2004 has life again been breathed into development ideas for Castello (see p8).

On to a darker subject altogether, Florentine tongues still wag about the Monster of Florence. Between 1968 and 1985 six related murders took place in the city, terrifying citizens and baffling the police. A prime suspect, Pietro Pacciani, got a life sentence on flimsy evidence in 1996 and died before his appeal could get under way in 1998. Even today, the police consider Pacciani's death may itself have been murder, to stop him raising the veil on the real answer to the killings. Some believe these were carried out by a group or sect that used Pacciani as a pawn.

FROM THE BEGINNING

Neolithic tribes of Liguri from northern Italy are thought to have inhabited the Arno valley where Florence would later be founded. This narrow but navigable stretch of the river was a busy crossing point, although the Etruscans preferred the heights to the valley and established a settlement at Fiesole (Faesulae to the Romans), possibly as early as the 9th century BC. The origins of the Etruscans remain mysterious but by the 6th century BC a dozen or so Etruscan towns had formed a powerful league in central Italy. The small Latin town of Rome was under Etruscan domination for a while, but its people turfed out their Etruscan kings in 509 BC. In the following decades this initially nondescript place began to bring neighbouring settlements under its control and soon felt the need to move against the Etruscans. They started with Veio, which fell in 392 BC. By 265 BC all of Etruria was firmly locked into Rome's system of conquest and alliance. At that point the peninsula south from modern Tuscany and Umbria was united under Rome.

FLORENTIA

By the time Julius Caesar was made a consul in 59 BC, much had changed. By force of arms and diplomacy, Rome had passed from being the head of a federation of two thirds of the Italian peninsula, to master of the greatest empire ever seen, stretching from Spain to the Middle East.

In 88 BC, civil war had induced the Empire to grant full Roman citizenship – and hence substantial equality of rights – to its federated Italian allies, including the Etruscan cities. The flip side was that, henceforth, Roman public and private law, along with the Latin language, came to dominate the peninsula and indigenous cultures were eased out of existence.

In the year he became consul, Caesar established a garrison town for army veterans on the Arno, naming it Florentia ('the flourishing one'). The project was part of his *lex Iulia* (which allotted farm plots to veterans) and construction probably began around 30 BC.

TOP FIVE BOOKS ON FLORENTINE HISTORY

- **April Blood: Florence and the Plot Against the Medici** (Lauro Martines; 2003) An intriguing, detective-style investigation into the Pazzi plot to assassinate Lorenzo de' Medici.
- **Florence: A Portrait** (Michael Levey; 1998) A city history with a leaning to its art rather than its wars.
- **The Merchant of Prato** (Iris Origo; 1957) Based on thousands of private documents, the life and times of a medieval Tuscan businessman, Francesco di Marco Datini, are brought to vivid life.
- **The House of Medici: Its Rise and Fall** (Christopher Hibbert; 1999) A classic on the fortunes of Florence's most famous family, written with witty anecdotes and easy grace.
- **The Stones of Florence** (Mary McCarthy; 1959) An opinionated look at modern Florence that has retained all its immediacy.

Lombards invade and occupy northern Italy, taking Florence two years later	Florence starts minting the florin, destined to become one of Europe's most favoured currencies

Whether or not Florentia was built on the site of a pre-existing village remains a matter of learned dispute.

Florentia lay on a strategic river crossing and was laid out in classic Roman form, with the main east–west street, the *decumanus*, intersected from north to south by the *cardo*. The first corresponds to Via del Corso and Via degli Strozzi, the latter Via Roma and Via Calimala. Piazza della Repubblica marks the site of the forum. The town walls followed Via del Proconsolo, Via de' Cerretani, Via de' Tornabuoni and, to the south, a rough line from Piazza Santa Trinita to the Palazzo Vecchio.

The first significant urban revolution came in the 2nd century AD under Hadrian, who graced the city with baths and an amphitheatre (which occupied most of the site of the Palazzo Vecchio, Via de' Gondi and part of Palazzo Gondi). Florentia had prospered on the back of brisk maritime trade along the Arno.

Under Diocletian in the late 3rd century, Florentia became the capital of the Regio Tuscia et Umbria (the name Etruria was banned), remaining so until the end of the Empire. The first Christian churches were raised in the following century, although Greco-Syriac merchants had brought the religion to pagan Florentia as early as AD 250, when St Minias (San Miniato) was martyred here.

By now Italy and the Western Roman Empire were in deep trouble. Barbarian invasions came in swift succession in the 5th century and culminated in Theodoric the Ostrogoth's coronation as king in 493. After a Byzantine interlude under Emperor Justinian, the Lombards came to control much of the northern half of Italy, including the region around Florentia.

MIDDLE AGES

After a period under Lombard rule, the duchy of Tuscia, which covered Tuscany, Umbria, much of Lazio and Corsica, fell under the control of the Holy Roman Empire, created in 800 when Charlemagne was crowned by the pope in Rome. By the end of the 11th century, particularly under the administration of Countess Matilda Canossa (see the boxed text, below), the duchy had achieved considerable independence. Florence, with a population of 20,000, was a robust regional capital.

The death of Matilda spelled the end of Tuscia as a political unit. In the wake of its disintegration, more-or-less independent and frequently quarrelling city-states emerged in Tuscany. Florence quickly reduced Fiesole to submission in 1123. Fifty years later a new set of defensive walls was built and Florentine troops were battling Sienese soldiers in the Chianti area over boundary disputes.

Emperor Frederick Barbarossa then waltzed into the Italian labyrinth, determined to reestablish imperial control. In Florence in 1173 he decreed the city's jurisdiction limited to the city *intra muros* and installed governors in most Tuscan cities. The latter, however, took little notice and pursued their own interests.

By now a system of corporatist government, the *comune*, was developing, a kind of oligarchy in which the top families (increasingly a mix of landed nobility and the

WALTZED BY MATILDA

'There's something wrong with this picture – I'm in it!' Holy Roman Emperor Henry IV must have mused if he ever laid eyes on the medieval miniature depicting him on bended knee before Pope Gregory VII and, worse, *that* woman. For Countess Matilda, ruler of Florence and close ally of the Papacy, played host in her castle at Canossa during a week of humiliation for the proud Teutonic despot, come to beg to have an excommunication revoked. Matilda, a mystic personality but no fool, had a long memory. Imprisoned for a time in Germany by Henry's predecessor, Emperor Henry III, she lived by the adage, 'don't get mad, get even'. Matilda savoured the sweet taste of revenge as the Pope let the emperor stew for three days before even considering his appeal. Henry had tried to have Gregory deposed in 1076. He himself would finally be ejected by his own son, Henry V, in 1105. Matilda, whom gossips suggested was the Pope's lover, ruled serenely over Florence until her death in 1115.

1260	1434
Siena defeats Florence at the Battle of Montaperti	Cosimo de' Medici returns from exile and takes effective control of the city

burgeoning merchant class) shared out the leading positions in government, or *signoria.* Powerful guilds, or *arti,* had also emerged and would long play a key role in the distribution of power.

Florentine family feuding as early as the 11th century crystallised as two main factions emerged, the pro-imperial Ghibellines (Ghibellini) and the pro-papal Guelphs (Guelfi). Traditionally the spark that set off this powder keg is identified as the murder of Buondelmonte dei Buondelmonti, a Guelph, on the south side of the Ponte Vecchio in 1216.

The Guelphs, generally wealthy merchants, sought greater independence than the Holy Roman emperor wished to countenance. The Ghibellines tended to be noble families whose sense of power rested in part on the notion of being part of the imperial order. By 1250 the Guelphs were in the ascendant in Florence and 20 years later had succeeded in having Guelph governors imposed on Siena, Pisa and other Tuscan cities.

Members of the seven senior *arti* by now furnished the city's governors, or *priori,* elected on a two-monthly rotational basis. From their ranks the *gonfaloniere* (standard-bearer) was selected as a kind of president. Together they formed the *signoria* and resided in the Palazzo della Signoria (today known as the Palazzo Vecchio) for the duration of their mandate. Representatives of the 14 lesser guilds had no political representation and still less the remaining three-quarters of the population, most of them wage slaves in the most unpleasant of wool industry jobs, like dyeing.

Renewed factional strife saw the reformist Bianchi (Whites) and conservative Neri (Blacks) in conflict over law proposals to block nobles' access to power in Florence. With French and Papal aid the latter prevailed and the Bianchi (including Dante Alighieri) were exiled.

At around this time, one of the great social-scientific revolutions was quietly taking place: towards the end of the 13th century reading glasses appear to have been invented in Tuscany.

A PLAGUE ON FLORENCE & THE PEOPLE REVOLT

In 1333 Giovanni Villani, the city's medieval chronicler, reports that a devastating flood ripped through the city, killing many and washing away the Ponte Vecchio. Around the same time the city's poorest were hard hit by a bout of plague. The city's response was, first and foremost, to authorise the importation of slaves to fill the shortage of servants in noble households caused by these disasters. These were mostly Turks, Greeks, Tartars and Circassians, bought at the markets of Venice and Genoa, Italy's major sea ports.

The massive bout of bubonic plague that then swept across Europe in 1348 no doubt further encouraged the practice of slave-ownership – disease halved Florence's population. Medieval Europeans seem to have had an unlimited capacity for absorbing punishment and over the next 17 years Florence went on the warpath, bringing San Gimignano, Volterra, Pistoia, Prato and Pisa to heel. War and peace were regular as clockwork and by 1430 Florence controlled much of Tuscany.

Quiet times were rare and fleeting. In 1375 a rather nasty band of unemployed mercenaries, led by Essex man Sir John Hawkwood, descended on Florence. In the end, Hawkwood, or Giovanni Acuto as the locals knew him, entered the pay of Florence and remained one of its more capable soldiers.

All the blood-letting, instability, tax rises and food shortages became increasingly hard to bear and a mob revolt in 1378 left city government in the hands, briefly, of the *ciompi,* as a militant section of the proletariat was known.

To pay more effectively for all its territorial expansion, the Florentines introduced the *catasto,* the world's first graduated income-tax system, in the early 15th century. Tax was assessed in proportion to wealth as measured in fixed goods and income-producing potential. Thus, tax avoidance and evasion in the modern sense were also born with the *catasto!*

1494	1571
A theocratic republic declared under Dominican friar Girolamo Savonarola	Cosimo I releases painters from legal obligation to belong to guilds

THE RISE OF THE MEDICI

In these first decades of the 15th century, the Albizi family called most of the shots in Florence. It was by now a given that the real power lay with people behind the scenes, not directly in the hands of any one *gonfaloniere*.

Another family, however, was growing in influence. Giovanni di Bicci de' Medici had steered his bank to becoming one of the most successful investment houses in Europe. His eldest son Cosimo became *paterfamilias* in 1429, by which time the increasing power of his family so upset the Albizi that they contrived to have him sent into exile in 1433.

The Albizi, however, had miscalculated. Not only were several powerful families allied to Cosimo, but he had enormous international support through his banking network. Within a year Cosimo was back and the Albizi expelled.

The Medici family crest was made up of six *palle* (balls), which must have been cause for some mirth through the years as Medici supporters would clatter down the street on horseback crying out: 'Balls! Balls! Balls!' The word has the same less-than-decorous meaning in Italian as it does in English.

For 30 years Cosimo de' Medici steered Florence on a course that served to increase the power and prosperity of the city. Although he chose to remain in the background he kept the government stacked with his own people. In the 1450s, Pope Pius II commented that Cosimo was 'master of all Italy'. Up until Cosimo's death in 1464, Florence enjoyed a rare and much appreciated period of peace. The population reached about 70,000, taxes fell and trade blossomed.

Even before Cosimo's rise to power, the artistic world had been in ferment. By the time he returned from exile in 1434, the Renaissance style had largely dislodged the Gothic. Two years later Brunelleschi completed the extraordinary dome that still graces the

The Medici crest, found all over Florence

Duomo (Cathedral) and from this time on Cosimo employed artists such as Donatello, Fra Angelico and Fra Filippo Lippi on various projects.

Cosimo was one of the few Florentine chiefs to be genuinely mourned by his people on his death. The *signoria* even went so far as to award Cosimo the posthumous title of *pater patriae* – Father of the Fatherland.

PIERO DE' MEDICI & LORENZO THE MAGNIFICENT

Within two years of succeeding his father as head of the family, Piero de' Medici put down a revolt and altered electoral laws, putting control of the elections of *priori* and *gonfalonieri* in the hands of selected people. Piero's successor in 1469, his 20-year-old son Lorenzo, attached the same importance to Florence's appearance as a democratic republic, but no-one was in doubt as to who was in charge.

1610	1769
Galileo Galilei publishes a treatise on the stars, dedicated to Grand Duke Cosimo II	Uffizi opened to the public

A BUGGER OF A BUSINESS

So what was it about the late Middle Ages? In Florence, as in other cities at the time, records show that homosexual practices flourished. The reasons? Aside from those with a genuine gay orientation, it seems that for some men it was the easiest way to get some action.

In medieval Florence, families married off their daughters at a high price, and otherwise tended to keep them under lock and key (which in turn led to widespread lesbianism, although records are less articulate on that subject). Men without the resources to consider marriage, or those who simply wanted to avoid the hassle (a high percentage of Florentine men put off marriage until into their 30s), turned to each other for their pleasure.

Such was the reputation of Florentine males that in distant Germany homosexuals were known by the slang term of *Florentiner*.

'Sodomy' was officially frowned upon and considered a threat to society (after all, sex was for procreation). Laws were passed against it and preachers inveighed against the apparently common practice in poorer families of prostituting their young sons. Many attributed the 1333 floods to divine wrath for the wayward ways of the Florentines.

In 1432 the town authorities set up the Ufficio di Notte (Night Office) to investigate and prosecute cases. The office stayed in business for 70 years and convicted thousands. From the records, however, it appears punishments were lenient (mostly fines) and often not applied.

For more on this side of Florentine life, check out Michael Rocke's *Forbidden Friendships: Homosexuality and Male Culture in Renaissance Florence.*

The Pazzi family, rivals of the Medici and backed by the papacy, plotted to murder Lorenzo and take over the city on 26 April 1478. Lorenzo's brother Giuliano was viciously torn to shreds in the assassination attempt during Mass in the Duomo, but Lorenzo escaped wounded and rallied his followers, who soon gave the Pazzi troops short shrift in the Palazzo della Signoria.

No sooner had he solved the Pazzi problem than Lorenzo found himself facing an allied Papal-Neapolitan army. Lorenzo chose to negotiate in Naples and spared Florence what looked like certain defeat. He then focused on home affairs, creating a Consiglio dei Settanta (Council of Seventy) with powers overriding those of the *signoria*. Lorenzo il Magnifico (the Magnificent), as he was now dubbed, had the reins of power in his hands.

Lorenzo continued the promotion of the arts (the young Michelangelo came to live in the Medici household for a time) but there were worrying signs on the horizon. Since the days of Cosimo, the Medici bank had declined. Branches across Europe continued to close through mismanagement and the family fortunes dwindled.

In the momentous year of 1492 Lorenzo expired, aged 43, to be succeeded by his nasty and incompetent son Piero, who ushered in a long period of mayhem.

A WHIFF OF HELLFIRE

Within two years Piero was out on his ear and the Medici family in disgrace after his abject submission to the invading French army of Charles VIII. The republic was restored and the constitution again remodelled in 1494. The flavour this time was altogether novel. A city of commercial families and luxury-lovers seemed to have lost its collective nerve as it meekly submitted to the fiery theocracy of Girolamo Savonarola. The republic was organised along the lines of the Venetian model and a Consiglio dei Cinquecento (Council of 500) set up as a parliament.

Savonarola, the Dominican friar with the staring eyes, big nose and fat lips, had arrived in Florence in 1481 to preach repentance in the Chiesa di San Marco. He found a susceptible audience that, over the years, filled the church to bursting to hear his bloodcurdling warnings of horrors to come if Florentines did not renounce their evil ways. He called on the government to act on the basis of his divine inspiration. Drinking, whoring, partying,

1823	1865
Florence Nightingale is born in...Florence	Florence becomes capital of Italy until 1870, when Rome is finally taken

AMERICA, AMERICA

No-one would claim that Florence, 85km inland from the nearest sea, has a proud naval history. And yet to one of the city's sons fell the honour of having a whole new world named after him – America.

Amerigo Vespucci had been sent to Seville, Spain, in 1491 to join a business associate of the Medici family, Giannotto Berardi. Little could he know that he would spend the rest of his days in the shipping business in Spain and Portugal. These were exciting times in Iberia. The last of the Muslims were thrown out of Granada in 1492 and that same year Columbus made his first voyage to what he was convinced was Asia, but was in fact the Caribbean. Vespucci helped fit out the next two of Columbus' voyages and in 1496 became head of the Medici Seville agency.

Between 1497 and 1504 Vespucci set out on his own expeditions. On one, in which he sailed down the South American coast into Patagonia and was the first European to lay eyes on the Río de la Plata (River Plate, between Uruguay and Argentina), Vespucci became convinced that this wasn't Asia or India, but a hitherto utterly unheard of world. In 1507 a humanist philosopher, Martin Waldseemüller, printed a treatise in which he described Amerigo as the 'inventor' of a new place called America. The name stuck, at first only to the southern continent, but later to all of what are to this day known as the Americas.

Vespucci had proved himself such a capable navigator that Spain awarded him citizenship and appointed him Pilota Mayor (Master Navigator) in 1508, with the task of organising further expeditions and coordinating the survey of the newly discovered (and conquered) territories. He remained in the post until his death in 1512.

---

gambling, wearing flashy clothes and other signs of wrongdoing were pushed well underground. Books, clothes, jewellery, fancy furnishings and art were burned on 'bonfires of the vanities', and bands of children marched around the city ferreting out adults still attached to their old habits and possessions.

No doubt feeling the sting of Savonarola's accusations of corruption and debauchery in the Church, Pope Alexander VI (the Borgia Pope was possibly the least religiously inclined pope of all time) was losing his cool. He demanded Savonarola be sent to Rome, and the *signoria* started to worry. Bad harvests were hurting the people, business was stagnant, and Savonarola seemed increasingly out to lunch with his claims of being God's special emissary.

The Franciscans, rivals of the Dominicans, had especially had enough. As 1498 wore on, street violence between the friar's supporters and opponents spread. The Franciscans challenged Savonarola to an ordeal by fire, an invitation he declined, although he had no problem with sending a deputy in his stead. The trial was washed out by rain but in the ensuing riots the *signoria* finally decided to arrest Savonarola. After weeks at the hands of the city's rack-master he was hanged and burned at the stake as a heretic. He died along with two supporters in Piazza della Signoria on 22 May. The spot is marked in the square today.

THE MEDICI STRIKE BACK

It took some time and a good deal of bloodshed, but Giovanni de' Medici returned home in 1512 backed by a Spanish-led army. He set about restoring the position of his family in Florence, which should have been further strengthened when Giovanni was elected Pope Leo X one year later. You can see the Pope's rooms in the Palazzo Vecchio today.

But the Medici line seemed to have lost much of its lustre. Florence was not the same city as that of Cosimo's day. Most of its banks had failed and business was bad. A series of Medici lads, culminating in the utterly useless bastards Ippolito and Alessandro, managed to so alienate Florentines that when Pope Clement VII (another Medici) was cornered in Rome by an uncompromising imperial army, the people rejoiced and threw the Medici family out. Alessandro soon returned as duke, but was assassinated by a jealous cousin, Lorenzino, in 1537.

1865–69	1896
Most of the old city walls pulled down	Sigmund Freud visits Florence in September and finds it 'in short, unbearable'!

A GRAND DUCHY

The Medici party activists decided on Cosimo (a descendant of the first Cosimo's brother Lorenzo) as successor, hoping he would prove easy to manipulate. They got that wrong. Cosimo, who in 1569 was declared grand duke of Tuscany after the definitive fall of Siena to Florence, brooked no opposition. In his long reign from 1537 to 1574 he was a despot, but a comparatively enlightened one. He sorted out the city's finances and promoted economic growth across Tuscany, with irrigation programmes for agriculture and mining.

Cosimo I reestablished his family's role as patron of the arts and sciences, and he also reformed the civil service, building the Uffizi to house all government departments.

His immediate successors, Francesco and Ferdinando I, between them managed to go some way to stimulating the local economy and promoting agriculture, building hospitals and bringing some relief to the poor. Cosimo II invited Galileo Galilei to

Arnolfo di Cambio's Palazzo Vecchio (p76)

History

A GRAND DUCHY

Florence, where the scientist could continue his research under Tuscan protection and undisturbed by the bellyaching of the Church.

Ferdinando II was ineffectual if well meaning – during the three terrible years of plague that scourged Florence from 1630, he stayed behind while anyone else who could was hotfooting it to the countryside.

Next in line was Cosimo III, a dour, depressing individual. Perhaps he had over-read his Savonarola, but in any event, this ill-educated bigot was not a fun date. Persecution of Jews was one of his contributions to Florentine society, and he also backed the Inquisition in its opposition to virtually any kind of scientific learning. A little stretch on the rack was the prescribed tonic for extramarital sex.

Before the drunkard grand duke, Gian Gastone de' Medici, had died, the European powers had decided the issue of the 'Tuscan succession' and appointed Francis, duke of Lorraine and husband of the Austrian empress Maria Theresa, as grand duke of Tuscany. The last significant act of the Medicis came six years after the death of Gian Gastone. His sister Anna Maria, who died in 1743, bequeathed all the Medici property and art collections to the Grand Duchy of Tuscany, on condition that they never leave Florence.

AUSTRIANS & NAPOLEON

The imperial Austrian couple visited for a three-month sojourn and liked Florence well enough, but from then until 1765 the city and Grand Duchy were ruled by regents.

They brought a feeling of (mostly) quiet discontent to their subjects. It is true that much-needed reforms swept away inequities in taxation, somewhat streamlined civil administration and curbed the powers of the Inquisition, but the regents' main task seemed to be the systematic plunder of Tuscany's resources in the service of the Austrian empire.

Matters improved in 1765, when Grand Duke Pietro Leopoldo arrived. He abolished torture and the death penalty, suppressed the Inquisition, embarked on a schools building programme for the poor, busied himself with agricultural matters and prodded Florence's

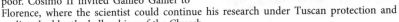

1926	1938
Fiorentina football club founded	Mussolini and Hitler pay Florence a state visit

THE GRANDILOQUENT TOURISTS

Florence has always invoked the most varied of reactions. Towards the end of the 18th century that self-appointed sexpert, the Marquis de Sade, passed through. His interest lay more with women than monuments and he was singularly unimpressed by what he found: 'They are tall, impertinent, ugly, dishevelled and gluttonous. There are not more than six beautiful women among the city's entire nobility. The rest are frightful and, worse, demanding and pretentious...'

Down through the years of the Grand Tour, the French (such as Stendhal, Mme de Staëhl and Anatole France) were outnumbered by the English and Americans. Lord Byron, who spent only a few days in the city in 1816 and 1821, thought the city already spoiled by English tourists, for whom it was 'their Margate'. Percy Bysshe Shelley, who composed his 'Ode to the West Wind' in the Cascine park, stayed longer and thought differently. Mary bore him a son here and as a mark of affection for the town he was named Percy Florence Shelley.

Robert and Elizabeth Barret Browning wound up in Florence in 1847 after becoming bored with Pisa. They soon moved in to Casa Guidi in the Oltrarno (it is possible to sleep there today too; see p181), where they would spend many years. Author of Casa Guidi Windows, and numerous other works of poetry, Elizabeth died here in 1861.

In 1868–69, without a word of Italian and perennially in debt, a somewhat lonely Fyodor Dostoyevsky finished The Idiot while lodging (accompanied by his wife Anna) opposite Palazzo Pitti. He missed his native Russia but he also observed: 'When the sun shines, it is almost Paradise. Impossible to imagine anything more beautiful than this sky, this air, this light...'

The year the Dostoyevskys packed their bags, Henry James turned up in the first of several visits and the city would, in the following years, inspire Portrait of a Lady. Curiously, he chose to pen The Aspern Papers in Florence, although the story is set in a city he loved at least as much, Venice.

The roll-call does not stop there. In later years EM Forster would visit with his mother (and wind up writing A Room with a View), and DH Lawrence with his lover. Rebecca West, Norman Douglas, Aldous Huxley, Sinclair Lewis and Hermann Hesse all spent greater or lesser periods here.

comune to clean up the city, improve lighting and introduce street names. He also made sure that some of the art and furnishings that had been removed to Austria under Grand Duke Francis were returned.

Pietro Leopoldo, as heir to the Austrian throne, had to leave Tuscany in 1790 upon the death of his brother, Emperor Josef II. His son and successor, Grand Duke Ferdinando III, was faced with Europe's new master of blitzkrieg, Napoleon Bonaparte. In 1800 Napoleon created the Kingdom of Etruria and then in 1809, by now Emperor of France, made his sister, Elisa Baciocchi, Grand Duchess of Tuscany: she remained so until Napoleon's defeat in 1814.

This whirlwind past, Ferdinando III returned from Vienna to take up where he had left off. He pushed through a raft of reforms at every level of city and grand ducal administration, and by every account was an all-round good fellow. His death in 1824 was greeted with dismay, not least because no-one knew what to expect from his gloomy son Leopoldo.

ITALIAN UNITY

Grand Duke Leopoldo II proved more able than anticipated, but as the years wore on his task grew more onerous. The independence of the Grand Duchy was menaced not only by more direct interference from Vienna, but also by the growing calls for a united Italian state.

Leopoldo took a lenient line in Florence, allowing dissent and so attracting to the city intellectuals from around the country, including writers such as Ugo Foscolo, Alessandro Manzoni and Giacomo Leopardi. And they weren't the only ones; a whole raft of foreign writers, musicians and artists descended on Florence, some for a few days, others for years.

The Grand Duke encouraged urban development and a series of improvements, including the introduction of gas street lighting, the widening of roads, and housing programmes for the poor.

August 1944	4 November 1966
Allied forces and Italian resistance fighters take Florence	Disastrous floods strike as Arno inundates Florence

The torment of the 1848 revolts across Europe convinced Leopoldo to repair to Vienna. He returned some months later but by then the writing was on the wall. In 1859 a combined French and Piedmontese army defeated the Austrians in two bloody battles at Magenta and Solferino, and the unification of Italy was set in motion. On 15 March 1860 the provisional government in Florence announced the adhesion of the Grand Duchy to the Kingdom of Piedmont. As other parts of Italy also joined, so in 1861 a united Italy under a constitutional monarch was born.

In February 1865 King Vittorio Emanuele and the national government arrived in Florence. Turin had been the first seat of the national parliament, but was deemed too far north to remain capital, and Rome, the natural choice, was yet to be wrenched from papal hands. So an 'army' of 30,000, including bureaucrats and their families, descended on Florence, a city of around 115,000, creating a sudden housing shortage and spurring an explosion of urban change.

In five brief years of 'occupation' (Rome was finally made the capital of a united Italy in 1870) the city was given much of its present appearance. Ring roads (the broad *viali*) that follow the line of the former city walls were paved. Large new squares appeared, including Piazzale Michelangelo, and the growth of whole new suburbs to the north and northwest of the centre got under way. In short, a modern middle-class Florence was born. By 1888 the first electric street lighting was going up.

Florentines continued in large measure to live poorly. Accounts suggest that in the 1860s and '70s delinquency was rife, with poverty and begging widespread. The economic crisis of the late 1890s pushed up the price of staples and led to bread riots. An 1892 report suggested that, of a total population of 180,000, 72,000 were officially considered poor.

THE TWO WORLD WARS

Italy's decision to enter WWI on 24 May 1915 had little initial impact on Florence, tucked far away from the front lines in the north, but by the end of the struggle some 11,000 young men from the city and its province had died in the field. By 1917 the situation on the home front had become grim too. All basic products were strictly rationed and that winter, a harsh one, heating fuel was virtually unavailable.

In Florence, postwar urban plans included creating a factory zone, to encompass the gasworks and the Pignone smelters, in the Rifredi area northwest of the centre. This in turn aided the growth of workers' groups and support for left-wing parties and action, creating the scene for clashes between right and left.

By 1920 Benito Mussolini's Fascists had established branches in Florence and in less than two years it would become one of their biggest strongholds. On 28 October 1922 Mussolini rolled the dice and marched on Rome. In Florence, 2000 Fascists took control of strategic buildings, the railway station and telecommunications posts. The Florentine version of Fascism was particularly virulent and Blackshirt violence became so bad that Mussolini had to shake out local organisations.

In the following years, the opposition went underground or was suppressed altogether. For its loyalty the city got a new stadium at Campo di Marte (1932) and the train station at Santa Maria Novella (1933–35). Then in 1938 the Florentines received another gift, a joint visit in all possible pomp and circumstance by Mussolini and his new buddy with the toothbrush moustache, Adolf Hitler. The multitude duly cheered and waved Florentine lilies with Nazi swastikas. They had no idea what they were heading for.

For Italy, the tragedy began in June 1940 when Mussolini decided to join Hitler's European tour. Things went Germany's way for a while, but for the Italians the difficulties began almost from the outset. Florence's war clothes included asbestos blocks and sandbags, placed to protect the city's monuments. In 1943 thousands of artworks, statues and other precious items were transported out of Florence as Allied bombing intensified. Michelangelo's *David* was encased in a brick shelter and a temporary bunker was built

1986	1993
Red Brigades assassinate Mayor Lando Conti	Car bomb attributed to Mafia kills 37 and damages Uffizi

around the Cappella Brancacci. About 500 people died in seven serious air raids between September 1943 and July 1944.

By 8 September 1943, when Italy surrendered to the Allies, the latter's troops were about to land at Salerno, south of Naples – a long way from Florence.

Italy surrendered, but not the Germans. They established their local military HQ in Piazza San Marco, while the SS (Schutzstaffel; Hitler's paramilitary forces) found a nice quiet place to carry out torture on Via Bolognese in the north of the city.

When Allied forces approached the German lines near Florence in July 1944, the German high command decided to blow up the city's bridges. They spared the Ponte Vecchio, blocking it at either end and mining its shops instead. Early in the morning of 4 August, the other bridges went up in smoke. Italian Resistance fighters harassed the Germans and later that day Allied scouts entered the city, but it would be two weeks before Florence was cleared. The last German forces finally fell back from Fiesole on 7 September. The war ended in May 1945.

AFTERMATH & THE FLOODS OF 1966

Within three months of the German exit from Florence, work began on restoration. Rebuilding bridges was paramount, and by August 1946 Ponte alla Vittoria was up. Ponte San Niccolò was finished in 1949 and Ponte alla Carraia two years later. Ponte Santa Trinita took another seven years, painstakingly reconstructed using copies of 16th-century tools.

Florentine postwar politics were dominated by the colourful Sicilian-born mayor, Giorgio La Pira, a centre-right politician with a strong religious inspiration who vowed to govern for the poor. His first electoral victory came in 1951, after a period in which the Communists and other left-wing forces had together dominated the city.

La Pira, who had been on the committee that wrote the new national constitution promulgated in 1948, was nothing if not controversial. He requisitioned empty buildings to house the homeless, distributed bread to the poor (a stunt in questionable taste) and, oddly enough for a Christian Democrat, sided with factory workers in their struggles with employers. He also indulged in international grand-standing, organising conferences with Third World leaders in favour of world peace.

Disaster struck in 1966. Torrential rain (the city absorbed 190mm in just 24 hours) turned the Arno into a raging torrent that, in the early hours of 4 November, crashed into Florence. When the floodwaters subsided, the city was left covered in a mantle of mud, oil and slime. Sixty-six people died, 14,000 families were left homeless and the impact on the city's art treasures was incalculable.

2003	2005
Restorers clean Michelangelo's *David*, using a specially designed aerial platform	Leonardo da Vinci's Florence workshop unearthed during restoration work in the monastery of the Chiesa della SS Annunziata

Sights ■

Sights

Florence is the proverbial chocolate cake in the way of 'all good things come in small packages'. The city is jammed with monuments and sights, most of them mercifully confined to a small area. There are so many of them that, unless you stay for a few weeks, you are unlikely to digest more than a modest portion. A lot of people zip around the classics more out of a sense of obligation than because they have a profound interest in Florentine art. Before you do anything, take the time to study what there is to see and make some choices.

Not everyone is an art buff. Perhaps you'd be better off concentrating on the grand churches. You like views from on high? Then give priority to the Campanile, the Palazzo Vecchio and the dome of the Duomo (Cathedral). If you are curious about ancient artefacts but not too crazy on painting, dare to be different, skip the Uffizi and head for the Museo Archeologico!

This chapter and the review chapters are divided into quarters, loosely based on the city's traditional parishes.

ITINERARIES

You could cobble together an endless variety of itineraries. If you have the time, just wander around the city to get a feel for it. It is compact so you can easily dedicate a day to a stroll and take note of sights you'd like to come back and visit another day – unless of course you're only in town for a day!

One Day

On a flying one-day visit? You'll have to make some tough choices. You will want to get a look at the Duomo (p65) but could probably skip visiting inside. You should visit the Baptistery though, and a climb to the top of either the Duomo's dome or the Campanile (p65) is in order. After that, go for a wander down through the old city to Piazza della Signoria (p77) and on to the Ponte Vecchio (p107) – which you might then cross for some lunch in the Oltrarno (p137) area. Depending on your stamina and the time you've got left you could, before heading across the bridge, squeeze in one of the midrange museums: it's a toss-up between the Galleria dell'Accademia (p94), the Museo Nazionale del Bargello (p74) or the Museo dell'Opera del Duomo (p67). The hard-core sightseers will then recross the bridge in the afternoon to tackle the Uffizi (p70). That should just about do you in, so from there you might like to just take a stroll – for instance to Piazza Santa Croce (p98), to catch the evening sunlight bathing the basilica of the same name. You could do a little leather shopping while in the area and head to one of the many tempting local eateries.

See also the Duomo to Piazza della Signoria walk (p114), which could serve as a good day route.

IT'S FREE

One week of the year (usually in spring), admission to state museums (musei statali) throughout Italy is free. Since dates change, it is impossible to plan a trip around this, but keep your eyes open. Admission to all state museums is always free for EU citizens under 18 and over 65. Admission is also free for non-EU citizens aged 12 years and under. In Florence these include the Cappelle Medicee, Galleria dell'Accademia, Giardino di Boboli, Museo Archeologico, Museo Nazionale del Bargello, Museo di San Marco, Opificio delle Pietre Dure, Palazzo Pitti (and its various components), Uffizi, and various of the cenacoli (Last Supper scenes).

In some other museums, EU citizens of differing ages get discounts. For EU-related discounts you must show your passport or national ID card. There are few discounts for non-EU citizens or nonresidents of Florence. Still, always ask to be sure.

It costs nothing to wander into the Basilica di Santa Croce, Chiesa di San Miniato al Monte, Chiesa di Orsanmichele, Duomo, some of the cenacoli and some of the lesser churches around Florence.

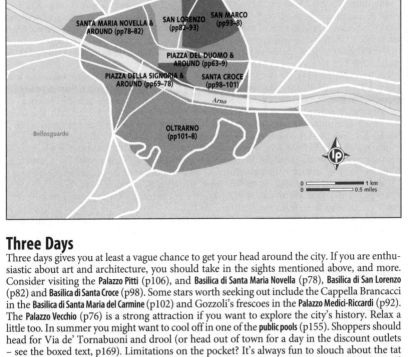

BEYOND CENTRAL
FLORENCE (pp109–112)

Fiesole

SANTA MARIA NOVELLA &
AROUND (pp78–82)

SAN LORENZO
(pp82–93)

SAN MARCO
(pp93–8)

PIAZZA DEL DUOMO &
AROUND (pp63–9)

PIAZZA DELLA SIGNORIA &
AROUND (pp69–78)

SANTA CROCE
(pp98–101)

Arno

Bellosguardo

OLTRARNO
(pp101–8)

0   1 km
0   0.5 miles

www.lonelyplanet.com

Sights

ITINERARIES

Three Days

Three days gives you at least a vague chance to get your head around the city. If you are enthusiastic about art and architecture, you should take in the sights mentioned above, and more. Consider visiting the **Palazzo Pitti** (p106), and **Basilica di Santa Maria Novella** (p78), **Basilica di San Lorenzo** (p82) and **Basilica di Santa Croce** (p98). Some stars worth seeking out include the Cappella Brancacci in the **Basilica di Santa Maria del Carmine** (p102) and Gozzoli's frescoes in the **Palazzo Medici-Riccardi** (p92). The **Palazzo Vecchio** (p76) is a strong attraction if you want to explore the city's history. Relax a little too. In summer you might want to cool off in one of the **public pools** (p155). Shoppers should head for Via de' Tornabuoni and drool (or head out of town for a day in the discount outlets – see the boxed text, p169). Limitations on the pocket? It's always fun to slouch about the tat and leather markets, such as **Mercato Nuovo** (p73) and the stands around **San Lorenzo** (p166). Head for the Oltrarno for some soothing views of the city. You can choose between the crowded **Piazzale Michelangelo** (p107), the **Forte di Belvedere** (p104) or **Bellosguardo** (p109).

One Week

OK, now we're talking. Although you could spend a month in Florence and still not feel you know it well, one week will definitely allow you to get to grips with the salient points, allowing you to mix the worthy with a little diversion. Basically take all of the above and add in your own extras. You should consider a couple of excursions out of town. Highly recommended is a day dedicated to Siena (p188) and one to Pisa (p195), which you might be able to combine with your flights in or out of the area, as well as Lucca (p195) and the Chianti (p192) – the latter is best done with your own transport. Back in Florence, you might like to search out a few of the lesser-known sights. The Museo Archeologico (p95) has extensive exhibits from the ancient world and the Museo di Storia della Scienza (p75) has all sorts of odds and ends. Art buffs looking for the unusual could search out some of the *cenacoli,* the Last Supper scenes painted in monastery refectories; see The Last Supper Trail (p119). Don't forget to take some time just to hang out in cafés on Piazza della Repubblica (p68) or in bars around Piazza Santo Spirito (p145).

ORGANISED TOURS

American Express (see p213) and various travel agents offer tours of the city. Call into one of their offices for information.

Central Sita Viaggi (Map pp242–3; ☎ 055 21 93 83; www.sitabus.it; Via Santa Caterina da Siena 17) runs half-day coach tours of Florence (€40) from the Sita bus station. It also runs day trips to destinations such as Il Chianti (€39) and Pisa (€38).

Arblaster & Clarke Wine Tours Ltd (www.winetours.co.uk) is a UK-based wine tour specialist that runs occasional tours in Tuscany, especially in the Chianti district.

Associazione Mercurio (Map pp244–5; ☎ 055 21 33 55; www.mercurio-italy.org; Via Cavour 8) organises daily (except Sunday) walking tours of the city centre and Galleria dell'Accademia, a guided visit of the Uffizi and one of the Palazzo Pitti and Oltrarno. Each takes two to three hours and costs €40.

For €65 you can join a half-day tour in the Chianti through Amici del Turismo (Map pp244–5; ☎ 055 238 27 53; Via Cavour 36/r).

CAF Tours (Map pp244–5; ☎ 055 21 06 12; www.caftours.com; Via Sant'Antonino 6/r) offers a variety of half-/one-day/evening tours of the city (walking and by coach) ranging from €24 to €69. It also offers guided museum visits and coach tours outside Florence.

Comune di Firenze tourist office puts on a series of guided tours. Generally the tours are for small groups and commentary is in Italian. You can get the latest programme and booking details from the tourist offices; see p218 for locations.

The city hall (☎ 055 262 59 55; www.comune.firenze.it/firenze900) also promotes a series of thematic walking tours called the Percorsi Culturali Firenze e il Novecento. The tours range from literature or cinema to historic stores, all with a 20th-century and contemporary bent.

Florence by Bike (Map pp242–3; ☎ 055 48 89 92; www.florencebybike.it; Via San Zanobi 120-122/r; 1-day tour adult/student €68/63) offers a Chianti tour with lunch and wine tasting. Groups tend to be from two to 10 people.

Florence Walks & Tours (☎ 800 50 11 72; www.tours-italy.com) does a three-hour walk (€20, Monday to Saturday). Just turn up at 9.50am outside the Louis Vuitton shop in Pi-

---

QUEUE JUMPING

If time is more precious than money, you can skip (or at least shorten) some of the museum queues by booking ahead. In summer especially, long queues can mean a sticky wait of up to four hours! Watch 'em sweat and swan on by.

For a fee of €3 per museum, you can book a ticket in advance to any of the 13 state museums *(musei statali)* in Florence. These include the Uffizi, the various museums of Palazzo Pitti, Museo Nazionale del Bargello, Galleria dell'Accademia, Museo Archeologico, Museo di San Marco, Cappelle Medicee, Museo Archeologico, Opificio delle Pietre Dure and the Medici villas. Phone Firenze Musei (☎ 055 29 48 83; www.firenzemusei.it; ⏱ 8.30am-6.30pm Mon-Fri, to 12.30pm Sat). When you arrive at the site, go to the window for those with prebooked tickets, quote your booking number, pay and away you go.

If you prefer electronic methods, Weekend a Firenze (www.weekendafirenze.com) is an online service for booking museums, galleries, shows and tours. For this you pay €7.80 on top of the normal ticket price; reserve at least one day in advance. Print out the email confirmation they send and present it on the day of your visit. You can get tickets for the Uffizi, Galleria Palatina, Museo di San Marco, Museo Nazionale del Bargello, Galleria dell'Accademia, Museo Archeologico, Cappelle Medicee and the Galleria d'Arte Moderna.

Many of the bigger hotels will also book entry tickets for you.

TOP FIVE FOR CHILDREN

- **Campanile** (p65) Kids will love to climb the tower.
- **Palazzo Vecchio – Museo dei Ragazzi** (Children's Museum; p77) Go back in time and play with the grand ducal toys.
- **Piazza dei Ciompi** (p100) Some great swings and things for the little 'uns.
- **Le Cascine** (p80) Let children loose in the parkland or take them to the Le Pavoniere pool to cool off on summer days.
- **Macchine di Leonardo** (p91) Kids (and not a few adults) will love twiddling knobs and pulling levers to make Leonardo's machines work.

azza degli Strozzi, just near Palazzo Strozzi (Map pp244–5).

I Bike Italy (☎ 055 234 23 71; www.ibikeitaly .com) offers full-day guided mountain-bike rides around Fiesole (US$85) and in the Chianti area (US$85), and a two-day trip down to Siena (US$280).

Terravision City Sightseeing (www.terravision .it; adult/6-15yr 24hr pass €20/10) is a set of two hop-on-hop-off circle-line tourist bus lines. Line A (every 20 to 30 minutes from 9am to 6.30pm and hourly from 7pm to 11pm) makes 15 stops around the historic heart of the city (50-minute circuit), while Line B does a longer route to Fiesole and back (two hours round-trip, hourly 9am-6pm and every 90 minutes from 6pm to 10pm). You can pick up either bus just outside the main train station (Map pp242–3)

or any other stop on the routes (the two lines have several common stops).

Accidental Tourist (☎ 055 69 93 76; www.accidentaltourist.com) organises walking (€60), cycling (€65) and half-day picnics (€40) into the Chianti region from Florence. You pay a €10 membership fee and are picked up in Florence and taken to a country estate for wine-tasting and nibbling, before being let loose for a few hours of afternoon strolling or bike riding. Alternatively, you can skip the exertion and join a cooking class (€70).

Walking Tours of Florence (Map pp244–5; ☎ 055 264 50 33; www.artviva.com; Piazza Santo de' Stefano 2) organises excellent three-hour walks of the city (€25 to €39) led by specialists. It can also plot all sorts of specific walks to suit your personal needs and tastes – at a price – and offers half-day guided cycle tours.

You can arrange a personal guide with, among others, the **Associazione Guide Turistiche Firenze** (☎ 055 264 52 17; www.florence-touristguides.com), the **Associazione Centro Guide Turismo** (☎ 055 28 84 48), the **Associazione Guide Turistiche e Accompagnatori** (☎ 055 448 69 71; www.agatour.it), or the **Associazione Culturale Guide Florence & Tuscany** (☎ 055 787 77 44; www.firenze-guide.com). The APT office (p218) can provide a full list of guide organisations in Florence.

PIAZZA DEL DUOMO & AROUND

Eating p128; Shopping p160; Sleeping p174

For more than 2000 years this has been the focal point of what started life as the Roman settlement of Florentia. Here, in the centre of the city and less than 500m north of the River Arno, it is believed a Roman temple once stood, replaced by a modest church after Emperor Constantine's conversion to Christianity in AD 313. As Florence emerged as one of the power centres of medieval Tuscany, so its epicentre gained in splendour. Romanesque, Gothic and Renaissance glories adorn this remarkable square.

Like bees to a honey pot, tourists from all over the world converge on the Duomo (Cathedral) and its surrounding sights. You will need patience to bear the queues

(unless you have come in the low season or are extremely lucky) and around €34 to visit all the following sights. It's heady stuff and will take up the better part of a day.

Orientation

The area covered in this section includes Piazza del Duomo and the adjoining Piazza di San Giovanni, as well as a few surrounding streets.

BAPTISTERY (BATTISTERO) Map pp244-5

☎ 055 230 28 85; www.operaduomo.firenze.it; Piazza di San Giovanni; admission €3; ☿ noon-7pm Mon-Sat, 8.30am-2pm Sun & holidays; ☐ 1, 6, 7, 10, 11, 14, 17, 23 & A

The Romanesque Baptistery may have been built as early as the 5th century on the site of a Roman temple. It is one of the oldest

OPENING TIMES

Museums and monuments tend to close on Monday, although due to the hordes of tourists that pour in year-round, quite a few have made an exception to this rule – the Azienda di Promozione Turistica (APT; p218) has a list of them (online too at www.firenzeturismo.it).

Opening times vary throughout the year, although many monuments stick to a vague summer/winter timetable. In the case of state museums, summer means 1 May to 31 October. For other sights it can be more like Easter to the end of September. It is impossible to be overly precise, because timetables change from year to year and from summer to winter. Museum staff frequently find out about changes only at the last minute. Get hold of the latest schedules, especially in winter (when opening times are generally less generous), from an APT office as soon as you arrive in Florence.

At most sights the ticket window shuts 30 minutes before the advertised closing time. Also, in some of these places (the Uffizi and Cappella Brancacci, to name a couple of the culprits) staff shuffle you out at least 15 minutes before closing time. Closing time means not when you have to start heading out the door, but when the door has to be bolted shut.

buildings in Florence and dedicated, as indeed was often the case with baptisteries in Italy, to St John the Baptist (San Giovanni Battista). Dante was among the many Florentine great and good to be baptised in this spot. The Roman-era north gate was close to here, about where Via de' Cerretani hits Piazza di San Giovanni. That street marks the line of the Roman north wall.

The present façade dates from about the 11th century. The white-and-green marble stripes that bedeck the octagonal structure are typical of the Tuscan Romanesque style. It is said that the eighth side represents the (nonexistent) eighth day of the week, which in turn symbolises birth, death and resurrection all in one.

More striking still are the three sets of bronze doors, conceived as a series of panels in which the story of humanity and the Redemption would be told.

The earliest set of doors, now on the south flank, was completed by Andrea Pisano in 1336. The bas-reliefs on its 28 compartments deal predominantly with the life of St John the Baptist.

Lorenzo Ghiberti tied with Brunelleschi in a competition in 1401–2 to do the north doors. Brunelleschi was so disgusted with the suggestion he share the job with Ghiberti that he flounced off in a huff to Rome, leaving his competitor to toil away for the next 20 years in an effort to get the doors just right. The top 20 panels recount episodes from the New Testament, while the eight lower ones show the four Evangelists and the four fathers of the Church.

Good as this late-Gothic effort was, Ghiberti returned almost immediately to his workshops to turn out the east doors. Made of gilded bronze, they took 28 years to complete, largely because of Ghiberti's intransigent perfectionism. The bas-reliefs on their 10 panels depict scenes from the Old Testament. So extraordinary were his exertions that, many years later, Michelangelo stood before the doors in awe and declared them fit to be the **Porta del Paradiso** (Gate of Paradise), which is how they remain known to this day. The Ghiberti doors you see here are copies. Visit the Museo dell'Opera del Duomo (p67) to view eight of the original restored panels.

Inside the Baptistery one is reminded of the Pantheon in Rome. The two-coloured marble facing on the outside continues within and is made more arresting by the geometrical flourishes above the Romanesque windows. The inlaid marble designs of the floor, reminiscent of those in the Chiesa di San Miniato al Monte (p103) are equally delightful. Look in particular for the sun and zodiac designs on the side opposite the apse.

But it is the glittering golden mosaics that most leave you pinned to the spot in admiration. Those in the apse were started in 1225 and are, admittedly, looking a little worse for wear. The glittering spectacle in the dome is, however, a unique sight in Florence. For some 32 years from 1270, Venetian experts in this delicate art executed with unusual genius the designs created by Tuscan artists. Among the latter was Cimabue (c 1240–1302), credited with taking the first steps away from Gothic to more natural painting.

Around the north, east and south sides of the dome, stories of the Old and New Testaments unfold, including Genesis, the Visitation, the Last Supper and the death of Christ. The western side is dominated by the figure of Christ Pantocrator enthroned. Around him the Last Judgement takes place. Anyone who has had the fortune to see the 12th- and 13th-century Byzantine mosaics in the Cattedrale di Santa Maria Assunta on the Venetian lagoon island of Torcello will notice uncanny similarities.

Donatello carved the tomb of Baldassare Cossa, better known as John XXIII the Antipope, which takes up the wall to the right of the apse. Despite his fall from grace, Cossa had powerful friends and Cosimo de' Medici commissioned the grand tomb for his deceased pal.

North across the road from the baptistery is the **Canonica di San Giovanni** (Canonry of St John), which is being converted into a visitors centre for all the religious monuments around the Duomo. It will contain displays on the history of these monuments and will contain modern amenities.

CAMPANILE Map pp244-5

☎ 055 230 28 85; www.operaduomo.firenze.it; Piazza del Duomo; admission €6; ☽ 8.30am-7.30pm Apr-Sep, 9am-4.30pm Oct-Mar; 🚌 1, 6, 7, 10, 11, 14, 17, 23 & A

Soaring gracefully by the side of the Duomo is the 84.7m-high Campanile (Bell Tower). You can admire its beauty from the outside and, if you're feeling fit, head inside and climb its 414 steps for some wonderful views of the Duomo and central Florence.

Having designed the bell tower, Giotto began work on it in 1334. His death only three years later cut his contribution cruelly short, and it was left to Andrea Pisano and Francesco Talenti to continue the work. The first tier of bas-reliefs around the base, carved by Pisano but possibly designed by Giotto, depicts the *Attività Umane* (Creation of Man and the Arts and Industries). Those on the second tier depict the planets, cardinal virtues, the arts and the seven sacraments. Many of these and the sculptures of the prophets and sibyls (by Donatello and others) in the niches of the upper storeys are actually copies – the originals are in the Museo dell'Opera del Duomo.

People with heart conditions or who are otherwise unfit should not undertake the climb upstairs. There is no lift should you get into difficulties.

CASA DI DANTE Map pp244-5

☎ 055 21 94 16; Via Santa Margherita 1; adult/child €4/2; ☽ 10am-5pm Tue-Sat, 10am-1pm Sun; 🚌 A

Dante would doubtless be unimpressed. Although the poet lived in this part of town,

this supposed House of Dante is an early-20th-century structure built on a site that more or less corresponds to the location of the great poet's lodgings. In other words, it's a fake. That said, it contains a recently renovated museum dedicated to Dante's work, life and times. Pictures and models of 12th- and 13th-century Florence, bristling with the house towers of the city's rival families, are completed by accounts of the interminable squabbles between Guelphs and Ghibellines and Dante's exile from the city. A video display shows illustrations of his *Divine Commedia* (Divine Comedy) by various artists down the years and the lift affords fine panoramic views over the neighbourhood.

DUOMO Map pp244-5

☎ 055 230 28 85; Piazza del Duomo; www .operaduomo.firenze.it; admission free; ☽ 10am-5pm Mon-Wed & Fri, to 3.30pm Thu, to 4.45pm Sat, 1-4.45pm Sun, closed during Mass; 🚌 1, 6, 7, 10, 11, 14, 17, 23 & A

You will probably already have spotted Brunelleschi's half-melon shaped, red-tiled dome – predominant on Florence's skyline – from afar but when you come upon the Duomo (Cathedral) from the crowded streets around its square, you will doubtless be taken aback by the ordered vivacity of its pink, white and green marble façade.

On 25 March 1436 the pope set off from his apartments in the monastery of Santa Maria Novella along a specially raised wooden walkway that had been laid out to the Duomo. Cardinals, bishops and the city's leading figures, including the *priori* (governors) led by the *gonfaloniere* (a kind of first minister) followed in solemn procession. They arrived at the Duomo to pay homage to Brunelleschi's remarkable feat of engineering, the dome, which had just been completed. Brunelleschi had won a public competition to design the enormous dome, the first of its kind since antiquity.

The great temple's full name is Cattedrale di Santa Maria del Fiore and it is the world's fourth-largest cathedral. It was begun in 1296 by Arnolfo di Cambio and took almost 150 years to complete. It is 153m long and 38m wide, except the transept, which extends 90m. The cathedral it replaced, dedicated to Santa Reparata, fitted into an area extending less than halfway down from the entrance to the transept.

The first 'disappointment', if you will, comes from the façade. It appears to blend perfectly well with the cathedral's flanks, the Romanesque facing of the Baptistery and the Gothic work on the Campanile, but the truth of the matter is that it was raised only in the late 19th century. Its architect, Emilio de Fabris, was inspired by the design of the flanks, which largely date from the 14th century.

Arnolfo began to raise a façade before his death; it remained incomplete and was stripped away in 1587 because it was considered old hat. The cathedral languished, exposed, for the next three centuries, largely because no-one could decide how the façade should look.

The southern flank of the church is the oldest and most clearly Gothic. The second doorway here, the **Porta dei Canonici** (Canons' Door) is a mid-14th-century High-Gothic creation. Wander around the trio of apses, designed to appear as the flowers on the stem that is the nave of the cathedral – hence reflecting the cathedral's name, Santa Maria del Fiore (St Mary of the Flower), which refers to the lily that is the city's symbol. The first door you see on the northern flank after the apses is the early-15th-century **Porta della Mandorla** (Almond Door), so named because of the relief of the Virgin Mary contained within an almond-shaped frame (you enter here to climb up inside the dome). Much of the decorative sculpture that graced the flanks of the cathedral (especially from the original façade that was dismantled in the 16th century) was removed. Some is now on display in the Museo dell'Opera del Duomo.

The vast and spartan interior of the Duomo comes as a surprise after the visual assault outside.

Down the left aisle are immense frescoes of equestrian statues dedicated to two mercenaries (condottieri) who fought in the service of Florence (for lots of dosh). The one on the left is Niccolò da Tolentino (by Andrea del Castagno) and the other is Giovanni Acuto, better known to the English as Sir John Hawkwood (by Paolo Uccello). The Florentines made his acquaintance in rather unpleasant circumstances in 1375, when he and his merry band of bloodthirsty marauders gave Florence two options: pay a huge ransom or we'll lay waste to Tuscany. The bankers coughed up and Hawkwood henceforth remained the city's leading soldier.

Although Florence had exiled him, Dante's La Divina Commedia (The Divine Comedy) fascinated generations of Florentines. Domenico di Michelino's Dante e i Suoi Mondi (Dante and His Worlds), the next painting along the left aisle, is one of the most reproduced images of the poet and his verse masterpiece.

The festival of colour and images that greets you as you arrive beneath Brunelleschi's dome is the work of Giorgio Vasari and Federico Zuccari. The fresco series depicts Il Giudizio Universale (The Last Judgement). Below that is the octagonal coro (choirstalls). Its low marble 'fence' also encloses the altar, above which hangs a crucifix by Benedetto da Maiano.

From the choirstalls, the two wings of the transept and the rear apse spread out, each containing five chapels. The pillars delimiting the entrance into each wing and the apse are fronted by statues of apostles, as are the two hefty pillars just west of the choirstalls.

Between the left (northern) arm of the transept and the apse is the **Sagrestia delle Messe** (Mass Sacristy), whose panelling is a marvel of inlaid wood created by Benedetto and Giuliano da Maiano. The fine bronze doors were executed by Luca della Robbia, showing he could turn his hand to materials other than just glazed terracotta. That said, the top of the doorway is decorated with one of his robbiane (terracotta medallions), as is the **Sagrestia Nuova** (New Sacristy) by the right transept (no access). It was through della Robbia's doors that Lorenzo de' Medici fled in the uproar following the assassination by the Pazzi conspirators of his brother Giuliano during Mass in 1478.

The Duomo (p65) from Via de Cerratani

Some of the finest stained-glass windows in Italy, by Donatello, Andrea del Castagno, Paolo Uccello and Lorenzo Ghiberti, adorn the windows.

A stairway near the main entrance of the Duomo leads down to the crypt (admission €3; ⏰ 10am-5pm Mon-Wed & Fri, to 3.30pm Thu, to 4.45pm Sat, closed during Mass), which is the site where excavations (which began in 1965) have unearthed parts of the 8th-century Chiesa di Santa Reparata. Brunelleschi's tomb is also in here (turn left into the bookshop rather than right into the main excavated area). Apart from the surviving floor mosaics, typical of early Christian churches in Italy and recalling their Roman heritage, the spurs and sword of Giovanni de' Medici were dug up here.

You can climb up into the dome (admission €6; ⏰ 8.30am-7pm Mon-Fri, to 5.40pm Sat) to get a closer look at Brunelleschi's engineering feat. You enter by the Porta della Mandorla from outside the north flank of the cathedral. The view from the summit over Florence is breathtaking. Be aware that you must climb 463 stairs – there is no lift. As with the Campanile, people with heart conditions should think twice about this climb.

On 8 September every year, a walkway that stretches around the sides and façade of the dome is opened to the public. You access it by the same entrance as to the dome.

LOGGIA DEL BIGALLO Map pp244-5
☎ 055 230 28 85; Piazza di San Giovanni 6; admission €2; ⏰ 10am-6pm Wed-Mon; 🚌 1, 6, 7, 10, 11, 14, 17, 23 & A

This elegant marble loggia (covered area; porch) was built in the second half of the 14th century for the Compagnia (or Confraternita) di Santa Maria della Misericordia, formed in 1244 to aid the elderly, the sick and orphans. Lost and abandoned children were customarily placed here so they could be reclaimed by their families or put into the care of foster mothers. In the meantime, the orphans were lodged upstairs. The members of the fraternity transported the ill to hospital and buried the dead in times of plague. In 1425 the fraternity was fused with another that had been founded by the same person, the Confraternita del Bigallo. The fusion lasted for a century, after which the Misericordia moved to its present position on Piazza del Duomo, from where they continue their ambulance vocation. They no longer

find themselves obliged to do the rounds with cries of 'bring out your dead!'.

The loggia houses the small museo del Bigallo containing a limited collection of artworks belonging to the two fraternities. Of particular interest are the two frescoes in the last room. One fresco, by Niccolò di Pietro Gerini (active 1368–1415), depicts the 'captains' of the Misericordia fraternity assigning orphans to their new mothers (for which the latter were paid). The other, Bernardo Daddi's *La Madonna della Misericordia,* is most interesting for the view of Florence at the feet of Our Lady. It is the earliest-known depiction of the city and shows the nearby Duomo with its (at the time) incomplete façade.

MUSEO DELL'OPERA DEL DUOMO
Map pp244-5
☎ 055 230 28 85; Piazza del Duomo 9; admission €6; ⏰ 9am-7.30pm Mon-Sat, to 1.40pm Sun; 🚌 14 & 23

Lurking modestly behind the cathedral is the treasure chest of sculptures that once adorned the Duomo, Baptistery and Campanile.

As you enter you see several 3rd-century marble fragments from funerary urns and sarcophagi. Some sculptural groups from the Baptistery follow these, and then various statues (ranging from 1335 to the 1380s) that once adorned the doorways of the Duomo.

You then enter the first main hall, devoted to statuary that graced Arnolfo di Cambio's original Gothic façade, which was never completed. Among the pieces, which, after the façade was dismantled in the 16th century, were scattered about churches and gardens across Florence, are some masterpieces, including several by Arnolfo himself. They include representations of Pope Boniface VIII, the Virgin and Child, and Santa Reparata. The long flowing beard of Donatello's St John stands out among the four mighty statues of the Evangelists.

Out in the courtyard are displayed eight of the original 10 panels of Ghiberti's masterpiece, the *Porta del Paradiso* of the Baptistery (what you see at the Baptistery itself are copies).

As you head up the stairs you approach the museum's best-known piece, Michelangelo's *Pietà*, which he intended for his own tomb and which was moved here from the Duomo in 1980. Vasari recorded in his *Lives of the Artists* that, unsatisfied with the quality of the marble or his own work, Michelangelo broke up the unfinished sculpture, destroying the arm and left leg of the figure of Christ. A student of Michelangelo later restored the arm and completed the figure of Mary Magdalene.

Continue upstairs to the next main hall, dominated by the two extraordinary *cantorie* (choir lofts; one by Donatello and the other by Luca della Robbia) that once adorned the Sagrestie in the Duomo. The panels of Luca della Robbia's *cantoria* have been removed and placed at eye level for closer inspection. They display children in joyous song and dance, and playing musical instruments, in what is one of the most remarkable pieces of Renaissance sculpture you are likely to see. In the same hall is Donatello's carving of the prophet Habakkuk (taken from the Campanile) and, in an adjoining room, his wooden impression of Mary Magdalene (formerly in the Baptistery) – another masterpiece, tense with the stress and emotion of a woman who has submitted herself to fasting and penitence.

MUSEO STORICO-TOPOGRAFICO 'FIRENZE COM'ERA' Map pp248-9

☎ 055 261 65 45; Via dell'Oriuolo 24; admission €2.70; ⏰ 9am-2pm Fri-Wed; 🚌 14 & 23

The mildly interesting 'Florence as it was' museum, behind the Duomo, charts the city's development, particularly from the Renaissance to the modern day. Paintings, models, topographical drawings (the earliest dating from 1594) and prints help explain the history of the city. The sketches and other pictures of the Mercato Vecchio (Old Market) and the old Jewish ghetto area are intriguing (and a little sad), showing as they do something of what was the bustling heart of the city before the town fathers had it all torn down to make way for the Piazza della Repubblica. A fine diorama and some maps complete the picture of destruction.

Another of the sections is dedicated to the evolution of the site from the times of the earliest-known settlement to Roman days, also providing information on what excavations have revealed about the city.

PALAZZO NONFINITO Map pp244-5

☎ 055 239 64 49; Via del Proconsolo 12; adult/child €4/2; ⏰ 9am-1pm Mon-Tue & Thu-Fri, to 5pm Sat; 🚌 14, 23 & A

Bernardo Buontalenti started work on this residence for the Strozzi family in 1593. He

and others completed the Palladian-style 1st floor and courtyard but the upper floors were never completely finished, hence the building's name. Buontalenti's window designs and other details constitute a mannerist touch that takes the building beyond the classicist rigour of the Renaissance. The obscure **Museo dell'Antropologia e Etnologia** is housed here. It contains all sorts of oddments, ranging from ancient crania to arms, boats and other objects from various indigenous peoples around the world. The fusty displays are sorted roughly by regions (Africa, America, Asia, India and Oceania). It is like a stroll through the late 19th century, and there are plenty of curious items, including the hunched-up Peruvian adult and child mummies.

PIAZZA DELLA REPUBBLICA Map pp244-5

🚌 A

On first sight this broad, breezy square seems perfectly acceptable as squares go, but the longer you look the more you realise that it probably isn't an ancient public space. Ever since this square was ruthlessly gouged from the city centre in the years following Italian unity in 1861, all and sundry have continued to execrate it.

On its western flank a huge memorial plaque atop a bombastic triumphal arch proclaims stridently: *l'antico centro della città da secolare squallore a nuova vita restituito* ('the ancient city centre returned to new life after centuries of squalor'). A polite way of saying: 'Hey, look! We've managed to rip out the heart of the old city and replace it with a soulless void!' Even today more sensitive Florentines remain embarrassed by this masterstroke of middle-class 19th-century arrogance.

To create the piazza and restructure the surrounding areas, 26 ancient streets and a further 18 lanes disappeared, along with 341 residential buildings, 451 shops, 173 warehouses and other buildings and services, while 5822 residents were forcibly relocated to other parts of the city. The entire Mercato Vecchio, which had inherited its function as a central market from the Roman forum, and the nearby lanes of the small Jewish ghetto were simply wiped from the map.

Just off the northwest tip of Piazza della Repubblica, where the Cinema Gambrinus is, excavators found a Roman ramp leading down to what must have been one of the Roman town's main cisterns, from which the populace would have drawn its fresh water.

THE MANY PARTS OF FLORENTINE NATURAL HISTORY

Florence's **Museo di Storia Naturale** (Natural History Museum) consists of several sites. By far the most curious is the **Museo di Zoologia La Specola** (p106), followed by the **Orto Botanico** (p97). Lovers of old-style museums might also want to have a peek at the **Museo dell'Antropologia e Etnologia** (see Palazzo Nonfinito, opposite) and/or the remaining sections of the **Museo di Storia Naturale** (p97), housed amid university buildings and incorporating sections on geology, paleontology, botany and mineralogy. You can save a few euros if you decide to visit two or more of these sections by getting the combined ticket (€6/3 per adult/child), which is valid for three months.

If you want some idea of what this part of town looked like before the 'squalor' was wiped away, the Museo Storico-Topografico 'Firenze Com'Era' (opposite) has a model, maps and late-19th-century pictures of the area.

PIAZZA DELLA SIGNORIA & AROUND

Eating p128; Shopping p162; Sleeping p175

Garnished with a slew of remarkable statues (some of them copies) raised here down the centuries, Piazza della Signoria has all the appearance of an outdoor art gallery, but the bustling air of the regional capital. Pedestrians and cyclists rule in the city's medieval heart, where chic shoppers and the café crowd mix with municipal bureaucrats and phalanxes of meandering tourists to create an agreeable buzz. It remains, as it has been since medieval times, the heart of the city's political life.

Orientation

The piazza lies at the core of the area covered in this section, which spreads south to the river, north to Via del Corso, east to Via dei Leoni and Piazza San Firenze and west to Piazza Santa Trinita. Just to the east of the square, stretching in a semicircle from Via de' Gondi to the junction of Via de' Castellani and Via dei Neri, was Roman Florentia's first theatre, built in the 1st century AD.

ARTE DEI GIUDICI E NOTAI Map pp244-5
☎ 055 240618; www.artenotai.org; Via del Proconsolo 16/r; admission €10; ☾ 9am-5pm Tue-Sun; ⌑ 14, 23 & A

During recent restoration on this building, historically the seat of the judges and lawyers guild, curious frescoes were uncovered, including a circular one on the central vault representing Florence, its quarters and masters. On one of the walls is what is thought to be the earliest portrait of Dante, along with fellow scribe Boccaccio. Dante is the one with the long nose. The place has been converted into the new home for one of the city's most distinguished restaurants, **Alle Murate** (p128), so you can opt to dine beneath the frescoes in the evening or call by during the day for a standard visit.

BADIA FIORENTINA Map pp244-5
Via del Proconsolo; admission free; ☾ 3-6pm Mon; ⌑ 14, 23 & A

The 10th-century Badia Fiorentina (Florence Abbey) was built on the orders of Willa, mother of one of the early margraves of Tuscany, Ugo. Willa was inspired to this act by calls for greater piety in the Church, which at the time was coming under hefty attack from some quarters for corruption. Ugo continued the work of his mother, investing considerably in the Benedictine monastery and church. He was eventually buried here.

This is one of several places where they say Dante first espied the object of his unrequited love, Beatrice. It is particularly worth visiting to see Filippino Lippi's *Apparizione della Madonna a San Bernardo* (Appearance of the Virgin to St Bernard), which is to the left as you enter the church through the small (and scaffolding-cluttered) Renaissance cloister.

At the left end of the transept is the monument to Margrave Ugo by Mino da Fiesole (1429–84).

CHIESA DI ORSANMICHELE
Map pp244-5
☎ 055 28 49 44; Via dell'Arte della Lana; admission free; ☾ 9am-noon & 4-6pm, closed 1st & last Mon of month; ⌑ A

Originally a grain market, the church was formed when the arcades of the granary building were walled in during the 14th century and the granary moved elsewhere. The granary was built on a spot known as Orsanmichele, a contraction of Orto di San Michele (St Michael's Garden). Under the Lombards a small church dedicated to St Michael and an adjacent Benedictine convent had indeed been graced with a pleasant garden. The *signoria* (the city's government) cleared the lot to have the granary built. It was destroyed by fire 20 years later and a finer replacement constructed. This was considered too good to be a mere granary, so it was converted into a church.

The *signoria* ordered the guilds to finance the decoration of the oddly shaped house of worship, and they proceeded to commission sculptors to erect statues of their patron saints in tabernacles placed around the building's façades.

The statues, commissioned over the 15th and 16th centuries, represent the work of some of the Renaissance's greatest artists. Some of the statues are now in the Museo Nazionale del Bargello. Many splendid pieces remain, however, including Giambologna's *San Luca* (St Luke; third on the right on Via de' Calzaiuoli), a copy of Donatello's *San Giorgio* (St George; last on the right on Via Orsanmichele), and Ghiberti's bronze *San Matteo* (St Matthew; first on the left on Via dell'Arte della Lana).

The main feature of the interior is the splendid Gothic tabernacle, decorated with coloured marble, by Andrea Orcagna. It is an extraordinary item; to look at the convulsed, twisting columns, you would swear you were looking at a scale prototype for the cathedral in Orvieto (Umbria). Classical music recitals are held here occasionally.

CHIESA DI SAN FIRENZE Map pp244-5
Piazza San Firenze; 🚌 14, 23 & A
From as early as 1645, the Oratorian Fathers wanted to expand the small parish church of San Firenze. For the next century, architects and finances came and went, and the design continued to change. The original church, which stood on the right flank of the present building, was to have a chapel and convent added. In the end, a new church, dedicated to St Philip Neri, was built on the left flank and the San Firenze church was reduced to an oratory. The two were then linked and the whole complex became known, erroneously, as Chiesa di San Firenze. The late-baroque façade that unites the buildings was completed in 1775. Today most of the building is occupied by law courts, although if you get lucky you may be able to enter the church.

CORRIDOIO VASARIANO Map pp244-5
☎ 055 265 43 21; Galleria degli Uffizi; ⏰ irregular; 🚌 B
When Cosimo I de' Medici's wife bought the Palazzo Pitti and the family moved into their new digs, they wanted to maintain their link – literally – with what from now on would be known as the Palazzo Vecchio. And so Cosimo commissioned Vasari to build an enclosed walkway between the two palaces that would allow the Medicis to wander between the two without having to deal with the public. Vasari's original project envisaged that it would take five years to complete. But Cosimo had other ideas: his son Francesco was to be married and father wanted everything ready sooner. Vasari always boasted about being fast with a canvas. Now he and his workshop managed to turn out this singular architectural feat in just five months – the kind of efficiency Florentines can only dream about nowadays.

When the makeover of the Uffizi (see the boxed text, p73) is complete, the corridor will be emptied of its numerous paintings (mostly self-portraits by artists such as Leonardo and Chagal that will be displayed together on the 1st floor) and opened as a link for visitors between the gallery and Palazzo Pitti.

GALLERIA DEGLI UFFIZI Map pp244-5
☎ 055 238 86 51; www.polomuseale.firenze.it /uffizi; Piazzale degli Uffizi 6; admission €6.50 (plus €3 for advance booking), audioguide per 1/2 people €4.65/6.20; ☎ 8.15am-6.50pm Tue-Sun; 🚌 B
Designed and built by Vasari in the second half of the 16th century at the request of

A living statue busker stops for lunch

Cosimo I de' Medici, the Palazzo degli Uffizi, south of the Palazzo Vecchio, originally housed the city's administrators, judiciary and guilds. It was, in effect, a government office building (*uffizi* means 'offices'). It now houses the world's single greatest collection of Italian and Florentine art. Be warned that if you don't book ahead you could be queuing for hours to get in. In busy periods the museum can be fully booked for a couple of days, making the line-up potentially fruitless, depending on how long those who have booked stay inside!

Vasari designed the private corridor, Corridoio Vasariano, linking Palazzo Vecchio with Palazzo Pitti, through the Uffizi and across the Ponte Vecchio.

Cosimo I's successor, Francesco I, commissioned the architect Buontalenti to modify the upper floor of the Palazzo degli Uffizi to house the Medicis' growing art collection. Thus, indirectly, the first steps were taken to turn it into an art gallery. It was first opened to selected public visits in 1591 – making it one of Europe's first functioning museums. Francesco also had a roof garden created – now a caféteria.

Before heading upstairs to the gallery, visit the restored remains of the 11th-century **Chiesa di San Piero Scheraggio**. The church's apse was incorporated into the structure of the palace but most of the rest was destroyed. It is occasionally possible to see the remains in special guided tours, otherwise you can get a fractional idea from what remains on the exterior of the northern wall of the palace.

On the 1st *(noble)* floor is the small **Galleria dei Disegni e delle Stampe** (Drawing and Print Gallery), in which initial draughts and sketches by the great masters are often shown. They tend to rotate the display frequently, as prolonged exposure can damage the drawings.

Upstairs in the gallery proper, you pass through two vestibules, the first with busts of several of the Medici clan and other grand dukes, the second with some Roman statuary.

The long corridor has been arranged much as it appeared in the 16th century. Below the frescoed ceilings is a series of small portraits of great and good men, interspersed with larger portraits, often of Medici family members or intimates. The statuary, much of it collected in Rome by the Medicis' agents, is either Roman or at least thought to be. **Room 1** (which used to hold archaeological treasures) is closed.

The first accessible rooms feature works by Tuscan masters of the 13th and early 14th centuries. **Room 2** is dominated by three paintings of the *Madonna in Maestà* (Madonna in Majesty) by Duccio di Buoninsegna, Cimabue and Giotto. All three were altarpieces in Florentine churches before being placed in the gallery. To look at them in this order is to appreciate the transition from Gothic to the precursor of the Renaissance. Also in the room is Giotto's polyptych *Madonna col Bambino Gesù, Santi e Angeli* (Madonna with Baby Jesus, Saints and Angels).

Room 3 traces the Sienese school of the 14th century. Of particular note is Simone Martini's shimmering *Annunciazione* (Annunciation), considered a masterpiece of the school, and Ambrogio Lorenzetti's triptych *Madonna col Bambino e Santi* (Madonna with Child and Saints). **Room 4** contains works of the Florentine 14th century.

Rooms 5 and **6** house examples of the International Gothic style, among them Gentile da Fabriano's *Adorazione dei Magi* (Adoration of the Magi).

Room 7 features works by painters of the early-15th-century Florentine school, which pioneered the Renaissance. There is one panel (the other two are in the Louvre and London's National Gallery) from Paolo Uccello's striking *La Battaglia di San Romano*

A LIGHTNING UFFIZI RAID

No time for inspecting each and every artwork in the Uffizi? A top 10 of the most outstanding works for the harried art-lover might include:

- **Cimabue** *Madonna in Maestà* (Madonna in Majesty; Room 2)
- **Simone Martini** *Annunciazione* (Annunciation; Room 3)
- **Paolo Uccello** *La Battaglia di San Romano* (Battle of San Romano; Room 7)
- **Piero della Francesca** *Federico da Montefeltro* (The Duke of Montefeltro; Room 7)
- **Fra Filippo Lippi** *Madonna col Bambino e due Angeli* (Madonna with Child and Two Angels; Room 8)
- **Sandro Botticelli** *La Nascita di Venere* (Birth of Venus; Rooms 10-14)
- **Leonardo da Vinci** *Adorazione dei Magi* (Adoration of the Wise Men; Room 15)
- **Michelangelo** *Tondo Doni* (Doni Tondo; Room 25)
- **Raphael** *Leo X* (Pope Leo X; Room 26)
- **Titian** *Venere d'Urbino* (Venus of Urbino; Room 28)

(Battle of San Romano). In his efforts to create perspective, he directs the lances, horses and soldiers to a central disappearing point. Other works include Piero della Francesca's portraits of *Battista Sforza* and *Federico da Montefeltro* (The Duke of Montefeltro), and a *Madonna col Bambino* (Madonna with Child) painted jointly by Masaccio and Masolino. In **Room 8**, devoted to a collection of works by Fra Filippo Lippi and Filippino Lippi, is Fra Filippo's delightful *Madonna col Bambino e due Angeli* (Madonna with Child and Two Angels). One of the angels has the cheekiest little grin.

Room 9 is devoted largely to Antonio de Pollaiuolo. His series of six virtues is followed by an addition by Botticelli, *Fortezza* (Strength). The clarity of line and light and the humanity in the face set the painting apart from Pollaiuolo's work and is a taster for the **Botticelli Room (Rooms 10 to 14)**, the gallery's most spectacular. Highlights are the *La Nascita di Venere* (Birth of Venus) and *Allegoria della Primavera* (Allegory of Spring). *Calunnia* (Calumny) is a disturbing reflection of Botticelli's loss of faith in humanity that came in later life. Some 15 of his works hang here.

Room 15 features Leonardo da Vinci's *Annunciazione* (Annunciation), painted when he was a student of Verrocchio. Perhaps more intriguing is his unfinished *Adorazione dei Magi* (Adoration of the Wise Men), which in 2002 narrowly escaped plans for restoration, and possible ruination (see the boxed text, p21).

Room 16 (blocked off, although you can peer in) once contained old maps and now houses an odd mix of Roman art and European Renaissance paintings.

Room 18, known as the **Tribuna**, houses the celebrated Medici *Venus*, a 1st-century BC copy of a 4th-century BC sculpture by the Greek sculptor Praxiteles. The room also contains portraits of various members of the Medici family. Access to the Tribuna is through a little room at whose centre is a Roman copy of an ancient bronze, *Ermafrodito Dormiente* (Sleeping Hermaphrodite).

The great Umbrian painter Perugino, who studied under Piero della Francesca and later became Raphael's master, is represented in **Room 19**, as is Luca Signorelli. Piero di Cosimo's *Perseo Libera Andromeda* (Perseus Frees Andromeda) is full of fantastical whimsy with beasts and flying heroes. **Room 20** features works from the German

Renaissance, including Dürer's *Adorazione dei Magi* (Adoration of the Wise Men). His depictions of Adam and Eve are mirrored by those of Lucas Cranach. **Room 21**, with a heavily Venetian leaning, has works by Giovanni Bellini and his pupil, Giorgione, along with a few by Vittorio Carpaccio.

In **Room 22**, given over to various German and Flemish Renaissance artists, you can see a small self-portrait by Hans Holbein.

The following room takes us back to the Veneto region in Italy's northeast with paintings mainly by Andrea Mantegna and Correggio. Peek into **Room 24** to see the 15th- to 19th-century works in the **Miniatures Room** and then cross into the west wing, which houses works of Italian masters dating from the 16th century.

The star of **Room 25** is Michelangelo's dazzling *Tondo Doni* (Doni Tondo), which depicts the Holy Family. The composition is highly unusual, with Joseph holding Jesus on Mary's shoulder as she twists around to watch him. The colours are so vibrant and the lines so clear as to seem almost photographic. This masterpiece of the High Renaissance seems to leap out at you as you enter, demanding attention.

In **Room 26** are works by Raphael, including his *Leo X* (Pope Leo X) and *Madonna del Cardellino*. The former is remarkable for the richness of colour (especially the reds) and detail. Also on display are some works by Andrea del Sarto. **Room 27** is dominated by the at times disquieting works of Florence's two main mannerist masters, Pontormo and Il Rosso Fiorentino.

Room 28 boasts eight Titians, including *Venere d'Urbino* (Venus of Urbino). His presence signals a shift in the weighting here to representatives of the Venetian school. **Rooms 29 and 30** contain works by comparatively minor painters from northern Italy, but **Room 31** is dominated by Venice's Paolo Veronese, including his *Sacra Famiglia e Santa Barbara* (Holy Family and St Barbara).

In **Room 32** it is Tintoretto's turn, accompanied by a few Jacopo Bassano canvasses. **Room 33** is named the Corridor of the 16th Century and contains works by a mix of lesser-known artists. A couple of pieces by Vasari appear, along with an unexpected foreign contribution, El Greco's *I Santi San Giovanni Evangelista e San Francesco* (Saints John the Evangelist and Francis). **Room 34** is filled mainly with 16th-century works by Lombard painters, although somehow the

Venetian Lorenzo Lotto managed to sneak in with three paintings.

Room 35 comes as a bit of a shock as you are confronted with the enormous and sumptuous canvasses of Federico Barocci (1535–1612) of Urbino.

For some reason the counting starts at **Room 41** after this. This room is given over mostly to non-Italian masters such as Rubens, Van Dyck and Spain's Diego Velázquez. There are two enormous tableaux by Rubens, sweeping with violence and power, representing the French King Henri IV at the Battle of Ivry and his triumphal march into Paris. The beautiful **Room 42** (also known as the Sala della Niobe), with its exquisite coffered ceiling and splendid dome, is filled with Roman statues.

Room 43 is given over to lesser-known Italian and European artists of the 17th century, while Rembrandt features in **Room 44**. **Room 45** takes us back to Venice, with 18th-century works by Canaletto, Guardi, Tiepolo, the two Longhi, and Crespi, along with a couple of stray pieces by the Spaniard Goya.

Downstairs on the 1st (noble) floor, the **Sala Caravaggio** presents three of his chiaroscuro masterpieces, including the Sacrificio d'Isacco (Sacrifice of Isaac) and a series of works by his followers. The theme of Caravaggio's admirers and imitators continues in the following four rooms. Work on the bulk of this floor to create the Nuovi Uffizi (New Uffizi) is still under way.

LOGGIA DELLA SIGNORIA Map pp244–5
Piazza della Signoria; B
Built in the late 14th century as a platform for public ceremonies, this loggia in Piazza della Signoria eventually became a showcase for sculptures. It also became known as the Loggia dei Lanzi because Cosimo I used to station his Swiss mercenaries (Landsknechte), armed with lances, in it to remind people who was in charge.

To the left of the steps stands Benvenuto Cellini's magnificent bronze statue of Perseus holding aloft the head of Medusa. To the right is Giambologna's mannerist Il Ratto delle Sabine (Rape of the Sabine Women), his final work. Inside the loggia proper is another of Giambologna's works, Ercole col Centauro Nesso (Hercules with the Centaur Nessus), in which the centaur definitely appears to be coming off second best. The statue originally stood near the southern end of the Ponte Vecchio. Among the other statues are Roman representations of women.

MERCATO NUOVO Map pp244–5
B
Leather goods of varying quality compete with trashy tourist trinkets at the 'New Market'. The loggia was built in the 16th century to cover the merchandise (including wool, silk and gold) traded here in the days of Cosimo I.

AN OLD STORY AT THE NEW UFFIZI

When, oh when, will the Nuovi Uffizi (New Uffizi) be complete? For decades they have been contemplating the expansion of the museum into largely unused space and the modernisation of its installations. The rise in the number of visitors (from 100,000 in 1950 to the current number of more than 1.5 million a year) has made the changes a matter of urgency.

The floors below the present gallery have been cleared of state archives and the Japanese architect Arata Isozaki are ready to go ahead with his controversial project for a starkly modern portico exit on to Piazza de' Castellani on the east side of the gallery. He won the 1998 competition for the job but his project unleashed a storm of protest from many who feel his monumental way out of the museum will be an equally monstrous eyesore. All the hullabaloo (in particular the opposition from the central government in Rome) and difficulties caused by archaeological studies around the site may sink the Isozaki project. At the moment, visitors now exit this way and a concrete ramp sweeps down above the excavation site on to Via de' Castellani.

When the gallery project is finished, exhibition space will be double its present size and cover three floors. The present core collection will largely remain as it is on the 2nd floor. On the 1st (noble) floor, much of the archaeological collection (statues and so on) will be grouped with minor artworks organised by theme (such as the self-portraits now in the Corridoio Vasariano). A new ground-floor restaurant will open on the Arno side of the building.

The €60 million project, partly funded by a property subsidiary of the Benetton group, will not be completed before mid-2007. The easiest part of the project so far has been the opening of the **Uffizi Center** (Map pp244–5) on Via de' Castellani. It is a modest, three-floor shopping centre incorporating a restaurant on the top floor and a café-restaurant on the ground floor that has seen the conversion of the city's one-time **Loggia del Grano** (grain market) into a pleasant covered terrace.

The **Fontana del Porcellino** (Piglet's Fountain) at the southern side of the market is a bit of a misnomer. This life-size bronze of a wild boar is supposed to have particular powers over those who chuck a coin into the small basin and rub the critter's shiny snout. Those who do this will, it is said, inevitably one day return to Florence. The statue is an early-17th-century copy of the Greek marble original that is now in the Uffizi.

Smack in the middle of the market is a stone symbol in the shape of a cartwheel in the pavement (visible if it has not been covered up with bags and other junk). In times of war, the city's old medieval war cart *(carroccio)* was placed here as a symbol of impending hostilities. On a less serious note (except perhaps for those on the receiving end), this was also the spot where dodgy merchants were punished. According to the law they were to drop their trousers, 'exposing the pudenda', and receive a sound thrashing on the bare buttocks. No doubt some disgruntled shoppers wish the law was still on the books today.

MUSEO NAZIONALE DEL BARGELLO

Map pp244–5

☎ 055 238 86 06; Palazzo del Bargello, Via del Proconsolo 4; admission €4; ⏰ 8.15am-1.50pm Tue-Sat, also alternating Sun & Mon; 🚌 14, 23 & A Begun in 1254, the Palazzo del Bargello, also known as the Palazzo del Podestà, was originally the residence of the chief magistrate

and then a police station. During its days as a police complex, many people were tortured near the well in the centre of the medieval courtyard. Indeed, for a long time the city's prisons were located here.

It now houses the most comprehensive collection of Tuscan Renaissance sculpture in Italy. The museum is absolutely not to be missed.

You enter the courtyard from Via Ghibellina and turn right into the ticket office. From here you end up in the ground-floor **Sala del Cinquecento** (16th-Century Room), dominated by early works by Michelangelo. His drunken *Bacco* (Bacchus), executed when the artist was 22, a marble bust of Brutus, and a tondo of the *Madonna col Bambino* (Madonna and Child) are among his best here. Other works of particular interest are Benvenuto Cellini's rather camp marble *Ganimede* (Ganymede) and *Narciso* (Narcissus), along with Giambologna's *Mercurio Volante* (Winged Mercury).

Among the statues lining the courtyard is Giambologna's powerful *Oceano* (Ocean), on the Via della Vigna Vecchia side. Cross the courtyard to the small **Sala del Trecento** (14th-Century Room) where, among other pieces, you can see Arnolfo's very Gothic group of *Acoliti* (Acolytes).

Head now up the grand staircase to the 1st floor. In the gallery (which, in the days when the building was a prison, was closed off and divided into cells) are a series of statues and bronzes destined for fountains

Rubbing the snout of Fontana del Porcellina (Piglet's Fountain; above), Mercato Nuovo

and gardens. They include a series of animal and bird bronzes by Giambologna.

Turn right into the majestic **Salone del Consiglio Generale** (Hall of the General Council). At the far end, housed in a tabernacle, is Donatello's famed *San Giorgio* (St George), which once graced the Chiesa di Orsanmichele. David (as in David and Goliath) was a favourite subject for sculptors. In this hall you can see both a marble version by Donatello and the fabled bronze he executed in later years. The latter is extraordinary – more so when you consider it was the first freestanding naked statue sculpted since classical times. This David doesn't appear terribly warrior-like. He looks rather like he is mincing up to the bar for a drinkie.

Another Donatello of note here is the *Marzocco,* the lion propping up the standard of Florence (a red lily on a white background). This originally stood on Piazza della Signoria, where it has been replaced with a copy.

From this hall you pass into a room given over to Islamic tapestries, ceramics and other items. There follows the Carrand collection, a mixed bag of items collected by a 19th-century French antiquarian in Florence. At the far end of this hall is the **Cappella di Santa Maria Maddalena** (Mary Magdalene's Chapel). The frescoes were created around 1340 by Giotto's workshop. The back-wall fresco depicting *Paradiso* (Heaven) includes a portrait of Dante.

Head back into the Carrand hall and then left into a room containing exquisite ivory pieces, some dating from Carolingian times (9th century AD). The closer you look at these miniature sculptures, the more astounding the workmanship appears.

Up on the 2nd floor you arrive in a room filled with glazed terracotta sculptures by the della Robbia family and others. The simplest and yet most captivating is the bust of a *Fanciullo* (Boy) in the annexe room to the left.

From that room you enter another filled with small bronzes. Among them, the two masterpieces are Antonio Pollaiuolo's *Ercole e Anteo* (Hercules and Anteus) and Cellini's *Ganimede* (Ganymede). Backtrack through the small room with the *Fanciullo* and continue into the next hall. Reliefs and sculptures by Mino da Fiesole and others play second fiddle to Verrocchio, among whose best efforts here is the *Madonna del Mazzolino* (Madonna with the bouquet of flowers).

MUSEO DI STORIA DELLA SCIENZA
Map pp244-5

☎ 055 26 53 11; Piazza de' Giudici 1; admission €6.50; ☼ 9.30am-5pm Mon & Wed-Fri, to 1pm Tue & Sat Jun-Sep, 9.30am-5pm Mon & Wed-Sat, to 1pm Tue, 10am-1pm 2nd Sun of every month Oct-May; ▣ 23 & B

Telescopes that look more like works of art; the most extraordinarily complex-looking instruments for the measurement of distance, time and space; and a room full of wax and plastic cutaway models of the various stages of childbirth are among the highlights in the odd collection that makes up this Museum of the History of Science.

If you have a genuine interest in the history of science, then you will almost certainly find at least some of the exhibits intriguing. Many, such as Samuel Morland's mechanical calculator, are from other parts of Europe. Indeed, after the golden age personified by the likes of Galileo, science in Florence and the rest of Tuscany declined in spite of occasional efforts on the part of the Medici and their successors to encourage research.

The centre of **Room VIII**, filled with globes of the world, is occupied by a huge solar-system globe with Earth at the centre and the moon, sun and other known planets, as well as astrological symbols, represented by wooden rotating 'spheres'.

Also on display in 21 rooms over two floors are astrolabes, clocks, pumps, microscopes and surgical instruments.

In summer there are tours (8pm Thursday June to September; in Italian) led by Galileo (well, an actor) that explain how he used some of the instruments housed in the museum and the importance of his discoveries.

PALAZZO DAVANZATI Map pp244-5
☎ 055 238 86 10; Via Porta Rossa 13; admission free; ☼ 8.15am-1.50pm Tue-Sat & alternating Sun & Mon; ▣ A

This 14th-century mansion has survived in its medieval state largely due to the intervention of antiquarian Elia Volpi, who bought and restored the building in 1904.

Closed in 1995 for restoration, it's gradually being reopened as work progresses. You enter via a vestibule and proceed into the small, columned courtyard. There and in an adjacent room are various pieces of centuries-old furniture. Up on the 1st *(noble)* floor are the most prestigious rooms.

The front room overlooking the street was the family's main reception room. The decorated beams of the timber ceiling are a masterpiece and five grand windows open on to the world. Next door and away from the street is the main dining room, or Sala dei Pappagalli (Parrot Room). It is so called because of the birds in the fresco decoration that, in semi–trompe l'oeil style, give the impression that the walls are covered in colourful drapes. Medieval documents suggest that in medieval nobles' houses at least one main room was always painted in this way.

Typically in medieval houses like this, the higher you went the simpler rooms got. Servants were housed in the top floor (often made of wood), exposed to the seasonal extremes of heat and cold. The kitchen was also kept on the upper floors because of the risk of fire and to prevent foul odours from filling the entire house. Although hard to determine, the 2nd floor may be open by mid-2006 and the 3rd shortly after.

PALAZZO VECCHIO Map pp244–5

☎ 055 276 82 24; Piazza della Signoria; admission €6 (combined ticket with Cappella Brancacci €8), audioguide €4.50; ☉ 9am-7pm Fri-Wed, to 2pm Thu; ⊟ B

Formerly known as the Palazzo della Signoria and built by Arnolfo di Cambio between 1298 and 1314, this palace is the traditional seat of the Florentine government. Its Torre d'Arnolfo is 94m high and, with its striking crenellations, is as much a symbol of the city as the Duomo.

Built for the *priori* (governors) who ruled Florence in two-month turns, the mansion came to be known as the Palazzo della Signoria as the government took on this name. The foundations of much of the building are in fact remains of the ancient Roman theatre. Excavations since 2003 have revealed parts of the theatre's seating, stage, subterranean corridors and more. It is hoped one day that these excavations will be opened to the public.

The fortresslike pile is a strange rhomboid shape, in part due to a government decree that nothing should be built on the razed land (now part of Piazza della Signoria near the palace) on which the Uberti family's residences had stood because the Uberti had been declared traitors.

In 1540 Cosimo I de' Medici moved from the Palazzo Medici into this building,

making it the ducal residence and centre of government. Cosimo commissioned Vasari to renovate the interior, creating new apartments and decorating the lot. In a sense it was all in vain, because Cosimo's wife, Eleonora de Toledo, was not so keen on it and bought Palazzo Pitti.

The latter took a while to expand and fit out as Eleonora wanted (she died before the work was finished), but the Medici family moved in anyway in 1549. Thus the Palazzo Ducale (or della Signoria for those with a nostalgic bent) came to be called the Palazzo Vecchio (Old Palace) as it still is today. It remains the seat of the city's power, as this is where the mayor is located.

Coming in from Piazza della Signoria, you arrive first in the courtyard, reworked in early Renaissance style by Michelozzo in 1453. The decoration came more than a century later when Francesco de' Medici married Joanna of Austria. The cities depicted are jewels in the Austrian imperial crown. The poor woman was much neglected by her unpleasant husband, who made no secret of his preference for various mistresses. The thin, pale and haughty Joanna, not much liked by anyone in Florence, died in this gilded cage at the age of 30.

From where you pass into the Cortile della Dogana (Customs Courtyard), off which you'll find the ticket office.

A stairway leads upstairs to the magnificent Salone dei Cinquecento, also known more simply as the Sala Grande (Big Hall). It was created within the original building in the 1490s to accommodate the Consiglio dei Cinquecento (Council of 500), called into being in the republic under Savonarola. Cosimo I de' Medici turned the hall, whose council had symbolised the end of Medici family rule, into a splendid expression of his own power. The elevated tribune at one end was where Cosimo held audiences. Vasari added the decorations, operating with a vast workshop of apprentices, and boasted of the speed with which he could turn out paintings, frescoes and whatever else might be required. Michelangelo once quipped that you could tell by the results.

Vasari and co slapped on the two sets of three panels depicting famous battles between Florence and Pisa (on the side you enter the hall) and Siena (on the opposite side). On the same side as the Siena painting is a statue, *Genio della Vittoria* (Genius of Victory), by the acid-tongued Michelangelo.

On the same side as the entrance, another door leads off to the windowless **Studiolo di Francesco I de' Medici** (Francesco's 'Little Study'), a mannerist gem whose design was also directed by Vasari. The best you can hope for is to peek inside if a museum employee leaves the door open (or by joining the small guided groups). Francesco lived in the shadow of his autocratic papa and sought solace in his claustrophobic hideaway.

Opposite the studiolo, you enter the **Quartiere di Leone X** by another door. The so-called 'Leo X Area' is named after the Medici pope. You can only see the one room as the others are given over to offices. Upstairs is the **Quartiere degli Elementi** (Elements Area), a series of rooms and terraces dedicated to pagan deities. The original *Putto col Delfino* (Cupid with Dolphin) sculpture by Verrocchio (a copy graces the courtyard of the building) is in the **Sala di Giunone**. Have a look at Vasari's *Venere* (Venus) in the central **Sala degli Elementi** and compare it with Botticelli's version – Michelangelo might have had a point.

From here a walkway takes you across the top of the Salone dei Cinquecento into the **Quartiere di Eleonora**, the apartments of Cosimo I's wife. The room most likely to catch your attention is Eleonora's chapel just off to the right as you enter the apartments. Il Bronzino's decoration represents the acme of his painting career (pity this is a copy of the original).

You pass through several more rooms until you reach the **Sala dell'Udienza** (Audience Room), where the *priori* administered medieval Florentine justice. The following room is the **Sala dei Gigli**, named after the lilies of the French monarchy that decorate three of the walls (the French were traditionally well disposed to Florence). Domenico Ghirlandaio's fresco on the far wall was to be matched by others, but they were never carried out. Donatello's restored bronze of *Giuditta e Oloferne* (Judith and Holofernes) stands in here. A small, bare study off this hall is the chancery, where Machiavelli worked for a while. The other room off the hall is a wonderful map room whose walls are covered by 16th-century maps of the known world.

Climb the stairs outside the Sala dei Gigli to the **battlements**, for views of the city. By following the stairs down towards the exit you'll see, at the mezzanine level, the **Loeser collection** of minor Tuscan art from the 14th to 16th centuries.

But there's more. By paying a little extra you can join in small guided groups to explore the *percorsi segreti* (secret ways), or head for the **Museo dei Ragazzi** (Children's Museum). The former consist of several options, including the possibility of visiting the Studiolo di Francesco and the nearby treasury of Cosimo I. Another walk takes you into the roof of the Salone dei Cinquecento.

In the Museo dei Ragazzi, kids and families can hang out with actors dressed up as Cosimo I and Eleonora de Toledo – kids are invited to dress up as their kids (Bia and Garcia) and play with the kinds of toys the two grand ducal imps used to enjoy. Other available activities include building and taking apart models of the Palazzo Vecchio and of bridges (for those children with an engineering bent), and peering through a remake of Michelangelo's binoculars. Another possibility is to follow around Giorgio Vasari (or rather a lookalike) for a personal explanation of his architectural and artistic work in the Palazzo.

For any one of these options and the standard visit you pay €8. If you want to add on more of the extras, each one costs an additional €1. Family tickets for two adults and two to three children (€21/25) are also available. Tickets and information on all these extra activities can be found in a room just back from the main ticket area.

PIAZZA DELLA SIGNORIA Map pp244-5
Piazza della Signoria; 🚌 B

Whenever Florence entered one of its innumerable political crises, the people would be called into Piazza della Signoria, the hub of the city's political life, as a *parlamento* to rubber-stamp decisions that frequently meant ruin for some ruling families and victory for others. Often one side or the other would make sure the square was cordoned off with loyal troops, just to hint in which direction votes should go. Here too the Ciompi (working class, or *popolo minuto*) rampaged in Florence's only proletarian uprising in the 14th century. Scenes of great pomp and circumstance alternated with others of terrible suffering – the puritan preacher Savonarola was hanged and fried along with two supporters here in 1498. A bronze plaque towards the middle of the piazza marks the spot.

The Palazzo Vecchio, with its crenellated walls and slender bell tower, stands watch over the square and the whole city. Seat of republican government and later of less democratic rule, it serves today as the mayoral offices. Directly connected is the Uffizi (p70), built under Cosimo I to house his public servants, and today the city's most important art gallery.

Bartolommeo Ammannati's huge *Fontana di Netuno* (Neptune Fountain) sits beside the Palazzo Vecchio. Although the bronze satyrs and divinities frolicking about the edges of the fountain are delightful, *Il Biancone* (The Big White Thing), as locals derisively refer to it, is universally considered a flop. Michelangelo couldn't believe Ammannati (1511–92) had ruined such a nice block of marble.

Flanking the entrance to the palace are copies of Michelangelo's *David* (the original is in the Galleria dell'Accademia) and Donatello's *Marzocco,* the heraldic Florentine lion (the original is in the Museo Nazionale del Bargello). To the latter's right is a 1980 copy of Donatello's bronze *Giuditta e Oloferne* (Judith Slays Holofernes) – the original is in the Sala dei Gigli inside the palace.

A bronze equestrian statue of Cosimo I de' Medici, rendered by Giambologna in 1594–98, stands towards the centre of the piazza.

SANTA MARIA NOVELLA & AROUND

Eating p130; Shopping p164; Sleeping p176

As you wander out of the Santa Maria Novella train station, you find yourself before the Basilica di Santa Maria Novella, one of the most important of Florence's churches,

the Dominican headquarters and often a temporary residence of visiting popes.

The broad squares on either side of the church, Piazza della Stazione and Piazza di Santa Maria Novella, are places of transit. The former is the city's principal arrival and departure point and temporary outdoor social club for some of the city's Latin American community. At night it is just plain seedy.

The atmosphere has rubbed off onto the largely pedestrianised Piazza di Santa Maria Novella, a grand open space dominated by the façade of the eponymous church that invites passers-by to pause in admiration but not to hang around. From the 16th to the 19th centuries, it hosted the annual Palio dei Cocchi (Chariot Race), which went around the two marble obelisks atop bronze turtles made by Giambologna in 1608. The town council has an ambitious plan to remodel the square, but no funds have been allocated or dates set.

Orientation

For the purposes of this book, this area stretches north to Viale Fratelli Rosselli, south to the Arno, west to Le Cascine and as far east as Via de' Tornabuoni.

BASILICA DI SANTA MARIA NOVELLA
Map pp244-5

☎ 055 21 59 18; Piazza di Santa Maria Novella; adult/child €2.50/1.50; ☽ 9am-5pm Mon-Thu & Sat, 1-5pm Fri, Sun & holidays; ᬵ 1, 7, 10, 11, 14, 17, 22, 23, 36, 37 & A

Just south of the main train station, Stazione di Santa Maria Novella, this church was begun in the late 13th century as the Florentine base for the Dominican order. Although mostly completed by around 1360, work on its façade and the embellishment of its interior continued well into the 15th century.

The lower section of the green-and-white marble façade is transitional from Romanesque to Gothic, while the upper section and main doorway were designed by Alberti and completed in around 1470. The highlight of the interior is Masaccio's superb fresco (restored in 2000) of *La Trinità* (The Trinity; 1428), one of the first artworks to use the then newly discovered techniques of perspective and proportion. It is about halfway along the northern aisle.

The first chapel to the right of the choir, the **Cappella di Filippo Strozzi**, features lively

THE URGE TO DISCOVER

In keeping with Cosimo I de' Medici's avid interest in the arts and sciences, the Medici family finally sponsored the creation, in 1657, of the Accademia del Cimento. Founded three years before the Royal Society in London, it was Europe's first research centre. Laudable though the idea was, the feverish activity carried out by its members – some 600 recorded experiments – lasted only 10 years. One area in which significant progress was made was in the study of vacuums. A long-held belief that nature abhorred vacuums was definitively put to rest. The Accademia folded in 1667 but the Royal Society proved somewhat more durable.

Basilica di Santa Maria Novella (opposite)

side of the cloister is the **museum** (☎ 055 28 21 87; adult/18-25yr & senior/child over 3yr/infant €2.70/2/1/free; ☷ 9am-5pm Mon-Thu & Sat, 9am-2pm Sun & holidays). Its two rooms used to be the convent's foyer and refectory and now contain vestments, relics and some art belonging to the Dominicans.

CASA GALLERIA Map pp248-9
Borgo Ognissanti 26; ☷ closed; ▤ A
Giovanni Micheluzzi breathed a rare moment of originality into Florentine architecture of the 20th century with a couple of town houses. This one, a few doors east of Chiesa di Ognissanti, is a pleasing Art Nouveau house whose façade, liberally laced with glass and iron, has striking curves and circular features. Most other buildings and villas built around Florence at this time have since been pulled down.

CENACOLO DI FOLIGNO Map pp242-3
☎ 055 28 69 82; Via Faenza 42; admission by donation; ☷ 9am-noon Mon, Tue & Sat (ring the doorbell); ▤ 4, 12, 25, 31, 32 & 33
Discovered in what had been a convent until the early 19th century, this Last Supper scene is thought to have been done around the end of the 15th century by students of the Umbrian Renaissance artist Il Perugino (1445–1523) to his design. The organisation of the scene is classic, with Judas (sans halo) sitting on the wrong side of the table, grasping the sack of coins (his reward for betraying Christ), and St John snoozing at Christ's side. Unusual are the light, bright colours, the decorated architectural scheme that frames the scene and the portrayal in the background of Christ praying in the Garden of Gethsemane while the Apostles sleep.

CHIESA DI OGNISSANTI Map pp248-9
☎ 055 239 68 02; Piazza d'Ognissanti; admission free; ☷ 9am-noon Mon, Tue & Sat; ▤ A
This 13th-century church was much altered in the 17th century and has a baroque façade, but inside are 15th-century works by Domenico Ghirlandaio and Sandro Botticelli. Of interest is Ghirlandaio's fresco above the second altar on the right of the *Madonna della Misericordia* (Mother of Mercy), protector of the Vespucci family. Amerigo Vespucci, who gave his name to the American continent (see the boxed text, p54), is supposedly the young boy whose head

frescoes by Filippino Lippi depicting the lives of St John the Evangelist and St Philip the Apostle. Restoration has infused the frescoes with renewed vibrancy. Another important work is Domenico Ghirlandaio's series of frescoes behind the main altar, painted with the help of artists who may have included the young student Michelangelo. Relating the lives of the Virgin Mary, St John the Baptist and others, the frescoes are notable for their depiction of Florentine life during the Renaissance. In the **Cappella Gondi**, the first chapel on the left of the choir, Brunelleschi's crucifix hangs above the altar.

The large painted wooden crucifix hanging from the ceiling in the middle of the central nave is a restored Giotto masterpiece.

To reach the **Chiostro Verde** (Green Cloister), exit the church and follow the signs to the 'Museo'. The porticoes' arches are propped by massive octagonal pillars. Three of the four walls are decorated with fading frescoes recounting Genesis. The cloister takes its name from the green earth base used for the frescoes. The most interesting artistically are those by Paolo Uccello on the party wall with the church, particularly *Il Diluvio Universale* (The Great Flood).

Off the next side of the cloister is the **Cappellone degli Spagnoli** (Spanish Chapel; Map pp244–5), which was set aside for the Spanish retinue that accompanied Eleonora de Toledo, Cosimo I's wife, to Florence. It contains well-preserved frescoes by Andrea di Bonaiuto and his helpers. On the western appears between the Madonna and the old man. He, along with Botticelli, are among the local celebs buried here.

Ghirlandaio's masterpiece, though, is *L'Ultima Cena* (The Last Supper) that covers most of a wall in the former monastery's cenacolo. You go through the cloister (lined with a fresco cycle on the life of St Francis of Assisi) to get to the refectory. It is an all too human scene, and touches like the transparent glasses and wine bottles are indicative of Ghirlandaio's eye. Art historians see in this work the main precedent set for Leonardo da Vinci's extraordinary Last Supper scene in Milan. When work was done to restore Ghirlandaio's fresco, a rare opportunity was seized to temporarily remove it and expose the *sinopia* (red-earth pigment sketch the artist used as a guide when slapping on the layers of wet plaster upon which he painted) below it. The *sinopia* is now on display on a side wall.

CHIESA DI SAN PANCRAZIO & MUSEO MARINO MARINI Map pp244-5

☎ 055 21 94 32; Piazza San Pancrazio 1; admission €4; ⏱ 10am-5pm Mon-Sat Oct-May, 10am-5pm Mon-Fri Jun-Sep; 🚍 A

As early as the 9th century a church stood here. The shabby-looking version you see today is what remains of the original building from the 14th and 15th centuries. The church, deconsecrated in the 19th century, now houses the Museo Marino Marini. Donated to the city by the Pistoia-born sculptor Marino Marini (1901–80), the collection contains about 200 of the artist's works, including sculptures, portraits and drawings. The overwhelmingly recurring theme appears to be man and horse, or rather man on horse. The figures are, in some cases, simple-looking chaps in various poses suggesting rapture or extreme frustration, the horses too seem to express a gamut of emotion. At times, man and horse seem barely distinguishable from one another.

CHIESA DI SANTA TRINITA Map pp244-5

☎ 055 21 69 12; Piazza Santa Trinita; admission free; ⏱ 8am-noon & 4-6pm Mon-Sat, 4-6pm Sun & holidays; 🚍 6, 11, 36, 37 & A

Although rebuilt in the Gothic style and later graced with a mannerist façade of indifferent taste, you can still get some idea of what the Romanesque original looked like by contemplating the façade wall from

the inside. Among its more eye-catching artworks are the frescoes depicting the life of St Francis of Assisi by Domenico Ghirlandaio in the Cappella Sassetti (in the right transept). The altarpiece of the *Annunziazione* (Annunciation) in the fourth chapel of the southern aisle is by Lorenzo Monaco, who was Fra Angelico's master. Monaco also painted the frescoes on the walls of the chapel.

Piazza Santa Trinita itself is faced by Palazzo Buondelmonti. The Buondelmonti family was at the heart of the Guelph-Ghibelline feud in Florence (see the boxed text, p50). More imposing is the Palazzo Bartolini-Salimbeni, an example of High Renaissance with a Roman touch (columns flanking the main door and triangular tympana).

CHIESA DI SS MICHELE E GAETANO
Map pp244-5

Via de' Tornabuoni; admission free; ⏱ 1.30-5.30pm; 🚍 6, 11, 22, 36, 37 & A

A church has stood on this site since the 11th century, but from 1604 it underwent a complete overhaul, resulting in the *pietra forte* ('strong stone') baroque façade (completed in 1683) you see today. More commonly known simply as San Gaetano, it is one of the most outstanding churches to be raised in 17th-century Florence. Whether or not you find it open could be a matter of luck, as restoration work is intermittently in progress.

LE CASCINE Map pp240-1

🚍 1, 9, 12, 13, 16, 26, 27, 80 & B

About 15 minutes' walk west along Borgo Ognissanti is Porta al Prato, part of the walls that were knocked down in the late 19th century to make way for the ring of boulevards that still surrounds the city. Through this gate many a Medici bride arrived in Florence in festive parade on her way to the Palazzo Vecchio or Palazzo Pitti.

A short walk south from here towards the Arno brings you to the eastern tip of Florence's great green lung, Le Cascine. The Medici dukes made this a private hunting reserve, but Pietro Leopoldo opened it to the public in 1776, with boulevards, fountains and bird sanctuaries. In the late 19th century horse racing began here (a British import it seems, since the locals referred to the sport as *le corse inglesi* – the English races). Queen Victoria was a fan of Florence and toddled along to Cascine during her stays.

At the extreme western end of the park is a monument to Rajaram Cuttiputti, an Indian maharajah who, while holidaying in Florence in 1870, managed to get a severe bout of gastroenteritis and died. His retinue requested, and surprisingly obtained, permission to cremate him by the river. This was quite a spectacle for the locals, who didn't understand a word of the ritual but were thoroughly fascinated by it. Four years later he got a statue and memorial designed by British artisans. At its opening the British imperial anthem sounded across the green expanses. To this day, the spot is called Piazzetta dell'Indiano. The nearby bridge is named after him too.

Nowadays the park fills with joggers, bladers, families and strollers, especially on warmer spring and summer days. At night a more furtive fauna of prostitutes and cruisers takes over, albeit in lesser numbers.

MUSEO DELLA STORIA DELLA FOTOGRAFIA FRATELLI ALINARI
Map pp244-5
www.alinari.com; Piazza di Santa Maria Novella; 🚌 1, 7, 10, 11, 14, 17, 22, 23, 36, 37 & A
Florence's Alinari family was one of the earliest in the world to enter the photography business. Their historical archives are an incredibly rich source of material but they have long been kept under lock and key. At the time of going to press, this new museum was still being completed on the site of the one-time Convento delle Leopoldine, behind the façade of the Loggia di San Paolo. It promises to be one of the world's great photography galleries.

MUSEO SALVATORE FERRAGAMO
Map pp244-5
☎ 055 336 04 56; www.salvatoreferragamo.it; Palazzo Spini-Ferroni, Via de' Tornabuoni 2; admission free; ⏰ 9am-1pm & 2-6pm Mon-Fri; 🚌 6, 11, 36, 37 & A
The forbidding Palazzo Spini-Ferroni was built in the 14th century with Guelph battlements and is owned by the Ferragamo shoe empire (see the boxed text, p165). The building is now just as intimidating for all the high-class fashion it exudes. If you don't feel like a pauper when entering the 2nd-floor shoe museum in your jeans and

A BRIDGE FOR ALL SEASONS
Cosimo I de' Medici put Vasari in charge of the Ponte Santa Trinita project, and he in turn asked Michelangelo for advice. In the end, the job was handed to Ammannati, who finished it in 1567. The statues of the seasons are by Pietro Francavilla. The bridge was one of those blown up by the Germans as they retreated in 1944. Rather than throw some slap-dash number back over the river, engineers rebuilt it as it had been, using copies of 16th-century tools and stone from the Boboli quarry. The statues were fished out of the Arno and the bridge completed in 1958.

All that was missing was the head from Francavilla's *Primavera* (Spring) statue on the northern bank. The fate of the head was long a source of anguished debate in Florence. Some eyewitnesses swore they had seen an Allied soldier make off with it after the city was liberated. Ads were even placed in New Zealand newspapers (New Zealanders were among the first Allied troops to enter the city in 1944) asking for whoever had made off with the head to send it back – no questions asked and a US$3000 reward! No-one owned up and three years later (in 1961) the missing head was discovered by chance in the Arno riverbed.

sandals, you never will! Although the museum advises booking by phone at least 10 days ahead, you may get lucky if you just wander in and climb the two floors of red-carpeted stairs. A maximum of 30 people are allowed in at any one time.

On display is a wide variety of some of Ferragamo's classic shoes, many worn by princesses and film stars. The *forme* (wooden model feet upon which tailor-made shoes were crafted) of everyone from Katherine Hepburn to Madonna are there to be seen.

PALAZZO CORSINI Map pp244-5
☎ 055 21 28 80; www.palazzocorsini.it; Via del Parione 11; admission free; ⏰ 9am-1pm & 4-7pm Mon-Fri; 🚌 A & B
For the best view of this grandiose late-baroque edifice, head to the south side of the Arno. It may seem a trifle curious, given that the U-shaped courtyard isn't in the middle. It would have been had the project been completed. The wing nearest Ponte alla Carraia was originally supposed to mirror the right wing. The building had belonged to the Medici family but they sold it in 1640. From then until 1735 work

on the exterior (the mighty façade on Via del Parione is a worthy counterpoint to the Arno frontage) dragged on at a snail's pace. By the time it was completed, the Corsini family was in the ascendant, with Lorenzo Corsini in the driving seat in Rome as Pope Clement XII. The most interesting feature inside the building is the spiral staircase known as the *lumaca* (literally 'slug'). You can take a look at it by entering the building at Via del Parione 11/b.

PALAZZO STROZZI Map pp244-5
Piazza degli Strozzi; admission varies; ⊗ varies; 🚌 6, 11, 22, 36, 37 & A

By far the most impressive of the Renaissance mansions is this earth-coloured palace, a great colossus of rusticated *pietra forte* ('strong stone'). The Strozzi family rivalled the Medici, but Filippo Strozzi was no fool. Before setting about the building of a structure greater than the Medici residence, he consulted Lorenzo de' Medici on some rather modest plans. Lorenzo advised Filippo to go for something grander, more befitting his family and the city. Filippo took this as carte blanche to massage his own ego – so began the construction of the city's greatest, if only in dimensions, Renaissance residence. It now houses offices and occasional art exhibitions.

SAN LORENZO
Eating p132; Shopping p166; Sleeping p179

The parish of San Lorenzo (St Laurence) was synonymous with Medici power. The basilica itself was heavily funded by Florence's top family, who eventually lavished upon it the glories of their family chapel and mausoleum. Strange that they never managed to find the funds to give the church a decent façade! Only a few blocks away is the Renaissance family mansion commissioned by Cosimo de' Medici, while a short hop to the north you strike the ebullient bustle of the city's 19th-century central produce market.

With its concentration of *pensioni*, eateries and sometimes almost down-at-heel cafés, the area is a strange mix. Just far enough away from the principal sights of the city not to feel wholly besieged by tourists, it is a bubbling pot of all sorts: locals on the make, variegated foreign residents, out-of-town students. There is a grittiness about the area that's wholly singular.

Orientation
For the purposes of the guide, we stretch the San Lorenzo boundaries north to Viale Filippo Strozzi, south to Via de' Cerretani, east to Via de' Martelli and its continuation Via Cavour, and west to Via Faenza.

BASILICA DI SAN LORENZO
Map pp244-5
☎ 055 21 66 34; Piazza San Lorenzo; admission €2.50; ⊗ 10am-5pm Mon-Sat; 🚌 1, 6, 7, 10, 11, 14, 17, 23 & A

The Medici family commissioned Brunelleschi to rebuild this church in 1425, on the site of a 4th-century basilica. It is considered one of the most harmonious examples of Florentine Renaissance architecture. Michelangelo prepared a design for the façade that was never executed, which is why this, as do so many other Florentine churches, appears unfinished from the outside. Many of the Medici family are buried in this, the family's parish church.

The church is a masterstroke of Brunelleschi's style. The nave is separated from the two aisles by columns in grey *pietra serena* ('tranquil stone') and crowned with Corinthian capitals. The whole is topped by a beautiful coffered ceiling. A visit to Brunelleschi's Basilico di Santo Spirito (p102) reveals uncanny similarities and curious difference. There the ceiling is a frescoed trompe l'oeil 'fake'.

The inside façade was done by Michelangelo, and above the main entrance is the Medici family coat of arms with the six balls. Il Rosso Fiorentino's *Sposalizio della Vergine* (Marriage of the Virgin Mary) dominates the second chapel on the right aisle after you enter. As you approach the transept, you will see two pulpits, or *pergami* (they look like treasure chests on Ionic columns), in what appears to be dark bronze. Some of the panels on each have been attributed to Donatello. Others, added later, are supposedly made of wood made to seem like bronze (the Medici money was obviously running short).

You enter the **Sagrestia Vecchia** (Old Sacristy) to the left of the altar. It was designed by Brunelleschi and mostly decorated by Donatello.

(Continued on page 91)

1 *Keeping company with the Arno, Ponte Vecchio (p107) and Ponte Santa Trinita (p81)* 2 *Florentine delicatessens offer fresh produce (p127)* 3 *Shopping on Ponte Vecchio (p107)* 4 *Motorini (p18) are a popular choice among Florentine motorists*

1 *Bridges over the Arno, seen from Piazzale Michelangelo (p107)*
2 *Detail on the 13th-century doors of the Baptistery (p63)* 3 *Sculptures adorning the Uffizi (p70)*
4 *Neo-Gothic, 9th-century façade of the Basilica di Santa Croce (p98)*

1 *Brunelleschi's great work, the Duomo (p65)* 2 *Michelangelo's David at the Galleria dell'Accademia (p94)* 3 *Rare modern sculpture in the Giardino di Boboli (p105)* 4 *Giardino di Boboli and the 17th-century Palazzo Pitti (p106)*

1 *Shops and restaurants abide over the Arno on the Ponte Vecchio (p107)* **2** *Basilica di San Lorenzo (p82)* **3** *Inside Basilica di San Lorenzo (p82)* **4** *Neptune by Ammannati, Piazza della Signoria (p77)*

Courtyard of Museo Nazion-
e del Bargello (p74) **2** Dawn
ew over Florence from the
azzale Michelangelo (p107)
The Ponte Santa Trinita (p81)
ver the Arno

1 Trippaio *(tripe stand; p41) on Via Aligherieri* 2 The terrace at JJ Cathedral (p146), the most coveted seat in Florence 3 Rivoire Café (p130) 4 Café latte, one of many ways to take your coffee (p126)

J.J. CATHEDRAL

1 *The cosy interior of Rex Caffè (p148)* **2** *Wine cellar, Da il Latini restaurant (p130)* **3** *A cameriere pours a glass of wine at Ristorante Beccofino (p139)* **4** *Sweets at Gilli (p130) on Piazza della Repubblica*

1 *Statue lies broken in the grounds of Basilica di Santa Croce (p98)*
2 *Delicate sculpted gravestone at Chiesa di San Miniato al Monte (p103)* 3 *L'Isolotto (Little Island) in the Medici's Giardino di Boboli (p105)* 4 *Roman amphitheatre at Fiesole (p110)*

(Continued from page 82)

From another entrance off Piazza San Lorenzo you enter the peaceful **cloisters**, off the first of which a staircase leads up to the **Biblioteca Medicea Laurenziana** (closed for restoration). This was commissioned by Cosimo I de' Medici to house the Medici library and contains 10,000 volumes. The real attraction is Michelangelo's magnificent vestibule and staircase. They are executed in grey *pietra serena* and the curvaceous steps are a sign of the master's move towards mannerism. Michelangelo wasn't around to oversee the execution of the project, which was entrusted to Florence's then leading resident architect, Bartolommeo Ammannati. He used stone rather than Michelangelo's preferred walnut.

Michelangelo also designed the main reading hall, covered by a magnificently carved timber ceiling, and the project would have been more striking still had he been able to finish it.

CAPPELLE MEDICEE Map pp244-5

☎ 055 238 86 02; Piazza Madonna degli Aldo-brandini; admission €6; ⏱ 8.15am-5pm Tue-Sat & alternate Sun & Mon, 8.15am-1.50pm public holidays; 🚌 1, 6, 7, 10, 11, 14, 17, 23 & A

It seems odd that the Medici chapels, built to balance the Brunelleschi sacristy on the other side of the church, have for organisational purposes been hived off from the church itself. Visitors are obliged to enter from another point behind the church rather than from inside and thus have difficulty picturing how the chapels fit in with the rest of the complex. Oh well.

You first enter a crypt after buying your ticket for the Medici chapels. The stairs from this take you up to the **Cappella dei Principi** (Princes' Chapel). The so-called chapel is actually the triumphalist mausoleum of some of the Medici rulers.

It is sumptuously decorated top to bottom with various kinds of marble, granite and other stone, and there are decorative tableaux made from painstakingly chosen and cut semiprecious stones, or *pietre dure*. It was for the purpose of decorating the chapel that Ferdinando I ordered the creation of the Opificio delle Pietre Dure (see p97).

Statues of the grand men were supposed to be placed in the still-empty niches, but only the bronze of Ferdinando I and partly gilt bronze of Cosimo II were done. The chapel's unfinished state lends it a gloomy air. Had the remaining statues been created, the chapel would no doubt have all the grandeur of the great royal pantheons.

A corridor leads from the Cappella dei Principi to the **Sagrestia Nuova** (New Sacristy), so-called to distinguish it from the Sagrestia Vecchia. It was in fact the Medicis' funeral chapel.

It was here that Michelangelo came nearest to finishing an architectural commission. His haunting sculptures, *Notte e Giorno* (Night and Day), *Aurora e Crepusculo* (Dawn and Dusk) and the *Madonna col Bambino* (Madonna and Child), adorn Medici tombs including that of Lorenzo the Magnificent. Michelangelo's sculptures are interesting for many reasons. In *Notte e Giorno* (the latter's face remains barely hinted at), Michelangelo goes to town in his study of human musculature. He liked boys so much that the female figures were modelled by lads. In the case of *Notte,* this is especially evident in the upper torso – the breasts seem to have been added as an afterthought. Still, as art experts point out, it was daring to place nude female figures in such a holy location. The statues of two Roman-looking princes (representative of two of the Medici clan) were another surprise – a pagan element in church!

CHIESA DI SAN BARNABA Map pp242-3

Via Panicale; admission free; ⏱ irregular; 🚌 4, 12, 25 & 33

It is no coincidence that this early 14th-century church lies on the corner of Via Guelfa, as it was built to celebrate a victory by the Florentine Guelphs over a Ghibelline (pro-Holy Roman Empire) army from Arezzo on 11 June 1289, the feast day of St Barnabus, to whose intercession Florence attributed victory. The entrance is topped by a ceramic *Madonna col Bambino* (Madonna and Child) by Giovanni della Robbia (added in the 16th century). Bright frescoes adorn part of the left wall as you enter. Used by the local Filipino community, the church is open intermittently.

MACCHINE DI LEONARDO Map pp242-3

☎ 055 29 52 64; www.macchinedileonardo.com; Via Cavour 21; adult/child €5/4; ⏱ 9.30am-7pm; 🚌 1, 6, 7, 10, 11, 114, 17, 23 & A

It started in his home town of Vinci, and now has spread to the Tuscan capital: museums with models (some on a life-size scale) of the extraordinary inventions that Leonardo da Vinci cooked up in his codices but rarely took past the drawing board. You can see some of his ideas for flying machines, a bicycle, a glider, a tank and other objects that were centuries ahead of their time. Strangely, the idea for this kind of private museum was so strong that there is another a few blocks away (see Il Genio di Leonardo, p95). This one is marginally better and cheaper.

MERCATO CENTRALE Map pp242-3

Piazza del Mercato Centrale; admission free;
⏲ **7am-2pm Mon-Fri, 7am-2pm & 4-8pm Sat;**
🚌 **4, 11, 12, 25, 31, 32 & 33**

Built in 1874, the city's central produce market seems to disappear amid the confusion of makeshift stands of the clothes and leather market that fill the surrounding square and streets during the day. At night all of this disappears, replaced instead by the contented munching of punters at the various eateries (which vary considerably in quality). The iron-and-glass architecture was something of a novelty in Florence when the market was first built.

PALAZZO MEDICI-RICCARDI

Map pp244-5

☎ **055 276 03 40; Via Cavour 3; admission €4;**
⏲ **9am-7pm Thu-Tue;** 🚌 **1, 6, 7, 10, 11 & 17**

When Cosimo de' Medici felt fairly sure of his position in Florence, he decided it was time to move house. He asked Brunelleschi to design him a new residence, but rejected the resulting design as too ostentatious. Cosimo had learned that the secret to long life in the politically fickle atmosphere of Florence was to keep a modest profile. With this in mind, he entrusted Michelozzo with the design in 1444. This palace is the result.

What Michelozzo came up with was ground-breaking and greatly influenced the construction of family residences in Florence thereafter. The fortress town houses with their towers that characterised Gothic Florence were no longer necessary. Cosimo's power was more or less undisputed, so Michelozzo created a self-assured, stout but not inelegant pile over three storeys.

The ground floor is characterised by its bulbous, rough surface (known as rustication) in *pietra forte*. The upper two storeys maintain restrained classical lines, which

Mercato Centrale (left), Piazza del Mercato Centrale

were already a feature of an emerging Renaissance canon, and are topped with a heavy timber roof whose eaves protrude well out over the street below.

The Medicis stayed here until 1540, and the building was finally acquired and somewhat re-modelled by the Riccardi family in the 17th century.

You can wander inside to the courtyard and to some of the rooms upstairs, although much of the building is given over to offices. The 1st-floor **Galleria** is a sumptuous example of late baroque, designed for the Riccardi family. The room glistens with gold leaf, and curvaceous figures loom out at you, especially from the ceiling frescoes by Luca Giordano (after whom the room is now usually named – **Sala Luca Giordano**).

The highlight is the **Cappella dei Magi**, a chapel with striking frescoes by Benozzo Gozzoli. Staff rotate 15 people through the chapel every 15 minutes as it is rather small inside.

Gozzoli never got a break like this again. Although he worked at a time when the Renaissance had taken off in Florence, he remained rooted in the International Gothic style. This magnificent fresco depicting the arrival of the Wise Men and a procession of the faithful to adore the newborn Christ betrays a number of jarring qualities.

On the rear wall he captures the natural essence of the Tuscan countryside (despite the subject, this is a very Florentine painting, filled with Medici family members and medieval dress), and yet on the lateral walls that same countryside seems bizarrely unreal. His characters mostly lack the realism and movement you might expect from greater Renaissance painters, and yet some of them are strikingly human.

The men in the lower right-hand corner on the left wall as you enter are exquisitely rendered, particularly the one with creased brow and quizzical expression. The colours are joyful and Gozzoli ensures immortality by penning his own name on one of the citizens' caps. He's the one looking straight out at you towards the back of the procession on the left side of the right-hand wall.

SAN MARCO

Eating p133; Shopping p167; Sleeping p179

Once the stalking ground of the fiery friar, Savonarola, the area around the former church and monastery of St Mark has some big artistic hitters. The Museo di San Marco, inside the former monastery, is a treasure chest of Fra (Beato) Angelico's works and people will want to get a gander at Michelangelo's *David* in the nearby Galleria dell'Accademia. Also close by is one of Italy's most important archaeological museums, with Egyptian and Etruscan collections. Close to the museums you can't help notice a youthful buzz in the air coming from students hanging around the university buildings in the area. Further away from the centre, the parish has a quiet, residential atmosphere.

Orientation

The area around Piazza San Marco stretches to the north around Piazza della Libertà and east to Cimitero degli Inglesi.

CENACOLO DI SANT'APOLLONIA

Map pp242-3

☎ 055 238 86 07; Via XXVII Aprile 1; admission free; ⏰ 8.15am-1.50pm Tue-Sat & alternate Mon & Sun; 🚌 7, 10, 20, 25, 31, 32 & 33

Seek out the Renaissance-style refectory (1445) of the former Benedictine convent that stands here. It is decorated with a remarkable fresco of the Last Supper (1447) by Andrea del Castagno, which is dominated by shades of red, blue and purple. Its existence had long been forgotten until

the convent was suppressed and the nuns turfed out in 1860. Three further frescoes above the Last Supper, depicting the crucifixion, burial and resurrection of Christ, were long covered by a layer of whitewash. Its painstaking removal revealed the frescoes, which include a rare image of a beardless Christ crucified. The backdrop of the dining hall has been made to look like grand slabs of veined and multicoloured marble. Also in the refectory are the *sinopie* (preparatory sketches) done for the three upper frescoes. To get to these, the frescoes had to be stripped off, the *sinopie* removed, and the frescoes put back.

CHIESA DELLA SS ANNUNZIATA

Map pp242-3

☎ 055 26 61 81; Piazza della SS Annunziata; admission free; ⏰ 7.30am-12.30pm & 4-6.30pm; 🚌 6, 31, 32 & C

Dedicated to the Virgin Mary, this church was established in 1250 by the founders of the Servite order and rebuilt by Michelozzo and others in the mid-15th century. In the ornate tabernacle, to your left as you enter the church from the atrium, is what is believed by the faithful to be a miraculous painting of the Virgin.

The painting, which is no longer on public view, is attributed to a 14th-century friar, but legend has it that an angel popped down from the heavens to add the finishing touches. Also of note are frescoes by Andrea del Castagno in the first two chapels on the left of the church, a fresco by Perugino in the fifth chapel and the frescoes in Michelozzo's atrium, particularly the *Nascita della Vergine* (Birth of the Virgin) by Andrea del Sarto and *La Visitazione* (The Visitation) by Jacopo Pontormo.

The square itself is one of the city's loveliest. Commanding the centre is Giambologna's equestrian statue of Grand Duke Ferdinando I de' Medici (largely created by Pietro Tacca on his master's design).

CHIESA E CONVENTO DI SANTA MARIA MADDALENA DE' PAZZI

Map pp242-3

☎ 055 247 84 20; Borgo Pinti 58; admission for lighting €1; ⏰ 9am-noon & 5-7pm Mon-Sat; 🚌 C

A convent was first raised on this site in 1257, where a variety of orders occupied it in turn. The Carmelites were turfed out

MONA LISA'S SMILE

Not long back in Florence after a protracted stint in Milan, Leonardo da Vinci was taken in by the friars at the monastery of the Chiesa della SS Annunziata. Here he set up a workshop and, it is thought, ran into the captivating Lisa Gherardini Giocondo, who would later pose for his Mona Lisa (known as La Gioconda to Italians because of her wealthy husband's surname). The location of the workshop had become one of the many mysteries of Leonardo's life, but this was swept away when it was discovered during restoration work in the monastery as recently as 2004.

when the present late-15th-century building (built by Giuliano da Sangallo) was expropriated and converted into a high school in 1888. The church, accessed via a sober courtyard lined with Ionic columns, is filled with frescoes but the real treat lies deeper inside. From the sacristy, through the door to the right just before the altar, you will be directed along corridors and up and down stairs to reach the chapter house (sala capitolare), which faces the main cloister and houses a remarkable three-part fresco of the crucifixion of Christ, done by Pietro Il Perugino in 1493–96. To Christ's left appear the Virgin Mary with St Bernard and to the right St John and St Benedict. In the background shimmers Lago di Trasimeno, the lake near the artist's hometown of Perugia. Note that this fresco has never been restored nor otherwise tampered with, although the 1966 floodwaters rose to within a couple of centimetres of its base!

CHIOSTRO DELLO SCALZO Map pp242-3

Via Cavour 69; admission free; ☼ 8.15am-1.50pm Mon, Thu & Sat; 🚌 6, 7, 10, 20, 25, 31, 32, 33 & C

This is one of those art-lover's treats, in which Florence is so rich. Hardly ever visited, this onetime cloister (chiostro) of a long-gone church is adorned with a monochrome fresco cycle carried out by Andrea del Sarto in on-and-off fashion throughout his career. Dedicated to the life of St John the Baptist, the images run from the annunciation of his birth, through his meeting with Jesus and on to his capture and beheading. John baptising Christ (1509–10) was the first of the images done and he finished the last in 1526. Fellow artist Franciabigio did two of the scenes.

CIMITERO DEGLI INGLESI Map pp242-3

☎ 055 232 14 77; Piazzale Donatello 38; admission by donation; ☼ 9am-noon Mon, 2-5pm Tue-Fri; 🚌 8 & 80

If you are a little sick of museums and need some air and a change of speed, you might consider heading east for the so-called English Cemetery. Located outside what were the city walls in 1828, and now effectively forming a large traffic island around which swarm thousands of hectic Florentine commuters, it is more accurately a Protestant cemetery and Swiss property. Several notable foreigners rest in (relative) peace here, including Elizabeth Barrett Browning and Walter Savage Landor, part of the clique of Anglo writers that made Florence home.

GALLERIA DELL'ACCADEMIA

Map pp242-3

☎ 055 238 86 09; Via Ricasoli 60; admission €6.50; ☼ 8.15am-6.50pm Tue-Sun; 🚌 C

You've seen the postcards and may feel you've already seen all you need of one of the greatest of all the Renaissance's sculptures, Michelangelo's David. Wrong. Make a date with this gallery, which is filled with all sorts of other intriguing items. The gallery occupies what was once a hospital and adjoining convent, converted into the seat of the Accademia di Belle Arti (Fine Arts Academy) under Grand Duke Pietro Leopoldo.

After collecting your ticket you enter the grand Sala del Colosso, dominated by a plaster model of Giambologna's Il Ratto delle Sabine (Rape of the Sabine Women) and lined by several interesting paintings. The latter include a fresco of the Pietà by Andrea del Sarto, a couple of pieces by Fra Bartolommeo and a Deposizione (Deposition) started by Filippino Lippi and finished by Il Perugino.

Immediately to the left off this first room a doorway leads into a long hall, at the end of which you can see David. Try to contain the urge to hurtle off in the giant-slayer's general direction and have a look at the four in the Prigioni (prisoners or slaves) series and the statue of San Matteo (St Matthew) between the two Prigioni on the right. The latter was sculpted about 1506, and the other from 1530.

The Prigioni were supposed to decorate the tomb of Pope Julius II, but ended up in the Giardino di Boboli. After the Prigioni comes another piece sometimes attributed to Michelangelo. It is an unfinished *Pietà* whose odd proportions have led several scholars to ascribe it to a not-so-successful employee of Michelangelo's.

All these pieces have in common the feature of not being completed. In the case of Michelangelo in particular, it is said he left many works 'unfinished' deliberately. Thus the observer is engaged in the process of creation, being obliged to 'complete' the work left undone by the master. It has been said that with Michelangelo this was in part due to his perfectionism. He could stop working on a project, but never truly finish.

David, however, is finished. Carved from one block of marble and weighing in at 19 tonnes, it's an exquisite, powerful figure that beggars description. While the statue still stood in Piazza della Signoria (it took four days in May 1504 to transport it on greased rollers from the Duomo, where it was carved and originally destined to stay, to its spot in Piazza della Signoria – and was only unveiled in September 1504), the left arm was hacked off during a riot and used to kill a peasant. You can see the break still, as well as one on the middle finger of the right hand (which was fixed in 1813).

Over the centuries, *David* has also suffered a couple of broken toes – the last one at the hands of a hammer attack carried out by a slightly emotional individual in 1991. The statue was moved to the gallery from Piazza della Signoria in 1873 and given a controversial restorative bath in 2003 (see p21). The statue has also had its critics. Many consider the head and hands to be too big, and still others his virile

member excessively small. DH Lawrence, who had the fortune to see the statue while it still dominated Piazza della Signoria, loved it but conceded that it could be seen as 'ugly, too naturalistic, too big…'

In the wing to the right of *David* are paintings by Florentine contemporaries of Michelangelo, including some by Botticelli.

In the wing to the left are more paintings of secondary importance. At the end of that wing, a hall hosts the **Gipsoteca Bartolini.** Lorenzo Bartolini was a major Italian sculptor of the 19th century. The works in here are plaster models created to help with the production of sculptures.

Another series of rooms off the left wing contains 13th- and 14th-century artworks. A triptych by Andrea Orcagna, which once hung in the Chiesa dei SS Apostoli, is particularly striking. From here you are led out into a small courtyard towards the exit. Just before you leave the building you can climb to the next floor to view mostly 14th-century Tuscan works, all with a religious theme. Among them is a small collection of Russian icons. There is also a fine collection of antique musical instruments.

IL GENIO DI LEONARDO Map pp242-3
☎ 055 28 29 66; www.mostredileonardo.com; Via dei Servi 66/r; adult/child €7/5; 🕙 10am-7pm; 🚍 C
Odd how two such museums have landed in Florence. This one is very similar to Le Macchine di Leonardo (see p91) though slightly less complete and a trifle more expensive. As in the other, you can see life-size models of Leonardo da Vinci's big ideas, from a glider to a tank. Whatever you do, do not visit both museums!

MUSEO ARCHEOLOGICO Map pp242-3
☎ 055 2 35 75; Via della Colonna 38; admission €4; 🕙 2-7pm Mon, 8.30am-7pm Tue & Thu, 8.30am-2pm Wed & Fri-Sun; 🚍 6, 31, 32 & C
A good deal of the Medici family's hoard of antiquities ended up here, in what would become one of Italy's most extensive archaeological museums. Further collections have been added in the centuries since. In each room you will find detailed explanatory sheets in several languages.

On the 1st floor you can either head left into the ancient Egyptian collection (Italy's most important collection after that of Turin's Museo Egizio), or turn right into the section on Etruscan and Greco-Roman art.

Sights

SAN MARCO

DAVID MIGHT HAVE BEEN BETTER OFF WITH A FIG LEAF

Florentines and foreigners alike have long sniggered at the size of Michelangelo's *David's* flaccid *pisello*. Given the statue is 4.34m high, 15cm does seem rather tiddly. In early 2005, the Dutch Institute for Art History announced it had made a study of the matter and found that, while *David* was no John Holmes, his limp willy was 'totally normal' for someone about to join combat with a giant (Goliath). Just what sort of a study the Dutch made is not entirely clear and the results are unlikely to convince the sceptics. *David's* privates have been on public display for several centuries so the dimensions in question have always been evident to all.

The former is an impressive collection of tablets inscribed with hieroglyphics, statues and other sculpture, various coffins and a remarkable array of everyday objects – it is extraordinary that sandals, baskets and all sorts of other odds and ends have survived to this day.

In the Etruscan section you pass first through two rooms dominated by funerary urns. Particularly noteworthy is the marble *Sarcofago delle Amazzoni* (Amazons' Tomb) from Tarquinia and the alabaster *Sarcofago dell'Obeso* (Fat Man's Tomb) from Chiusi. Etruscan and Roman art throw up some noticeable differences. You may notice an oriental touch in the depiction of battle and other scenes on the Etruscan urns that is absent from Roman artwork. Frequently the appearance of the characters and their attire is anything but Roman.

From the funerary urns you pass into a hall dedicated to bronze sculptures, ranging from miniatures depicting mythical beasts through to the life-size *Arringatore* (Orator). Dating from the 1st century BC, the figure, draped in Roman garb, illustrates the extent to which the empire had come to dominate the Etruscans at this point.

A successive corridor is lined on one side by ancient rings, pendants and amulets, many made of chalcedony. When you reach the end, swing left and walk back along another corridor with windows overlooking the museum's gardens. Here you can admire a selection of the museum's treasure of ancient gold jewellery.

The 2nd floor is taken up with an extensive collection of Greek pottery (in large part the characteristically red-and-black Attic type) from various epochs.

MUSEO DI SAN MARCO Map pp242-3

☎ 055 238 86 08; Piazza San Marco 1; admission €4; ☾ 8.15am-1.50pm Tue-Fri, to 6.50pm Sat, to 7pm alternate Sun, to 1.50pm alternate Mon; ☐ 6, 7, 10, 20, 25, 31, 32, 33 & C

In the centre of the university area, this museum is housed in the now-deconsecrated Dominican convent and the Chiesa di San Marco. The church was founded in 1299, rebuilt by Michelozzo in 1437, and again remodelled by Giambologna some years later. It features several paintings, but they pale in comparison with the treasures in the adjoining convent.

Famous Florentines who called the convent home include the painters Fra (or Beato) Angelico and Fra Bartolommeo. Fra Angelico, who painted the radiant frescoes on the convent walls, was of the Dominican order. The convent now serves as a museum of Fra Angelico's works, many of which were moved there in the 1860s, and should be up there on every art lover's top-priority list.

Almost 30 years after Fra Angelico's death in 1455, the rather ugly and intense little Dominican friar Girolamo Savonarola turned up in Florence with a post as lector at the Chiesa di San Marco (see the boxed text, p53).

You find yourself in the **Chiostro di Sant'Antonio** (St Anthony's Cloisters), designed by Michelozzo in 1440, when you first enter

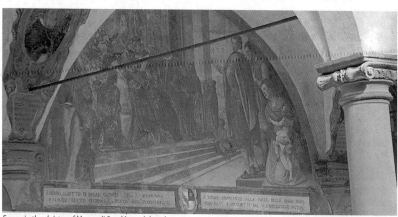

Fresco in the cloister of Museo di San Marco (above)

the museum. Turn immediately to the right and enter the Sala dell'Ospizio. Paintings by Fra Angelico that once hung in the Galleria dell'Accademia and the Uffizi have been brought together here. Among the better-known works are *La Deposizione di Cristo* (Deposition of Christ) and the Pala di San Marco, an altarpiece for the church paid for by the Medici family. It did not fare well as a result of 19th-century restoration.

More of Angelico's works, including a *Crocifissione* (Crucifixion), are on display in the Sala del Capitolo (Chapter House) on the opposite side of the cloister. In here is also La Piagnona, the bell rung the night Savon-arola was arrested on 8 April 1498.

The east wing of the cloister, formerly the monks' rectory, contains works by various artists from the 14th to the 17th centuries. Paintings by Fra Bartolommeo are on display in a small annexe off the refectory rooms. Among them is a celebrated portrait of Savonarola.

You reach the upper floor by passing through the bookshop. This is, in a sense, the real treat. Fra Angelico was invited to decorate the monks' cells with devotional frescoes aimed as a guide to the friars' meditation. Some were done by Fra Angelico, others by aides under his supervision including Bennozo Gozzoli. You can peer into them today and wonder what sort of thoughts would swim through the minds of the monks as they prayed before these images.

However, the true masterpieces up here are on the walls in the corridors. Already at the top of the stairs you climbed to the 1st floor is an *Annunciazione* (Annunciation), faced on the opposite wall with a *crocifisso* (crucifix) featuring St Dominic (San Domenico). One of Fra Angelico's most famous works is the *Madonna delle Ombre* (Madonna of the Shadows), to the right of cell No 25.

MUSEO DI STORIA NATURALE
Map pp242-3

☎ 055 275 74 62; www.unifi.it/msn; Via Giorgio La Pira 4; adult/child €4/2; ⏰ 9am-1pm Mon-Fri; 🚌 1, 7, 10, 11, 17, 20, 25 & 33
Four sections of the Natural History Museum are scattered across one of the central university campuses. The ticket office is in the paleontology and geology section, a musty old museum replete with skeletons of ancient beasts, models of same, prehistoric tusks and glass cases laden with fossils. The

equally ancient botany (visits by appointment only) and mineralogy sections are in separate buildings a short way down the same drive from the faculty street entrance.

OPIFICIO DELLE PIETRE DURE
Map pp242-3

☎ 055 26 51 11; Via degli Alfani 78; admission €2; ⏰ 8.15am-2pm Mon-Wed, Fri & Sat, 8.15am-7pm Thu; 🚌 C
For centuries a workshop that took pride of place in Florence's high-class handicrafts industry, the Opificio was established by Ferdinando I in 1588 in the Uffizi to create decorative pieces in *pietre dure* (see p107) for the Cappella dei Principi in the Basilica di San Lorenzo. These pieces were such a hit that soon artisans were making everything from tabletops to sculptures, and so-called 'paintings in stone' (by the 17th century mostly still lifes of flower vases) for sale in Florence and for export across Europe.

The Opificio moved to its present home in the 18th century, and in 1975 was fused with the Laboratori di Restauro in 1975 to become, officially at least, the Istituto Specializzato per il Restauro (Specialised Institute for Restoration). It remains known to most as the Opificio, and has developed a worldwide reputation for its instruction in art restoration. Specialist students from around the world flock here.

In the museum you can see a broad range of items in *pietre dure* (or *scagliola*, a method that produces results similar in appearance).

ORTO BOTANICO Map pp242-3

☎ 055 275 74 02; www.unifi.it/msn; Via Pier Antonio Micheli 3; adult/child €4/2; ⏰ 9am-1pm Mon-Fri; 🚌 1, 7, 10, 11, 17, 20, 25 & 33
Also known as the Giardino dei Semplici, this small botanical garden was the Medici herb garden, where all sorts of medicinal plants were grown for the city's pharmacies. It now belongs to the university and is an unexpectedly curious green patch in this part of the city. You can see a good deal of the garden from Via Giorgio la Pira.

ROTONDA DEL BRUNELLESCHI
Map pp242-3

Piazza Brunelleschi; 🚌 C
This neglected-looking hexagonal building was going to be the Rotonda di Santa

Maria degli Angioli and, lined with chapels, would have been one of Brunelleschi's most original buildings had money not run out. The university now has offices here.

SPEDALE DEGLI INNOCENTI
Map pp242-3

☎ 055 249 17 08; Piazza della SS Annunziata 12; admission €4; ⏰ 8.30am-2pm Thu-Tue; 🚌 6, 31, 32 & C

For the bulk of medieval Florence's urban poor, as elsewhere in Europe, having children was frequently a charge too onerous to bear. Many of the newborn ended up abandoned and so orphanages began to spring up in cities across Europe. Among the first was this 'hospital of the innocents', founded in 1421.

Brunelleschi designed the portico, which Andrea della Robbia decorated with terracotta medallions of a baby in swaddling cloths. Under the portico to the left of the entrance is the small revolving door where unwanted children were left. A good number of people in Florence with surnames such as degli Innocenti, Innocenti and Nocentini, can trace their family tree only as far back as the orphanage. Undoubtedly life inside was no picnic, but the Spedale's avowed aim was to care for and educate its wards until they turned 18.

A small gallery on the 2nd floor features works by Florentine artists. If you are already overdosing on the seemingly endless diet of art in Florence, you could skip this stop. Those truly interested will find it worthwhile.

The most striking piece is Domenico Ghirlandaio's L'Adorazione dei Magi (Adoration of the Wise Men) at the right end of the hall. This is one of those paintings that truly repays close inspection. The main image of the Wise Men come to adore the Christ child distracts most observers from such secondary scenes as Herod's massacre of the innocents – the city and port detail in the background is remarkable.

SANTA CROCE
Eating p134; Shopping p167; Sleeping p180

Piazza Santa Croce is an unusually large space that was opened out before the Franciscan basilica of the same name to accommodate hordes of the Sunday faithful who could not cram inside the church (Mass must have been quite an event in those days). From the 14th century it was the stage for all sorts of festivals, jousts and other merriment. On a more sober note, it came in handy for the execution of heretics in Savonarola's day.

Most curious of all were the ancient matches of calcio storico – a combination of football (soccer) and rugby with no rules. They still play it today (see the City Calendar, p9). Below the gaily frescoed façade of the Palazzo dell'Antella (Map pp248-9), on the south side of the piazza, is a marble stone embedded in the wall – it marks the halfway line on one of the world's oldest football pitches.

Today the surrounding streets are jammed with inviting restaurants, osterie and bars, making it one of the more enticing quarters to wander around in search of sensory joys.

Orientation

Spread out to the east of the old city centre and north of Ponte alle Grazie, Piazza Santa Croce lies at the heart of a web of long, narrow lanes that spin out to the busy boulevards marking the line of the former city walls.

The Romans used to have fun in much the same area centuries before. The city's 2nd-century amphitheatre took up the area facing the western end of Piazza di Santa Croce. To this day, Piazza de' Peruzzi, Via Bentaccordi and Via Torta mark the oval outline of the theatre's northern, western and southern sides.

BASILICA DI SANTA CROCE Map pp248-9

☎ 055 246 61 05; Piazza di Santa Croce 16; adult/child €4/2, audioguide €3; ⏰ 9.30am-5.30pm Mon-Sat & 1-5.30pm Sun & holidays; 🚌 C

Attributed to Arnolfo di Cambio, Santa Croce was started in 1294 on the site of a Franciscan chapel, but not completed until 1385. The name stems from a splinter of the Holy Cross donated to the Franciscans by King Louis of France in 1258. Today the church is known as much for the celebrities buried here as its captivating artistic gems.

The magnificent façade is a neo-Gothic addition of the 19th century, as is the bell tower. The architect, Niccola Matas, had a hard time even getting his façade design passed. Rather austere compared with the contemporary job done on the Duomo, the main source of jollity is the variety of colour in the different types of marble used. A commission set up in 1837 to study the urgent question of dressing the front of the church, apparently loathe to make any decision, was finally moved to do so when Matas produced the old designs for a façade by Il Cronaca, found in the church's archives. Matas was a clever fellow, for it seems he created these designs in the hope of finally getting some action!

Brooding at the foot of the left side of the church (as you gaze upon the façade) is a dazzling white statue of Dante. It is as though his ghost has returned to the ungrateful city that exiled him. There he stands with crumpled brow and acid gaze, contemplating the ebb and flow of his fellow citizens across the square.

The church's massive interior is divided into a nave and two aisles by solid octagonal pillars. The ceiling is a fine example of the timber A-frame style used occasionally in Italy's Gothic churches.

The protagonists of EM Forster's *A Room with a View* stumbled across one another beneath the silent vaults in here. Today you'll be lucky to squeeze through the seemingly endless hordes that mill at the front end of the church before being raced through by their tour guides. Try to get here early in the morning or leave it till late in the day – you could easily spend an hour or more wandering around inside.

The celebrity roll call of those buried or at least commemorated here is impressive. Heading down the right aisle you will see, between the first and second altar, Michelangelo's tomb, designed by Vasari. The three muses below it represent his three principal gifts – sculpting, painting and architecture. Michelangelo, apparently, would have preferred to be buried in Rome. Next up is a cenotaph to the memory of Dante. Having exiled the poet, Florence spent centuries trying to convince the city of Ravenna to return his cadaver, to no avail. There follows a monument to the 18th-century poet Vittorio Alfieri sculpted by Antonio Canova in 1810. After the fourth altar is Machiavelli's tomb. Following the next is Donatello's sculpture of *L'Annunciazione* (Annunciation), uniquely done in grey *pietra serena* ('tranquil stone').

Dogleg round to the right as you approach the transept and you find yourself

before the delightful frescoes by Agnolo Gaddi in the **Cappella Castellani** (in all, the church is covered in more than 2500 sq metres of frescoes). Taddeo Gaddi created the frescoes, depicting the life of the Virgin, and the stained-glass window in the adjacent **Cappella Baroncelli**. Next, a doorway designed by Michelozzo leads into a corridor off which is the **Sagrestia**, an enchanting 14th-century sacristy dominated on the right by Taddeo Gaddi's fresco of *La Crocifissione* (Crucifixion).

Through the next room, now serving as a bookshop, you can get to the **Scuola del Cuoio** (School of Leather; see p169). At the end of the Michelozzo corridor is a Medici chapel, featuring a large altarpiece by Andrea della Robbia.

Back in the church, the transept is lined by five minor chapels on either side of the **Cappella Maggiore** (Main Chapel). The two chapels nearest the right side of the Cappella Maggiore, belonging to the Bardi and Peruzzi clans, are decorated with partly fragmented frescoes by Giotto.

In the ninth chapel along, there's a glazed terracotta altarpiece by Giovanni della Robbia, while the final chapel is frescoed by Maso di Banco. These frescoes, among them *Miracolo del Santo che Chiude le Fauci del Drago e Risuscita due Maghi Uccisi dall'Alito del Mostro* (Miracle of the Saint who Shuts the Dragon's Jaws and Brings Back to Life the Magi Killed by the Monster's Breath), burst with life.

In the central chapel of the northern transept (also a Bardi chapel) hangs a wooden crucifix by Donatello. Brunelleschi thought it ugly and, to get his point across, went and sculpted another for the Basilica di Santa Maria Novella.

From the entrance, the first tomb in the left aisle is Galileo Galilei's. You will also have noticed by now that the floor is paved with the tombstones of famous Florentines of the past 500 years. Monuments to the particularly notable were added along the walls from the mid-16th century. They include composer Gioacchino Rossini, writer Ugo Foscolo and architect Leon Battista Alberti.

Brunelleschi designed the serene **cloisters**, dominated by his **Cappella de' Pazzi**, just before his death in 1446. Off the first cloister is the **Museo dell'Opera di Santa Croce**, which features a partially restored crucifix by Cimabue, badly damaged during the 1966 flood. Donatello's gilded bronze statue of *San Ludovico di Tolosa* (St Ludovich of Toulouse) was originally placed in a tabernacle on the Orsanmichele façade. Also on view is Taddeo Gaddi's somewhat faded Last Supper fresco *(cenacolo)*, surmounted by a more intriguing one depicting Christ crucified on the background of the Tree of Life.

CASA BUONARROTI Map pp248-9
☎ 055 24 17 52; Via Ghibellina 70; admission €6.50; 🕑 9.30am-2pm Wed-Mon; 🚌 14
Michelangelo bought himself this rather nice residence in Florence but never lived in it. Upon his death, it went to his nephew and eventually became a museum in the mid-1850s.

Although not uninteresting, the collections are a little disappointing given what you pay to get in. On the ground floor on the left is a series of rooms used for temporary exhibitions, usually held once a year from May to September. To the right of the ticket window is a small archaeological display. The Buonarroti family collected about 150 pieces over the years, many of which were for a long time in the Museo Archeologico (see p95). The last of them were returned to this house in 1996. The most interesting items are the Etruscan urns, but if you have seen the collection in the Museo Archeologico you don't really need to come here.

A scowling Dante, outside Basilica di Santa Croce (p98)

Upstairs you can admire a detailed model of Michelangelo's design for the façade of the Basilica di San Lorenzo – as close as the church came to ever getting one.

CHIESA DI SANT'AMBROGIO
Map pp248-9
Piazza Sant'Ambrogio; 🕑 Mass only; 🚌 C
A rather dull 18th-century façade hides centuries of church history on this site. The first church here was raised in the 10th century, but what you see inside is a mix of 13th-century Gothic and 15th-century refurbishment. The name comes from the powerful 4th-century archbishop of Milan, Sant'Ambrogio (St Ambrose), who stayed in an earlier convent on this site when he visited Florence. The church is something of an artists' graveyard too. Among those who rest in peace here are Mino da Fiesole, Il Verrocchio and Il Cronaca. Nearby is the local produce market, **Mercato di Sant'Ambrogio**, on Piazza Ghiberti.

MUSEO HORNE Map pp248-9
☎ 055 24 46 61; Via de' Benci 6; admission €5; 🕑 9am-1pm Mon-Sat; 🚌 13, 23, B & C
Herbert Percy Horne, an eccentric Brit abroad with cash, bought this building on Via de' Benci in 1911 and installed his eclectic collection of 14th- and 15th-century Italian paintings, sculptures, ceramics, coins and other odds and ends, creating this museum. Horne renovated the house in an effort to recreate a Renaissance ambience. Although the occasional big name pops up among the artworks, such as Giotto, Luca Signorelli and Giambologna, most of the stuff is minor. More interesting than many of the paintings is the furniture, some of which is exquisite. On the top floor is the original kitchen.

PIAZZA DEI CIOMPI Map pp248-9
🚌 A & C
Cleared in the 1930s, the square was named after the textile workers who used to meet in secret in the Santa Croce area and whose 14th-century revolt, which had seemed so full of promise, came to nothing. Nowadays it is the scene of a busy flea market called **Mercato dei Pulci** (see the boxed text, p167). The **Loggia del Pesce** (Fish Market) was designed by Vasari on the orders of Cosimo I de' Medici for the Mercato Vecchio (Old

Market), which was at the heart of what is now Piazza della Repubblica. The loggia was set up here in 1955. Kids love the swings and other rides set up in this park.

PONTE ALLE GRAZIE Map pp248-9
Piazza Carlo Goldini; 🚌 23 & C
In 1237, Giovanni Villani tells us, Messer Rubaconte da Mandella, a Milanese then serving as external martial (*podestà*) in Florence, had this bridge built. It was swept away in 1333 and on its replacement were raised chapels, one of them dubbed Madonna alle Grazie (Our Lady of the Graces), from which the bridge then took its name. Eventually the chapel, at one end of the bridge, was expanded into a small convent whose Benedictine nuns lived in isolation. Their food was passed to them through a small window and so the nuns became known as Le Murate (The Walled-in Ones). In 1424 they left for larger premises on Via dell'Agnolo, which took on their name, Le Murate (Map pp248–9). Much later that building was turned into a women's prison and in 2004 was completely renovated to create smallish rent-assisted apartments for low-income earners.

The bridge, in the meantime, had filled up with chapels, shops and other buildings much in the manner of the Ponte Vecchio. These were demolished in 1876 to allow street-widening across it. The Germans blew up the bridge in 1944, and the present version was constructed in 1957.

SINAGOGA & MUSEO DI STORIA E ARTE EBRAICA Map pp248-9
☎ 055 24 52 52; Via Luigi Carlo Farini 4; adult/child €4/2; ⏱ 10am-6pm Sun-Thu, to 2pm Fri Jun-Aug, 10am-5pm Sun-Thu, to 2pm Fri Apr-May & Sep-Oct, 10am-3pm Sun-Thu, to 2pm Fri Nov-Mar; 🚌 C
This late-19th-century synagogue is a fanciful structure with playful Moorish and even Byzantine elements. Although Florence was home to a Jewish community since at least the 14th century, serious discussion on the building of an appropriate temple only began around 1850, after the town authorities had definitively dropped all discriminatory regulations against the Jews.

The playfulness of the exterior of the synagogue that resulted is matched inside by the prayer hall, sumptuously (if a little gloomily) decorated with Arabesques and

www.lonelyplanet.com

A LONDONER WITH A PENCHANT FOR BOTTICELLI
Friend of the likes of John Ruskin, Oscar Wilde and William Morris, London-born Herbert Percy Horne (1864–1916) was a poet, critic, architect and canny merchant. His two-volume study of Botticelli is considered one of the key works on that artist. The first volume came out in 1908 and the second about 80 years later! He moved into the Via de' Benci home in 1915, only a year before his death.

held together by Moorish-style arches. Up on the top floor is the small museum. You can see Jewish ceremonial objects and some old codices, as well as follow the story of Florence's Jews down through the centuries. There are also various photos and models that transmit something of the appearance of the old centre of town, which was destroyed to make way for Piazza della Repubblica – it was in this area that Florence's ghetto had long been located.

TEATRO VERDI Map pp248-9
Via Giuseppe Verdi; 🚌 14 & A
Heading north from the Arno river along Via de' Benci (which after Piazza di Santa Croce becomes Via Giuseppe Verdi), you come across this 19th-century theatre at the intersection with Via Ghibellina. It stands on the site of the 14th-century prison, Le Stinche, which had also been used as a horse-riding school. Building work on the theatre began in 1838 and it was finally inaugurated in 1854. The theatre is still going strong (see p154).

OLTRARNO
Eating p137; Shopping p169; Sleeping p181
Literally 'beyond the Arno', the Oltrarno encompasses the part of the city that lies south of the river. Protected from much (but not all!) of the chaos north of the river, it is in some regards the most charming side of Florence. Green and hilly, in parts it gives the impression that you have already left the city behind. It bristles with restaurants and bars (for those in need of a break from the sightseeing) and more than a respectable clutch of important churches and art. And beyond the monuments and crowds

TRANSPORT

ATAF's No 13 circular line bus runs from Stazione di Santa Maria Novella to Piazzale Michelangelo Via Ponte alle Grazie, past the Chiesa di San Miniato al Monte and on to Porta Romana before turning north again for the station via Ponte al Prato. Minibus D runs back and forth between the train station and Oltrarno, ranging between Ponte di Vespucci and Piazza Ferrucci on its travels.

come to see them, you get the feeling some-thing of the real Florence lives on, especially around Borgo San Frediano. Wander the lanes and feel the pulse…

Orientation

The lie of the land has largely dictated the way the Oltrarno has developed. It stretches along the entire south bank of the Arno, with the Ponte Vecchio marking the half-way point. A series of streets funnels south past the Palazzo Pitti to the ancient south gate and the road to Rome. Otherwise, the area is dominated by gardens and green hills with a surprisingly rural feel – it's as though the Chianti were invading the city!

BASILICA DI SANTA MARIA DEL CARMINE Map pp248-9

☎ 055 276 82 24; Via Santa Monaca; church admission free, Cappella Brancacci €4, incl Palazzo Vecchio €8; ☒ 10am-5pm Wed-Mon, 1-5pm Sun & holidays; 🚌 D

West from Piazza Santo Spirito is Piazza del Carmine, an unkempt square used as a car park. On its southern flank stands this church, high on many art-lovers' list of Florentine must-sees because of the Cappella Brancacci. This chapel is a treasure trove of paintings by Masolino da Panicale, Masaccio and Filippino Lippi. Above all, the frescoes by Masaccio are considered among his greatest works, representing a defini-tive break with Gothic art and a plunge into new worlds of expression in the early stages of the Renaissance. His *Cacciata dei Progenitori* (Expulsion of Adam and Eve), on the left side of the chapel, is the best-known work. His depiction of Eve's anguish in particular lends the image a human touch hitherto little seen in European painting. In times gone by, prudish church

authorities had Adam and Eve's privates covered up.

Masaccio painted these frescoes in his early twenties and interrupted the task to go to Rome, where he died aged only 28. The cycle was completed 60 years later by Filippino Lippi.

That you can even see these frescoes today is little short of miraculous. The 13th-century church was nearly destroyed by a fire in the late 18th century. About the only thing the fire spared was the chapel.

The church interior is something of a sac-charine baroque bomb. Take a look up at the barrel-vaulted ceiling above the single nave. There is an excessive architectural trompe l'oeil fresco painting, with arches, pillars, columns and tympana all crammed in together. Opposite the Cappella Bran-cacci is the Cappella Corsini, one of the first (and few) examples of the extremes of billowing Roman baroque executed in Florence. The fresco in the cupola after the statuary is by Luca Giordano.

BASILICA DI SANTO SPIRITO
Map pp248-9

☎ 055 21 00 30; Piazza Santa Spirito; admission free; ☒ 10am-noon Mon-Fri, also 4-5.30pm Thu-Tue; 🚌 11, 36, 37 & D

It's a shame the authorities concerned could never get their act together suf-ficiently to provide this fine church with a dignified façade, but the inside is a Renais-sance masterpiece.

The church was one of Brunelleschi's last commissions. Its entire length inside is lined by 40 semicircular chapels. The architects who succeeded the master were not entirely faithful to his design. He wanted the chapels to form a shell of apses around the church, which clearly would have been revolution-ary. Instead they chose to hide them behind a rather ad hoc wall, flattening off the flanks of the church in an unsatisfying fashion.

More than the chapels, the colonnade of 35 columns in *pietra serena* is particularly striking. Not only do they separate the aisles from the nave, they continue round into the transept, creating the optical im-pression of a grey stone forest. Look closely at the high 'coffered' ceiling above the nave. It is simply painted – a trompe l'oeil 'fake' (funds were limited).

Noteworthy is Filippino Lippi's *Madonna col Bambino e Santi* (Madonna with Child and Saints) in one of the chapels in the right transept.

BORGO SAN FREDIANO Map pp248-9
🚌 6 & D

Just north of Piazza del Carmine stretches Borgo San Frediano. The street and surrounding area have, to a degree, retained their feel of a working-class quarter where small-scale artisans have beavered away over the centuries. Many continue to do so.

At the western end of the street stands the lonely **Porta San Frediano**, one of the old city gates left in place when the walls were demolished in the 19th century. Before you reach the gate, you'll notice the unpolished feel of the area neatly reflected in the unadorned brick walls of the **Chiesa di San Frediano in Cestello** (Piazza di Cestello; admission free; 🕿 9am-11.30am & 4.30-6pm Mon-Sat, 5-6.30pm Sun & holidays), whose incomplete façade hides a restrained version of a baroque interior. The western side of Piazza di Cestello is occupied by granaries built under Cosimo III de' Medici.

CASA GUIDI Map pp248-9
🕿 055 35 44 57; Piazza San Felice 8; admission free (donation appreciated); 🕙 3-6pm Mon, Wed & Fri Apr-Nov; 🚌 11, 36, 37 & D

Welcome to chez Browning. Robert and Elizabeth Barrett rented rooms in 1847 and lived and scribbled here for many years. Elizabeth died here in 1861. The house, run by Eton College and the Landmark Trust, has been restored in 19th-century style and some of the furnishings belonged to the poetic couple. If you like it enough you can stay (see p181).

CASA RODOLFO SIVIERO Map pp248-9
🕿 055 234 52 19; Lungarno Serristori 1/3; admission free; 🕙 9.30am-12.30pm Mon, 9.30am-12.30pm & 4.30-7.30pm Sat; 🚌 11, 36, 37 & D

This shady mansion on the Arno was until 1999 the house of the family of Rodolfo Siviero, an art collector of eclectic taste and, during and after WWII, a key figure in the recovery of art stolen from Florence by the Nazis. The collection is a hodgepodge, ranging from Renaissance church furniture to Roman busts, from Etruscan objects to paintings by Giorgio de Chirico, a personal friend who on the back of one work wrote that the painting was a gift but that Siviero had to pay for the frame!

CENACOLO DI SANTO SPIRITO
Map pp248-9
🕿 055 28 70 34; Piazza Santo Spirito 29; admission €2.20; 🕙 9am-2pm Tue-Sun Apr-Nov, 10.30am-1.30pm Tue-Sun Dec-Mar; 🚌 D

Housed in a refectory next door to the basilica of the same name, the Cenacolo is a grand fresco depicting the Last Supper and Crucifixion by Andrea Orcagna. In 1946 the building was enriched by the creation of the Fondazione Romano when the Neapolitan collector Salvatore Romano left his hoard of sculpture to Florence's town council. Among the most intriguing pieces are rare pre-Romanesque sculptures and works by Jacopo della Quercia and Donatello.

CHIESA DI SAN FELICE Map pp248-9
🕿 055 22 17 06; Piazza San Felice; 🕙 8-11am Mon-Sat, 6.30pm Sun for Mass; 🚌 11, 36, 37 & D

This unprepossessing church has had several makeovers since the Romanesque original was ruined in 1066. The simple Renaissance façade is by Michelozzo. Inside you can admire an extraordinary early 14th-century crucifix by Giotto's workshop. This giant cross dominates the altar area by its sheer size and colour.

CHIESA DI SAN MINIATO AL MONTE
Map pp248-9
🕿 055 234 27 31; Via delle Porte Sante; admission free; 🕙 8am-7.30pm May-Oct, 8am-noon & 3-6pm Nov-Apr; 🚌 12 & 13

A steep climb up from Piazzale Michelangelo will bring you to this wonderful Romanesque church, surely the best surviving example of its type in Florence. The church is dedicated to San Miniato (St Minius), an early Christian martyr in Florence who is said to have flown to this spot after his death down in the town.

The church, started in the early 11th century, has a typically Tuscan marble façade featuring a mosaic depicting Christ with the Virgin and St Minius, added 200 years later. The eagle at the top represents the Arte di Calimala, the guild that financed the construction.

Inside you will see 13th- to 15th-century frescoes on the right wall, intricate inlaid marble designs down the length of the nave and a fine Romanesque crypt at the back, below the unusual raised *presbiterio* (presbytery). The latter boasts a fine marble

Sculpted gravestone, Chiesa di San Miniato al Monte (p103)

pulpit replete with intriguing geometrical designs. The sacristy, to the right of the church (they suggest you make a small donation to get in), features marvellously bright frescoes. The four figures in the cross vault are the Evangelists.

The **Cappella del Cardinale del Portogallo** (Chapel of the Portuguese Cardinal), to the left side of the church, features a tomb by Antonio Rossellino and a striking ceiling decorated in terracotta by Luca della Robbia. The chapel was created for the Portuguese Prince James, who also happened to be a cardinal. When on his deathbed in Florence, he requested (and no doubt paid for) a suitably regal burial place.

It is possible to wander through the cemetery outside. Some of Michelangelo's battlements remain standing around here too.

CHIESA DI SANTA FELICITA Map pp244–5
Via de' Guicciardini; admission free; ⏱ 9am-noon & 3-6pm Mon-Sat, 9am-1pm Sun & holidays; 🚌 D
The most captivating thing about the façade of this 18th-century remake of what had been Florence's oldest (4th-century) church is the fact that the Corridoio Vasariano passes right across it. The Medici could drop by and hear Mass without being seen!

Inside, the main interest is in the small **Cappella Barbadori**, designed by Brunelleschi, immediately on the right as you enter. Here Pontormo left his disquieting mark with a

fresco of the *Annunciazione* (Annunciation) and a *Deposizione* (Deposition). The latter depicts the taking down of Christ from the cross in disturbingly surreal colours. The people engaged in this operation look almost as if they have been given a fright by the prying eyes of the onlooker.

The good thing about coming into a 'minor' church like this is that you'll probably find it empty, with one or two seniors perhaps muttering a few prayers in the silence. Shame it's not like that all over town!

FORTE DI BELVEDERE Map pp248–9
Costa di San Giorgio; adult/child €8/5, incl temporary art exhibitions; ⏱ 10am-10pm Wed-Mon Sep–mid-Jul, 10am-midnight mid-Jul–Aug, exhibitions 10am-7pm Wed-Mon; 🚌 D & C
Bernardo Buontalenti helped design the rambling fortifications here for Grand Duke Ferdinando I towards the end of the 16th century. From this massive bulwark soldiers could keep watch on all fronts, and indeed it was designed with internal security in mind as much as foreign attack. Set high on a hill, the views across the city are, for this writer's money, better than the much-touted ones from Piazzale Michelangelo (see p107).

The entrance is near **Porta San Giorgio**, and you can approach from the east along the walls or by taking Costa di San Giorgio up from near the Ponte Vecchio. If you take the latter, you will pass, at Nos 17 to 21, one of the houses where **Galileo Galilei** lived while in Florence. The Raccolta d'Arte Contemporanea Alberto Ragione of contemporary art (an extra €2) is housed in the fort. Among the work of Italian artists from the first half of the 20th century, a few Giorgio Morandis stand out. Fans of Carlo Levi's classic book, *Cristo si è Fermato ad Eboli* (Christ Stopped at Eboli), may be curious to see the trio of paintings he did while in exile in southern Italy. Mario Mafai, Ottone Rosai and Virgilio Guidi are well represented. Temporary exhibitions are held here and in summer the fort is sometimes used as an outdoor cinema – check this before heading up though!

As you take in the sweep of the view south of the fort, you can identify clearly the marble Romanesque façade of the Chiesa di San Miniato al Monte (opposite) to the southeast. More or less directly south on a distant height is a watchtower. Known as the **Torre del Gallo** (Map pp240–1), it belonged to the Galli clan, a Ghibelline family. Galileo carried out some of his astronomical observations there and lived his last years in a nearby villa. The tower is a bit of a travesty – a medieval-style reconstruction built in 1906 – but will one day be at the centre of the future Museo dell'Universo, an interactive astronomy museum with modern planetarium. Optimistic guesses suggest part of it will open by 2009.

GIARDINO DELLE ROSE Map pp248-9
Via di San Salvatore al Monte; admission free; 8am-8pm May–mid-Jun; 12 & 13
For a brief spring moment, this pungent garden comes to colourful life. A plethora of rose varieties and a modest Japanese garden are on show, and you are high enough here to enjoy views over the city too. The main entrance is a about halfway along the pedestrianised street leading up to Viale Galileo Galilei from the San Niccolò area.

GIARDINO DI BOBOLI Map pp248-9
055 265 18 16; Piazza Pitti; admission incl Museo delle Porcellane & Museo degli Argenti €4; 8.15am-7.30pm Jun-Aug, 8.15am-6.30pm Apr-May & Sep-Oct, 8.15am-5.30pm Mar, 8.15am-4.30pm Nov-Feb; closed 1st & last Mon of each month; D

A relaxing antidote to cultural overdose in the Palazzo Pitti is a stroll in the palace's Renaissance Giardino di Boboli (Boboli Gardens). The garden was laid out in the mid-16th century and based on a design by the architect known as Il Tribolo. Buontalenti's noted artificial grotto, the **Grotta del Buontalenti**, with *Venere* (Venus) by Giambologna, is curious. In June, concerts of classical music are sometimes held in the gardens.

Before you leave, you can visit the **Museo degli Argenti** (see p107) in the north wing of Palazzo Pitti on the same ticket.

At the southeast end of the garden is the **Museo delle Porcellane**, housing a varied collection of porcelain collected over the centuries by the illustrious tenants of Palazzo Pitti, from Cosimo I de' Medici and Eleonora de Toledo onwards. The exhibits include exquisite Sèvres and Vincennes pieces, as well as Meissen, Vienna and local collections from Doccia. The views south from the museum add a soothing bucolic flavour to your visit; the hilly country at your feet is dotted with olive trees and cypresses.

At a vantage point in the east end of the garden is the **Kaffeehaus**, a 19th-century conceit installed by Grand Duke Pietro Leopoldo. It has been restored and is waiting for the green light to reopen for business as a café.

In summer the gardens are frequently the setting for concerts and other events.

THE WORLD TURNS
'Eppur si muove', Galileo is supposed to have muttered after having been compelled to recant his teachings on astronomy before the Inquisition in Rome in 1633. 'And yet it *does* move.' He was referring to the earth, whose exalted position at the centre of the universe he maintained was a falsehood. He further espoused Copernicus' theory that the earth, along with other planets, rotated around the sun.

As long ago as 1616 Galileo had been ordered not to push this theory, which Vatican conservatives, not overly well disposed to the 'new learning', saw as a threat to the Church. If teachings long held dear about the position of the world in God's universe were debunked, it could lead to further uncertainty. The capacity to reveal what makes things tick, rather than simply remaining awestruck by divine majesty, threatened those intent on maintaining the Church's position of pre-eminence in worldly and spiritual affairs.

Galileo was born in Pisa on 15 February 1564, the son of a musician. He received his early education at the monastery of Vallombrosa near Florence and later studied medicine at the University of Pisa. During his time there he became fascinated by mathematics and the study of motion, so much so that he is regarded as the founder of experimental physics. He became a teacher of mathematics in Pisa and then taught in Padua for 18 years.

Having heard of the invention of the telescope in 1609, he set about making his own, the first used to scan the night skies. In the coming years he made discoveries that led him to confirm Copernicus' theory that the planets revolve around the sun. In 1610 Galileo moved to Florence, where he had many supporters; however this was not enough to prevent his astronomical works being placed on the 1616 index of banned books. In 1632 he was confined to exile within Florence until his death 10 years later, when he was buried in the Basilica di Santa Croce. No doubt he was touched (in spirit) when, 350 years after his death, Pope John Paul II acknowledged that Galileo's theories had largely been correct.

MUSEO ZOOLOGICO LA SPECOLA

Map pp248-9

☎ 055 228 82 51; www.unifi.it/msn; Via Romana 17; admission €4; ☒ 9am-1pm Thu-Fri & Sun-Tue, 9am-5pm Sat; ☒ 11, 36, 37 & D

Down Via Romana from Piazza San Felice is this fusty but fascinating museum. On the top floor are hundreds of stuffed animals and other critters. The range is extraordinary, from giant South American insects to a rhinoceros, from crocodiles to emus, from sharks and sea mammals to Prince Vittorio Emanuele's African hunting trophies. The museum includes people as well. The highlight is the collection of late-18th-century wax models of assorted bits of human anatomy, created as teaching aids for doctors. The life-size human bodies, laid out as if taking a lie-down and stripped back to muscles, organs and veins, are particularly gruesome. The section devoted to the genitals is enough to put you off sex forever. Downstairs in the courtyard is a skeleton collection, including kids' favourites like whales, an elephant and a giraffe.

PALAZZO PITTI Map pp248-9

☎ 055 238 86 14; Piazza de' Pitti 1; combined ticket to all galleries & museums €10.50, after 4pm €8, see individual sights for costs; ☒ 8.15am-5.30pm Mar, 8.15am-6.30pm Apr-May & Sep-Oct, 8.15am-6.50pm Tue-Sun (Galleria Palatina), 8.15am-1.50pm Tue-Sat & alternating Sun & Mon (Galleria d'Arte Moderna & Galleria del Costume), 8.30am-1.50pm Tue-Sat & alternating Sun & Mon (Museo degli Argenti & Museo delle Porcellane), 8.15am-7.30pm Jun-Aug, 8.15am-4.30pm Nov-Feb, closed 1st & last Mon of each month (Giardino di Boboli); ☒ D

When the Pitti, a wealthy merchant family, asked Brunelleschi to design the family home, they did not have modesty in mind. Great rivals of the Medici, there is not a little irony in the fact that their grandiloquence would one day be sacrificed to the bank account.

Begun in 1458, the original nucleus of the palace took up the space encompassing the seven sets of windows on the 2nd and 3rd storeys.

In 1549 Eleonora de Toledo, wife of Cosimo I de' Medici, finding Palazzo Vecchio too claustrophobic, acquired the palace from a by-now rather skint Pitti family. She launched the extension work, which ended

up crawling along until 1839! Throughout that time the original design was respected and today you would be hard-pressed to distinguish the various phases of construction.

After the demise of the Medici dynasty, the palace remained the residence of the city's rulers, the dukes of Lorraine and their Austrian and (briefly) Napoleonic successors.

When Florence was made capital of the nascent Kingdom of Italy in 1865, it became a residence of the Savoy royal family, who graciously presented it to the state in 1919.

The palace houses five museums. The **Galleria Palatina** (Palatine Gallery; admission incl Appartamenti Reali €6.50) has paintings from the 16th to 18th centuries, hung in lavishly decorated rooms. The works were collected mostly by the Medici and their grand ducal successors.

After getting your ticket, head up a grand staircase to the gallery floor. The first rooms you pass through are a seemingly haphazard mix of the odd painting, sculpture and period furniture.

The gallery proper starts after the **Sala della Musica** (Music Room; created under the short reign of Elisa Baciocchi as a reception room for her brother, the Emperor Napoleon, who never had the time to come and try it out). The paintings hung in the succeeding rooms are not in any particular order. Among Tuscan masters you can see work by Fra Filippo Lippi, Sandro Botticelli, Giorgio Vasari and Andrea del Sarto (who is represented in just about every room!). The collection also boasts some important works by other Italian and foreign painters. Foremost among them are those by Raphael, especially in the **Sala di Saturno**. A close second is Titian (particularly in the **Sala di Marte**), one of the greatest of the Venetian school. Other important artists represented include Tintoretto, Paolo Veronese, José Ribera, Bravo Murillo, Peter Paul Rubens and Van Dyck. Caravaggio is represented with the striking *Amore Dormiente* (Love Sleeping) inside the **Sala dell'Educazione di Giove**. Although probably overwhelmed by all the art hanging on the walls, you should scrape together some energy for the ceilings too – many of the wonderfully airy frescoes are by Pietro da Cortona, who came from Rome to do the job.

From the gallery you can pass into the **Appartamenti Reali**, a series of rather sickeningly opulent furnished and decorated rooms, where the Medici grand dukes and their successors slept, received guests and generally hung about. It was redecorated by the Hapsburgs: the style and division of tasks assigned to each room is reminiscent of Spanish royal palaces, all heavily bedecked with curtains, silk and chandeliers. Each room has a colour theme, ranging from aqua green to deep wine red and dusty mellow yellow.

The other galleries are also worth a look if you have plenty of time at hand.

The **Museo degli Argenti** contains collections of glassware, silver, ivory and amber objects (mostly imported from Germany in the 17th century), *pietre dure* (literally 'hard stones'; an artistic technique in which semi-precious stones are fragmented, melded together and polished to a fine surface to create all sorts of decorative objects, from table tops to bracelets) from the Medici collections and those of the Dukes of Lorraine who succeeded the Medici as Grand Dukes of Tuscany. Cosimo Medici got the ball rolling in the 15th century. His successors, especially starting with the first Grand Duke Cosimo I, actively sponsored an industry in the 'minor arts', promoting the ingenious work of jewellers, goldsmiths and others, and so hoarding this endless array of expensive trinkets.

The **Galleria d'Arte Moderna** (Gallery of Modern Art; admission incl Galleria del Costume €5) covers mostly Tuscan works from the 18th to the mid-20th century (including numerous works by the Macchiaioli), while the **Galleria del Costume** (Costume Gallery) features high-class ballroom threads from the 19th century and curious outfits from as late as the 1960s, including ones worn by Jacqui Onassis and Audrey Hepburn. The gallery is housed in the Meridiana, a low-slung neoclassical addition to the Palazzo Pitti made under the Hapsburg Pietro Leopoldo. The **Museo delle Carrozze** contains ducal coaches and the like but has been closed for years and shows no signs of reopening any time soon.

From Palazzo Pitti you also access the Giardino di Boboli (p105) and the Museo delle Porcellane.

PIAZZALE MICHELANGELO Map pp248-9
🚌 12 & 13
Since its creation in the 19th century, this grand viewpoint-cum-car park has been a favourite with locals and visitors alike for gazing down over the Arno and city. It is dominated by a bronze copy of Michelangelo's *David* and littered with snack bars and cafés. The statue was dragged up here from central Florence in 1873 in a wagon pulled by eight pairs of oxen. You can get up here by following the winding paths up from Piazza Giuseppe Poggi (marked by the medieval gate tower, the Porta San Niccolò).

PONTE VECCHIO Map pp244-5
Via de Guicciardino; 🚌 B, C & D
The first documentation of a stone bridge here, at the narrowest crossing point along the entire length of the Arno, dates from 972 AD. The Arno looks placid enough but when it gets mean, it gets very mean. Floods in 1177 and 1333 destroyed the bridge, and in 1966 it came close again. Newspaper reports of the time highlight how dangerous the situation was: one couple who owned a jewellery shop on the bridge described the crashing of the waters just below the floorboards as they tried to salvage some of their goods. *Carabinieri* (military police) on the river bank excitedly warned them to get off, but they retorted that the forces of law and order should do something. They did get off in the end, fearful they'd be swept away.

Those jewellers were among several on the bridge who inherited the traditional business in the 16th century when Grand Duke Ferdinando I de' Medici ordered a replacement to the rather malodorous presence of the town butchers. The latter tended to jettison unwanted leftovers into the river.

The bridge as it stands was built in 1345, and those of us who get the chance to admire it can thank...well, someone...that it wasn't blown to smithereens in August 1944. Retreating German forces blew up all the other bridges on the Arno, but someone decided that sending the Ponte Vecchio to the bottom would have been going too far! Instead they mined large areas on either side of the bridge, evident today in the ugly architecture that replaced the rubble.

It was on the Oltrarno side of the bridge that Buondelmonte dei Buondelmonti was assassinated beneath the statue of Mars that stood here then, sparking the conflict between the Guelphs and Ghibellines that subsequently tore the city and Tuscany apart. Mars was washed away by the 1333 flood.

The enduring Ponte Vecchio (p107)

Among the buildings to survive the Nazis' mines are two medieval towers. The first, **Torre dei Mannelli**, just on the southern end of the bridge, looks very odd, as the Corridoio Vasariano was built around it, not simply straight through it as the Medici would have preferred. Just south of here across Via de' Bardi as your eye follows the Corridoio you espy **Torre degli Ubriachi** (Drunks' Tower). On the intersection of Borgo San Jacopo and Via de' Guicciardini you will see an unassuming fountain, the **Fontana di Bacco** (Bacchus Fountain). Giambologna's *Ercole col Centauro Nesso* (Hercules with the Centaur) statue was here until transported to the Loggia della Signoria (see p73).

PORTA ROMANA Map pp248–9
Via Romana; 🚌 11, 36 & 37

Pilgrims to Rome headed down Via Romana leaving Florence behind them. The end of the road is marked by the Porta Romana, an imposing gate that was part of the outer circle of city walls knocked down in the 19th century. A strip of this wall still stretches to the north from the gate. If you head along the inside of this wall (the area is now a car park), you will find an entrance that allows you to get to the top of the Porta Romana.

The square below was traditionally a fairground for peasants in the surrounding county *(contado)*. By far the most curious of

these fairs was the *Fiera dei Contratti* (Contracts Fair), when country folk from near and far dragged sons and daughters along to contract marriage. They would haggle keenly over dowries and, much to the amusement of the not-too-respectful city folk who had taken the day off to come and gawk, compel prospective brides to walk up the hill towards the Poggio Imperiale (see p112) to see how well they swayed their hips!

VIA MAGGIO Map pp248–9
🚌 11, 36, 37 & D

No, it doesn't mean May St, but rather Via Maggiore (Main St). In the 16th century this was a rather posh address, as the line-up of fine Renaissance mansions duly attests. **Palazzo di Bianca Cappello**, at No 26, has the most eye-catching façade, covered as it is in graffiti designs. As a fugitive from Venice and Francesco I de' Medici's lover and later wife, Ms Cappello didn't know too many dull moments (see the boxed text, p110). Across the street, a series of imposing mansions more or less follow the same Renaissance or Renaissance-inspired style. They include the **Palazzo Ricasoli-Ridolfi** (No 7), **Palazzo Martellini** (No 9), **Palazzo Michelozzi** (No 11), **Palazzo Zanchini** (No 13; Map pp244–5) and **Palazzo di Cosimo Ridolfi** (No 15; Map pp244–5). All were built and modified, not always favourably, over the 14th, 15th and 16th centuries. Another impressive one is the **Palazzo Corsini-Suarez** (No 42).

BEYOND CENTRAL FLORENCE

Eating p141; Shopping p170; Sleeping p182

Beyond the cramped quarters of historic Florence lies rolling country and farmland. Over the centuries, monasteries, villas and even a giant fortress have been raised amid the bucolic bliss. Since ancient times the village of Fiesole, a cool and pretty escape hatch for Florentines and foreigners with cash, had stood sunnily aloof above Florence. From the late 19th century the city began to spread rapidly along the broad valley floor; much of it today is drab urban sprawl. However, the surrounding picture-postcard Tuscan countryside is quite another story.

Orientation

About 8km northeast of the old city centre lies the hillside town of Fiesole. To the immediate north of old central Florence stand the unlikely pair of the massive Fortezza da Basso and the onion-domed Russian Chiesa Russa Ortodossa, while further away is the quietly eccentric Museo Stibbert. Beyond

the line of the south walls spreads the hilly beauty spot known as Bellosguardo, the one-time villa Poggio Imperiale and, a few kilometres away, the Certosa di Galluzzo, a still-functioning monastery. To the east, in amid modern 'burbs, is the unexpected haven of the Cenacolo di San Salvi, while scattered in a more distant arc north and west is a series of lavish villas of the once all-powerful Medici.

BELLOSGUARDO Map pp240-1

A favourite spot for 19th-century landscape painters was the hill of Bellosguardo (Beautiful View), southwest of the city centre. A narrow winding road leads up past a couple of villas from Piazza Tasso to Piazza Bellosguardo. You can't see anything from here, but if you wander along Via Roti Michelozzi into the grounds of the Albergo Torre di Bellosguardo, you'll see what the fuss was about. The hotel (p182) is the latest guise of what was once a 14th-century castle – try to get a glimpse of the view before you are not-so-kindly requested to be on your way by hotel staff. There are no buses to Bellosguardo.

CENACOLO DI SAN SALVI Map pp240-1

☎ 055 238 86 03; Via San Salvi 16; admission free; ⏰ 9am-2pm Tue-Sun; 🚌 3, 6, 20 & 34

Dominating the refectory wall in what was once a part of the San Salvi monastery is one of Andrea del Sarto's most extraordinary frescoes (1527). In this scene of the Last Supper, the diners gather at an austere table beneath a grand trompe l'oeil vault. Curiously, the tavern owner and an employee are peering at the proceedings from a window above and behind them. They watch as Jesus hands Judas (who sits among the apostles and not customarily alone on the other side) a piece of bread to indicate that he is the apostle who will betray him. There is a collection of other works by Andrea del Sarto's contemporaries on show. You are more than likely to have the place to yourself.

CERTOSA DI GALLUZZO Map p238

☎ 055 204 92 26; admission by donation; ⏰ 9am-noon & 3-6pm Tue-Sun May-Oct, 9am-noon & 3-5pm Tue-Sun Nov-Apr; 🚌 37

Dominating the village of Galluzzo, about 3km south along Via Senese from Porta Romana, is this quite remarkable 14th-century

Sights

BEYOND CENTRAL FLORENCE

TRANSPORT

ATAF bus 7 from Stazione di Santa Maria Novella connects with Piazza Mino da Fiesole in Fiesole. If you are driving, find your way to Piazza della Libertà in Florence and follow signs to Fiesole. ATAF bus 28 from Stazione di Santa Maria Novella runs to the Villa Medicea La Petraia and Villa Medicea di Castello. Bus 14C, which you can pick up at Piazza C Beccaria, the Duomo or Stazione di Santa Maria Novella, runs past Villa Careggi.

The easiest way to reach Villa di Poggio a Caiano without your own transport is with the COPIT bus service running between Florence and Pistoia (€2, 30 minutes). There is a bus stop right outside the villa.

No buses run to Bellosguardo – you need your own wheels or the patience to walk for an hour or so from central Florence. ATAF bus 37 runs from Stazione di Santa Maria Novella to Galluzzo and 38 from Porta Romana to Poggio Imperiale. Among the buses that head for the Cenacolo di San Salvi, the 20 can be picked up from Piazza San Marco. The easiest way to the Museo Stibbert is with bus 4 from Piazza dell'Unità Italiana (get off along Via Vittorio Emanuele II).

THE COMPLICATED LOVE LIFE OF BIANCA CAPPELLO

When the ravishing Bianca Cappello (1547–87) was seduced by a low-paid Florentine clerk in Venice, she probably knew she was getting into hot water. Fearful of how her noble family would react, she left the lagoon city for Florence, where her lover, Paolo Bonaventuri, married her but whose family treated the young noblewoman with contempt. The Venetian authorities did not take kindly to the situation and their spies were soon hot on the couple's trail. Both feared for their lives and so approached Grand Duke Francesco for protection. A ladies' man and unhappily hitched to a hunchbacked harridan from Austria, Joanna, Francesco moved the fugitive couple into a mansion in Via Maggio and employed them at court. In exchange, Bianca became his lover. Bonaventuri was later murdered in mysterious circumstances. On Joanna's death Francesco married Bianca and made her Grand Duchess. The Florentines took no more kindly to her than they had to her unpopular Austrian predecessor and when she and here husband died of fever within a day of each other, he was buried with full honours but Bianca's remains were dumped in an unmarked grave.

monastery. The Carthusian order of monks once had 50 monasteries in Italy. Of these, only two are now inhabited by monks of that order. The Certosa passed into Cistercian hands in 1955.

The Certosa can only be visited with a guide (reckon on about 45 minutes) who will take you first to the Gothic hall of the **Palazzo degli Studi**, now graced by a small collection of art, including five somewhat weathered frescoes by Pontormo. It is a little depressing to think that, until Napoleon's troops looted the place in the early 19th century, more than 500 important works of art graced the monastery. The **Basilica di San Lorenzo**, with 14th-century origins, has a Renaissance exterior. To one side of it is the **Colloquio**, a narrow hall with benches. Here the Carthusian monks were permitted to break their vow of silence once a week (they got a second chance on Mondays when they were allowed to leave the monastery grounds for a gentle stroll). You end up in the **Chiostro Grande**, the biggest of the complex's three cloisters. It is flanked by 18 monks' cells and decorated with busts from the della Robbia workshop.

CHIESA RUSSA ORTODOSSA
Map pp242-3

☎ 055 49 01 48; Viale Giovanni Milton; admission free; ☼ 3.30pm 3rd Sun of month for Mass; ☐ 4, 8, 13 & 20

The onion-shaped domes are a bit of a giveaway on this Russian Orthodox church. Built in 1902 for the Russian populace resident in Florence, it was designed in the northern Russian style, with two interior levels decorated in part by Florentine artists but mostly by Russians who were expert in iconography.

FIESOLE Map p239
Founded at the latest in the 5th century BC, Fiesole had a five-century head start on Florence. The main northern Etruscan settlement, Fiesole was in many respects a far more pleasant site for a town than the sweaty malarial river valley in which Roman Florentia was founded. As the stoic Romans set about building their town, the Etruscans sat back and regarded them with a mixture of ambivalence and incomprehension.

Then, as now, the view over the Roman city is a drawcard. Add the olive groves and pretty valleys and you can understand why the likes of Boccaccio, Marcel Proust, Gertrude Stein and Frank Lloyd Wright (it's unlikely they have anything else in common!) have resided here.

The **APT office** (☎ 055 59 87 20; www .comune.fiesole.fi.it/infoturismo; Via Portigiani 3; ☼ 9am-6pm Mon-Sat, 10am-1pm & 2-6pm Sun Apr-Oct, 9am-5pm Mon-Sat, 10am-4pm Sun Nov-Mar) is just off Piazza Mino da Fiesole, the heart of the village. For more information on the town, its history and sights, check out the **Fiesole Life & Art** (www.fiesolelifeart.it) and **Fiesole Musei** (www .fiesolemusei.it) websites.

In the piazza itself is the **Cattedrale di San Romolo** (admission free; ☼ 7.30am-noon & 3-6pm). Much of its medieval splendour was lovingly erased by 19th-century renovation. Inside, a statue of San Romolo (St Romulus; 1521) by Giovanni della Robbia sits above the entrance.

Behind the cathedral, the **Museo Bandini** (Map p239; ☎ 055 5 94 77; Via Duprè 1; admission incl Zona Archeologica €6.70; ☼ 9.30am-7pm daily Apr-Sep, 9.30am-5pm Wed-Mon Oct-Mar) features an impressive collection of Tuscan artwork, most of it pre-dating the early Renaissance period. Among the paintings is also a collection of ceramics from the della Robbia clan.

Opposite the entrance to the museum is the **Zona Archeologica** (☎ 055 5 94 77; Via Portigiani 1; admission incl Museo Bandini €6.70; ⌚ 9.30am-7pm Apr-Sep, 9.30am-5pm Wed-Mon Oct-Mar). At its centre is the 1st-century-BC **Roman theatre** – built not long after the Romans took the Etruscan settlement. It's still used today from June to August for the Estate Fiesolana, a series of summer concerts and performances. Also in the complex are a small Etruscan temple, Roman baths and a small archaeological museum, the **Museo Civico Antiquarium Constantini**, containing finds ranging from Etruscan funeral stones through Greek-era ceramics and on to Lombard tombs.

Far in time and style from the Renaissance splendours of the valley below, the **Museo Primo Conti** (☎ 055 59 70 95; www.mega.it/primo.conti/contiho.htm; Via Dupré 18; admission €3; ⌚ 9am-1.30pm Tue-Sat), a 10-minute walk north of Piazza Mino da Fiesole, was the home of the eponymous avant-garde 20th-century artist and houses over 60 of his paintings. His style was eclectic but always bursting with colour, as these works show.

A short, steep walk west of Piazza Mino da Fiesole takes you past a fine lookout over the Florentine valley and up to the **Convento di San Francesco**, a tranquil spot with a pretty little church, two cloisters and the curious **Museo Missionario Francescano** (☎ 055 5 91 75; Via San Francesco 13; admission free; ⌚ 9am-noon & 3-6pm), which contains, among other odds and ends, an Egyptian mummy, Roman coins and a collection of Chinese art (gasp at the gruesome torture scenes!) and carvings brought back to Europe by Franciscan missionaries to China down the centuries.

About half a kilometre downhill from Piazza Mino da Fiesole on the road to Florence spread the lovely gardens of the **Villa Medici** (☎ 055 59417; Via Fra Giovanni Angelico 2; admission €6; ⌚ 8am-1pm Mon-Fri). The villa itself, also known as Il Palagio, is a private home and closed to visits.

At certain times of the year it is possible to join guided tours of some of the fine country villas around Fiesole. Inquire at the tourist office.

FORTEZZA DA BASSO Map pp242-3

Viale Filippo Strozzi; 🚌 4, 12, 13, 14, 20, 23, 28, 33 & 80

Alessandro de' Medici ordered this huge defensive fortress built in 1534, and the task went to a Florentine living in Rome, Antonio da Sangallo il Giovane. The Medici family in general and Alessandro in particular were not flavour of the month in Florence at the time, and construction of the fortress was an ominous sign of oppression. It was not designed to protect the city from invasion – Alessandro had recently been put back in the saddle after a siege by papal imperial forces. The idea of this fort was to keep a watchful eye over the Florentines. Nowadays it is used for trade fairs, exhibitions and cultural events.

MEDICI VILLAS Map p238

You can tell things are going well for the fat cats by the number and glory of their residences. The Medicis were no exception and built several opulent villas in the countryside around Florence as their prosperity grew during the 15th and 16th centuries. Most are now enclosed by the city's suburbs and industrial sprawl and are easily reached by bus (see the boxed text, p109).

One of the finest is **Villa Medicea La Petraia** (☎ 055 45 26 91; Via della Petraia 40; admission incl Villa Medicea di Castello €2; ⌚ 8.15am-7.30pm Jun-Aug, 8.15am-6.30pm Apr-May & Sep, 8.15am-5.30pm Mar & Oct, 8.15am-4.30pm Nov-Feb; closed 2nd & 3rd Mon each month). Commissioned by Cardinal Ferdinando de' Medici in 1576, this former fortress, about 3.5km north of the city, was converted by Buontalenti and features a magnificent sculpted garden from where you can take in the entire Florentine plain (it is easy to see why there was a fort here). Brunelleschi's dome and Giotto's Campanile are perfectly visible, as are the planes taking off from Florence's airport. Inside, the bulk of what you see was redecorated in the time of King Vittorio Emanuele's rule, when the Italian capital shifted temporarily to Florence in 1865. The most stunning aspect is the first entrance into the fresco-plastered former courtyard. Vittorio Emanuele had any wall space not already frescoed covered with more. Then he had a glass and metal roof built to cover the area so that his guests could use it as a ballroom under the stars. His morganatic wife, the Duchess of Mirafiori, took up residence here. Take bus 28 to get here.

Barely 1km west is **Villa Medicea di Castello** (☎ 055 45 47 91; Via di Castello 47; admission incl Villa Medicea La Petraia €2; 🕙 8.15am-7.30pm Jun-Aug, 8.15am-6.30pm Apr-May & Sep, 8.15am-5.30pm Mar & Oct, 8.15am-4.30pm Nov-Feb, closed 2nd & 3rd Mon each month). Also known as the Villa Reale, it was Lorenzo the Magnificent's favoured summer retreat. You can visit the gardens only. Again, take bus 28.

Access to **Villa Careggi** (☎ 055 427 97 55; Viale Pieraccini 17; admission free; 🕙 9am-6pm Mon-Fri, 9am-1pm Sat), where Lorenzo the Magnificent breathed his last in 1492, is limited as it is used as administrative offices for the local hospital. You can wander about outside the villa and visit two halls, one of them with 18th-century frescoes. The villa has been sold to the Tuscan regional government and will eventually be handed over, restored and opened as a museum, although hospital staff expect to remain until at least 2006. Take bus 14C.

Another Medici getaway was the **Villa di Poggio a Caiano** (off Map p238; ☎ 055 87 70 12; Piazza dei Medici 12; admission €2.50, grounds free, interior tours hourly 9.30am-6.30pm Jun-Aug, 9.30am-5.30pm Apr-May & Sep, 9am-4.30pm Mar & Oct, 9am-3.30pm Nov-Feb). About 15km from Florence on the road to Pistoia, and set in sprawling gardens, the interior of the villa is sumptuously decorated with frescoes and furnished much as it was early in the 20th century as a royal residence of the Savoys. Work began on the villa in 1445 and continued, with interruptions, until 1520. It became the family's main summer residence from the early 16th century and the scene of big family events, such as the marriage of Cosimo I to his Spanish bride Eleonora de Toledo. They say that Napoleon's sister, Elisa Baciocchi, whom he had made Grand Duchess of Tuscany in 1809, had a love affair with the violinist Nicolò Paganini here.

MUSEO STIBBERT Map pp240-1
☎ 055 47 55 20; Via F Stibbert 26; admission €5, gardens free; 🕙 10am-2pm Mon-Wed, 10am-6pm Fri-Sun, gardens 10am-dusk; 🚌 4

Frederick Stibbert (1838–1906) was one of the big wheeler-dealers on the European antiquities market in the 19th century and unsurprisingly had quite a collection himself. Born in Florence to an officer of the Coldstream Guards and a Florentine mother, Stibbert was forced through the English public school system and at 20 inherited a huge fortune from his grandfather. He bought and expanded the Villa di Montughi with the intention of creating a museum-home. His obsessions (apart from fast women and parties) revolved around the study of costume and armour. And so he built up a unique collection of European and Middle Eastern armour. The centrepiece of the display is the **Sala della Cavalcata** (Parade Room), with life-size mannequins of mounted knights, more than a dozen of them, on parade in German, French, Italian and Turkish armour. It is a unique sight and the hall is topped at one end with a figure of St George slaying the dragon – the latter is made of hundreds of snakeskins!

The exhibits, which spread out over a seeming infinity of rooms, also include clothes, furnishings, tapestries, ceramics and paintings (among them a good dose of Flemish and Dutch works) from the 16th to the 19th centuries. One of the most important items is the ceremonial cape in which Napoleon had himself crowned King of Italy (a short-lived honour as it turned out). It cost Stibbert 800 lire at auction.

Set in magnificent gardens, the museum lies about 1.5km north of the Fortezza da Basso.

POGGIO IMPERIALE Map p238
🚌 30

From Porta Romana a straight boulevard, Viale del Poggio Imperiale, leads directly to this once-grand Medici residence, the 'Imperial Hill'. The neoclassical appearance is due to changes wrought in the 18th and 19th centuries. It is now home to a high school and girls boarding school. If you turn up alone you will probably be able to wander around this somewhat neglected site.

Walking Tours

Walking Tours

The Florence of our dreams is a compact place and you will rarely find yourself wanting to hop on to a bus, except perhaps to return to a central point after a long meander. In this chapter a selection of possible walks is suggested, from general strolls of discovery to specific thematic searches. However you choose to wander this town, the used shoe leather will pay wonderful dividends.

THE DUOMO TO PIAZZA DELLA SIGNORIA

What follows is a serpentine route across old Florence from its religious to its political heart. The big sights are dealt with in detail in the Sights chapter, here we explore another, less obvious face of the medieval centre.

From the apse of the **Duomo** 1 (p65) head south down Via del Proconsolo. The first grand mansion on your left is the **Palazzo Nonfinito** 2 (p68). Across Borgo degli Albizi stands the equally impressive **Palazzo dei Pazzi** 3, which was completed a century earlier than the Palazzo Nonfinito and is influenced by the Palazzo Medici-Riccardi. The striking difference is in the sumptuous sculpting of the cornices on the windows, a departure that places the building's design, attributed to Giuliano da Maiano, in the late 15th century. It now houses offices, but you can wander into the courtyard. The Pazzi family lived up to their surname (which literally means 'mad') when they decided to assassinate Lorenzo de' Medici and usurp power in Florence (see p52). The assassins managed to kill Lorenzo's brother Giuliano, but the Medici revenge was swift. Most of the conspirators were caught and executed, and the family name and coat of

WALK FACTS

Start Duomo
Finish Piazza della Signoria
Distance 4.5km
Duration 1¼ hours

The Campanile (p65) and spread of Florence as seen from the Duomo

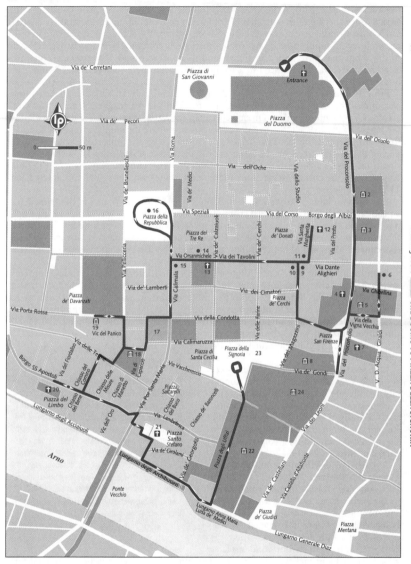

Via de' Cerretani

Piazza di
San Giovanni

1
Entrance

Via de' Pecori

Piazza
del Duomo

Via dell' Oriuolo

0   50 m

Via Roma

Via de' Brunelleschi

Via dell'Oche

Via del Proconsolo

Via de' Medici

Via dello Studio

2

Via del Corso   Borgo degli Albizi

Via Speziali

16
Piazza della
Repubblica

Piazza
de' Donati

12
Via del Presto

3

Piazza dei
Tre Re

Via de' Calzaiuoli

Piazza
de' Cerchi

Via Santa Margherita

14
Via Orsanmichele

Via dei Tavolini

11

Via de' Cerchi

15

13

Via Pellicceria

10 9
Via Dante
Alighieri

6

4

Via Ghibellina

Via de' Lamberti

Via dei Cimatori
Piazza
de' Cerchi

Via Calimala

5

Via della
Vigna Vecchia

Piazza
de' Davanzati

Via della Condotta

Via Porta Rossa

19

Via del Panico

17

Via Calimaruzza

Piazza di
Santa Cecilia

Piazza della
Signoria   23

7

Piazza
San Firenze

Via delle Terme

18

Via di Capaccio

Via Vacchereccia

Via dei Magazzini

8

Via de' Gondi

Borgo SS Apostoli

Via del Fiordaliso

Chiasso del Cornino

Chiasso delle Misure

Chiasso di Manetto

Via Por Santa Maria

Piazza
Saltarelli

Chiasso del Buco

24

20

Chiasso
del Bene

Via del Oro

Via Lambertesca

Via de' Leoni

Via de' Girolami

21
Piazza
Santo
Stefano

22

Lungarno degli Accaiuoli

Piazza del
Limbo

Chiasso de' Baroncelli

Piazza degli Uffizi

Via de' Georgofili

Arno

Via de' Castellani

Via Castello d'Altafronte

Lungarno degli Archibusieri

Ponte
Vecchio

Lungarno Anna Maria
Luisa de' Medici

Piazza
de' Giudici

Piazza
Mentana

Lungarno Generale Diaz

arms were ordered removed forever from all buildings in Florence. The family's destruction was complete.

Diagonally across from Palazzo dei Pazzi is one of the oldest churches in Florence, the **Badia Fiorentina 4** (p69), fronted by a building that was once the city prison and is now a grand museum, the **Palazzo del Bargello 5** (p74). A block east and then north of the latter is **Palazzo Borghese 6**. This long, low building is an early-19th-century neoclassical pile built for the family of the same name.

A few metres further south of Palazzo del Bargello is Piazza San Firenze, dominated by the law courts which are made up of two churches in one, most commonly known as the

Chiesa di San Firenze 7 (p70). Across the piazza (on the west side) is the main façade of **Palazzo Gondi 8**, once the site of the merchants' tribunal, a court set up to deal with their quarrels. Off Via de' Gondi you can enter a beautiful courtyard with fountain and staircase in *pietra serena* (grey 'tranquil stone'). The whole courtyard is crammed with tourist tat, especially in the shops that have nested in the ground floor; what would Leonardo da Vinci, who as a young lad was apprenticed to a painter's workshop here (before Palazzo Gondi was built) think of it all?

From Piazza San Firenze, turn west along Via della Condotta, which in medieval times was one of the main fashion shopping streets. Take Via dei Magazzini north and you'll arrive at Via Dante Alighieri. On one corner of the latter street and Via dei Magazzini is the **Torre della Castagna 9**, all that remains of the *palazzo* where the medieval republic's leaders, the *priori*, met until the Palazzo della Signoria (nowadays the Palazzo Vecchio) was built. Facing the tower across Via dei Magazzini is the **Oratorio di San Martino 10**, a chapel on the site of the former Chiesa di San Martino, Dante's parish church. North across Via Dante Alighieri, on the corner of Via Santa Margherita, stands what is touted as the **Casa di Dante 11** (Dante's House; p65).

Just up Via Santa Margherita from Dante's alleged former home, is the **Chiesa di Santa Margherita 12**, which dates at least from 1032. Some say that it was in this small single-nave church that Dante met his muse, Beatrice Portinari, although he himself claimed that he bumped into her in the Badia. However, he may have married Gemma Donati in this church. Members of both families, and conceivably Beatrice and Gemma themselves, are buried here.

Continuing along Via Dante Alighieri, which leads into Via dei Tavolini, you come across the **Chiesa di Orsanmichele 13** (p69) and opposite it the **Arte dei Beccai 14**, the 14th-century headquarters of the Butchers' Guild. Far more important was the Wool Guild, or **Arte della Lana 15**, the medieval headquarters of which still stand proudly on the corner of Via Orsanmichele and Via Calimala. It is made up of a tower-house, echoing that Florentine preoccupation with self-defence that clearly affected the guilds as much as it did feuding families.

Just south of where Via Calimaruzza runs into Via Calimala is where the Roman city's south gate stood. Some think the word 'Calimala' is a distortion of *callis maius*, itself a badly pronounced version of the Roman *cardo maximus*, the name given to the standard main cross-street in a Roman garrison town.

A short way north, along Via Calimala, is **Piazza della Repubblica 16** (p68). If you stroll back south down Via Calimala you'll arrive at the **Mercato Nuovo 17** (New Market; p73). Just off to the southwest of the Mercato Nuovo, **Palazzo dei Capitani di Parte Guelfa 18** (Palace of the Guelph Faction's Captains) was built in the early 13th century, and was later

> ## ALONG THE WAY
>
> Along this route you are spoilt for choice with rest and lunch stops. Just before you hit the Chiesa di Orsanmichele you might be tempted by a gelato at **Perchè No** (p142). Special mention should be made of the grand historic cafés on Piazza della Repubblica, such as **Gilli** (p130) and **Giubbe Rose** (p130). Or you could hold out until you emerge in Piazza della Signoria and sit down for a cup of sticky chocolate at **Rivoire** (p130), another Florentine icon. If you're after lunch during, or at the end of your walk, give serious thought to **Gustavino** (p129), or **Frescobaldi** (p129), both as good for their wines as the grub.

tinkered with by Brunelleschi and Vasari. The leaders of the Guelph faction raised this fortified building in 1265, using land and houses that had been confiscated from the Ghibellines (for more on this medieval faction-fighting, see p50). About a block west is a remarkable leftover from the 14th century, **Palazzo Davanzati 19** (p75).

The modest 11th-century **Chiesa dei SS Apostoli 20** is dwarfed by the houses built around it in Piazza del Limbo. The plain exposed brick of the Romanesque façade is complemented by a Renaissance entrance. Inside, columns of green Prato marble set apart two aisles from the considerably higher central nave. At the end of the left aisle is a glazed terracotta tabernacle by Giovanni della Robbia.

If you hike back east to Via Por Santa Maria, cross into the little square presided over by the part-Romanesque, part-Gothic façade of the now deconsecrated **Chiesa di Santo Stefano 21**.

It's only ever open when concerts are held, during which you could get a look at the rather heady baroque interior. From here, wind on to Lungarno degli Archibusieri and then between the wings of the **Uffizi 22** (p70) into **Piazza della Signoria 23** (p77), which is dominated by the fortified hulk of the **Palazzo Vecchio 24** (p76).

AN OLTRARNO STROLL

When you come off the **Ponte Vecchio 1** (p107) on the Oltrarno side of the river you are on Via de' Guicciardini. This street has had its fair share of VIP residents. At No 18 is **Machiavelli's home 2**; exiled for a time, he ended up back in Florence and breathed his last here. At No 15 is **Palazzo Guicciardini 3**, one of several mansions belonging to the family of the same name. In this one the 16th-century intriguer and historian, Francesco, had his home.

Russian novelist **Fyodor Dostoyevsky** stayed at **No 22 Piazza de' Pitti 4** to write *The Idiot* in 1868-69. A few doors down, opposite **Palazzo Pitti 5** (p106), was the **home of Paolo dal Pozzo Toscanelli 6** (1397-1482), cosmographer, scientist, engineer and all-round extremely clever chap. They say Columbus used his theoretical maps on the explorations that led to the discovery of the Americas.

WALK FACTS

Start Ponte Vecchio
Finish Porta San Miniato
Distance 3.6km
Duration One hour

Walking Tours

AN OLTRARNO STROLL

Dogleg west, down Via Sor de' Pitti, cross Via Maggio and head along Via de' Michelozzi to reach **Piazza Santo Spirito 7**. On a summer afternoon here you could almost feel yourself to be in Spain. The bars attract a mixed and largely local crowd of students, layabouts, artists, misfits and the odd foreigner. The feel is laid-back, with tables tumbling out on to the square and music humming from one corner or another. It gets more animated as the night sets in.

During WWII, the Deutsches Institut (German Institute) had its offices and library in a building on this square. The staff had a risky habit of sheltering anti-Fascists in its library. At its northern end, the square is fronted by the flaking façade of the **Basilica di Santo Spirito 8** (p102). The southeast corner of the square is graced by a fine Renaissance residence, the **Palazzo Guadagni 9**, also home to a *pensione* (p182).

Stroll west from Piazza Santo Spirito and you'll wind up in Piazza del Carmine, whose star attraction is the **Cappella Brancacci 10** in the Basilica di Santa Maria del Carmine (p102). To the north runs Borgo San Frediano, a busy street dotted with the workshops of artisans, ranging from shoemakers to jewellers. Nip around baroque **Chiesa di San Frediano 11** (p103) to reach the Arno again. Here you turn right (east) and head back towards the Ponte Vecchio. Along the way you pass several grand family mansions, including **Palazzo Guicciardini 12** at Lungarno Guicciardini 7 and the 13th-century **Palazzo Frescobaldi 13** in Piazza de' Frescobaldi. The latter played host to Charles de Valois in 1301, when he came to mediate peace between the Bianchi and Neri in one of Florence's interminable squabbles.

Round this palazzo you continue east along Borgo San Jacopo, on which still stand two 12th-century towers, the **Torre dei Marsili 14** and **Torre de' Belfredelli 15**. On Via de' Ramaglianti once stood a synagogue.

Continuing east from the Ponte Vecchio, the first stretch of Via de' Bardi shows clear signs of its recent history. The entire area was flattened by German mines in 1944 and hastily rebuilt in questionable taste after the war. The street spills into **Piazza di Santa Maria Soprarno 16**, which takes its name from a church that has long ceased to exist. Follow the narrow Via de' Bardi (the right fork) away from the square and you enter a pleasantly quieter corner of Florence. The Bardi family once owned all the houses along this street, but by the time the chubby Cosimo de' Medici married Contessina de' Bardi in 1415, the latter's family was in decline. They were among the banking dynasties ruined by the habit of debtors, such as England's King Edward III, of defaulting on huge loans. Cosimo and Contessina moved into a Bardi mansion on this street, but it was later pulled down. Buying up the original plot had clearly been a medieval bargain as, until the de' Bardi family

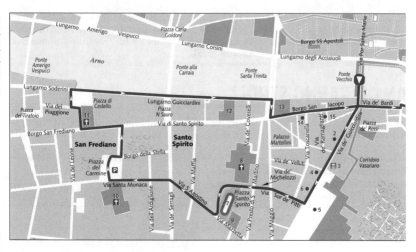

built their mansions, the street had been known as Borgo Pidiglioso (Flea St), one of the city's poorest quarters.

A couple of 15th-century mansions on the left, the **Palazzo Capponi delle Rovinate 17** at Via de' Bardi 36 and **Palazzo Canigiani 18** at No 28, are typically Renaissance structures, with heavy *pietra forte* ('strong stone') façades and jutting eaves. A little further on, the **Chiesa di Santa Lucia dei Magnoli 19** has a striking glazed terracotta relief above the portal of Santa Lucia in the style of the della Robbia workshop.

Via de' Bardi expires in Piazza de' Mozzi, which is also surrounded by the sturdy façades of grand residences belonging to the high and mighty. The southern flank of the piazza is occupied by the **Palazzi de' Mozzi 20**, where Pope Gregory X stayed whilst brokering peace between the Guelphs and Ghibellines. The western side is lined by the 15th-century **Palazzo Lensi-Nencioni 21**, **Palazzo Torrigiani-Nasi 22** (with the graffiti ornamentation) and **Palazzo Torrigiani 23**.

Across the square, the long façade of the **Museo Bardini 24** is the result of an eclectic 19th-century building project by its owner, the collector Stefano Bardini. The collection has been closed for years.

From here turn east down Via dei Renai, past the leafy **Piazza Demidoff 25**, which is dedicated to Nicola Demidoff, a 19th-century Russian philanthropist who lived nearby in Via di San Niccolò. Demidoff and his two sons rained money on philanthropic works in Florence and restored a beautiful country getaway north of the city – the former Medici Villa of Pratolino, now known as the Villa Demidoff.

It is open to the public as a **park** (☎ 055 40 91 55; admission €3; 🕙 10am-7.30pm Thu-Sun & holidays, 10am-6pm Sun & holidays Mar-Oct). The 16th-century **Palazzo Serristori 26** in Via dei Renai was home to Joseph Bonaparte in the last years of his life (he died in 1844). At the height of his career he had been made king of Spain by his younger brother Napoleon.

Turn right and you'll end up in Via di San Niccolò. Here, the bland-looking **Chiesa di San Niccolò Oltrarno 27** is interesting if for nothing else than the plaque indicating how high the 1966 flood waters reached (about 4m). Go east along Via San Niccolò and

ALONG THE WAY

The best options for eating and drinking are found at either end of this walk. The bars and restaurants on and around Piazza Santo Spirito could be used to fuel up at lunchtime before setting off. While wandering along Borgo San Jacopo you could drop into **Azzarri** (p127) to pick up some delicatessen goods. Or, at the end of your exertions, you could opt for one of the places around Porta San Miniato, like the **Osteria Antica Mescita San Niccolò** (p139), or the **Enoteca Fuoriporta** (p138). A relaxing coffee or cocktail stop in the same area is **Il Rifrullo** (p146)

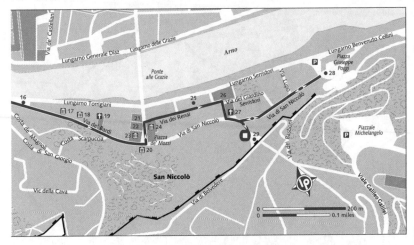

you'll emerge at the tower marking the **Porta San Niccolò 28** – all that is left of the medieval city gate here.

To get an idea of what the old walls were like, walk south from the Chiesa di San Niccolò Oltrarno through **Porta San Miniato 29**. The wall extends a short way to the east and quite far further west, up a steep hill that leads to the **Forte di Belvedere** (see p104). Less strenuous are the back roads, such as Via dell'Erta Canina, that wend southwards into a paradise of olive groves and vineyards. Those who live in the few villas scattered about in what is virtually Florence's back garden must know people in the right places to keep developers out!

THE LAST SUPPER TRAIL

In the convents and monasteries of medieval Italy, and indeed much later, it was customary to decorate the *cenacolo* (refectory), or dining hall, with a scene of *L'Ultima Cena* (Last Supper). In this way, dining friars or sisters could contemplate the importance of physical *and* spiritual nutrition. From the early 14th century on, the standard model for the scene had Christ seated between St Peter and a sleeping St John. Alone on the other side of the table, with his back to the observers of the fresco, was a furtive Judas Iscariot. On rare occasions artists elected to abandon that scheme (as in the Cenacolo di San Salvi).

Although many of Florence's religious houses were shut down over the course of the 19th century – and the buildings handed

Architectural detail of the Duomo (p65)

WALK FACTS
Start Piazza Santo Spirito
Finish Via di San Salvi
Distance 5.8km
Duration 1¾ hours

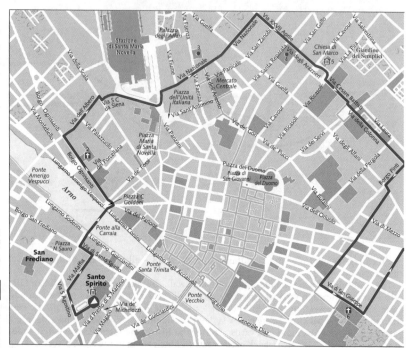

over to public institutions such as schools, or sold to private entrepreneurs – some fine examples of these frescoes have survived (albeit with most having to be restored). A tour of these, aside from the pleasure of contemplating fine works of art, brings the added joy of being able to do so in peace (hardly anyone bothers to seek these sights out), almost with a sense of discovering the unknown, and (with one modest exception) it's all for free. Most open only in the morning, so you need to get off to an early start if you want to digest the lot in one day!

Start in the Oltrarno, with **Cenacolo di Santo Spirito 1** (p103), in which the central scene by Andrea Orcagna is accompanied by a museum display of sculpture – this is the

ALONG THE WAY

You could have your breakfast at one of the lively bar-eateries on Piazza Santo Spirito before embarking on this walk, which will soon leave you feeling hungry again, given the constant supper theme! **Cabiria** (p145) is a fun spot to start the day. If you feel peckish by the time you exit the Cenacolo di Foligno, pop down to **Da Nerbone** (p133), in the Mercato Centrale, for a *lampredotto* (tripe) roll. There's also no shortage of places to refuel around Piazza di Santa Croce before embarking on the last long stretch of this walk; among the more enticing are **Osteria Cibrèo** (p136) and **Il Pizzaiuolo** (p136).

only time you'll need to pull out a few euros during the tour. From here, head across Ponte alla Carraia to Piazza C Goldoni. Turn left and make for the **Chiesa di Ognissanti 2** (p79), in the refectory of which you will find an extraordinary fresco of the Last Supper by Domenico Ghirlandaio. You pass through the equally fresco-rich cloister to reach the refectory.

After that, stroll another block west and then swing around to the northeast, past the front of the train station and down Via Nazionale. Turn left (north) into Via Faenza for the least known and visited of the city's *cenacoli*, **Cenacolo di Foligno 3** (p79), a delightful scene created at the very end of the 15th century by Il Perugino's workshop. Thereafter it's a short stroll up Via Nazionale and right along Via XXVII Aprile Via degli Arazzieri to Andrea del Castagno's startling **Cenacolo di Sant'Apollonia 4** (p93). Shortly thereafter, in the small refectory of the former

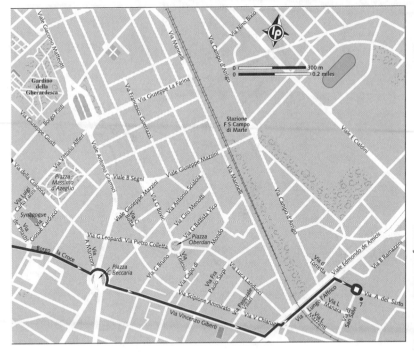

convent that is now the **Museo di San Marco 5** (p96) you can see a Last Supper scene by Domenico Ghirlandaio, completed around 1482. From there, make your way down to the **Basilica di Santa Croce 6** (p98) for the Last Supper scenes held in its Museo dell'Opera di Santa Croce. Then it's a longish walk east, out of the historic centre, to Andrea del Sarto's **Cenacolo di San Salvi 7** (p109).

SUNSET VIEWS & A COUNTRY MILE

From **Ponte Vecchio 1** (p107), walk along Via de' Guicciardini then take a quick left and head along the left flank of **Chiesa di Santa Felicita 2** (p104), under the Corridoio Vasariano. Stroll up central Florence's only hill, Costa di San Giorgio, lined with lovely small *palazzi*, and take in the city view at the intersection of Costa Scarpuccia. A little further, at No 19, is the beautifully restored former **home of Galileo 3** (see Forte di Belvedere, p104). At the top is the 13th-century city gate, **Porta di San Giorgio 4** (p000). Passing the entrance to **Forte di Belvedere 5** (p104) on your right, walk along Via di San Leonardo – lined with villas, olive groves and cypress trees – to the 11th-century **Chiesa di San Leonardo 6**, whose 13th-century marble pulpit was taken from another church, San Piero Scheraggio (largely demolished to make way for the Uffizi). They say the likes of Dante and Boccaccio spoke from that pulpit. The church only opens for occasional services. Further along the road you will pass, on the right, the **villa 7** where Russian composer Tchaikovsky stayed on his 1890 visit to Florence. Here he wrote his opera, *Queen of Spades*. The sojourn later inspired his *Souvenir of Florence*. Another 150m further on and you turn left into the tree-lined Viale Galileo Galilei for 800m of views, before climbing the

WALK FACTS

Start Ponte Vecchio
Finish Piazza Santa Felicita
Distance 5km
Duration One hour

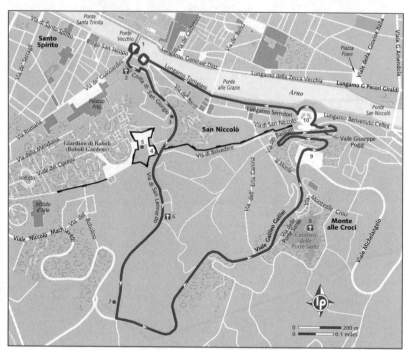

steps on your right to the captivating **Chiesa di San Miniato Al Monte 8** (p103). If your timing is right, it will gently resound to the monks' Gregorian chanting. With the sun setting, rejoin the busier Florentine tourist trail at **Piazzale Michelangelo 9** (p107) – dominated by the giant copy of Michelangelo's *David* – for refreshments and more stunning views. Take the western steps and winding path down to **Porta San Niccolò 10**, a lone tower that was one of the city's medieval gates (now without walls) and head back along the Arno to **Piazza Santa Felicita 2**.

ALONG THE WAY

If you pay to enter Forte di Belvedere, you could take the weight off your feet early in your trek and enjoy a cuppa in the fort's bar. Otherwise wait until you reach **Piazzale Michelangelo** (p107) and drink in the views at one of several cafés. If you're feeling hungry, hang on until you get down to Porta San Niccolò – a quick stroll west will bring you to a gaggle of eating and drinking options, including **Osteria Antica Mescita San Niccolò** (p139) and the fashionable **Negroni** (p148).

CINEMA SCENES

Such a pretty face, Florence has frequently lent its good looks to film-makers. According to one local academic, the most popular sites chosen to shoot film scenes are Piazza della Signoria, Ponte Vecchio, Piazza del Duomo and Piazzale Michelangelo, in that order. The first full-length feature film shot on location in the city was *Fiorenza Mia* (1915), directed by Enrico Novelli. Many have followed since, although frequently they have assigned Florence little more than bit roles.

Starting in Piazza Santo Spirito, look up to the gallery of **Pensione Bandini 1** (p182), used as a set in Franco Zeffirelli's *Tea with Mussolini*. More than a century before that film was shot the Lumière brothers presented films to the honeymooning Italian royal prince Vittorio, and his wife Elena, in the Sala Meridiana in **Palazzo Pitti 2** (p106). Indeed Florence was one of the first cities in Europe to open movie houses. Behind the palace, the

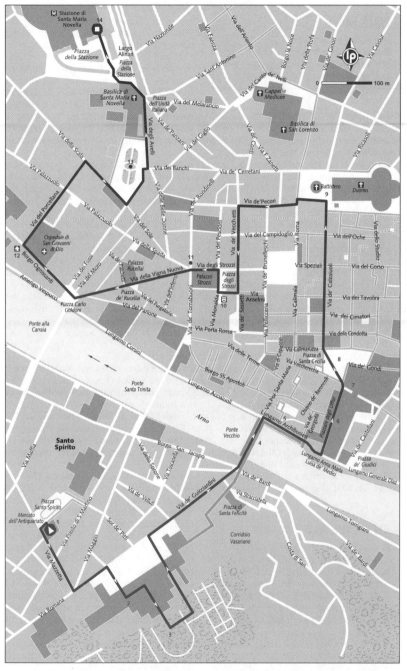

Stazione di
Santa Maria
Novella

14

Piazza
della Stazione

Largo
Alinari

Piazza
della Stazione

Via Nazionale

Via Faenza

Via Sant'Antonino

Via dell'Ariento

Via del Canto de' Nelli

Borgo la Noce

Via della Stufa

Via de' Ginori

Via Cavour

Cappelle
Medicee

Basilica di
Santa Maria
Novella

Piazza
dell'Unità
Italiana

Via del Melarancio

Via de' Panzani

Via de' Conti

Basilica di
San Lorenzo

Via F. Zanetti

Via Ricasoli

Via della Scala

Via Palazzuolo

Via del Porcellana

Via Palazzuolo

13

Via delle Belle Donne

Via del Sole

Via dei Banchi

Via de' Rondinelli

Via de' Cerretani

Battistero
9

Duomo

Via de' Pecori

Via dello Studio

Ospedale di
San Giovanni
di Dio

12 Borgo Ognissanti

Via de' Fossi

Via della Spada

Via dei Federighi

Palazzo
Rucellai

Via della Vigna Nuova

11

Via dei Pescioni

Via de' Vecchietti

Via de' Tornabuoni

Via degli Strozzi

Via del Campidoglio

Via de' Brunelleschi

Via Roma

Via dell'Oche

Via del Corso

Via de' Calzaiuoli

Via Speziali

Via dei Tavolini

Amerigo Vespucci

Via del Moro

Via dell'Inferno

Palazzo
Strozzi

Piazza
degli
Strozzi

10

Via de' Sassetti

Via della Pelliceria

Via Calimala

Via Anselmi

Via dei Cimatori

Piazza
de' Rucellai

Via del Purgatorio

Via del Parione

Piazza
Carlo
Goldoni

Via della Condotta

Ponte alla
Carraia

Lungarno Corsini

Via Monalda

Via Porta Rossa

Via delle Terme

Via di Capaccio

Via di Santa Maria

Calimaruzza

Piazza di
Santa Cecilia

8

Via de' Gondi

Borgo SS Apostoli

Lungarno Acciaiuoli

Via Pon. Santa Maria

Vacchereccia

Chiasso de' Baroncelli

7

Ponte
Santa Trinita

Arno

Ponte
Vecchio

4

Via de' Georgofili

5

Piazzale degli Uffizi

Lungarno Archibusieri

6

Via de' Castellani

Piazza
de' Giudici

Santo
Spirito

Borgo San Jacopo

Lungarno Anna Maria
Luisa de' Medici

Lungarno Generale Diaz

Via Maffia

Via dello Sprone

Via Toscanella

Via de' Velluti

Via de' Guicciardini

Via de' Bardi

Via Stracciatella

Piazza di
Santa Felicità

Lungarno Torrigiani

Via de' Bardi

Piazza
Santo Spirito

Mercato
dell'Antiquariato

1

Via Presto di S. Martino

Sor de' Pitti

Corridoio
Vasariano

Costa di San

Via Mazzetta

Via Romana

Via Maggio

2

3

0 ————————— 100 m

WALK FACTS

Start Piazza Santo Spirito
Finish Stazione Santa Maria Novella
Distance 4.5km
Duration One hour

Giardino di Boboli 3 (p105) was used to shoot scenes for *Paisà,* the second part in Roberto Rossellini's postwar trilogy. It tells of the taking of Florence from the Germans in 1944 and the feeling of immediacy and authenticity in the set stems partly, perhaps, from the fact that the movie was shot in 1946. Cross the **Ponte Vecchio 4** (most recently seen in spectral winter fashion in Ridley Scott's *Hannibal,* 2001), which the Germans spared from destruction in the year *Paisà* is set. If you are a buff of 1970s Italian cinema, you might remember the winter scenes of Marcello Mastroianni and Natasha Kinsky together on the bridge in Alberto Lattuada's flop *Così Come Sei* (Just As You Are; 1978).

Turn right into **Lungarno Archibusieri 5**. Here stood the Pensione Quisisana e Ponte Vecchio, used in some of the scenes from James Ivory's *Room with a View* (1985). The film crew also stayed here. The *pensione,* in which interior shots were done (the views were taken from another location in a bit of artistic licence), was later badly damaged in the 1993 mafia bomb blast in Via de' Georgofili.

Entering **Piazzale degli Uffizi 6** (Map pp244–5), also shot in *Hannibal* and *Paisà,* we approach the site of one of the most horrible film scenes in Florentine history. Inside **Palazzo Vecchio 7** (p76) Hannibal Lecter (Anthony Hopkins) eviscerates police inspector Rinaldo Pazzi in *Hannibal.* In a double wink at history, Lecter hangs the body from the palace walls (the fate reserved for Pazzi's namesakes, the Pazzi conspirators, after their failed attempt to assassinate Lorenzo il Magnifico – see p52) and his innards drip onto the spot in **Piazza della Signora 8** (Map pp244–5) below, where Savonarola was burned at the stake (see p53). Many Florentines (including the Greens and some left-wing politicians) didn't want the scenes shot in one of the city's most emblematic buildings, fearing they would give their city a blood-thirsty reputation.

Much more light-hearted are images of David Niven in the same square, where a six-metre statue of his character is made by his wife in the 1971 farce, *The Statue.* Lucy (Helena Bonham Carter) wanders through here too, in *Room with a View.*

From there, move on to another frequent backdrop in Florentine movies, **Piazza del Duomo 9** (Map pp244–5). In *Paisà,* the square is empty and desolate, while in Jane Campion's *Portrait of a Lady* (1996), John Malkovich and Nicole Kidman glide ethereally past the Duomo as Malkovich's Gilbert sets about seducing Kidman's Isabel.

A short walk away, on the south side of Piazza degli Strozzi, is the city's best cinema for undubbed foreign movies, the **Odeon Cinehall 10** (p153). Most Florentines have forgotten that the cinema was used in scenes from the Taviani brothers 1987 *Good Morning Babilonia,* which took a quirky look at the mammoth silent-film production, *Intolerance,* created by D W Griffith in Hollywood in 1916.

Perhaps some cinema fans will get a strange sense of déjà vu in **Via de' Tornabuoni 11** (Map pp244–5). That's because Al Pacino was filmed wandering down here as a tourist in Sidney Pollack's *Bobby Deerfield* (1977), in which he plays a somewhat disillusioned car-racing champ with an Italian lover and no end of problems. A little further west, on Piazza d'Ognissanti, the **Excelsior 12** (see the Grand Hotel, p177) has long been the preferred hotel of film stars and crews in town to shoot. **Piazza Santa Maria Novella 13** (Map pp242–3) will probably be familiar to those who have seen *Tea with Mussolini,* and train station **Stazione Santa Maria Novella 14** (Map pp242–3) got a bit part on screen with stunning Ornella Muti in torment over her troubled love life in the 1978 *Eutanasia di un Amore* (aka *Break Up*).

ALONG THE WAY

Piazza Santo Spirito (Map pp248–9) makes a good starting point for any walk, as the serried ranks of eateries and bars give you breakfast, lunch and snack options. Should hunger strike while wandering along Via de' Bardi, **I Tarocchi** (p139) is a handy lunch stop. Take hot chocolate at **Rivoire** (p130) and jump at the chance for a little fashion shopping along Via de' Tornabuoni and Via della Vigna Nuova. A couple of fine eateries along Via del Porcellana are **La Sostanza** (p131) and **Trattoria dei 13 Gobbi** (p131).

Eating

Eating

Florence presents plenty of opportunities to wrap your mandibles around fine local food and to savour the exquisite fruit of the Tuscan vine. Tourist traps abound in the city centre, but even there you will discover cosy trattorias, snack bars and fancy restaurants. Edge just a short way from the central pole of the Duomo and Piazza della Signoria, and you will soon turn up all sorts of goodies.

Opening Hours & Meal Times

Italians rarely eat a sit-down *colazione* (breakfast). They tend to drink a cappuccino and eat a *cornetto* (croissant) or other type of pastry (generically known as a *brioche*) at a bar.

For *pranzo* (lunch), restaurants usually open from 12.30pm to 3pm. Virtually none take orders after 2.30pm. Traditionally lunch is the main meal of the day and many shops and businesses close for two or three hours to accommodate it.

A full meal will include some type of *antipasto*, which can vary from a classic dish, such as *prosciutto e melone* (cured ham and melon), to *crostini*. After this comes the *primo piatto*, generally a pasta or risotto, followed by the *secondo piatto* of meat or fish. This is not necessarily accompanied by vegetables and Italians often order a *contorno* (vegetable dish) to go with it. *Insalate* (salads) have a strange position in the order. They are usually ordered as separate dishes and, in some cases, serve as a replacement for the *primo piatto*.

Opening hours for *cena* (dinner) vary, but people start sitting down around 8.30pm. With a few exceptions, you'll be hard pressed to find a place still serving after 10.30pm. The evening meal follows a similar pattern to lunch. It was once a simpler affair, but habits are changing because of the inconvenience of travelling home or going out for lunch every day.

Restaurants and bars are generally closed one day each week; the day varies depending on the establishment. Closing days (where applicable) are listed here, but opening times are only mentioned where they vary substantially from the norm.

Cafés and bars that serve sandwiches and other snacks generally open from 7.30am to 8pm, although some stay open after 8pm and turn into pub-style drinking and meeting places.

A lot of restaurants close for part or all of August, another reason for steering clear of Florence at this stifling time of year.

CONFUSED OVER COFFEE

Coffee in Italy is complex. An *espresso* is a small cup of strong black coffee. A *doppio espresso* is a double. A *caffè lungo* is more watery, and an approximation of bland filter coffee is a *caffè americano*.

A *caffè latte* is coffee with milk. Cappuccino is a frothy version. You can ask for it *senza schiuma* (without froth), in which case the froth is scraped off the top. It tends to come lukewarm, so if you want it hot, ask for it to be *molto caldo*. Both are breakfast drinks to Italians. *Caffè macchiato* is an *espresso* with a dash of frothy milk. In summer you can opt for a *caffè freddo*, a long glass of cold coffee with ice cubes. Good on winter afternoons is a *corretto* – an *espresso* 'corrected' with grappa or similar hard liquor.

After lunch and dinner it wouldn't occur to Italians to order either *caffè latte* or a cappuccino – but an *espresso*, *macchiato* or *corretto* are all perfectly acceptable. If you want a cappuccino there's no problem – but you might have to repeat your request a couple of times to convince disbelieving waiters that they have heard correctly.

An *espresso* at a regular bar costs 80 to 90 cents; it costs up to €3.50 (cappuccino €4.50) if you sit at one of the grand café terraces, such as Gilli, Giubbe Rosse or Rivoire.

How Much?

Florence offers a broad range of eating options in terms of quality and price. Although it can on occasion be an expensive business, all sorts of curious eateries will feed you well at a reasonable cost.

Some bars serve filling snacks with lunchtime and pre-dinner drinks. At others you can pick up reasonable *panini* (filled rolls or sandwiches), costing from €2 to €3.50 if you eat them standing up or takeaway. You'll also find numerous outlets where you can buy pizza *a taglio* (by the slice) for not more than a couple of euros.

For a sit-down meal there are several options. Numerous restaurants offer a *menù turistico* or *menù a prezzo fisso*, a set-price lunch costing €10 to €15 excluding drinks. Generally, choice is limited and the food is unspectacular (there are exceptions). In some cases it is downright awful (see the boxed text, p129). From your taste buds' point of view, and as long as you are not overly hungry, you'd be better off settling for a plate of pasta, some salad and wine at a decent restaurant.

Prices throughout this guide are given for a full meal, by which we mean a *primo*, a *secondo*, a dessert and some house wine. You could also add an *antipasto* (starter) at the front end of your meal, but these are generally expensive and will simply stunt your appetite. At modest restaurants a full meal is unlikely to cost less than €25 a head. Any place where you could probably eat for under €25, and places where you would mainly eat pizza, have been classified as 'cheap eats'. At good midrange places expect to part with up to €50 a head. Much depends on your choice of dish and wine; you can easily hit €80 to €100 (and more) in the top-flight joints.

Even many Italians are breaking with the habit of the full meal – preferring instead, say, a *secondo* with a side dish – although curiously, the change in Italian habits is one reason cited by restaurateurs for the rise in prices in the past few years.

Booking Tables

For much of the year, Florence is full of visitors, so you should consider booking ahead. You can often get a table when you walk in off the street, but you can by no means bank on it.

Tipping

Most eating establishments have a cover charge, ranging from €1 up to €6 per head. You also have to factor in the service charge of 10% to 15%. Since most places include this on the bill, further tipping is strictly optional. Most locals don't bother adding any more unless they have been particularly overwhelmed by service and quality. Remember this if you are presented with a credit-card receipt with space to add in the tip. In any case, it is always preferable to leave a tip in cash for the person who has waited your table.

Self-Catering

Making your own snacks is the cheapest way to keep body and soul together. For salami, cheese and wine, shop in *alimentari, salumerie* or *pizzicherie,* which are a cross between grocery stores and delicatessens. Fresh bread is available at a *forno* or *panetteria* – bakeries that sell bread, pastries and sometimes groceries. The following places offer tasty produce for your picnic basket.

Ask the friendly folks at Tassini (Map pp244–5; ☎ 055 28 26 96; Borgo SS Apostoli 24/r; ⊙ Mon-Sat; ☒ A) to make up a *panino* or two for with the fresh products on display and you won't regret it. Or just stock up on the basics and do it yourself. Delicious hams hang behind the counter out the back. Standa (Map pp248–9; ☎ 055 234 78 56; Via Pietrapiana 42-44; ⊙ 8am-9pm Mon-Sat & 9am-8pm Sun; ☒ 14 & 23) is about the only major supermarket within the old town centre of Florence. It does a roaring trade, especially with the resident foreign students. Another delicatessen is Azzarri (Map pp244–5; ☎ 055 238 17 14; Borgo San Jacopo 27/b; ⊙ Mon-Sat; ☒ D). If you're hankering to put together your own gourmet snacks or lunches while traipsing around the Oltrarno, this is the place. The Azzarri family have been purveying fine foodstuffs, wines and other goodies for generations, so your taste buds will leap with appreciation.

PIAZZA DEL DUOMO & AROUND

There's no shortage of eateries to be found immediately near the Duomo, but few are of real quality. As a rule, it is worth investing some shoe leather to track down better trattorias a little further from the epicentre of old Florence.

CAFFÈ COQUINARIUS Map pp244-5 Wine Bar
☎ 055 230 21 53; Via dell' Oche 15/r; meal €25; ⏰ 9am-midnight, kitchen open noon-11pm; 🚌 A

An excellent choice outside rigid meal times, this laid-back and comfy café in a former stables has light and substantial dishes of *crostini,* salads, pasta and the usual meaty mains, as well as more than a dozen wines by the glass.

CHEAP EATS

RISTORANTE SELF-SERVICE LEONARDO Map pp244-5 Canteen
☎ 055 28 44 46; Via de' Pecori 35/r; pasta €3.30, mains €4-5; ⏰ 11.45am-2.45pm & 6.45-9.45pm Sun-Fri; 🚌 A

When it comes to eating a full meal while you pinch pennies, it's hard to beat this refectory-style spot. Queue up with a tray and choose from a limited range of *primi* and *secondi* and wash it down with a simple Tuscan tipple – it beats McDonald's any day of the week.

PIAZZA DELLA SIGNORIA & AROUND

You won't find anything much actually on this square (right at the heart of Florence's turbulent political life), but hidden away in various surrounding streets and lanes are a few eating dens that reward a little hunting. Piazza della Signoria *does* host one of the city's great cafés. And just a caffeine-induced hop, skip and jump away are the grand cafés of Piazza della Repubblica.

ACQUA AL 2 Map pp248-9 Tuscan
☎ 055 28 41 70; Via della Vigna Vecchia 40/r; meal €25-30; ⏰ dinner only; 🚌 14 & A

A long-standing favourite, this is a cheerful old eating den known for its *assaggi di*

primi (mini portions of first courses for tasting). Although well populated with out-of-towners, it retains much of its atmosphere and still attracts Florentines.

ALLE MURATE Map pp244-5 Mediterranean
☎ 055 24 06 18; Via del Proconsolo 16/r; meal €80; ⏰ dinner only Tue-Sun; 🚌 14, 23 & A

Recently moved into this historic building, the Arte dei Giudici e dei Notai (p69), one of the city's most distinguished restaurants now has an address to match. Come for creative, light homemade pasta dishes and seafood mains (particularly in winter, when fish dishes rule here). A special emphasis is laid on the preparation of vegetables and side dishes. Dine in class surrounded by vivacious frescoes.

ANGELS Map pp244-5 Modern Tuscan
☎ 055 239 87 62; www.ristoranteangels.it; Via del Proconsolo 29-31/r; meal €40; ⏰ noon-2am; 🚌 A

Sturdy stone columns prop up an exquisite timber ceiling in this cavernous restaurant, where the centuries-old structure is combined with a contemporary look. Grand picture windows open the place up to natural light, and the dark tables and white seats suggest hard modern angles. Elegant Tuscan faves are often accompanied, later in the evening, by some DJ-spun music.

Rivoire café (p130) on Piazza della Signoria

WHERE NOT TO EAT

Many tourist restaurants – especially in the centre of town – have a ruthless attitude to food, their customers and their employees. Some *pizzerie* employ foreigners without papers at slave rates to churn out pre-prepared pizzas. The base and sauce are ready to go, just tip tinned mushrooms on the top, heat and serve. Delicious. The process with other dishes in some trattorias is similar. Mountains of precooked pasta is reheated – you can be sure most of the ingredients are canned and your hosts will do their best to make sure the elements of your salad have been well aged.

We don't want to spoil your appetite, but this is the state of affairs. So, how do you recognise these places before it's too late? Many of those on the most visited squares and streets, especially if they have outdoor dining, tend to fall roughly into this category. If no locals are eating in the place you are considering, ask yourself why. If you see tour groups gobbling down identical meals – stay away! Places that need to advertise themselves loudly or that display menus in a variety of languages are often suspect. There are some noble exceptions to these rules, so you need something of a sixth sense and a little luck.

FRESCOBALDI

Map pp244–5   Modern Tuscan & Wine Bar

☎ 055 28 47 24; Via de' Magazzini 2-4/r; meal €30–35; ☙ Tue-Sat, dinner only Sun-Mon; 🚌 A

One of Tuscany's great wine-making families has dared to place a quality restaurant and wine bar within sniffing distance of Palazzo Vecchio, no doubt to the joy of public servants and a Godsend to tourists otherwise largely surrounded by dross. Beneath the broad vaults of this hushed restaurant you can savour artichoke risotto or a juicy beef dish, all washed down, of course, with Frescobaldi tippling material.

GUSTAVINO Map pp244–5   Italian & Wine Bar

☎ 055 239 98 06; www.gustavino.it; Via della Condotta 37/r; meal €40; ☙ Tue-Sun; 🚌 A

A young team have created this fresh dining idea, a modern *enoteca*-cum-restaurant, in which the menu covers all sorts of regional dishes, often with an unexpected twist. The *tagliolini neri al riccio di mare con pesto* (black pasta with sea anenome and pesto) are a good example. Metallic chairs and glass-topped tables lend a crisp air to the place, in which visibility indeed dominates. You can see the kitchen and passers-by can see you!

LA CANOVA DI GUSTAVINO

Map pp244–5   Snacks

☎ 055 239 98 06; Via della Condotta 29/r; meal €25; ☙ noon-midnight daily; 🚌 A

Next door, the Gustavino team run this place with an altogether more traditional air. This is the place to try some cheese and cold meat platters, soups, hams, and – of course – some of the wines from next door!

OSTERIA DEL GATTO E LA VOLPE

Map pp248 9   Tuscan

☎ 055 28 92 64; Via Ghibellina 151/r; meal €25; ☙ Tue-Sun; 🚌 14 & A

On the corner of Via de' Giraldi, this is a small and welcoming spot where the food is reasonable and the prices are stable. It gets its fair share of tourists but this hasn't yet ruined what's on offer. Pizzas are reliable too.

TRATTORIA DA BENVENUTO

Map pp244–5   Tuscan

☎ 055 21 48 33; Via della Mosca 16/r; meal €25; ☙ Mon-Sat; 🚌 B

Eating here, on the corner of Via dei Neri, is hardly an ambient experience, but the food is reliable and modestly priced. Mains include some Florentine favourites, including *lampredotto* and *bistecca,* while the pasta dishes are innovative, for example the *rigatoni alla siciliana* (with a slightly spicy Sicilian sauce). It is wise to reserve a table.

CHEAP EATS

CAFFÈ ITALIANO Map pp244–5   Italian

☎ 055 28 90 20; Via della Condotta 56/r; salad €8, meal €20; ☙ 8am-8.30pm Mon-Sat; 🚌 A

Full of glamorous locals and a few savvy tourists who see beyond the stand-up bar, upstairs here is a lovely relaxed café with small antique tables, velvet sofas and soft lighting. The food – tangy soufflés, pastas, and hearty salads – is a light alternative to the norm. Otherwise, drop by for the tempting range of coffees, chocolate, smoothies and *acquantica* – a lightly sparkling flavoured water.

Eating

PIAZZA DELLA SIGNORIA & AROUND

VINI E VECCHI SAPORI Map pp244-5 Tuscan
☎ 055 29 30 45; Via dei Magazzini 3/r;
meal €20; ⏰ 1-11pm Tue-Sat & Sun lunch; 🚌 A
Within about 10 seconds' walk of Piazza della Signoria, one of the city centre's last surviving, and more or less genuine, *osterie* stubbornly remains in business. Inside this tiny den of 'wines and old tastes' there is barely room to swing a Florentine rat, but you can eat decently and taste some solid local wines at low prices.

YELLOW BAR Map pp244-5 Pizzeria
☎ 055 21 17 66; Via del Proconsolo 39/r;
pizza €5-8; ⏰ Wed-Mon; 🚌 A
It's cheerful here, although about all that's yellow are the outside lights. Inside, folks cram good-naturedly around long, sociable timber tables or into slightly less gregarious snugs, mostly for the pizza.

SANTA MARIA NOVELLA & AROUND

There's no end of cheap and cheerful Italian diners in streets like Via della Scala and Via Palazzuolo. They get more interesting to the south and southeast of the basilica, with some of the city's more popular nooks and crannies frequented by Florentines with a nose for good value.

CANTINETTA ANTINORI
Map pp244-5 Tuscan
☎ 055 29 22 34; Piazza degli Antinori 3;
meal €35-40; ⏰ Mon-Fri; 🚌 6, 11, 22, 36, 37 & A
Feeling posh? This might be the place for you. The *enoteca* and restaurant on the ground floor of 15th-century Palazzo Antinori offers a reasonable meal, along with some fine wines – it is for the latter that most people come here.

DA IL LATINI Map pp244-5 Tuscan
☎ 055 21 09 16; Via dei Palchetti 6/r; meal €25-30;
⏰ Tue-Sat; 🚌 6 & A
Hiding away just off Via del Moro, this place remains something of a classic for Florentines, in spite of the queues. The food is largely Tuscan but the dining area has a truly Spanish touch – all those legs of ham dangling off the ceiling! A trattoria since 1964, the place began as a wine store in 1898. It doesn't take bookings and can get packed.

I QUATTRO AMICI Map pp242-3 Seafood
☎ 055 21 54 13; Via degli Orti Oricellari 29;
meal €35-40; ⏰ Mon-Sun; 🚌 26, 27, 35 & D
Finding reasonable seafood in Florence is no easy task, but this spot, virtually in the shadow of the train station, there's not a *bistecca fiorentina* in sight! It's all fish, *mazzancolle* (king prawns) and other delights from the deep.

TOP FIVE CAFÉS
- **Café Concerto Paszkowski** (Map pp244–5; ☎ 055 21 02 36; Piazza della Repubblica 31-35/r; ⏰ 7am-2am Tue-Sun; 🚌 A) With more than 150 years of history, this is one of the class café acts of the city and makes a stylish way to start the day. It is worth making the trip to the square for the café's interior alone.
- **Colle Bereto** (Map pp244–5; ☎ 055 28 31 56; Piazza degli Strozzi 5/r; ⏰ 8am-9pm Mon-Sat, noon-3pm brunch Sun; 🚌 A) A grand café over two floors in the heart of chic Florence, this place is run by a Chianti wine producer. You can have sweet pastries for breakfast, and a light snack and fine wine during the day or early evening.
- **Gilli** (Map pp244–5; ☎ 055 21 38 96; Piazza della Repubblica 39/r; coffee on the square €3.50; ⏰ 8am-1am Wed-Sun; 🚌 A) This is one of the city's finest cafés. Founded in 1733 by a Swiss family in Via de' Calzaiuoli, it moved to its present location in the latter half of the 19th century.
- **Giubbe Rosse** (Map pp244–5; ☎ 055 21 22 80; Piazza della Repubblica 13-14/r; ⏰ 8am-2am; 🚌 A) The early-20th-century futurist movement, despite not making as big an impact in Florence as elsewhere in Italy, nevertheless had its following – and this is where its die-hard members used to drink and debate. Inside, long vaulted halls lined with old photos, sketches and artwork make this a great place for coffee over the daily papers. The red jackets of the place's name are still in evidence on the waiting staff, along with red shirts and tablecloths.
- **Rivoire** (Map pp244–5; ☎ 055 21 44 12; Piazza della Signoria 4/r; ⏰ Tue-Sun; 🚌 B) Founded in 1872 by a chocolate-maker from Turin, Enrico Rivoire, this is the place to sip on a cup of sticky *cioccolata* (€5.50) after overdosing on art in the Uffizi.

MASA Map pp248-9 *Japanese*
☎ 055 29 09 78; Borgo Ognissanti 1/r;
meal €40-50; ⏲ Wed-Mon; 🚌 A
About the most refined and well-prepared
Japanese you will find in Florence. Head
downstairs to the fussily efficient dining
room – all hushed chat and serious concentration on good grub. You'll probably feel a
little underdressed without a tie.

NANAMUTA Map pp240-1 *Tuscan*
☎ 055 267 56 12; Corso Italia 35; meal €35; ⏲ lunch
& dinner Mon-Fri, dinner only Sat & Sun; 🚌 B
Walk in and take a left, past the open
kitchen, into a spacious dining area with
high ceiling, mezzanine level and cream-
and-maroon décor. Some interesting dishes
come your way here, like *tortelloni di coniglio alla Vernaccia* (pasta packets of rabbit
cooked in white wine).

OSTARIA DEI CENTO POVERI
Map pp242-3 *Tuscan*
☎ 055 21 88 46; Via Palazzuolo 31/r; meal €35-40;
⏲ dinner only Tue-Sat, lunch & dinner Sun;
🚌 11, 36, 37 & A
A congenial spot in a not-so-congenial part
of town, the 'hostel of the hundred poor
people' sits apart from most other places
around here as a quality dining option.
Tuck in to creative Tuscan food in a down-
to-earth setting.

PROCACCI Map pp244-5 *International*
☎ 055 21 16 56; Via de' Tornabuoni 64/r;
⏲ Tue-Sat; 🚌 6, 11, 22, 36, 37 & A
For a century the chefs here have been
tickling Florentine palates with *panini tartu-
fati* (*panini* spread with truffle paste). Not so
much a nutritional exercise as a ritual, these
tasty numbers can be accompanied by a
drop of Tuscan wine or cup of tea. The green
marble used for the bar and table tops is the
same used in the city's great monuments.
It's definitely more of a winter place, when it
stays open until about 9pm (door open no
later than 8pm in the warmer months). You
can shop here too (see p166).

SOSTANZA Map pp248-9 *Tuscan*
☎ 055 21 26 91; Via del Porcellana 25r; meal
€25-30; ⏲ noon-2pm & 7-9.45pm Mon-Sat; 🚌 A
This traditional Tuscan eatery is a good
spot for *bistecca alla fiorentina* if you are not

fussy about your surrounds. A no-nonsense
approach dominates. The minestrone (€5.50)
is also good. Locals know it as Il Troia – the
(Male) Slut – because they say its 19th-
century owner had the habit of touching up
his guests. Don't worry, he's long gone.

TRATTORIA COCO LEZZONE
Map pp244-5 *Tuscan*
☎ 055 28 71 78; Via Parioncino 26/r; meal €30-40;
⏲ lunch & dinner Mon, Wed-Sat, lunch only Tue;
🚌 A
This tiny place, tucked away off Via del
Purgatorio is a cheerful, down-to-earth spot
where you can find yourself rubbing shoul-
ders with out-of-towners and local busi-
nesspeople seeking genuine, old-fashioned
home-cooking. *Ribollita* (vegetable stew)
is the house speciality, but the kitchen will
do you a *bistecca alla fiorentina* for €40
(enough for two in most cases) if you book
it ahead. They don't serve coffee.

TRATTORIA DEI 13 GOBBI
Map pp248-9 *Tuscan*
☎ 055 21 32 04; Via del Porcellana 9/r;
meal €25-30; ⏲ Tue-Sat; 🚌 A
There is an almost bucolic feeling inside
this trattoria, especially in the plant-filled
courtyard out the back. Inside, hunker
down with the locals under the low ceilings
with typical Tuscan treats. What about a
peposo di manzo con carote brasate (a pepper steak stew with braised carrots)? There
is a good set lunch for €13 too.

CHEAP EATS
AMON Map pp248-9 *Egyptian*
☎ 055 29 31 46; Via Palazzuolo 26-28/r; sandwiches
€2.50-3.50; ⏲ Tue-Sun; 🚌 11, 36, 37 & A
Here you can pick up Egyptian sandwiches
such as *felafel* or *fuul* (fava beans) – a couple
of these will fill most reasonable paunches.

I' VINAIO Map pp242-3 *Tuscan*
☎ 055 29 22 87; Via Palazzuolo 124/r; meal €20;
⏲ Mon-Sat; 🚌 11, 36, 37 & A
A sociable spot where you sit at close
quarters over tiny square timber tables, this
is a long-time favourite. Servings of such
choices as *penne all'ortolana* (pasta and
vegetables) or *spaghetti alla carrettiera* (a
spicy Sicilian sauce) are generous.

TRATTORIA IL CONTADINO

Map pp242-3   Italian

☎ 055 238 26 73; Via Palazzuolo 71/r; set menu with wine €11; 🕙 Mon-Sat; 🚌 11, 36, 37 & A

The set menu price says it all. Don't expect gourmet grub, but if you need to fill up without inflicting fiscal damage, this is a good place to do it. A favourite with local workers, who know where to find value for their euro, it is one of several cheapies around here.

SAN LORENZO

The Mercato Centrale is naturally a hub in this part of town and surrounding trattorias of all sorts cater to the tourist trade and market workers. The whole gamut is run – from trusty and good-value institutions that locals still pile into at lunchtime, through to the worst of all limp-lettuce traps for the unsuspecting.

CAFÉ CARACOL Map pp244-5   Mexican

☎ 055 21 14 27; Via de' Ginori 10/r; meal €20; 🕙 6pm-2am Tue-Sun; 🚌 1, 6, 7, 10, 11 & 17

For a slightly cheesy Tex-Mex atmosphere you could drop by this place for a plateful of nachos, *fajitas* and other Mexican flavours. It's not going to win any food prizes, but there aren't many places in Florence where you can get corn chips and salsa, and the atmosphere is jolly enough. Happy hour for Mexican cocktails is 4pm to 8.30pm.

I' TOZZO…DI PANE Map pp242-3   Tuscan

☎ 055 47 57 53; Via Guelfa 94/r; meal €25; 🕙 lunch & dinner Tue-Sat, dinner only Mon; 🚌 4, 12, 25 & 33

A young and friendly team run this simple neighbourhood place, where cool jazz warbles in the background. For starters, go for the *zuppa toscana,* a thick gruel of vegetables and barley. Although not to all tastes, the *trippa alla fiorentina* (tripe) follows on a treat. The small rear garden is a pleasant retreat.

OSTERIA PEPÒ Map pp242-3   Tuscan

☎ 055 28 32 59; Via Rosina 6/r; meal €20-25; 🕙 Mon-Sat; 🚌 1, 6, 7, 10, 11 & 17

Pepò is a classy rendering of a Tuscan eatery and makes a pleasant stop for reasonable serves of Tuscan food with the occasional slight twist – instead of a *tagliata di manzo* (prime beef cooked medium in chunky slices), try the *pollo* (chicken) version, with melted parmesan.

RISTORANTE ZÀZÀ Map pp242-3   Italian

☎ 055 21 54 11; Piazza del Mercato Centrale 20; meal €20-25; 🕙 Mon-Sat; 🚌 1, 6, 7, 10, 11 & 17

This place gets its produce fresh from the covered Mercato Centrale, just across the square. It's a great spot for combining outdoor dining with a little people-watching. In winter, head inside for some exposed-brick cosiness. The menu changes regularly and often presents imaginative Italian dishes.

Florentines dining alfresco

FLORENTINE FAST FOOD & FINE-WINE DINING

Some habits die hard. When Florentines feel like a fast snack instead of a sit-down lunch, they might well stop by a *trippaio* or *tripperia* (often just a mobile stand) for a nice tripe burger (well, tripe on a bread roll). It may sound nauseating to the uninitiated, but it's really not that bad. McDonald's has arrived in Florence, but it has yet to snuff out local preferences. Who knows what a generation fed on Big Macs might think of tripe rolls in years to come? To try your tripe, head for **Da Nerbone** (below) or, better still, the mobile **Tripperia da Sergio e Pier Paolo** (p137). For a sit-down lunch of the stuff, another specialist is **Il Magazzino** (p141).

Savouring fine wines is one of the great pleasures of the palate in Florence, and for many there is nothing better than a couple of glasses of a good drop accompanied by simple local snacks – sausage meats, cheeses, *ribollita* and the like. And the good news is that the tradition of the *vinaio* (wine bar) has won new life in the past few years in Florence. You may never see the word 'vinaio' on the doorway, but the idea remains the same. The old traditional places still exist too – often dark little grog shops where you can also get a bite to eat. Look out for the sign 'Mescita di Vini' (roughly, 'wine outlet'). You could start your search with any of the following: **Enoteca Fuoriporta** (p138), **Le Volpi e l'Uva** (p141), **Vini e Vecchi Sapori** (p130), **Osteria Antica Mescita San Niccolò** (p139).

CHEAP EATS

CASA DEL VINO Map pp244-5   Tuscan
☎ 055 21 56 09; Via dell'Ariento 16/r; meal €10-15;
☻ 9.30am-7pm Mon-Fri; 🚍 1, 6, 7, 10, 11 & 17
Step back in time at this traditional *vinaio*, one of the few examples of the genuine article left in Florence. Join market workers in the morning for a heart starter, or pop in around lunchtime for *panini* and other snacks over a traditional *gottino* (tumbler) of fine wine. Via dell'Ariento was lined by such wine shops from the mid-19th century. Here the original walnut furnishings remain in place, but instead of simple plonk the wine served is a choice of fine Tuscan drops.

DA NERBONE Map pp242-3   Tuscan
☎ 055 21 99 49; Mercato Centrale; meal €15-20;
☻ 7am-2pm Mon-Sat; 🚍 1, 6, 7, 10, 11 & 17
Way back in 1872 this corner stall was set up in the market as a snack stop for toiling market workers. They still pile in for breakfast on market days and are joined at lunch by a growing troupe of curious outsiders. Breakfast at Da Nerbone means a *lampredotto* roll, but at lunch you can fill up on soups and boiled meats. Friday is fish day.

MARIO Map pp242-3   Tuscan
☎ 055 21 85 50; Via Rosina 2/r; meal €15-20;
☻ lunch only Mon-Sat; 🚍 1, 6, 7, 10, 11 & 17
For an eternity Mario has been serving up plentiful, hearty lunches to market workers and a host of passers-by. Something of a culinary icon, it offers some pasta options and Tuscan classics, followed by a few meat-dominated mains. No credit cards.

SAN MARCO

The pickings are fairly slim around Savonarola's old haunts, and things don't get much better as you proceed further away from the centre to the north, east and west. A couple of exceptions confirm the rule.

CAFAGGI Map pp242-3   Tuscan
☎ 055 29 49 89; Via Guelfa 35/r; meal €30;
☻ Mon-Sat; 🚍 1, 6, 7, 10, 11 & 17
Not an awful lot has changed since Cafaggi was launched back in Mussolini's big year (1922, time of the great dictator's March on Rome). An old-style attention to service, a menu dominated by meat and a muted elegance (beige table linen, dark timber décor) make this a decent, if unsung, choice. Try some old favourites like *cervello di vitella fritto con zucchini fritti* (fried calf's brain and courgettes).

SAMOVAR Map pp242-3   Fusion
☎ 055 24 49 35; Via della Mattonaia 51/r;
meal €45; ☻ dinner only Mon-Sat; 🚍 6, 31 & 32
Head through the heavy red drapes into this intriguing Med-Russian-fusion den; a low-lit Buddha Bar from the steppes, where you might opt for a steaming stroganoff or sashimi on a skewer. There's no culinary reverence in this deliberately iconoclastic, big-city style, chilled-out dining locale.

SEMIDIVINO Map pp242-3   Tuscan
☎ 055 462 00 16; Via di San Gallo 22/r; meal €30;
☻ 11am-midnight; 🚍 1, 6, 7, 10, 11 & 17
The pickings get a little slim as you edge away from Piazza San Marco, so this place

is a welcome option. A blend of new and old, it offers the option of sidewalk dining, or sitting deep inside under low lights. It's as much about ambience as tickling the palate.

CHEAP EATS

DIONISO Map pp242-3   Greek
☎ 055 21 78 82; Via San Gallo 16/r; meal €15; ☺ Mon-Sun; ▣ 1, 6, 7, 10, 11 & 17
Feel like a big Greek salad full of feta? Or perhaps some *taramasalata* and other similar dips to accompany typical meat dishes like souvlaki? Dioniso can be a lively and filling stop. On Fridays and Saturdays it stays open until 3am, taking on more the air of a bar, where you can sate yourself with snacks and appetizers.

IL VEGETARIANO Map pp242-3   Vegetarian
☎ 055 47 50 30; Via delle Ruote 30/r; meal €20; ☺ lunch & dinner Tue-Fri, dinner only Sat & Sun; ▣ 4, 12 & 20
One of the few restaurants to seriously cater to vegetarian needs, this is an unassuming locale with a great selection of fresh food, salads and mains. The menu changes regularly, in part dictated by the availability of fresh products. Try things like the *gazpacho* (a cool Spanish, tomato broth) or *risotto integrale con radicchio rosso* (whole rice risotto with red lettuce).

SANTA CROCE

Several of the city's finest restaurants await discovery in the streets east of the centre and around Piazza Santa Croce. But the area is full of diversity too: you can spend €100 or more, or enjoy a quick *felafel*.

ANTICO NOÈ Map pp248-9   Tuscan
☎ 055 234 08 38; Arco di San Piero 6/r; panini €3.80-4.50, meal €25-30; ☺ noon-midnight Mon-Sat; ▣ 14 & 23
This legendary sandwich bar, just off Piazza San Pier Maggiore, has two sections. The sandwich bar is takeaway only, but next door there's a cosy restaurant where you can enjoy fine cooking to slow jazz and blues tunes. Don't let the loitering drunks outside bother you, as they're generally pretty harmless.

BOCCADAMA Map pp248-9   Italian
☎ 055 24 36 40; www.boccadama.it; Piazza di Santa Croce 25-26/r; meal €30; ☺ Mon-Sat; ▣ C
Located inside the medieval Palazzo dell'Antella is this surprise packet. Sweep away the lunchtime tourists and underneath you find a quality restaurant with a classy wine list. The menu is limited, but changes regularly. One good way to accompany your choice of wine is to opt for the cold meat platter, perhaps with a selection of Italian and French cheeses.

BOCCANEGRA Map pp248-9   Modern Italian
☎ 055 200 10 98; Via Ghibellina 124/r; meal €45; ☺ dinner only Mon-Sat; ▣ 14 & A
Like a dark den, the 'Black Mouth' invites you to taste modern, original spins on Italian combinations. The furniture has an antique feel and molten candles shed light on the surprises in your dishes, like *piccione in rete* (grilled pigeon). For vegetarians there are some tasty options as well, like the *torta di asparagi e seitan su velluta di zafferano* (asparagus and seitan pie on a saffron sauce).

DANNY ROCK Map pp248-9   Pizzeria
☎ 055 234 03 07; www.dannyrock.it; Via de' Pandolfini 13/r; meal €20; ☺ 7pm-3am; ▣ A
This place does not sound promising, but it's actually an immensely popular venue for pizza, pasta and, best of all, its €6.90 *insalatoni* (huge salads). One of these with a drink or two could make a filling and ultra-healthy meal. Then you could undo all the good dietary work with a wicked crepe. Be prepared to queue for a bit.

TOP FIVE FOREIGN EATS
The availability of ethnic cuisine in Florence is limited, aside from the ubiquitous Chinese option. Still, a few possibilities do present themselves, including Japanese, Indian, Cuban, Mexican, Israeli and a couple of *felafel* and *shwarma* (kebab) bars. Among the best are:
- **Masa** (p131) Japanese.
- **Ashoka** (p138) Indian.
- **Fontanka** (p138) Russian.
- **Café Caracol** (p132) Mexican.
- **Ruth's** (p137) Middle Eastern kosher.

Eating
SANTA CROCE

DOLCI E DOLCEZZE Map pp248-9   Cakes

☎ 055 234 54 58; Piazza C Beccaria 8/r;
⏲ 8.30am-8pm Tue-Sat, 9am-1pm & 4.30-7pm Sun;
🚍 8, 12, 13, 14, 31, 32, 33, 80 & A

This place claims its *torta di cioccolato* (chocolate cake) is the 'best in the world'. Hyperbole aside, it is damned good, made with fine Swiss and Belgian ingredients and creamy Maremma butter. There are no tables so it's takeaway only.

ENOTECA PINCHIORRI Map pp248-9   Italian

☎ 055 24 27 77; www.enotecapinchiorri.com; Via Ghibellina 87; meal €120-150; ⏲ Tue-Sat; 🚍 14

Glide upstairs to the grand foyer that fronts Florence's premier address (and Michelin champ) for food buffs. Your wallet will have a date with destiny here, but every now and then you just have to do it. Elegant dress is the preferred sartorial option for this excursion into Italian nouvelle cuisine. What about lightly grilled lobster with a crust of bread and capers?

FINISTERRAE Map pp248-9   Fusion

☎ 055 24 19 32; Via de' Pepi 3-5/r; meal €25-30; ⏲ lunch & dinner Wed-Sun, dinner only Mon-Tue; 🚍 C

The attraction here is the setting. Come for dinner and enjoy the different candle-lit spaces: the bigger dining areas, with aqua green tables, contrast well with the North African–style chill-out lounges. Food ranges across the Maghreb, from couscous and *tajine* to old Italian favourites. It also puts on a chilled Sunday brunch.

LA BARAONDA Map pp248-9   Modern Tuscan

☎ 055 234 11 71; Via Ghibellina 67/r; meal €30-35; ⏲ lunch & dinner Tue-Sat, dinner only Mon; 🚍 14 & A

As the name implies, a 'convivial chaos' prevails at this handsome trattoria, where the friendly owner floats between three connecting dining rooms, articulating the seasonal Tuscan menu. Spare his voice box and order the *polpettone* (meatloaf).

LA TERRAZZA DEL PRINCIPE

Map pp248-9   Tuscan & Sicilian

☎ 055 22 41 04; Viale Niccolò Machiavelli 10; meal €45-55; ⏲ Mon-Sun; 🚍 12 & 13

From this well-placed villa, high up on the winding thoroughfare of Oltrarno, you can enjoy bucolic views across a valley towards

THE BRUNCH BRIGADE

With so many Anglo-American tourists and residents in Florence, it is hardly surprising that the concept of the Sunday brunch has become a fixture in various spots around town. **Angels** (p128) stages an All American Brunch, complete with pancakes, omelettes and steak sandwiches, while **Finisterrae** (left) takes a more laid-back Maghreb-Med approach to the event. **Danny Rock** (opposite) pours out unlimited American-style coffee with its pancakes and muffins, while **Capocaccia** (p145) attracts its fashion-victim customers to the Arno for its stylish offerings. The **Colle Bereto** café (see the boxed text, p130) also puts on a reasonable effort. Hotel restaurants are not far behind either. The **Hotel Excelsior** (see the Grand Hotel, p177) puts on a big spread, including bubbly. **Gallery Hotel Art** (p175) stages its Fusion Brunch in the hotel bar of the same name, while The Lounge, attached to **JK Place** (p177) offers an elegant brunch option on Saturday and Sunday.

the Forte di Belvedere and remnants of the medieval city walls. Dishes are given a bit of an inventive kick. A tangy tempter is the *tagliata di anatra in aceto balsamico* (slices of duck char-cooked to seal in the juice and bathed in balsamic vinegar).

OSTERIA DE' BENCI Map pp248-9   Tuscan

☎ 055 234 49 23; Via de' Benci 13/r; meal €30-35; ⏲ Mon-Sat; 🚍 13, 23, B & C

This *osteria* is a consistently good bet. The menu changes frequently, although it has a few core dishes. The young team offer up generous slabs of meat, such as the ubiquitous *bistecca alla fiorentina* to a *braciolone piccante* (steak in olive oil, lemon juice, parsley and hot pepper). They also run a pleasant corner café and snack spot, Osteria de' Benci Café (☎ 055 21 68 87; Via de' Benci 9/r; ⏲ 8am-midnight), next door.

OSTERIA VINI E CUCINA DI TOSCANA

Map pp248-9   Tuscan

☎ 055 28 93 68; Via Isola delle Stinche 11-13/r; meal €25; ⏲ Tue-Sun; 🚍 A

The old-time lettering on the windows invites you to peer into this welcoming restaurant, with dark timber tables scattered about spaciously. An ever-changing daily menu, including some vegetarian options like *melanzane alla parmigiana* (eggplant slices oven-cooked with parmesan cheese), keeps you on your toes.

RISTORANTE CIBRÈO Map pp248-9 Italian
☎ 055 234 11 00; Via de' Macci 118/r; meal €75-90;
☽ Tue-Sat Sep-Jul; 🚍 C
Over the years, this quietly elegant, but unpretentious, locale has made an international name for itself. Warm timber dominates the décor, but the table settings are a notable sign of the class that this place exudes. The underlying philosophy here is that pasta is not a traditional Tuscan dish, so no pasta for you! But fine, elegantly presented local cooking, with the freshest possible ingredients, is another pillar in the philosophy.

SÉSAME Map pp248-9 Fusion
☎ 055 200 18 31; Via delle Conce 20/r;
meal €30-45; ☽ dinner only Tue-Sun; 🚍 C
Confusion might be the best word. Wend your way inside this Arabised food temple and take your pick from two food cultures. The Moroccan dishes work out cheaper, while the creative Mediterranean menu (filet tartare followed by *tarte tatin* for dessert) come in close to €50 with wine. A serving of six oysters (€15) might be your preferred starter.

TEATRO DEL SALE Map pp248-9 Tuscan
☎ 055 200 14 92; www.teatrodelsale.com;
Via de' Macci 111/r; meal €30-40; ☽ dinner only
Mon-Sun; 🚍 C
The Cibrèo folk have branched out into a new dining experience with this combined entertainment-food option. First you become a member (€5 annual fee for nonresidents) and then you check out the concert programme to see what suits. You might be treated to light jazz or world music to go with a well-prepared but no-nonsense Tuscan buffet. Once a member you need to reserve a spot at the mostly communal tables by noon.

TRATTORIA CIBRÈO Map pp248-9 Tuscan
☎ 055 234 11 00; Via de' Macci 122/r; meal €35-40;
☽ Tue-Sat Sep-Jul; 🚍 C
Located next door to the posher restaurant of the same name (see above), this branch is also known to locals as Cibreino ('little Cibrèo'). It offers no pasta, but has some enticing first courses, such as *sformato di patate e ricotta* (oven-cooked potato and white cheese). There follows a variety of seafood and meat options (the latter are better) for the main course.

A BAKERY WITH NO NAME

Need a pastry at 4am? A couple of bakeries open to sell their wares straight out of the oven. One, without a name or street number, is at Via del Canto Rivolto (Map pp248–9), just north of Via dei Neri. As you will see, the people want you to be quiet and get out quickly. Should the neighbours become vexed by the street noise, the bakery may have to stop the practice.

CHEAP EATS

CAFFELLATTE Map pp242-3 Italian
☎ 055 47 88 78; Via degli Alfani 39/r; meal €15;
☽ 8am-8pm Mon-Sat; 🚍 C
A tiny, charming place for a long *caffè latte* (or indeed a cappuccino if your prefer) over the morning paper. Or come by for a tasty lunch, such as *crema di zucca* (pumpkin soup). This is a health-food haven and it doesn't serve alcohol, so you can feel virtuous while you eat.

CAFFETTERIA PIANSA Map pp248-9 Italian
☎ 055 234 23 62; Borgo Pinti 18/r; set lunch
€10.50; ☽ lunch only Mon-Sat; 🚍 14 & 23
At this ebullient, vaulted local workers' diner, you basically point and choose from a limited number of cheap and tasty first and main courses. Get in early as it's all over by 2.30pm.

IL NILO Map pp248-9 Egyptian
☎ 055 24 16 99; Arco di San Piero 9/r;
shwarma & *felafel* sandwiches €2.50-3.50;
☽ noon-10pm Mon-Sat; 🚍 14 & 23
Revellers, dropouts and a host of other weird and wonderful beings wander in and out of this place in the course of the evening for a takeaway *felafel*. Some hang around and eat it here, although there's nowhere to sit.

IL PIZZAIUOLO Map pp248-9 Pizzeria
☎ 055 24 11 71; Via de' Macci 113/r;
pizza €4.50-8.50, meal €25; ☽ Mon-Sat; 🚍 C
Good pizza is not always easy to come by, but this is the top spot in the Santa Croce area. In particular it is known for its Neapolitan pizzas (thick and soft crusts), but the chefs also do a reasonable line in fish dishes.

LA TRIPPERIA DA SERGIO E PIER
PAOLO Map pp248-9   Tripe Stand
Via de' Macci; panini €2.30, 200gr dish €3;
🕒 8.30am-7pm Mon-Sat Sep-May, 8.30am-3pm
Mon-Sat Jun-Jul; 🚌 C
You don't get much more Florentine than
this. Sergio and Pier Paolo's road stand
serves up succulent portions of tripe, *trippa*
or *lampredotto,* depending on which bit
exactly of the innards you are indulging
in. Have it in a roll with hot sauce, or in a
container prepared in different ways each
day – with boiled potatoes on Friday or
beans and sauce on Wednesday, for instance. Wash it down with a plastic cup of
wine for 70c.

RUTH'S Map pp248-9   Middle Eastern Kosher
☎ 055 248 08 88; Via Luigi Carlo Farini 2/a;
meal €15; 🕒 lunch & dinner Sun-Thu,
lunch only Fri; 🚌 C
For something different try out this place,
offering Middle Eastern fare down by the
synagogue. It serves tasty kosher food,
bearing a strong resemblance to other
Middle Eastern cuisine, and makes a good
choice for vegetarians. You can have a
plate of mixed dips with couscous, *felafel*,
filo pastry pie and potato salad (quite filling in itself) for €10. The *fattoush* (a finely
chopped and liquidy salad mixed with
pitta croutons) is a tad bitter.

SEDANO ALLEGRO Map pp248-9   Vegetarian
☎ 055 234 55 05; Borgo della Croce 20/r;
meal €18-25; 🕒 Tue-Sun; 🚌 A
Clearly not that many vegans are circulating in Florence, as this vegetarian hangout
has found it necessary to add a fish and
seafood menu to its vegetarian specials
(many of which don't meet vegan needs
either). If you don't want fish you could try
a *filetto di formaggio al whisky* (cheese 'fillet'
done in whisky). There is a pleasant, shady
courtyard out the back.

OLTRARNO
Piazza Santo Spirito (Map pp248–9) is one
of the most attractive squares in the city and
clustered on and around it are a nice range of
restaurants, snack places and café-bars. This
is the headquarters of laid-back Florentines.
Heading east you will find several other spots
on the way to Ponte Vecchio (Map pp248–9)
and much further east again, near Porta San
Niccolò (Map pp248–9), is another cluster of
places well worth seeking out.

ALL'ANTICO RISTORO DI CAMBI
Map pp248-9   Tuscan
☎ 055 21 71 34; Via Sant'Onofrio 1; meal €25;
🕒 Mon-Sat; 🚌 6 & D
The food here is traditional Tuscan and the
bistecca alla fiorentina is succulent. This

Da il Latini restaurant (p130)

is one of those places a local might take a newcomer to impress them with local knowledge. You can eat out on the square or inside, where the bright, vaulted tavern-like atmosphere can edge towards the raucous. Don't come looking for fish unless it's cod you're after. The *panzanella* is a good starter and the *fiori di zucca ripieni* (stuffed pumpkin flowers) are a light, meaty main.

ASHOKA Map pp240-1 Indian
☎ 055 22 44 46; Via Pisana 86/r; meal €20; ☽ 6pm-midnight, lunch Sun; 🚌 6
For fine Indian dining at comparatively reasonable prices it is hard to surpass this place, one of the few Indian options in Florence. A reasonable range of predictable dishes, from tandoori to *biryanis* and *kormas*, can be washed down with cold Kingfisher beer.

BORGO SAN JACOPO
Map pp244-5 Modern Italian
☎ 055 28 16 61; Borgo San Jacopo 62/r; meal €70; ☽ dinner only Wed-Mon; 🚌 D
The designer folks behind the Gallery Hotel Art and Co have brought similar design concerns to their restaurant. You'll be wearing your name gear here: get in early and you may score a riverside table for your *brodetto de pesce alla marchigiana* (Marche-style fish soup). Young waiters will swish about you in this modern, elegant locale.

ENOTECA FUORIPORTA
Map pp248-9 Tuscan
☎ 055 234 24 83; Via del Monte alle Croci 10/r; meal €25; ☽ Mon-Sat; 🚌 13, 23 & D
In this fine *enoteca* – lovingly carved out of what was once just a simple local bar, now an obligatory stop on any wine-lover's stay in Florence – the wine list comprises hundreds of different drops (plus an impressive roll call of whiskies and other liquors). You can order from a limited list of *primi piatti* for a pleasant evening meal. The desserts are also good; it sometimes opens on Sunday too.

FONTANKA Map pp240-1 Russian
☎ 055 233 62 10; Via Pisana 9/c; meal €30; ☽ Tue-Sun; 🚌 6
Feeling nostalgic for the Siberian steppes? In need of more bracing alcohol than the Tuscan grape can provide? For a real warp out of Florence, head for this out-of-the-way rep of all things Russian, from *blinis* to Stoly. Makes a definite change!

YOU NEED NEVER LEAVE YOUR HOTEL
Following a worldwide trend to turn drab hotel diners into name eateries with acclaimed chefs, Florence too is playing the game. Among the high fliers are **The Fusion Bar** in the Gallery Hotel Art (p175), the restaurant at the **Hotel Savoy** (p174), **Hostaria & Bibendum** in the Hotel Helvetia & Bristol (p174), **Incanto** in the Grand Hotel (p177), **Il Cestello** in the Excelsior (p177), **I Chiostri** in the Grand Hotel Minerva (p177), the **Terrazza Brunelleschi** in Grand Hotel Baglioni (p177) and **The Lounge**, attached to JK Place (p177).

HEMINGWAY Map pp248-9 Sweets
☎ 055 28 47 81; www.hemingway.fi.it; Piazza Piattellina 9/r; ☽ 4.30pm-1am Tue-Sun; 🚌 D
This is a chocolate-lover's haven. You can choose from all sorts of goodies to take home and munch in private, or sit down for a glorious cup of hot chocolate. The home-made ice cream, crepes, cocktails, fruit shakes *(frullati)* and endless pastries and tarts are enough to make you skip dessert at your dinnertime restaurant and head here instead.

IL GUSCIO Map pp248-9 Tuscan
☎ 055 22 44 21; www.il-guscio.it; Via dell'Orto 19; meal €35; ☽ dinner only Tue-Sat; 🚌 6 & D
The meat here comes from a traditional local butcher, the fish is provided by Viareggio fishermen and the remaining ingredients are fresh from the market. A light hand in the kitchen produces feather-weight *filetti di gallinella* (a tangy white fish) or marshmallow-soft cuts of beef: it's your choice.

IL SANTO BEVITORE Map pp248-9 Tuscan
☎ 055 21 12 64; Via dello Spirito Santo 64-66/r; meal €30-35; ☽ Tue-Sun; 🚌 6 & D
Settle in at the spaciously set dark timber tables for a bottle of fine Tuscan wine beneath the vast vaults of this young, bustling *enoteca,* and then choose from a limited list of generous dishes. The thick, hearty *pappa al pomodoro* (tomato and bread soup) will be enough for a limited appetite, while the hungry might follow with a *tartare di Chianina* of top-grade minced Tuscan beef.

www.lonelyplanet.com

Eating OLTRARNO

138

IL VICO DEL CARMINE Map pp240-1 Pizzeria
☎ 055 233 68 62; Via Pisana 40/r; pizza €5-8, meal €30; ⏰ Tue-Sun; 🚌 6
Away from the madding crowds of central Florence they have created a little piece of Naples here – quite literally a lane typical of the southern city. This makes the ideal setting for good Neapolitan pizza and the ingredients for all their dishes are said to come from the Campania region around Naples.

I TAROCCHI Map pp248-9 Pizzeria
☎ 055 234 39 12; Via dei Renai 12-14/r; pizzas around €6-8, meal €25; ⏰ lunch & dinner Tue-Fri, dinner only Sat & Sun; 🚌 13, 23 & D
Most people drop by this place for the pizzas. In summer you can gobble one up on the pavement terrace (if you can find a seat), or squeeze in along the benches inside. Aside from the pizza, the kitchen churns out immensely filling pasta dishes and a handful of main courses – only those with an abyss opening up inside them will be capable of ingesting pasta *and* a main!

LA BEPPA FIORAIA Map pp248-9 Italian
☎ 055 234 76 81; Via dell'Erta Canina 6/r; meal €30-35; ⏰ Wed-Mon; 🚌 13, 23 & D
For some inventive Italian cooking, in what feels like the countryside, La Beppa Fioraia is worth going the extra mile. The homemade pasta dishes are all equally tempting, and the meat mains (sorry, no fish fare) ooze flavour. Try the *filetto di cinta senese con aceto balsamico* (a thick, juicy pork fillet in a dark, tangy balsamic vinegar sauce, served with spinach). Before or after your meal, it's worth taking a stroll along this back lane through old olive groves and retiring villas. You feel as though you're already deep in Chianti country.

L'BRINDELLONE
Map pp248-9 Tuscan & Vegetarian
☎ 055 21 78 79; Piazza Piattellina 10-11/r; meal €25-30; ⏰ dinner only Tue-Sun; 🚌 D
Surrounded by dangling garlic strands and old chianti bottles, this is a truly Tuscan spot with a slightly vegetarian bent too. Alongside such classics as *bistecca di maiale* (pork steak) you can get vegetable couscous. The house red is good and the atmosphere welcoming, with soft lighting.

MOMOYAMA Map pp248-9 Japanese & Fusion
☎ 055 29 18 40; Borgo San Frediano 10/r; meal €40-50; ⏰ dinner only Tue-Sun; 🚌 6 & D
Technically operating as a club, this place also touts itself as a sushi bar offering 'inventive food'. When you come the first time you fill out a form and may have to show some form of ID to become a member. It is an offbeat dining experience for Florence, with its bare minimalist ochre-coloured décor and tables spread over floors reaching well into the back.

OSTERIA ANTICA MESCITA SAN NICCOLÒ Map pp248-9 Tuscan
☎ 055 234 28 36; Via di San Niccolò 60/r; meal €25; ⏰ Mon-Sat; 🚌 13, 23 & D
A limited but tasty range of home-style cooking awaits in this wine den. Centuries ago this spot was a customs post for wine arriving in the city from the Chianti area, and in the early 1800s it became a general store. Now you can sit down at the timber tables, choose from an endless range of Tuscan tipples and place your order.

OSTERIA SANTO SPIRITO
Map pp248-9 Tuscan
☎ 055 238 23 83; Piazza Santo Spirito 16/r; meal €30-35; ⏰ Mon-Sun; 🚌 D
If you prefer a slightly higher-quality meal than what's on offer in the bustling locales across the square, or the occasional non-Italian surprise dish, head here. Osteria Santo Spirito, set over two cosy floors, is the place to try an adventurous, tangy *tagliata di salmone con curry e cocco* (salmon steak with curry and coconut).

RISTORANTE BECCOFINO
Map pp248-9 Modern Italian
☎ 055 29 00 76; Piazza degli Scarlatti 1/r; meal €50-60; ⏰ Tue-Sun; 🚌 6
A ground-breaker in design restaurants on the Arno (check out the stainless steel, floor-lit loos!), Beccofino allows you to try a vaguely adventurous style of Tuscan cooking. The pasta dishes in particular represent a departure from tradition – try the *gnocchetti* with sweet onions. And go to town on the wine, with some powerful Super Tuscans that thumb their noses at the DOC establishment.

RISTORANTE PANE E VINO

Map pp248-9   Modern Tuscan

☎ 055 247 69 56; Piazza di Cestello 3/r;
meal €40-50; 🕑 Mon-Sat; 🚍 D

Having moved from the San Niccolò end
of Oltrarno, this gourmet magnet has
emerged as one of the star attractions for
well-dressed Florentines looking to see,
and be seen while indulging in, imaginative
Tuscan cuisine. Dine inside, where light-
coloured clothes hang on the wall as
decorative lamp-shades, or outside in the
summer heat. You might like to try the
saltimbocca di rana (a breaded frog dish)
or *taglierini in zimino* (pasta with cuttlefish,
tomato and spinach cream).

TRATTORIA CAVOLO NERO

Map pp248-9   International

☎ 055 29 47 44; Via dell'Ardiglione 22;
meal €35-40; 🕑 Tue-Sat; 🚍 11, 36 & 37

Hidden away in a back street, the 'Black
Cabbage' is a gem. Try the entrecote of
Angus steak, prepared with assorted herbs.
Soups and tarts are also tempting, but
it's probably best to skip the house wine.
Homemade desserts by Michela are worth
the extra notch in your belt.

Waiter at work, Piazza della Signoria (p69)

TRATTORIA NAPOLEONE

Map pp248-9   Tuscan & Pizzeria

☎ 055 28 10 15; Piazza del Carmine 24; meal €30;
🕑 dinner only Mon-Sun; 🚍 D

A spacious restaurant that has Florentines
in ecstasy for several reasons: the *filetto alla
Napoleone* is a handsome steak dressed
in a vinegar and mustard sauce and, perhaps best of all, you can order one until
12.30am!

TRATTORIA QUATTRO LEONI

Map pp244-5   Tuscan

☎ 055 21 85 62; Piazza della Passera 1/r; meal €30;
🕑 Mon-Sun; 🚍 C & D

It's long been a byword for good, cheap
Tuscan grub, and many Florentines still
mention this place with a satisfied smile. It
has a pleasingly busy backstreet feel, but
is far from a local secret nowadays. Meats
dominate but you can opt for a handful of
reasonable seafood and fish dishes too.

TRATTORIA I RADDI Map pp248-9   Tuscan

☎ 055 21 10 72; Via dell'Ardiglione 47/r;
meal €30-35; 🕑 Mon-Sat; 🚍 11, 36 & 37

Just off Via de' Serragli, this trattoria serves
traditional Florentine meals in an intimate
and quiet location. Generous slabs of meat
in the form of *bistecca* (steak) or hashed up
as *peposo* lead the way in this carnivore's
paradise.

CHEAP EATS

AL TRANVAI Map pp248-9   Tuscan

☎ 055 22 51 97; Piazza Torquato Tasso 14/r;
meal €20-25; 🕑 Mon-Fri; 🚍 12, 13 & D

If you don't mind eating elbow to elbow
with complete strangers on benches set up
along the walls, this is a wonderful rustic
Tuscan eatery. It serves a limited range
of pastas as *primi,* along with classics like
pappa al pomodoro and *ribollita*. It also specialises in animal innards, including *trippa
alla fiorentina*. If that doesn't attract, there
are some meat alternatives.

CAFFÈ LA TORRE Map pp248-9   Snacks

☎ 055 68 06 43, Lungarno Benvenuto Cellini 65/r;
meal €10-15; 🕑 8.30am-4am Mon-Sun; 🚍 13,
23 & D

If you are in need of snack food of indifferent quality in the wee hours of the morning,

or a meal as late as 3am, this is about the only choice you have. It is also a busy bar and a great deal of fun (see p145).

IL MAGAZZINO Map pp244-5 Tripe
☎ 055 21 59 69; Via dei Sapiti 20/r; set lunch €9, meal €15-20; ♥ Mon-Sun; 🚍 C & D
This is an utterly unassuming eatery, and those in search of the Florentine tripe experience will not be disappointed here. Start with *tagliatelle con ragù di lampredotto* (ribbon pasta with a kind of tripe-based bolognaise sauce) and follow with trays more tripe: *trippa alla fiorentina* or *lampredotto*, for example, with mushrooms.

LE VOLPI E L'UVA Map pp244-5 Snacks
☎ 055 239 81 32; Piazza de' Rossi 1/r; snacks €2-4; ♥ 11am-8pm Mon-Sat; 🚍 D
At 'The Foxes and the Grape', hidden away off the Oltrarno end of the Ponte Vecchio, you can sample from an impressive stock of cheeses, try a gourmet *tramezzino* (sandwich triangle) and taste new wines the owners have discovered in the vast backyard that is Tuscany (along with a few from further afield in Italy, and even France).

TRATTORIA CASALINGA
Map pp248-9 Tuscan
☎ 055 21 86 24; Via de' Michelozzi 9/r; meal €15-20; ♥ Mon-Sat; 🚍 11, 36 & 37
People jostle to get into this cheerfully bustling eatery for a taste of its standard Florentine mainstays at bargain-basement prices. Don't expect to linger over a meal, as there is usually a queue of people waiting for your table.

BEYOND CENTRAL FLORENCE

In summer especially, choking Florentines seek escape and solace in the marginally cooler, hilly area of Fiesole, the 5th-century town overlooking Florence and the Arno. Around the central Piazza San Tommaseo you'll find no end of pizzerias, terraces and other eateries, all of them perfectly cheerful. A couple of quality restaurants with a penchant for slabs of meat are well worth the effort of traipsing beyond Florence in any season. Other worthwhile alternatives are located a little closer to central Florence.

DA RUGGERO Map pp248-9 Tuscan
☎ 055 22 05 42; Via Senese 89/r; meal €30-35; ♥ Thu-Mon mid-Aug–mid-Sep; 🚍 37
Locals love this straightforward and homely Tuscan eatery, where the emphasis is on consistently good home cooking using fresh market produce. A large dining area is followed by a smaller one, and the daily menu is scribbled in chalk on a board in the window. A perennial favourite with local workers and students, it is often full at lunchtime.

DA STEFANO Map p238 Seafood
☎ 055 204 91 05; Via Senese 271, Galluzzo; meal €50-60; ♥ dinner only Mon-Sun; 🚍 37
Well known among Florentines for its fish dishes, this welcoming spot prides itself on using fresh produce imported from around the Mediterranean. Instead of the usual first and second courses you can opt for an abundant single course, mixing various kinds of fish and seafood. In summer head out to the garden.

EDI HOUSE Map pp242-3 Pizzeria
☎ 055 58 88 86; Piazza Savonarola 8/r; pizza €5-8, meal €25; ♥ 7pm-1.30am Mon-Sun; 🚍 13 & 33
Out on its own to the north of the city centre, this big bright place is a lighthouse for starving locals. They mainly come to feast on the broad variety of pizzas and *focaccia* (how about the one with *gamberetti* – tiny prawns – and pesto?), preferably on the pavement terrace in the warmer months.

LA CAPPONCINA Map p238 Tuscan
☎ 055 69 70 37; Via San Romano 17/r, Settignano; meal €40; ♥ dinner only Tue-Sun year round, dinner only Tue-Sat, lunch & dinner Sun Oct-Apr; 🚍 10 & 67
Up in the hills overlooking Florence from the northeast, Florentines often gather for a bit of a splurge on this restaurant's *tagliata di manzo* – succulent beef fillets sliced up and served on a bed of rocket lettuce. Sitting in the garden is a true pleasure in summer, when you are sure of being several degrees cooler than everyone else down in Florence. The restaurant is a few steps off Piazza San Tommaseo, where the bus terminates.

TOP FIVE GELATO STOPS

- **Baroncini** (Map pp240–1; ☎ 055 48 91 85; Via Celso 3/r; ☷ Thu-Tue; ▣ 4, 8, 14, 20 & 28) If you happen to be in the area, drop in to one of Florence's most popular *gelaterie*. Fresh fruit is used in the fruit-flavoured options, and there's also great yogurt and *sorbetto al limone*.
- **Gelateria Carabé** (Map pp244–5; ☎ 055 28 94 76; Via Ricasoli 60/r; ☷ Mon-Sat; ▣ 14 & 23) For the best and most varied *granite* in town, head to this Sicilian specialist. You can get the standard lemon and coffee versions of this slushy crushed ice 'drink', but why not try the melon, fig or almond flavours? They do plenty of other Sicilian sweets too, such as *cannoli*.
- **Gelateria Veneta** (Map pp248–9; ☎ 055 234 33 70; Piazza C Beccaria 7/r; ☷ 8am-8pm Wed-Mon Oct-Apr, 8am-midnight Wed-Mon May-Sep; ▣ 8, 12, 13, 14, 31, 32, 33, 80 & A)
- **Gelateria Vivoli** (Map pp248–9; ☎ 055 29 23 34; Via dell'Isola delle Stinche 7; ☷ 9am-1am Tue-Sun; ▣ A) People queue outside this place, near Via Ghibellina, to delight in the broad range of creamy *gelati*. It even has a kind of rice-pudding flavour.
- **Perchè No** (Map pp244–5; ☎ 055 239 89 69; Via dei Tavolini 19/r; ☷ Wed-Sun; ▣ A) This *gelateria*, off Via de' Calzaiuoli, is excellent.

L'ERTA DEL MANGIA Map p239   Italian
☎ 329 449 84 76; Giardino di San Francesco, Fiesole; meal €40; ☷ Tue-Sun; ▣ 7
Up the lane leading to the Convento di San Francesco from Piazza Mino da Fiesole, this place's pleasant location is an immediate plus. The warm terracotta and timber interior adjoins the airy, chianti wine bottle–lined terrace with views over Florence. Some dishes make surprising departures from the standard canons, like the *tagliatelle con fiori di zucca, piccione e pomodorini* (ribbon pasta with pumpkin flowers, grilled pigeon meat and cherry tomatoes).

TRATTORIA LE CAVE DI MAIANO
Map p239   Tuscan
☎ 055 5 91 33; Via Cave di Maiano 16, Fiesole; meal €30; ☷ Mon-Sun; ▣ 7
This place is not dissimilar, in terms of price, atmosphere and clientele, to La Capponcina. Tables are arranged across a variety of interconnected dining rooms and out on to terraces. Getting here without a car is tricky as the restaurant is actually in Maiano, a *frazione* (division) of Fiesole, and

off the bus routes. You could try getting a taxi from central Fiesole.

TRATTORIA VITTORIA Map pp240-1 Seafood
☎ 055 22 56 57; Via della Fonderia 52/h; meal €40; ☷ Thu-Tue; ▣ 6 & D
A simple family-run place, this is one of the few Florentine locations where locals head to satisfy their marine desires with genuine fresh fish and seafood. It's a little out of the way, but if you are sick of Florentine steaks and dining among other foreigners, it is worth making the effort to wander here. Try the *spiedino misto*, a handsome tray of mixed seafood.

VINANDRO Map p239   Tuscan
☎ 055 5 91 21; Piazza Mino da Fiesole 33; meal €25; ☷ Tue-Sun; ▣ 7
Here they have gone to some lengths to recreate a sense of the old Tuscan tavern, with long, timber *fratina* tables conducive to convivial eating. The menu consists of Tuscan staples and snacks, all washed down in tumblers of chianti. In summer you can sit outside too.

Entertainment

Entertainment

For a provincial capital, Florence has a variegated palette of entertainment. Bars of all sorts, from wine outlets to cool cocktail coves, keep the young and not-so-young of Florence in tipples. A wide mixture of live music and clubs will keep you swinging through the wee hours. Theatre, the occasional opera and cinema are also on hand.

In summer, the scene changes somewhat. The city organises open-air concerts (located in places like the ever-convivial Piazza di Spirito Santo), theatre and modern dance performances.

Information

The tourist office produces a bimonthly publication, *Turismonotizie* (which is nominally 50c, but is often available free); a free monthly events flyer, *Eventi;* and an annual brochure, *Avvenimenti,* covering major events in and around the city. There is also the monthly freebie *Informacittà* – check out its website (www.informacittafirenze.it, in Italian) for the latest updates.

Florence Concierge Information is a more compendious, privately published free bimonthly that runs a good what's-on website, www.florence-concierge.it, with plenty of links.

Firenze Spettacolo (www.firenzespettacolo.it), the city's monthly definitive entertainment publication, is available for €1.60 at newsstands. You will soon start finding other backyard publications, distributed in places like bars and restaurants. Some can be quite useful, such as the monthly *Zero* and *Nightfly,* which concentrate on bars and clubs.

TOP FIVE DRINKING ESTABLISHMENTS

- Negroni (p148)
- Rex Caffè (p148)
- La Dolce Vita (p147)
- Capocaccia (opposite)
- Slowly (p148)

Sbandieratori *(flag-throwers) in front of the Duomo (p65)*

144

DRINKING

Inveterate bar-hoppers and night owls will find plenty to fill their wee hours. You could sip on endless selections of fine Tuscan wine in a relaxed *enoteca* (wine bar), perhaps over a tasty snack or two. At the other end of the scale, you might choose from one of several UK-style pubs. The latter are a reflection of a double phenomenon in Florence: the considerable Anglo-Saxon presence in town (made up of both language students or travellers) and a certain Italian fondness for bars dressed up as Anglo-Irish pubs. These pubs offer everything from UK football games live on screen, through to mostly Italian punters sipping on pints of McCaffrey's in genteel fashion.

Otherwise bars are distinctive in their own style. They range from a chintzy one-time brothel (all leopard skins and puffy cushions at Montecarla) to low-lit cocktail bars.

Drink prices don't vary much. A good rule of thumb is €4 to €5 for a pint-sized glass of beer on tap, while mixed drinks and cocktails typically cost around €6 to €8.

Many bars and pubs tend to shut around 1am or 2am, but there are enough exceptions to this rule (especially on a Friday and Saturday) to keep you going til 3am and, on a few occasions, later.

Starting in late May, quite a few bars shut for summer and don't open their doors again until September.

ASTOR CAFFÈ Map pp244-5
☎ 055 239 90 00; Piazza del Duomo 5/r;
🕐 10am-3am; 🚌 14 & 23
You can have breakfast here, but the nocturnal folk gather round for loud music and cocktails, both inside and out, right by the solemn walls of the Duomo. You can keep an eye on the big red clock to see how near it is to closing time.

BARCELÓ Map pp240-1
☎ 055 436 93 81; Viale Morgagni 1/b;
🕐 7am-1am Mon-Sat; 🚌 8, 14, 20 & 28
Not much goes on here in winter, but from late May the team from Rex Caffé move in to create a busy summertime atmosphere. Although in action all day, it only swings into the groove from the early evening *aperitivo* on, attempting the noisy clamour of a Spanish bar (something a certain class of young Italians seem to hold in some awe).

BETTY BOOPS Map pp242-3
☎ 055 21 33 52; Via Taddea 13; 🕐 midnight-6am;
🚌 1, 6, 7, 10, 11 & 17
A luminous pink sign glows sickly across this quiet lane, but it's a sign that says you might be able to get a last very late tipple without having to resort to a club. It's a cramped little bar touting itself as a club, and opening days can be variable. When we last swung by it was opening throughout summer. Although open from midnight, it can be quite dead until 4am.

CABIRIA Map pp248-9
☎ 055 21 57 32; Piazza Santo Spirito 4/r;
🕐 11am-2am Wed-Mon; 🚌 D
This popular daytime café converts into a busy music bar by night. In summer the buzz extends onto Piazza Santo Spirito, which itself becomes a stage for an outdoor bar and regular free concerts.

CAFÉ DE PARIS Map pp240-1
☎ 055 422 05 05; Piazza Dalmazia 7/r;
🕐 6pm-2am; 🚌 8, 14, 20 & 28
A modern café-bar that is especially busy for the summer evening *aperitivo*, and until about 10pm. On Friday and Saturday nights it can also get busy much later.

CAFFÈ LA TORRE Map pp248-9
☎ 055 68 06 43; Lungarno Benvenuto Cellini 65/r;
🕐 8.30am-4am; 🚌 12, 13, 23 & D
Hang out into the wee hours, drinking and listening to all kinds of music – from cool jazz to Latin rhythms. Find your spot within the red-lit ambience of the bar or head outside to the terrace. Drinks are reasonable, and this is one of the only places in Florence where you can snack after midnight.

CAPOCACCIA Map pp244-5
☎ 055 21 07 51; Lungarno Corsini 12-14/r;
🕐 noon-1am Tue-Sun; 🚌 B
The fashion set of Florence gather here, especially on a balmy spring or summer evening, for a riverside nibble and cocktail before heading on to dinner and clubs. It can be a curious exercise in people-watching, but you might want to dress up a little to avoid feeling like a hick from the sticks. A DJ swings into action most nights from about 11pm.

CHEQUERS PUB Map pp244-5

☎ 055 28 75 88; Via della Scala 7-9/r;
⊙ 6pm-1.30am Sun-Thu, 6pm-2.30am Fri & Sat;
🚍 11, 36, 37 & A

Mainly foreigners hang out in this big and busy UK-style pub, although Italians sometimes frequent it too. In the background the big-screen TV will feature anything from European football to American basketball.

CLURICANE PUB Map pp244-5

☎ 055 28 45 09; Piazza dell'Olio 2;
⊙ 2pm-2am; 🚍 A

Touting itself as a Guinness bar, this is really a warm, dark, drinking cubicle, with a fan over the bar and Latin music. But the Guinness (warm and cold) and Kilkenny are there. A handful of tables are set up outside in the warmer months.

EBY'S LATIN BAR Map pp248-9

☎ 055 24 00 27; Via dell'Oriuolo 5/r;
⊙ noon-3am Mon-Sat; 🚍 C

Bright blues and reds greet you in a festive Mexican fashion in this lively Latin bar. Cocktails are good and the music tropical. Burritos (€3.50) and other snacks are on hand and the place is a hit with locals.

FISH Map pp242-3

☎ 055 265 40 29; Piazza del Mercato Centrale 44/r;
⊙ 6pm-2am; 🚍 1, 6, 7, 10, 11 & 17

A boisterous pub-style bar with a strong American air about it, the Fish attracts hordes of people, mostly young foreigners but also a sprinkling of youthful Italians. The terrace on the square is relatively peaceful, while inside the bar goes to some lengths to keep business humming, offering countless shots at a pittance and organising events such as its Friday night Free Crazy Party, when the drinking is free from 9pm to 11pm.

FLOR Map pp242-3

☎ 055 47 59 02; Viale Filippo Strozzi 28/a-b;
⊙ 7.30am-1.30am Mon-Sat, 6pm-1.30am Sun;
🚍 4, 12, 13, 14, 23, 28 & 80

The locals call it a 'cooking bar' and they certainly seem to think something is cooking here. Apart from a light and easy buffet lunch, a trendy set gather in this postage stamp–sized redoubt for the evening aperitivo, spilling out onto the pavement terrace (in spite of the traffic). From 10.30pm on it's

cocktail time, and Sunday night is particularly festive.

IL RIFRULLO Map pp248-9

☎ 055 234 26 21; Via di San Niccolò 55/r;
⊙ 9am-1am Tue-Sun; 🚍 12, 13, 23 & D

A cool corner bar, nicely placed off the main tourist trail. The bar snacks are generous and the evening cocktails good. You can sit by the bar or wind your way out to the back garden on summer nights.

JAMES JOYCE Map pp248-9

☎ 055 658 08 56; Lungarno Benvenuto Cellini 1/r;
⊙ 6pm-1am; 🚍 12, 13, 23 & D

This is a rather pleasant version of the Irish-pub theme, with a beer garden and largely local punters, if only because it's a bridge too far for most interlopers. Beamish is the main drop on tap, which you can mix with Florence-style bar snacks.

JJ CATHEDRAL Map pp244-5

☎ 055 28 02 60; Piazza di San Giovanni 44/r;
⊙ 11am-1am; 🚍 1, 6, 7, 10, 11, 14, 17 & 23

Get here early if you want the balcony table overlooking the Baptistery – possibly the most coveted drinking spot in Florence. Otherwise make do with the narrow interior, cluttered with ripped wallpaper and fiddly bits of Irish paraphernalia. Usually filled with international students and local lads making moves.

APERIMADNESS

The aperitivo has always been a key feature of Florentine, and indeed Italian, social life. That early evening drink, perhaps over a snack or two with friends, comes at the end of a day's pain or pleasure, before heading off for dinner. It might last the length of a glass of wine, or go on for hours. Florence's bars and restaurants have reinvented the aperitivo, turning something that was taken for granted into a key social statement. Aperitivo theme nights rule. If Capocaccia (p145) presents Aperifish (seafood snacks) on Fridays, Flor (left) has AperiNutella on Wednesdays. Negroni (p148) does a generous range of bar food in the Milanese aperitivo tradition and in summer Barceló (p145) offers Greek snacks on Thursdays. Several hotel bars are following the trend and are worth keeping an eye on too. Check out the Apericena by the rooftop pool at the Grand Hotel Minerva (p177), for example.

JOSHUA TREE Map pp242-3

Via della Scala 41; ☾ 4pm-1am; 🚍 11, 36, 37 & A
A dark, conspiratorial air pervades this
place, with its U2 reminders scattered
about. The crowd is mixed, although you
can expect a predominance of young
foreigners.

KIKUYA PUB Map pp248-9

☎ 055 234 48 79; Via de' Benci 43/r;
☾ 7pm-3am; 🚍 13, 23, B & C
The cocktails in Kikuya are unusually generous and occasionally you can hear live
music. It invites a predominantly foreign
crowd, but it at least avoids the overtly
UK-style-pub identity. Indeed it is a strange
mix, with Brazilian bar staff and a rocky
ambience.

LA DOLCE VITA Map pp248-9

☎ 055 28 45 95; Piazza del Carmine 6/r;
☾ 8pm-1am Mon-Thu, 8pm-3am Fri-Sun; 🚍 D
Just a piazza away from Santo Spirito,
this place attracts voguish people. During the week it's a tame affair, with the
30-something clientele looking carefully
dressy over a cocktail. Things get busier
from Thursday night on, as impossibly suntanned charmers in hunting mode jostle for
space with equally suntanned ladies in a
similarly provocative mood.

LA ROTONDA Map pp242-3

☎ 055 265 46 44; Via il Prato 10-16; ☾ 7.30pm-
1am; 🚍 1, 2, 9, 16, 17, 26, 27, 29, 30, 35 & D
This cavernous place spreads over two
floors. Part pub, part music bar (sometimes
with live action), it offers simple grub and
attracts a largely Italian crowd.

LION'S FOUNTAIN Map pp248-9

☎ 055 234 44 12; Borgo degli Albizi 34/r;
☾ 6pm-2am; 🚍 A
This pub tends to attract a young, rowdy
and substantially English-speaking crowd
which, as it spews out into the streets
towards closing time, is highly reminiscent
of 11pm closing in the UK.

LOCHNESS Map pp248-9

www.lochnessclub.com; Via de' Benci 19/r;
☾ 10pm-5am Sep-May; 🚍 13, 23, B & C
Look for the green door. Loonees' patrons
(see the next entry) often end up here.

You'll need to pay a one-off membership
fee of €8. Those with unlimited drinking
capacity, but who are short on cash, could
combine the Loonees happy hour, from
8pm to 10pm, with more of the same until
11pm at Lochness.

LOONEES Map pp244-5

☎ 055 21 22 49; Via Porta Rossa 15; ☾ 10pm-3am
Wed-Sat; 🚍 A
You wouldn't know this place existed if you
had not been told. Walk into the building
and the door is to the left of the staircase.
It's a fairly small 'club' – basically just a
bar with an expat bent and occasional live
music of dubious taste. Still, it's a personable enough spot for a pint.

MAMMA Map pp248-9

☎ 055 233 67 76; Lungarno Santa Rosa;
☾ 7pm-2am Mon-Thu, 7pm-3am Fri & Sat; 🚍 6 & D
You might be wondering where all the
Florentines disappear to in summer, as
you do the round of city centre bars. Well,
apart from the various squares (see the
boxed text, p150), half of them seem to be
at Mamma, a series of bars in the shadow
of the old city walls, with tables set up on
a grass strip, a couple of tents and lots of
tanned Florentines sipping cocktails and
checking one another out.

MAYDAY Map pp244-5

☎ 055 238 12 90; Via Dante Alighieri 16/r;
☾ 8pm-2am; 🚍 A
This stylish lounge bar, often the scene of
art exhibitions, is primarily a funky stage for
an evening out, with great music and even
the occasional live show. Much of the décor
comes from bits and pieces donated by the
mostly foreign punters at the end of their
Florentine sojourns.

MONTECARLA Map pp248-9

☎ 055 234 02 59; Via de' Bardi 2; ☾ 8pm-4am
Thu-Tue; 🚍 13, 23 & D
One of the weirder locations to get a
late-night cocktail, this place has remained
faithful to the baroque kitsch aesthetic
that inspired Montecarla's supposed
originator – a prostitute of some fame in
years gone by (hence the feminine version
of the bar's name). It's all leopard skins,
gaudy cushions, plush drapes and moody
corners.

MOYO Map pp248-9

☎ 055 247 97 38; Via de' Benci 23/r; ☼ 8am-3am;
🚌 13, 23, B & C

Aside from being the city's first free-access wifi bar, this trendy number (run by the people from Zoe across the Arno – see opposite) has Florentines quaffing out of its tumblers. Snacks for the evening are laid along a high table just inside the main entrance. For your cocktail-sipping you can opt to perch on high stools, lounge out the back or sit on outdoor tables.

NEGRONI Map pp248-9

☎ 055 24 36 47; Via dei Renai 17/r; ☼ 8am-2am Mon-Sat, 6pm-2am Sun; 🚌 12, 13, 23 & D

A smart bar, named after the Campari and gin–based cocktail, Negroni has evolved into one of the city's hippest venues. Generous Milan-style bar snacks are laid on in the early evening for the *aperitivo*, and a relaxed, good-looking crowd hangs out here late into the night, attracted by the cocktails and the local DJs' mixes.

NOVABAR Map pp244-5

☎ 055 28 98 80; Via de' Martelli 14/r;
☼ 9am-2am; 🚌 1, 6, 7, 10, 11, 14, 17, 23 & A

The waiters are in black, the walls are black, even the floor is black in parts. Red lights and loud DJ-spun tracks of a distinctly hippity hoppity nature all help attract a predominantly foreign crowd into this watering hole, divided into two separate drinking spaces.

PICCOLO CAFÉ Map pp248-9

☎ 055 200 10 57; Borgo Santa Croce 23/r;
☼ 5pm-2am; 🚌 C

What's behind the purple doors? A relaxed place to hang out and get acquainted with the city's gay scene. The bar is by no means gay-male exclusive though lesbians and straights are equally welcome.

A COCKTAIL FOR FLORENCE

Negroni is basically one part sweet vermouth, one part Campari and one part gin, with a twist of lemon to top it off. Invented in Florence in the early 20th century, it was named after one Camilo Negroni, a prominent tippler whose favourite indulgence was precisely this mix. This Negroni Classico is hard to find, as the vermouth used is something of a rarity and in its stead Martini is generally added.

REX CAFFÈ Map pp248-9

☎ 055 248 03 31; Via Fiesolana 25/r;
☼ 5pm-3am Sep-May; 🚌 C

A top stop on the cocktail circuit and a hip place to slip into for your favourite mixed concoction. Occasionally you'll strike live music and when the sounds are vinyl based the taste is eclectic. You get a mixed crowd, including an arty, grungy lot, as well as students and a sprinkling of the fashion set.

ROSE'S Map pp244-5

☎ 055 28 70 90; Via del Parione 26/r;
☼ 12.30pm-1am Mon-Sat, 7pm-1am Sun; 🚌 A & B

A casual and smoke-free New York–style café, with salads and pastas available during the day, Rose's undergoes a metamorphosis after dark, when it turns into a hip and lively sushi bar (food on until 11pm) and fills up with a trendy crowd.

SALAMANCA Map pp248-9

☎ 055 234 54 52; Via Ghibellina 80/r;
☼ 5pm-2am; 🚌 14

The tapas here have a vaguely Italian flavour about them, but otherwise the place manages to exude an almost convincing pseudo-Spanish atmosphere with plenty of hearty flamenco rock and South American sounds to keep punters returning to the bar for more – it's a favourite with Latin Americans living in Florence. Sangria and Latin American cocktails predominate.

SANT'AMBROGIO CAFFÈ Map pp248-9

☎ 055 24 10 35; Piazza Sant'Ambrogio 7/r;
☼ 9am-2am Mon-Sat; 🚌 C

A good source of snacks, Sant'Ambrogio Caffè is especially dedicated to the sipping of cocktails. On summer nights tables are set up outside and the place is popular with a mix of Italian students and arty types.

SLOWLY Map pp244-5

☎ 055 264 53 54; Via Porta Rossa 63/r;
☼ noon-2.30am Mon-Sat, 6pm-2.30am Sun; 🚌 A

Frizzy-haired ladies with euro-trash wardrobes trip their way in on high heels, while brillo'd Don Giovannis check out the talent from behind their designer shades. The barman has a heavy hand with the cocktails and the place is so hip they have even brought out their own Buddha Bar–style CD, *Slowly Café*.

LADS IN PARADISE

Lad tourism – blokes (and often lasses) whose principal idea of cultural diversion while abroad is to absorb the greatest quantity of alcohol possible in the shortest possible time – aided and abetted by low-cost air travel, has many a continental town hall in despair. But in Florence one almost gets the impression it's being encouraged. In the past couple of years the number of central Florentine bars, largely aimed at a young and foreign clientele and tempting customers with bargain basement booze, has grown. When one offers 'five shots for €5 – all night!', the others are quick to follow. Pint and shot combinations, all-you-can-drink happy hours (that go on for hours) and ladies' nights (free booze for the girls) all feature in certain pubs' and bars' armoury. Who gives a fig for the Uffizi?

UNIVERSALE Map pp240-1
☎ 055 22 11 22; www.universalefirenze.it; Via Pisana 77/r; admission €10-15 (includes first drink); ⏱ 8pm-3am Wed-Sun Sep-May; 🚌 6
This old cinema, which has a restaurant upstairs and a bar in the middle of the downstairs area – around which gather a mixed set of very fashionable locals – has been converted by the owners. In the background a screen plays clips from classic black-and-white movies.

UNIVERSO SANCHEZ Map pp242-3
☎ 055 28 34 53; Via Il Prato 57/r; ⏱ 8pm-2am Tue-Sat; 🚌 1, 2, 9, 12, 17, 26, 27, 29, 30 & 35
Florentines in their finest frippery flock here (but not in summer, when it is usually half-empty) to sip cocktails in a series of different bars, stretching back from the vaguely North African–styled chill area in the front. There are dance spaces, the chance to do a little yoga and more intimate rooms towards the back, for couples with eyes (and hands) only for one another.

VINARIUS Map pp248-9
☎ 055 200 12 16; www.vinarius-it.com; Borgo Santa Croce 15/r; ⏱ 10am-7pm; 🚌 C
If you're after a civilised wine stop in the course of the day, drop by here and indulge in a little tasting. They put out more than a dozen reds and several whites by the glass for you to choose from – a combination of Tuscan and national labels.

WILLIAM Map pp248-9
☎ 055 246 98 00; Via Magliabechi 7/r; ⏱ 6pm-2am; 🚌 C
This is a loud UK-style pub, but it has found quite a following among twenty-something Florentines in search of a pint of ale, rather than Anglos in search of six.

Y.A.G. BAR Map pp248-9
☎ 055 246 90 22; Via de' Macci 8/r; ⏱ 7pm-3am; 🚌 C
Barely a stone's throw away from the Piccolo Café, this gay bar is a relaxed and mixed location. It claims to be the largest gay bar in Florence and is one of the city's best. There are two video screens, and on Mondays you can exchange written messages with strangers to make new friends.

ZOE Map pp248-9
☎ 055 24 31 11; Via dei Renai 13/r; ⏱ 3pm-2am Apr-Oct, 6pm-2am Tue-Sun Nov-Mar; 🚌 12, 13, 23 & D
Florentines in their 20s converge on this hopping Oltrarno bar from all corners of town, and they spill out on to the street amid a friendly atmosphere. When we passed by plans were afoot to convert the place into a mixed bar/restaurant, so you may find the atmosphere changed when you check it out.

Enjoying an outdoor drink

SUMMER FROLICS

While some clubs and bars close for two or so months in summer, all sorts of places spring to life to keep Florentines occupied from June to early September.

About four kilometres east of the city centre, in parkland on the south bank of the Arno, **Parco Sud** (Map pp240–1; Parco dell'Anconella; 🚌 8, 23 & 71) is the scene of almost nightly performances from June to August; look for fliers in the tourist office. Shows range from DJ sets to live world music, dance and theatre – they start at 9pm.

For a poolside atmosphere, take your swimming gear to **Le Pavoniere swimming pool** (Map pp240–1) in Le Cascine Park. From 8pm (especially on Thursday) this turns into an open-air dip and sip session. With liquid on the outside and inside, punters admire the purple lights in the trees and the stars beyond, watch the beautiful people swanning around and chat away. Entrance is free.

Just off Piazza della Libertà, the odd-looking collection of buildings and performance spaces known as **Parterre** (Map pp242–3) comes to life as a kind of all-in-one entertainment scene in summer. Nightly performances of varied music, theatre (for adults and kids) and so on are the order of the evening.

In **Piazza di Santo Spirito** (Map pp248–9) a bar is set up in the middle of the square every night for **Notti d'Estate** (Summer Nights) and frequent live-music acts keep the punters coming. The fun (free) lasts from 8pm to 1am. A similar scene is played out at the other end of town, around the La Vasca (the Pond) on the eastern flank of **Fortezza da Basso** (Map pp240–1). **Piazza Ghiberti** (Map pp248–9), in the Santa Croce district, is the scene for the **Sant'Ambrogio Summer Festival** concert programme.

Rime Rampanti (free) is a mixed programme of music and theatre on **Piazza Giuseppe Poggi** (Map pp248–9) by the Porta San Niccolò in Oltrarno. Again, temporary bars and snack stands are put in place and the activity runs from 7pm to 2am, but the main performances start at 10pm.

Teatro dell'Acqua (Map pp248–9; ☎ 055 234 34 60; Lungarno G Pecori Giraldi 1) opens up for fun and music from mid-May to September. It attracts a mixed crowd and you can also get a bite to eat. This is a popular place for summertime liquid refreshment too.

In Fiesole, the **Estate Fiesolana** (Fiesole Summer; ☎ 055 5 91 87; www.estatefiesolana.com) programme is busy with opera, jazz and classical music concerts, mostly in the Roman theatre.

LIVE MUSIC

In some music venues you may be asked to pay for membership – effectively a one-off cover charge. If you are staying in Florence for any length of time give a local address so that you receive your card – generally valid for a year. Establishments do this to maintain their status as 'clubs', which brings tax breaks. Check out *Firenze Spettacolo* to see what's on.

JAZZ

Several bars provide Florentines with a regular aural diet of jazz. The Jazz Club is the main bastion for the genre, but a couple of other locales occasionally chime in.

BEBOP Map pp242–3

☎ 055 239 65 44; Via dei Servi 76/r; admission free–€10; ⏰ 8pm-2am Mon-Sat; 🚌 C

A mellow underground music cavern, this is a nice spot to catch a little jazz, blues or whatever else pops on to the often eclectic programme. Basically the music consists of light covers but it can be quite pleasant, and the place doesn't seem to get too crowded.

CARUSO JAZZ CAFÉ Map pp244–5

☎ 055 28 19 40; www.carusojazzcafé.com; Via Lambertesca 14-16/r; ⏰ 9.30am-4pm & 6pm-midnight Mon-Sat; 🚌 C

Thursday to Saturday nights this mellow café, with a vaguely baroque feel, offers jazz concerts from 9pm. The Gallery room, with its red sofas and low lights, is perfect for cosying up to your partner. They also have an internet café next door and serve food.

JAZZ CLUB Map pp242–3

☎ 055 247 97 00; Via Nuova de' Caccini 3; admission €6 membership; ⏰ 9.30pm-1am Sun-Thu, 9.30pm-2am Fri & Sat; 🚌 C

The name says it all. This is Florence's top jazz venue and it gets some quality acts, both local and from out of town. The atmosphere is low-lit and the music can be enjoyed without necessarily killing the conversation – a good mix. At the weekend you should book a table if you are going in a group.

ROCK & OTHER

A handful of big venues, including the football stadium on occasion, host major concerts at various times throughout the year. Otherwise you must dig around a handful of spots spread thinly around town to hear a little live music.

AUDITORIUM FLOG Map pp240-1

☎ 055 49 04 37; www.flog.it; Via M Mercati 24/b; admission free-€10; ☯ 10pm-4am; ☒ 4, 8, 14, 20 & 28

A major venue for bands that was born out of a workers' society created in 1945, Flog is in the Rifredi area, quite a way north of the centre. It has a reasonable stage and dance area, and a swimming pool sometimes operates in summer.

CHIODO FISSO Map pp244-5

☎ 334 364 60 88; Via dell'Anguillara 70/r; admission free; ☯ 10pm-3am Tue-Sun; ☒ 14, 23 & A

Singer-songwriter and local legend Andrea Ardia has converted the medieval vaults of this one-time wine cellar into a cosy gathering place for wine and song. He sings his own material and covers Italian classics from Fabrizio de Andrè to Francesco de Gregori – sometimes alone, sometimes with guests. If it's open, this offers a singular opportunity to bathe in Italian musical culture over a bottle of red. Opening times can be loose.

TENAX Map p238

☎ 055 30 81 60; www.tenax.org; Via Pratese 46; admission up to €20; ☯ 10pm-4am Tue-Sun; ☒ 29 & 30

Located well northwest of the centre, Tenax has been staging big local and international acts since the early 1980s. Although the emphasis has moved to clubbing in recent years, Tenax still attracts live shows by noted performers, such as Bob Geldof and Grace Jones. Keep an eye on the programme. It also operates as a club (see p152).

CLUBBING

An odd mix of little dance clubs are scattered across the city. You can get down to Latin rhythms, squeeze up in dance clubs no bigger than your average bathroom, or join the glitzy things in a couple of good old-fashioned meat markets.

Two of the city's main clubs, Central Park and Meccanò, are in Le Cascine park. They are fun without exactly being the last word in European nightlife. In both you will be given a card on entry, which you use to get drinks (and food if you want). It is swiped on your way out, which is when you pay. You will be obliged to pay for at least one drink whether you have one or not – this is effectively your admission charge. A word of warning about Le Cascine – it is a haunt for prostitutes, pimps and other interesting folk.

The pay-on-your-way-out system operates in some other clubs too, so bear this in mind. Beware of the claim that entry is free; literally this may be true, but the exit generally won't be! You'll often get a chit when ordering your first drink – you must keep hold of this chit (with all subsequent drinks also totted up on it) and pay for it before you can leave.

CENTRAL PARK Map pp240-1

☎ 055 35 35 05; Via Fosso Macinante 2; admission up to €20; ☯ 11pm-6am Tue-Sat; ☒ 1, 9, 12, 13, 16, 26, 27, 80 & B

What kind of music you hear in this club, one of the city's most popular, will depend partly on the night; although as you wander from one dance area to another (there are four) you can expect a general range from Latin and pop through to house. In summer you can dance inside or under the stars. In the opinion of locals it has gone somewhat downhill recently and Florentines who consider themselves a cut above the average prefer nearby Meccanò (p152).

CRISCO Map pp248-9

☎ 055 248 05 80; Via Sant'Egidio 43/r; ☯ 8pm-4am Sun-Mon & Wed-Thu, 8pm-6am Fri & Sat; ☒ 14 & 23

A somewhat furtive air seems to reign in this strictly men-only club. After a few

GAY & LESBIAN OPTIONS

Florence isn't memorable for its gay nightlife, but there are a handful of possibilities. A couple of relaxed bars to include on your gay pilgrimage are **Piccolo Café** (p148) and **Y.A.G. Bar** (p149). In summer especially, Florence's gays head for the clubs of Viareggio on the coast instead. They especially make for Torre del Lago, which boasts four main spots: Bocachica, Mama Mia, La Plaza and Priscilla. A big gay disco at Marina di Pisa is Pappafico.

warm-up tipples and body-grinding dance routines, explore the dark rooms. As the night wears on, the punters seem less abashed about the place and the doors swing wide open to welcome all (male) comers.

EXMUD Map pp248-9

☎ 055 263 85 83; www.exmud.it; Corso dei Tintori 4; admission €10-15; ☷ 9pm-4am Mon, Thu-Sat; ▣ B & C

One of central Florence's hotter clubs, this place introduces an impressive array of local and international DJs. Monday nights are free in, Thursdays is Apnea Drum 'n' Bass night, and Friday features the popular PUSH Soulful House night. Although really a winter place, this postage stamp–sized venue has a small courtyard area that allows them to open in summer too.

FULL UP Map pp248-9

☎ 055 29 30 06; Via della Vigna Vecchia 23-25/r; ☷ 10pm-4am Wed-Sat; ▣ 14 & A

Full-up by name and…you guessed it. This tiny venue is very popular with a largely Florentine crowd, made up of Fabios and the skimpily clad objects of their desire. It's a good place to go if you're looking for a Mediterranean orgasm (and we're not talking cocktails).

JARAGUA Map pp248-9

☎ 055 234 36 00; Via dell'Erta Canina 12/r; admission free; ☷ 8pm-3am; ▣ 12, 13, 23 & C

Somewhat hidden from the main tourist stream, this is a cool Latin locale where you can admire the slick dance moves or even join in – definitely the place to practise your salsa and merengue. Sip on a Banana Mama, Jaragua or Culo Bello ('Nice Ass'). The Latin thing is extremely popular with Florentines.

KLYK Map pp248-9

☎ 338 691 91 39; Via dell'Oriuolo 19/r; admission free; ☷ 11.30pm-5am Tue-Sun; ▣ 14, 23 & A

In winter especially, this hole-in-the-wall club is appreciated by locals above all for its opening hours. For you can choose simply to sip your drinks at the tiny bar, or penetrate out the back to shake your thing around to a variety of sounds, depending on the evening. House nights alternate with mainstream pop, R 'n' B and hip-hop.

MECCANÒ Map pp240-1

☎ 055 33 13 71; Viale degli Olmi 1; admission up to €20; ☷ 11pm-5am Tue-Sat; ▣ 1, 9, 12, 13, 16, 26, 27, 80 & B

Three dance spaces offer house, funk and mainstream music to appeal to a fairly broad range of tastes. The main dance floor is dominated by go-go dancers. From here you can meander your way through the other dance floors. Thursday is house night and, for Florentines' money, this is the pick of the two big Cascine clubs.

TABASCO Map pp244-5

☎ 055 21 30 00; www.tabascogay.it; Piazza di Santa Cecilia 3/r; ☷ 8pm-4am, disco until 6am Tue, Fri & Sat; ▣ A

For some time this place stood alone as Florence's only serious gay club (indeed it was Italy's first gay disco), and it remains one of the best. In a building dating to the 16th century, you dance beneath stone vaults and among ageing statues. The old well still works! Here you have a space for dancing, a cocktail bar and dark room. Wednesday is leather night.

TENAX Map p238

☎ 055 30 81 60; www.tenax.org, in Italian; Via Pratese 46; admission up to €25; ☷ 10pm-4am Tue-Sun; ▣ 29 & 30

Tenax isn't just the main venue for major live bands; it is also one of the hottest and longest-standing clubs in town. It still gets plenty of live acts, but in recent years the emphasis has shifted to clubbing. Upstairs you'll find a cool wine bar and chill-out area, as well as MUM – a club within the club featuring DJs from around Europe. On Friday night clubbers go behind the bars for The Cage, while Saturday is run by DJs, such as Alex Neri, of Nobody's Perfect – basically it's a house night.

YAB Map pp244-5

☎ 055 21 51 60; Via de' Sassetti 15; admission up to €20; ☷ 9pm-4am Mon-Sat Oct-late May, Mon only Jun-Sep; ▣ 6 & A

Remember those '80s disco years? Well, in some respects Yab never moved on from them – in spite of the hip-hop rage that dominates nowadays. With a local reputation as a meat market, it grinds on with a hormonally charged crowd of local dons

Florentine nightlife (p151)

and gals, mixed with tipsy out-of-towners. Beyond hip-hop nights, music can range from live sax shows to R 'n' B, soul and a middle-of-the-road mix of rock.

CINEMAS

There are a few venues that show films in their *versione originale* (original language), which generally means in English with Italian subtitles. At most cinemas there are three or four sessions daily, the latest starting between 10pm and 10.45pm. Wednesday is cheap cinema day, when tickets cost €5. Normally they cost around €7.20.

BRITISH INSTITUTE Map pp244-5
☎ 055 26 77 82; Lungarno Guicciardini 9; 🚌 6 & D
The British Institute will sometimes put on English-language films in its library.

CINEMA FULGOR Map pp242-3
☎ 055 238 18 81; Via Maso Finiguerra 22/r; 🚌 B
You'll find films in English screened here on Thursday evenings.

ODEON CINEHALL Map pp244-5
☎ 055 21 40 68; www.cinehall.it;
Piazza degli Strozzi; 🚌 6 & A
This is the main location for seeing subtitled films, which are screened on Mondays, Tuesdays and Thursdays. The Odeon chain has cinemas spread all over town, but this is the best for original English-version films.

CLASSICAL MUSIC & OPERA

From October to April the city's main theatres provide Florentines with a programme of opera and classical music. Come the warmer months, special performances and music festivals take over the scene (see p9). In summer especially, concerts of chamber music are held in churches across the city. Keep an eye out for programmes of the Orchestra da Camera Fiorentina (Florentine Chamber Orchestra), whose performance season runs from March to October.

Tickets & Reservations

A handy central ticket outlet is **Box Office** (Map pp242-3; ☎ 055 21 08 04; www.boxol.it; Via Luigi Alamanni 39; ⏱ 3.30-7.30pm Mon, 10am-7pm Tue-Sat). Call by the office or book events online. Another Web service, **Ticket One** (www.ticketone.it), allows you to book tickets for theatre, football and other events on the Internet.

CHIESA SANTA MARIA DE' RICCI CONCERTI Map pp244-5
☎ 055 28 93 67; Via del Corso; admission €11;
⏱ 9.15pm; 🚌 A
Although they can be a little cheesy, the concerts of baroque and classical music staged in this church (the proceeds go, in part at least, to the church's restoration),

---

CINEMA UNDER THE STARS

From mid-June to early September, several places set up outdoor cinemas (programmes are available from tourist offices) as most indoor cinemas shut for the summer break. Tickets generally cost €5. Some of the main locations:

Arena Chiardiluna (Map pp240-1; ☎ 055 233 70 42; Via di Monte Uliveto 1; 🚌 12 & 13)

Arena di Marte (Map pp240-1; ☎ 055 67 88 41; Viale Pasquale Paoli, Terrazza Palasport at Campo di Marte; 🚌 10)

Esterno Notte (Map p000; ☎ 055 48 12 85; www.flog.it; Via M Mercati 24/b; 🚌 4, 8, 14, 20 & 28)

Arena Parco Demidoff (☎ 055 40 91 55; Parco di Pratolino; 🚌 25/a) A cinema set up in a beautiful park north of Florence.

may be your only chance to sample a little musical culture while in Florence. Quality is variable, but on the whole a night of favourites (such as *The Four Seasons*, a little Bach or Paganini) can make for a pleasant evening out. Arrive a little before showtime to get your ticket.

TEATRO COMUNALE Map pp240-1

☎ 800 11 22 11; Corso Italia 12; 🚍 B

Concerts, operas and dance shows are performed at various times of the year here, on the northern bank of the Arno. In May and June the theatre hosts **Maggio Musicale Fiorentino** (www.maggiofiorentino.com), an international concert festival. Contact the theatre's box office for more.

TEATRO DELLA PERGOLA Map pp242-3

☎ 055 247 96 51; www.pergola.firenze.it; Via della Pergola 18; 🚍 C

With a main auditorium and the smaller Saloncino, this theatre puts on a varied programme of opera, drama and recitals. Classics of Italian manufacture that have been put on recently range from Toscanini's *La Traviata* to Pirandello's *Sei Personaggi in Cerca d'Autore*.

TEATRO VERDI Map pp248-9

☎ 055 21 23 20; www.teatroverdifirenze.it; Via Ghibellina 99; tickets up to €15 for classical music concerts; 🕑 Oct-Apr; 🚍 14 & A

For decades this classy 19th-century theatre has been the focal point of classical music, drama, opera, and dance. It is the permanent home of the Orchestra della Toscana. Most performances start around 8.30pm.

THEATRE & DANCE

The theatre season runs from October into April/May. Which is not to say that Florence comes to a standstill outside of that time, but many of the main stages stay quiet while more festive cultural events take centre billing in summer (see p9 and also the boxed text, p150).

The theatres mentioned in the Classical Music & Opera section above, also frequently stage drama. You will find productions at these, and several other smaller theatres dotted about town, advertised in *Firenze Spettacolo*. Most theatre is in Italian.

EX-STAZIONE LEOPOLDA Map pp240-1

www.stazione-leopolda.com; Viale Fratelli Rosselli 5; 🚍 1, 9, 12, 13, 16, 26, 27, 80 & B

This former train station is divided into several performance spaces, used to present a mix of avant-garde theatre, concerts and big city fairs, such as the Pitti Uomo fashion extravaganza in June. For programmes and tickets go to Box Office (see p153) or any of the tourist offices in Florence.

TEATRO DELLA LIMONAIA Map p238

☎ 055 44 08 52; www.teatrodellalimonaia.it, in Italian; Via Gramsci 426, Sesto Fiorentino; admission €8-12; 🚍 2 & 28A

This place, well beyond the centre of Florence, is one of the leading avant-garde theatres in Italy. It puts on a wide variety of new drama (pretty much all in Italian) and also runs a series of small theatre spaces elsewhere in the city. On Sundays, and some matinée sessions, children's theatre predominates – but remember, it's all in Italian. Take the bus from Stazione di Santa Maria Novella.

Buskers on Piazza della Repubblica.

ACTIVITIES

Travellers may not flock to Florence for its sport, but to watch the local football team in action you can purchase tickets at the football stadium, Chiosco degli Sportivi (see p156), or Ticket One (p153).

HEALTH & FITNESS

Cycling

Cycling around Florence and across Tuscany is becoming increasingly popular. In Florence, ask for a copy of *Viaggio in Toscana – Discovering Tuscany by Bike* at the APT office. For details of where to rent a bike see p204, or for bike tours outside of Florence, see p62. The city is slowly increasing its cycling lanes, although the experience of pedalling around Florence remains a little hairy.

Gyms

A handful of gyms around central Florence will allow you to work off a little extra sweat.

PALESTRA RICCIARDI Map pp242-3
☎ 055 247 84 62; www.palestrariccardi.com; Borgo Pinti 75; admission €10; 9am-10pm Mon-Fri, 9.30am-6pm Sat, closed Aug; C
Pump weights, attach yourself to exercise machines or join a class at this central gym. Aerobics, spinning and sauna are also available.

Rowing

Should you wind up staying in Florence for any length of time, a wonderful way to keep fit and meet locals is to join one of the city's rowing clubs. The cost of joining either of the main clubs that indulge in river activities is prohibitive, though, if you don't plan to stay in the city for at least a couple of months.

SOCIETÀ CANOTTIERI FIRENZE
Map pp244-5
☎ 055 28 21 30; www.canottierifirenze.it, in Italian; Lungarno Anna Marisa Luisa de' Medici 8; office 10am-1pm & 2-5pm Mon-Fri; B
This is the prestige club of the two, with impressive installations virtually under

the Uffizi. Unfortunately, to take rowing courses and use its small pool and gym you have to become a full member, a rather costly exercise with a one-year minimum.

SOCIETÀ CANOTTIERI COMUNALI
Map pp240-1
☎ 055 681 21 51; www.canottiericomunalifirenze.it; Lungarno Francesco Ferrucci 6; office 3-6pm Tue & Thu; 12, 13, 23 & C
Here too you need to become a member (€100 join-up fee and €28 per month) to use the facilities – which include a gym – and get rowing lessons.

Swimming

In the scorching summer months a dip in a pool can come as welcome relief. From mid-September to June is winter for Florentine pools though, and gaining access becomes rather complicated. You have to take out one-month (or longer) subscriptions, and access is restricted to certain times on no more than four days a week. Which is pathetic, as most Florentines would agree.

LE PAVONIERE SWIMMING POOL
Map pp240-1
☎ 055 36 22 33; Viale della Catena 2; adult/child €7.50/4.50; 10am-6pm & 8pm-2am Jun–mid-Sep; 1, 9, 12, 13, 16, 26, 27, 80 & B
This pool, Florence's most attractive, is a little small for serious lap swimming. Florentines are just as inclined to turn up here at night, as the pool becomes the centre for late-evening summer happenings, with its pizzeria and bar (see the boxed text, p150).

NANNINI SWIMMING POOL
Map pp240-1
☎ 055 67 75 21; Lungarno Aldo Moro 6; adult/child €6.50/4.50 or book of 10 tickets €45; 10am-6pm Jun-Aug; 14 & 34
In summer, when they pull back the movable roof from over this Olympic-sized pool, it becomes a watery haven on those torrid Florentine days, just the place for a hangout. Opening times tend to change from month to month; it's a good idea to ring up and check.

Tennis

CAMPO SPORTIVO ASSI Map pp240-1
☎ 055 68 78 58; Viale Michelangelo 64;
per hr €11; ☯ 8am-10.30pm Mon-Fri, 8am-5pm
Sat, 8am-2pm Sun; 🚌 12 & 13

This is a pleasant spot to book a court (but
not equipment) for a bit of therapeutic ball
bashing – a great antidote for museum-
overload.

WATCHING SPORT
Football

Your average Florentine is as passionate about football as the next Italian, but
their side, **AC Fiorentina** (www.acffiorentina
.it) has had a rocky few years. It finished
the 2005 season low down the ladder in
Serie A (the top division), which is still not
bad, considering the club had collapsed
several divisions in earlier years as it went
into bankruptcy. For more on the club's
story, see p15.

Match tickets are available directly at the
Stadio Comunale Artemio Franchi (Map pp240–1;
☎ 055 50 32 61; Viale Manfredo Fanti 4,
Campo di Marte) or at the ticket outlet at **Chiosco degli Sportivi** (Map pp244–5; ☎ 055 29 23
63; Via Anselmi, off Piazza della Repubblica;
☯ 9am-1pm and 3pm-6pm Mon, Tue-Thu,
9am-7.30pm Wed, 9am to 7pm Fri, 9am-
1pm & 3pm-8pm Sat, 10am-12.30pm Sun).
You can also have a flutter on the Totocalcio,
or football pools.

Motorsport

Approximately 30km north of Florence is the
Ferrari-owned **Mugello track** (☎ 055 849 91 11;
www.mugellocircuit.it; Via Senni 15, Scarpe-
ria), host to Formula 3000 car racing, and the
world-championship motorcycle competi-
tions in early summer. Tickets for one day of
championship motorcycle racing cost from
€60 to €175. The nearest train stations are
at Borgo San Lorenzo and San Piero, from
where you will have to get a cab.

Shopping

Shopping

Your credit-card Geiger counter is likely to start pulsating as you near Florence. Suckers for style and lovers of luxury are going to have a hard time resisting the goodies on display, while name-droppers and label-seekers may well find themselves permanently distracted from all the art and architecture.

Florence is one of Italy's principal homes of fashion and has given the world some of its greatest names in clobber. In addition to the name stores for threads, shoes and accessories in the city, the cut-price outlets outside town are becoming shoppers' meccas too (see p169).

And there is plenty of other stuff to make your pockets jingle. Leather is still a big draw, even if bargains are not as easy to come by as they were once were. Also hunt around for ceramics, mouth-watering food and drink products, classy stationery and jewellery.

What to Buy

Clothes, shoes, accessories and leather goods lead the way to your retail undoing. Local boys Gucci, Pucci and Ferragamo are joined by a host of other labels you'll recognise (and some you might not). One thing you should not expect is outrageous or avant-garde threads. Florentines are a fairly conservative lot and prefer classic style over zany innovation.

The same goes for shoes and leather. Whether you seek out your footwear in a workshop in Oltrarno or at a high-fashion store around Via de' Tornabuoni, you can be sure your new shoes have been made to last. That said, each season in Italy brings new and at times off-the-wall novelty and before you know it *everyone* is wearing the latest foot look.

As Florence tried to pick itself up by the bootstraps after WWII, local leather workshops began to crank out all sorts of goodies. The process accelerated with the increase in tourism in the 1960s and for a while the city had a name for low-priced, high-quality leather goods. At the top end of the market the quality remains exceptional, but the bargain days are largely a matter of wistful memory. However, the city *is* jammed with leather so, if only for the sheer quantity and choice, it is well worth looking around. It can be fun to hunt in the leather markets, such as **Mercato Nuovo** and around **San Lorenzo** (p167), and the shops of **Santa Croce** (p167), as sooner or later you will turn up a deal with appeal. Make like you're in a Middle Eastern *souq* and always bargain (prices in the markets drop considerably under the merest whiff of bargaining pressure), and keep your eyes peeled for defects in the production.

For those with unlimited bank accounts, gold and jewellery might be an option. Back in 1563, Grand Duke Ferdinando I ordered that goldsmiths install themselves in the shops of the Ponte Vecchio. He had decided that enough was enough – for centuries butchers and greengrocers had sold meat and vegies to the good citizens of Florence on the bridge (and dumped rubbish in the river below) but now they had to go – the stench and rotting mess of dead flesh was not for central Florence, rather the glamour of all that glistens. The gold merchants haven't budged since.

In line with its reputation for style, Florence has a name for elegant stationery and paper products. This could be the place to look if you want to turn back the clock and do a little high-class letter writing.

Florence is graced with a fair sprinkling of private art galleries, but many deal in a staid diet of typical 'Tuscan' scenes and the like. A handful of galleries dedicate themselves to contemporary art and freely display the work of artists from all over the world.

Various shops about the city turn out highly distinctive pottery and porcelain, from practical vases to purely decorative items. Florence itself is not known for its ceramics, but in the nearby town of Montelupo, west along the Arno, the locals have been pottering about since the Middle Ages, and a good deal of their stuff makes its way to Florentine stores.

Gourmets and gourmands should trail around the specialist food and wine stores. Florence offers a cornucopia of goods designed to tantalise the palate, as you may have already noticed at the city's dinner tables.

Finally, there is no shortage of tourist tat. Some of us are suckers for the stuff. Anything from 'I Love Florence' T-shirts to snow-scenes (those little models of the Duomo encased in plastic that you turn upside down to make it snow) can be picked up in shops around the centre of town. Or what about your very own David statuette-cum-pencil-sharpener?

Shopping Areas

The medieval heart of Florence is mainly dedicated to fashion, with the streets of **Via de' Tornabuoni** and **Via della Vigna Nuova** (Map pp248–9) forming the altar of *haute couture*. There you'll find more designer shops than you can shake your platinum card at.

Many Florentines head to **Borgo San Lorenzo** (Map pp244–5) for their shoes, although you will also find quality shoe stores on another major shopping street, **Via Roma** (Map pp244–5). Santa Croce is the heart of the leather merchants' district; see the **Scuola del Cuoio**, p169. Streets near **Piazza della Signoria**, **Borgo de' Greci** and **Via de' Gondi** (p162) in particular, are lined with leather shops and stands offering gear of every possible description (and quality). Leather stands are also abundant in the outdoor market around the **Basilica di San Lorenzo** and at **Mercato Nuovo** (p162), but remember, caveat emptor – let the buyer beware.

Borgo Ognissanti, **Via de' Fossi** and **Via Maggio** (Map pp248–9) are the antique strips, while the whole surrounding area of Oltrarno abounds with traditional artisans' shops and studios, cherished by locals and turning out everything from shoes to jewels.

Ponte Vecchio (Map pp244–5) is laden with gold and jewellery stores, though goldsmiths no longer actually work in them. To find higher quality jewellers and artisans, you'll need to get off the bridge and search about; a few options appear in this chapter.

How to Shop

Florentine shopkeepers will try to sell you anything they can, from extreme kitsch to serious art. One basic rule applies to all purchases – shop around before making your mind up.

When shopping in the markets, haggle. Paying the asking price is bad karma and makes things tougher for everyone else! Haggling won't get you anywhere in a department store, but you'd be surprised how often you can wangle a discount in many fashion shops. Just asking 'is that the best price you can do?' will sometimes produce surprising effects. In many central Florence stores you can do this in English, as at least some shop employees speak it well enough to fully understand market banter.

If you're dizzy from the fashion boutique prices but would still like to invest in some clothes, there are a couple of options. Do

CLOTHING SIZES

Measurements approximate only, try before you buy

Women's Clothing

Aus/UK	8	10	12	14	16	18
Europe	36	38	40	42	44	46
Japan	5	7	9	11	13	15
USA	6	8	10	12	14	16

Women's Shoes

Aus/USA	5	6	7	8	9	10
Europe	35	36	37	38	39	40
France only	35	36	38	39	40	42
Japan	22	23	24	25	26	27
UK	3½	4½	5½	6½	7½	8½

Men's Clothing

Aus	92	96	100	104	108	112
Europe	46	48	50	52	54	56
Japan	S		M	M		L
UK/USA	35	36	37	38	39	40

Men's Shirts (Collar Sizes)

Aus/Japan	38	39	40	41	42	43
Europe	38	39	40	41	42	43
UK/USA	15	15½	16	16½	17	17½

Men's Shoes

Aus/UK	7	8	9	10	11	12
Europe	41	42	43	44½	46	47
Japan	26	27	27½	28	29	30
USA	7½	8½	9½	10½	11½	12½

what many locals do and visit the department stores, like **La Rinascente** (p163) and **COIN** (p162). These don't necessarily carry many big label items, but you can often find quality clothing at reasonable prices. Another fun option is to explore the so-called 'stock houses', loaded with brand name cast-offs.

Heavy, cumbersome and fragile items (such as ceramics and some antiques) need to be shipped home. Many stores will take care of this for you and include the costs of shipping in the price. Ask before you buy, as shipping it yourself can be a pain. If you do find yourself with something that you need to ship, head for the **central post office** (Map pp244–5).

Opening Hours

In general, shops are open from about 9.30am to 7.30pm Monday to Saturday. Some close for a couple of hours at lunchtime, from around 1.30pm to 3.30pm. Some open only from 3.30pm on Monday, while a few may choose to close on Wednesday and/or Saturday afternoon. Laws on opening hours are fairly flexible, so shopkeepers exercise a large degree of personal discretion. Although the summer sales keep shops busy through July and into early August, many take off at least part of the latter month.

Department stores such as La Rinascente and COIN open longer hours and, often, on Sunday too.

PIAZZA DEL DUOMO & AROUND

You only need go a few steps from the grand cathedral to start spending your hard-earned cash on classic watches, fine food and ceramics.

ARTE CRETA Map pp244-5   Ceramics
☎ 055 28 43 41; Via del Proconsolo 63/r;
🚌 14, 23 & A
Elisabetta di Costanzo turns out original work, breaking with tradition in her use of predominantly green floral scenes on the majority of the objects for sale. They make a refreshing change from the usual stuff.

CALZOLERIA BOLOGNA Map pp244-5 Shoes
☎ 055 238 18 49; Via de' Cerretani 50/r;
🚌 1, 4, 6, 7, 10, 11, 12, 13, 14, 22, 23, 25, 36 & 37
Sneak inside here if you have a hankering for something different to attach to your feet. Classic styles in women's footwear are on show, but more intriguing are some of the crazier cuts. Try on the silver slippers and go to the ball, or step out in floral-motif boots. How much will you dare?

CARNICELLI
Map pp244-5   Photographic Equipment
☎ 055 21 43 52; Piazza del Duomo 4/r;
🚌 1, 6, 7, 10, 11, 14, 17, 23 & A
For serious photography needs, traditional and digital, you could try this camera emporium. It also provides the standard services.

EDISON Map pp244-5   Books
☎ 055 21 31 10; www.libreriaedison.it; Piazza della Repubblica 27/r; ⏰ 9am-midnight Mon-Sat, 10am-midnight Sun; 🚌 A
This place right on the Piazza boasts a grand array of Italian literature on Florence and Tuscany, plus some foreign-language books, all arranged over three floors. And it's open extra-long hours. Once you've made your purchase, head upstairs for a coffee while you look your new books over.

ENRICO VERITÀ Map pp244-5   Watches
☎ 055 28 78 62; Via de' Calzaiuoli 122/r; 🚌 A
This is one of the eight oldest watchmakers in all of Italy, and a wander around in here is a trip through time. Apart from selling a broad range of timepieces, from the most prestigious modern brands to antique items, the shop also specialises in repairs to just about any kind of ticker you care to bring in.

TOP FIVE SHOPPING AREAS

- **Antiques** Borgo Ognissanti and around (Map pp248–9).
- **Gold** Ponte Vecchio and around (Map pp244–5).
- **Designer Fashion** Via de' Tornabuoni and around (Map pp248–9) and outlets (p169).
- **Leather** Santa Croce (Map pp248–9).
- **Shoes** Borgo San Lorenzo and Oltrarno (Maps pp244–5 & pp248–9).

FRATELLI ROSSETTI Map pp244-5   Shoes
☎ 055 21 66 56; Piazza della Repubblica 43-45; 🚍 A
For one of the last words in classic elegant footwear, made to last a lifetime, you should have a browse here.

LA GALLERIA DEL CHIANTI
Map pp244-5   Wine
☎ 055 29 14 40; Via del Corso 41/r; 🚍 A
In spite of the name, this shop has on its shelves a selection of fine wines from all around Tuscany, as well as top-quality drops (such as Poli Grappa from Bassano del Grappa in the Veneto region) from other parts of the country.

LIBRERIA ANTIQUARIA GONNELLI
Map pp244-5   Antique Books
☎ 055 21 68 36; www.gonnelli.it;
Via Ricasoli 14/r; 🚍 C
One of the temples to old books and manuscripts in Florence, the Gonnelli business has been going since 1875. Step inside and see the ancient volumes stacked on the shelves, precious manuscripts on show and knowing clients discussing rare texts in hushed tones. It is as though time has stood still.

LUISA Map pp244-5   Clothes
☎ 055 21 78 26; www.luisaviaroma.com;
Via Roma 19-21/r; 🚍 A
For quality men's and women's clothing, of a none-too-daring but classic and self-assur cut, this is a regular stop on Florence's shopping circuit.

OFFICINE PANERAI Map pp244-5   Watches
☎ 055 21 57 95; Piazza San Giovanni 16/r;
🚍 1, 6, 7, 10, 11, 14, 17, 23 & A
This purveyor of watches has a special place in Italian hearts. The watches were first produced for Italy's navy divers in WWII. Nowadays the chunky nautical timepieces are collectors' items that can easily cost €3000. Upstairs from the store is a small archive with WWII photos of Italian navy commandos and their deadly (often for their crew) little manned torpedoes.

PEGNA Map pp244-5   Food & Drink
☎ 055 28 27 01; www.pegna.it;
Via dello Studio 26/r; 🚍 A
Pegna has an interesting selection of Tuscan wines and Italian produce, such as bottled

Adventurous footwear design (p158)

ribollita (vegetable stew). It's pricey though, so don't go buying your De Cecco pasta (which you can get in any supermarket) here.

RASPINI Map pp244-5   Clothes
☎ 055 21 30 77; www.raspini.com;
Via Roma 25-29/r; 🚍 A
A classic Florentine purveyor of fine footwear, with an enticing range of quality fashion for both sexes. They carry such designer names as Prada, Miu Miu and Armani. Now a prosperous chain across town, Raspini first got into business in 1965.

RICORDI MEDIASTORE Map pp244-5   Music
☎ 055 21 41 04; Via de' Brunelleschi 8/r; 🚍 A
This nationwide chain store is Italy's vague equivalent of Virgin or HMV. It stocks a solid range of Italian and international CDs and tapes, plus sheet music.

SERGIO ROSSI Map pp244-5   Shoes
☎ 055 29 48 73; Via Roma 15; 🚍 A
For women after footwear that's adventurous (but not outrageous), this is the place to visit. Extra pointy and impossibly high, the footwear can make a statement about the person attached to the feet in the shoes.

PIAZZA DELLA SIGNORIA & AROUND

A real mixed bag of shops are scattered around the medieval streets surrounding Piazza della Signoria. Everything from camera equipment, through food and wine, to jewellery and stationery wait to be discovered.

ARTPELL COKE Map pp244-5   Leather
☎ 055 239 66 60; Via dei Neri 25/r; 🚍 A
No, this place has nothing to do with beverages. Since 1938 they have been crafting handmade leather bags and other accessories in this unassuming little shop. It is well worth casting your eyes over the goods here.

BARTOLUCCI Map pp244-5   Crafts
☎ 055 21 17 73; www.bartolucci.com; Via della Condotta 12/r; 🚍 A
The Bartolucci clan use pine to create a remarkable range of toys, models and trinkets that may appeal as much to adults as to kids. How about a life-sized *motorino*, or a larger-than-life Pinocchio for the lounge room? This is one of two stores in Florence and several around the country.

BIZZARRI Map pp244-5   Herbs & Chemicals
☎ 055 21 15 89; Via della Condotta 32/r; 🚍 A
Bizzarri by name… Since 1842, the family has been in the business of flogging herbs, chemicals, potions and all sorts of other products. You are unlikely to want to buy anything here, but just peering in the windows is a trip into another century.

BOTTEGA DELL'OLIO
Map pp244-5   Olive Oil Products
☎ 055 267 04 68; Piazza del Limbo 2/r; 🚍 A
Only the best of central Italy's extra virgin olive oil arrives in this tiny store, tucked away in an equally tiny square. There are also aromatic oils, olive soap (the best imported from Aleppo, Syria) and balsamic vinegar.

CHEBÀ Map pp244-5   Ceramics
☎ 055 28 18 55; Via de' Cerchi 8/r; 🚍 A
There is no shortage of ceramic stores around central Florence, many purveying classic and antique (or antique-style) stuff that becomes a little laboured. Barbara and Cristina Chelazzi do their own thing: hand-painting plates, dishes and other objects

with bright, sunny Tuscan scenes – like a typical country house surrounded by fields of poppies, sunflowers or grapevines. Some items have a more impressionist look.

COIN Map pp244-5   Department Store
☎ 055 28 05 31; Via de' Calzaiuoli 56/r; 🚍 A
A slightly downmarket version of La Rinascente, this place is for the practical shopping most visitors probably won't need to do while in Florence. You could look at the clothes department; it's standard stuff, but the standards are Italian and you can find some quality gear at prices Marks & Spencer could not afford to consider.

ENOTECA ROMANO GAMBI
Map pp244-5   Food & Drink
☎ 055 29 26 46; Borgo SS Apostoli 21-23/r; 🚍 B
Selling quality foodstuffs and wine, this *enoteca* claims to have the 'best Tuscan biscuits', among a broad selection of other products ranging from olive oil to chocolate.

IL GATTO BIANCO Map pp244-5   Jewellery
☎ 055 28 29 89; Borgo dei SS Apostoli 12/r; 🚍 B
Get off the Ponte Vecchio and you can do better by your bank manager while searching for all that glistens. At the White Cat, an attractive back-street jewellery workshop, you can pick up all sorts of wonderful and affordable jewellery. Contemporary designs incorporate gold, silver and semiprecious stones.

LANZO CAFFÈ Map pp244-5   Food & Drink
☎ 055 29 08 34; Via dei Neri 69/r; 🚍 B
This shop offers a mix of attractively packaged foodstuffs, such as *panforte* ('strong bread', made of almonds, candied fruit, spices and honey) and various regional products like honey – as well as a wine selection from Tuscany and beyond.

DON'T DO THE CRIME IF YOU CAN'T PAY THE FINE

Florence, along with several other Italian municipalities, is getting tough on the sale of fake name-brand accessories on the streets. Rather than continually chasing the poor and generally illegal migrants who sell contraband Gucci bags and Ferragamo sunglasses, the city has switched its attention to those who cheerfully buy the fakes. If you're caught in the act, fines run from €3300 to €10,000!

TAKING STOCK

Vertigo-inducing prices can take the fun out of fashion. But, if you can't afford the name shops and can't be bothered heading out of town to the discount outlets, you do have another option. Lots of fallen-off-the-back-of-a-rack clothing is crammed into so-called stockhouses, rag-trade stores stuffed to the rafters with all sorts of goodies in generally disorderly fashion. Finding something you like can take a time but that can be part of the fun. Some handy stores include the following.

Stockhouse Il Giglio (Map pp242–3; ☎ 055 21 75 96; Borgo Ognissanti 86/r; 🚌 A) Cheap is a relative term in Florence, but you can pick up some interesting men's and women's fashion items here, and occasionally turn up some genuine bargains. Name labels can come in at a considerable discount. Florentines consider it one of the best stockhouses for picking up labelled items at off-the-back-of-a-lorry rates.

Stockhouse Il Guardaroba (Map pp248–9; ☎ 055 234 02 71; Via Giuseppe Verdi 28/r; 🚌 14, 23 & A) Across town, this is another spot worth dropping by, although the range is not as great. The place is arranged more like a standard fashion boutique than a higgledy-piggledy threads lucky dip.

Stockhouse One Price (Map pp248–9; ☎ 055 28 46 74; Borgo Ognissanti 74/r; 🚌 A) Although more densely stocked (in a smaller space) than the others, the idea basically remains the same.

LA RINASCENTE Map pp244-5 Department Store
☎ 055 239 85 44; www.rinascente.it; Piazza della Repubblica 1; 🚌 A
The prince of Italian department stores, the Florence branch is rather modest but worth a look around for fashion, perfumes and similar items. Check out their rooftop café while you're there too.

LUCA DELLA ROBBIA Map pp244-5 Ceramics
☎ 055 28 35 32; Via del Proconsolo 19/r; 🚌 14, 23 & A
Since the end of the 19th century this shop, with the famous surname, has been creating handmade reproductions of *robbiane* (terracotta medallions) and other Renaissance and classical ceramics. They also offer a broad range of more general pottery. The shop occupies what is thought to have been a 15th-century sculptor's workshop in the Badia Fiorentina complex.

MANETTI & MASINI Map pp244-5 Ceramics
☎ 055 21 22 54; Borgo SS Apostoli 45/r; 🚌 B
Since 1948 this classic ceramic store has been producing top-quality porcelain, specialising in reproduction antique majolica and restoring the genuine articles. Tucked away just off chic Via de' Tornabuoni, you could easily miss it.

PINEIDER Map pp244-5 Paper & Stationery
☎ 055 28 46 55; www.anticheofficinepineider.it; Piazza della Signoria 13/r; 🚌 B
Purveyors of paper and related products, Pineider has been in business since 1774.

The shop is housed in what was the seat of one of the city's most important medieval guilds, the Arte di Calimala. In an age where handwriting is a rapidly dying art, the store has extended its range into all sorts of quality office materials. Among the customers to have wandered in for a browse here are Lord Byron and Stendhal.

PUSATERI Map pp244-5 Gloves
☎ 055 21 41 92; Via de' Calzaiuoli 25/r; 🚌 A
Chic leather gloves in an array of colours, ranging from the vaguely loud and pastel to more subdued hues, will have ladies dreaming it is winter again.

VANNUCCHI Map pp244-5 Paper
☎ 055 21 67 52; Via della Condotta 26-28/r; 🚌 A
Via della Condotta was long known as the paper-vendors' street in Florence, and at this historic shop they know a thing or too about the business. Apart from quality writing materials (pens and other accessories) you can splash out on high quality gift-wrapping paper, stationery and *carta fiorentina* (Florentine paper, with floral motifs).

VETTORI Map pp244-5 Gold & Jewellery
☎ 055 28 20 30; Ponte Vecchio 37/r; 🚌 B, C & D
This is one of the big names weighing down the Ponte Vecchio with its treasure chests of gold. You can order pieces to be handcrafted here, but be aware that none of the Ponte Vecchio stores is a workshop any more – they buy and sell the stuff, while generally having the work done elsewhere.

SANTA MARIA NOVELLA & AROUND

The area between the basilica and the Arno is a particularly rich retail hunting ground. Via de' Tornabuoni is at the heart of high-fashion shopping, and all the favourite names cluster here. Inject a little variety by checking out the purveyors of classy leather goods, antiques and gourmet snacks, and browse a couple of good bookshops.

BIAGIOTTI Map pp244-5   Art Gallery
☎ 055 21 47 57; www.artbiagiotti.com; Via delle Belle Donne 39/r; 🚌 A
For truly adventurous art exhibitions, this place – tucked away in a street named after the one-time trade in pearly-hawking that went on here – is well worth checking out.

BM BOOKSHOP Map pp248-9   Books
☎ 055 29 45 75; Borgo Ognissanti 4/r; 🚌 A
This bookshop claims to have the broadest range of English language books in town, and it may be right. You can find a fair spread of books on Florence and Tuscany, as well as fiction and speciality books on art.

Leather goods at Florentine market stall (p167)

BOJOLA Map pp244-5   Leather
☎ 055 21 11 55; www.bojola.it; Via de' Rondinelli 25/r; 🚌 6, 11, 22, 36, 37 & A
For more than 150 years, Bojola has been turning out high-quality items for the discerning lover of animal hides. From classic belts and wallets (which start at around €40) to classy travel bags, this is one of Florence's top stops in the search for fine leather gifts.

CESARE PACIOTTI Map pp244-5   Shoes
☎ 055 21 54 71; Via della Vigna Nuova 14/r; 🚌 6 & A
Although a few pairs of men's shoes sneak in here, the bulk of the show is a ladies-only affair. Classic footwear, that knows no fashion fade, sits alongside funkier gear that will put a spring in your step but might look silly in a couple of years' time.

COLTELLERIA BIANDA Map pp248-9   Knives
☎ 055 29 46 91; Via della Vigna Nuova 86/r; 🚌 6 & A
The Bianda family has been selling one thing or another at this end of the street since 1820, but the knife speciality really only took off in the early 1900s. The shop remains pretty much as it was when it was given an overhaul in the 1930s.

DESMO Map pp244-5   Leather
☎ 055 29 23 95; Piazza de' Rucellai 10; 🚌 6 & A
For those with a full wallet, and perhaps the desire to replace it with a new one, this is a good address for leather accessories. It has a range of clothes on offer as well.

EMILIO PUCCI Map pp244-5   Clothes
☎ 055 265 80 82; Via de' Tornabuoni 20-22; 🚌 6, 11, 22, 36, 37 & A
The marquis Emilio Pucci is a Florentine aristocrat and jet-set clothes designer who was big in the 1960s and bounced back in the 1990s. He keeps his *haute couture* stuff at home but for his 1960s-revisited psychedelic colours, pop into the shop. Just looking at his women's fashions and accessories (anything from swimwear to umbrellas) will make you think you've dropped acid.

ERMANNO SCERVINO Map pp244-5   Clothes
☎ 055 260 87 14; Piazza degli Antinori 10/r; 🚌 6 & A
Scervino hit the big time in the mid-1990s with a youthful, plugged-in approach to fashion. The options swing broadly, from high-class grunge (designer jeans that hang

THE FERRAGAMOS' FLUCTUATING FORTUNES

Born in 1898 outside Naples, Salvatore Ferragamo made his first pair of shoes for his sister's first communion at the age of nine. Four years later he was in charge of a shoe shop with six workers.

Ferragamo, hoping for bigger things, moved to the USA in 1914. After a brief stint in Boston with his brothers, he headed to Hollywood, where he started designing for the film industry – everything from Egyptian sandals to cowboy boots. From there it was a short step to making footwear for the stars when they were off the screen, and he began to build up an elite clientele, from Mary Pickford to John Barrymore.

Back in Italy in the early 1930s, Ferragamo set up a 'factory' in Via Mannelli in Florence, with 60 employees all making certain parts of the shoes by hand. Ferragamo designed and created the shoes in Florence and sold them in the USA. But the Great Depression hit and brought bankruptcy in 1933. He was soon back in business though, and patented the cork wedge in 1936.

Two years later Ferragamo bought the Palazzo Spini-Ferroni on Via de' Tornabuoni, where he had already moved his shop. By the 1950s he had 700 employees producing 350 pairs of shoes per day, entirely by hand. Everyone from Audrey Hepburn to Sophia Loren was wearing Ferragamo's designs.

Salvatore died in 1960 and the business passed to his wife, Wanda, and then Fiamma, their eldest daughter. Under Fiamma the company expanded into accessories and by the time she died in 1998, it had a turnover of more than US$500 million. The family later launched a line in children's fashion and opened flagship stores in Tokyo and New York's Fifth Avenue.

Back in the heartland, the empire took fashion into the hotel business, opening a series of Florence's hippest designer digs (see p175).

around the lower end of your buttocks) to other lines that the designer says are influenced by his globe-trotting experiences.

SALVATORE FERRAGAMO

Map pp244-5   Fashion, Shoes & Accessories
☎ 055 29 21 23; www.salvatoreferragamo.it;
Via de' Tornabuoni 14/r; 🚌 6, 11, 36, 37 & A
Another grand Florentine name (see the boxed text, above), the one-time shoe specialists now turn out a range of clothes and accessories for the serious fashion aficionado: man, woman or child. You can even order shoes to suit your taste, selecting the material (crocodile hide?) to style yourself! It also has a curious shoe museum – see p81.

GUCCI Map pp244-5   Clothes
☎ 055 26 40 11; www.gucci.com; Via de' Tornabuoni 73/r; 🚌 6, 11, 22, 36, 37 & A
Only the name remains of the great Florentine fashion house. Of course the soap-opera family saga has put a lot of spice into Gucci (see the boxed text, p14), but the fashion-conscious take little notice and just keep on buying. The Japanese especially can be seen lining up to pay homage.

IL BISONTE Map pp244-5   Leather
☎ 055 21 57 22; Via del Parione 31/r; 🚌 A
Here the concentration is on accessories, ranging from elegant bags in natural leather to distinguished desktop items, leather-bound notebooks, briefcases etc.

LIBRAIRIE FRANÇAISE Map pp248-9   Books
☎ 055 21 26 59; http://users.libero.it/libfranflorence; Piazza d'Ognissanti 1/r; 🚌 A
Housed within the city's French cultural institute, this is easily the best place for French texts, with a range of books on Florence and Tuscany and a welter of Gallic prose.

L'IPPOGRIFO Map pp244-5   Books
☎ 055 29 08 05; Via della Vigna Nuova 5/r; 🚌 6 & A
Lovers of old and rare books, maps and manuscripts should mosey around here. You may not want to buy, but the place is laden with curios redolent of other, less frenetic times.

LORETTA CAPONI Map pp244-5   Clothes
☎ 055 21 36 68; Piazza degli Antinori 4/r; 🚌 6, 11, 22, 36, 37 & A
If nothing is too good for your infant or small child, this is your store. It sells exquisite small persons' (particularly girls') clothing (and a few things for big people too), some of it finely embroidered. Your three-year-old may not fully appreciate it, but rest assured; they will be dressed to impress when they leave here.

Shopping

SANTA MARIA NOVELLA & AROUND

OFFICINA PROFUMO FARMACEUTICA DI SANTA MARIA NOVELLA

Map pp242-3   Pharmacy & Perfumes

☎ 055 21 62 76; Via della Scala 16; 🚍 11, 36, 37 & A

This ancient pharmacy, set up by Domini-can monks in the 13th century, opened to the public in the 17th century. When Napoleon confiscated Church property early in the 19th century, the business went into private hands, in which it has contin-ued to prosper. All sorts of traditional and herbal potions, made to recipes handed down by the monks right through to the present owners, treat everything from sore feet to bad breath. Need any *amamelide* (witch hazel) or *iperico* (St John's Wort)? Extract of heliotrope? This is the place for you. From the entrance you pass through a long hall to the 'pharmacy', a magnificent room with a high vaulted and frescoed ceiling. Here you may buy mainly essences and perfumes. Pass on to the *erboristeria* (natural medicine shop), which backs onto the cloister of the Basilica di Santa Maria Novella, for your herbal remedies.

PARENTI Map pp244-5   Jewellery

☎ 055 21 44 38; Via de' Tornabuoni 93/r; 🚍 6, 11, 22, 36, 37 & A

Since 1855 the Parenti clan has steered this exclusive store down the decades, provid-ing Florence's high and mighty with jewel-lery, silverware and gift items. The Italian royal family and Italian aristocrats would often seek out unusual and one-off pieces here. You can emulate them today.

PROCACCI Map pp244-5   Food & Drink

☎ 055 21 16 56; Via de' Tornabuoni 64/r; 🚍 6, 11, 22, 36, 37 & A

Come to nibble and sip (see p131) or buy some stuff to take away, from fine Tuscan wines to homemade honey and jams. The star is the truffle. You can obtain white truffles here in season or content yourself with a *panino tartufato* (little bread roll with truffle spread).

ROBERTO CAVALLI Map pp244-5   Clothes

☎ 055 239 62 26; www.robertocavalli.net; Via de' Tornabuoni 83/r; 🚍 6, 11, 22, 36, 37 & A

Housed in the noble Palazzo Viviani, this is a temple to edgy men's and women's fash-ion. Cavalli has a penchant for jungle safari décor, evident in this flagship store and

in the Café Giacosa by Roberto Cavalli (Via della Spada 10/r; 🕒 7.30am to 11pm Monday to Saturday), a shoppers' café he runs next door. The fashion is young and unabashed: men's suits that look suitable for a Star Trek trip, with green crocodile-leather jackets, and flowing, on-the-hip threads for her.

SHOWROOM FRATELLI ALINARI

Map pp244-5   Photography, Old Prints & Books

☎ 055 2 39 51; www.alinari.com; Largo Fratelli Alinari 15; 🚍 4, 12, 25 & 33

Head down the arcaded lane to get to the showroom of Florence's fathers of photog-raphy. The Alinari brothers got the world's first photographic store up and running in 1852. Today you can get a hold of grand coffee-table books featuring photos of 19th-century Florence and other locations around Italy. It also stocks wonderful prints. This same dynasty is behind the creation of the city's new Museo della Storia della Fotografia (see p81), and you may want to call by here after visiting the museum.

SAN LORENZO

The main shopping attractions here are the stands set up just outside the basilica. If you dare, bargain for a leather jacket of potentially dubious origins and quality, or just have fun watching others haggle. A couple of interest-ing speciality stores are worth checking out.

CAVUROTTO ARGENTERIA

Map pp244-5   Silverware & Jewellery

☎ 055 21 31 95; Via Cavour 26-28/r; 🚍 1, 6, 7, 10, 11 & 17

The location has been home to a store since as early as the 18th century but this, one of the city's senior names in the silver busi-ness, has been going since 1919. Nothing much has changed since then, when the town's aristocracy and Jewish community converged here for their silver needs – even the Savoy royal family shopped here.

CECCHERINI & CO

Map pp242-3   Musical Instruments

☎ 055 21 00 31; Via de' Ginori 31/r; 🚍 1, 6, 7, 10, 11, 14, 17, 23 & A

Florentines with a musical bent converge on this classic store in search of guitars and most other imaginable instruments. You can also just pick up some replacement strings.

DREONI Map pp244-5   Toys
☎ 055 21 66 11; Via Cavour 33/r;
🚌 1, 6, 7, 10, 11, 14, 17, 23 & A

Florence's leading toy store ain't exactly Manhattan's FAO Schwarz, but it's full of fun stuff for kids and also has models that seem to attract just as many adults (well, blokes).

FELTRINELLI INTERNATIONAL
Map pp244-5   Books
☎ 055 21 95 24; Via Cavour 12/r;
🚌 1, 6, 7, 10, 11, 14, 17, 23 & A

This place has a good selection of books in English, French, German, Spanish, Portuguese and Russian, as well as a reasonable travel section and plenty of Italian literature.

JOHNSONS & RELATIVES STAMPERIA
TOSCANA Map pp242-3   Paper
☎ 055 21 16 50; Via Cavour 25;
🚌 1, 6, 7, 10, 11, 114, 17, 23 & A

For a high-quality selection of paper products, it's hard to go past this long-established Florentine company with the oh-so English name. Along with common stationery items you can browse for hand-decorated paper, books, photo albums and other items covered in decorated paper.

SAN MARCO
There's not a lot of serious shopping action in this part of town, although we have picked one exception to prove that rule!

STEFANO ALINARI
Map pp242-3   Gold & Jewellery
☎ 055 28 49 96; Via San Zanobi 24/r;
🚌 1, 6, 7, 10, 11, 14, 17, 23 & A

Mr Alinari is a craftsman in the old mould. He creates his pieces with all the temperament of a great sculptor and the results are often extraordinary.

SANTA CROCE
Traditionally the heart of Florence's leather production, Santa Croce is also home to other curious shops. This is a good part of town to hunt out books in English too.

MILLING IN MARKETS

Florence has many markets. The daily displays of **San Lorenzo** (Map pp244–5; Piazza San Lorenzo; 🕙 9am-7.30pm Tue-Sat; bus 4, 11, 12, 25, 31, 32 & 33) and **Il Mercato Nuovo** (Mercato del Porcellino, or 'Piglet's Market'; Map pp244–5; 🕙 8am-7pm Tue-Sat; 🚌 A) are the most visible in town, and the curious but uncommitted shopper can enjoy a rather tacky browse at either, any day of the week. Next to the predictable stocks of cheap (and sometimes nasty) leather gear are phalanxes of tourist tat and other far-from-useful paraphernalia. To get the feel for a real Florentine market, you need to look elsewhere.

Mercato Centrale (Map pp242–3; Piazza del Mercato Centrale; 🕙 7am-2pm Mon-Fri, 7am-2pm & 4-8pm Sat; 🚌 4, 11, 12, 25, 31, 32 & 33) This, the main daily-produce market, is under cover in the 19th-century market hall. Outside are spread the clothes, leather and tourist-tat stalls of the San Lorenzo market. For more information, see p92.

Mercato dei Pulci (Map pp248–9; Piazza dei Ciompi; 🕙 10am-7pm Thu-Sun; 🚌 A & C) This flea market is where the townsfolk gather to poke about amid the mountains of junk and bric-a-brac that every self-respecting household should be able to cough up sooner or later. From antique furniture to ancient comic books, all sorts of jumble turns up here. It's fun for a browse and occasionally you'll find genuinely interesting little items.

Mercato dell'Antiquariato (Map pp248–9; Piazza Santo Spirito; 🕙 2nd Sun of the month; 🚌 D) A cheerful little antiques market with all sorts of odds and ends is held in this delightful square.

Mercato delle Cascine (Map pp240–1; Le Cascine, Viale Abramo Lincoln; 🕙 8am-noon Tue; 🚌 B) This is Florence's only all-in-one market. Sufficiently far from the city centre to put most tourists off, it specialises in knock-down clothes and fabrics, along with other household products and a modest produce section. Some Florentines come here in search of bargains.

Mercato di Sant'Ambrogio (Map pp248–9; Piazza Ghiberti; 🕙 8am-2pm Mon-Sat; 🚌 C) Buzzy and without the tourist-tat element, this produce market is the best place to do your daily hunting for fresh products, from fruit and veg to all sorts of local cheeses, sausages and other goodies.

ANDREINI Map pp248-9 — Ceramics
☎ 055 234 08 23; Borgo degli Albizi 63/r; 🚍 A
A century ago the statues and ceramics crafted here adorned the gardens of Tuscan nobility. Even today you'd need a lot of money to afford most of the work on show in this workshop-gallery. It is tempting to imagine that in this kind of place lies the heritage of the great Renaissance sculptors' workshops. For those eager to add a special touch to their houses, this is where to come for a fine copy of a David or Venus. If nothing else, it is worth dropping by for a browse in this wonderful relic of another epoch.

FILISTRUCCHI Map pp248-9 — Masks & Theatre
☎ 055 234 49 01; Via Giuseppe Verdi 9; 🚍 14, 23 & A
Need a wig or other theatrical devices? This has been the place to come for masks and theatre accessories since the early 18th century. In the 1720s, when it opened, it was a barber's and make-up shop in one, but gradually specialised in make-up and wigs for the theatre. It is one of Florence's oldest stores to have kept in constant business.

ITALIANLOVES Map pp248-9 — Wine & Olive Oil
☎ 055 200 11 92; Via de' Pepi 4-6/r; 🚍 C
Lurking just off the bustling Piazza di Santa Croce, this long gallery of a shop sells a good selection of Tuscan farm products, but above all wine and olive oil. Out the back you can taste both products before making a purchase. The same shop also runs an Internet service.

LIBRERIA DELLE DONNE
Map pp248-9 — Books
☎ 055 24 03 84; Via Fiesolana 2/b; 🚍 14, 23 & A
Florence's main women's bookshop is also something of a lesbian info centre. Most of the literature is in Italian, but you may find the listings on the notice board useful.

MCRAE BOOKS Map pp248-9 — Books
☎ 055 238 24 56; www.mcraebooks.com; Via dei Neri 32/r; 🕙 9am-7.30pm; 🚍 B
A great and well-stocked English-language bookshop, just a stone's throw from Piazza della Signoria. A relative newcomer to the English-language bookshop scene in Florence, it has the distinct advantage on Sundays too. So, if you feel like a lie in and a read on the Lord's day of rest, no problem!

PAPERBACK EXCHANGE Map pp242-3 Books
☎ 055 247 81 54; www.papex.it; Via Fiesolana 31/r; 🕙 Mon-Sat; 🚍 C
This is the place to track down bargains in English. The store has a vast selection of new and secondhand books in English, including classics, contemporary literature, reference, bestsellers and travel guides.

PERUZZI Map pp248-9 — Leather
☎ 055 28 90 39; www.peruzzispa.com; Borgo de' Greci 8-20/r; 🚍 14, 23 & A
This barnlike leather emporium has been selling everything from cheap accessories to high-quality shoes since the end of WWII. Its sheer size alone makes it an interesting one-stop leather shop, even if you're only browsing for an idea of prices. It also carries name-brand accessories.

Pineider stationery shop (p163)

OUTLETS FOR YOUR EVERY DESIRE...

Have you got champagne tastes on a beer budget? If you want the high-fashion look of central Florence without the price tag, you may be able to satisfy your modish retail cravings if you flee the metropolis. Southeast of Florence are clustered several discount outlets for big names in fashion. These basically sell off last year's fashion at more reasonable prices than you can hope to find in their Florence stores. The ranges are not always wonderful, but you can come away with bargains on name goods. The phenomenon has grown over the years and you can find information on the following and more on www.outlet-firenze.com.

Dolce & Gabbana (☎ 055 833 13 00; Località Santa Maria Maddalena, Via Piana dell'Isola 49, Rignano sull'Arno; ⏰ 9am-7pm Mon-Sat, 3-7pm Sun) Mostly interesting for accessories, it is really only worth coming here if you have your own transport, as it is close to The Mall (see below). In itself, it does not warrant the effort from Florence if you are relying on public transport. Less than 1km south of Leccio, turn right and you arrive at a T-junction, on your left is a long building with no signs whatsoever: this is the Dolce & Gabbana outlet. If you do want to do it by public transport, catch a train to Rignano sull'Arno, and from there it is about 4km south (see the directions for Fendi below). About 1km north, at Via Pian dell'Isola 66, is an outlet store for **Celine** and **Loewe** (☎ 055 834 71 55).

Prada (Map p186; ☎ 055 9 19 01; Località Levanella, Montevarchi; ⏰ 9.30am-7pm Mon-Sat, 3-7pm Sun) This outlet, although set in an industrial estate just outside the village of Levanella, has the elegance of a high-street store with a café and taxis waiting. It's best for women's accessories and classic suits for men. The women's clothing can be disappointing and mostly comes in small sizes. A queuing ticket system operates, so you may find yourself waiting in line. By car you could follow the SS69 south from Leccio (see The Mall below) to Montevarchi (28km). As you edge south through this sprawling town you will enter Levanella (no signs and virtually soldered onto Montevarchi), whose southern end is an industrial estate. Turn left at Via Levanella Becorpi and pass the warehouses to the car park at the end of the street. If you pass under the rail bridge on the SS69, you have overshot the turn-off by a few hundred metres. Alternatively, if you want to come here direct from Florence, take the A1 motorway and exit at Montevarchi. From the exit it's 7km to the outlet, following the same directions. Otherwise take an Arezzo-bound train from Florence, get off at Montevarchi and grab a cab.

Roberto Cavalli (☎ 055 31 77 54; www.robertocavallioutlet.it; Via Volturno 3, Osmannoro; ⏰ 10am-7pm Mon-Fri, 10am-4pm Sat) This features all the best in the previous season's men's and women's fashion, and has a range of tempting accessories. Bus 29 runs from the train station in Florence to Via Volturno in Osmanoro. If driving from central Florence, head for the A1 motorway (Firenze Nord) and keep an eye out for the Sesto Fiorentino exit, and then follow signs to Osmannoro.

The Mall (☎ 055 865 77 75; Via Europa 8, Leccio Reggello; ⏰ 10am-7pm Mon-Sat, 3-7pm Sun) Gucci leads the way at this mixed-bag emporium, by far the most serious of the outlets and looking more like a regular fashion store. Gucci accessories, from belts and bags to shoes and sunglasses, are well worth sifting through. Also represented here are Agnona, Ermenegildo Zegna, Tod's, Yves Saint Laurent, Sergio Rossi, Armani, Ferragamo, Valentino, Loro Piana and Bottega Veneta. Clothes tend to be from the previous season but can be incredibly good value. Check out the Armani suits. Take a train to Rignano sull'Arno and then it's a 10-minute taxi ride. The Mall also runs a daily shuttle bus from Florence (€25 return) – call to book; they can pick you up at most hotels or from other points in central Florence. A public bus service (€2.60 each way; 9am & 12.30pm, Mon-Fri, 9am Sat) runs from the SITA bus station, returning at noon and 5pm. If driving, take the SS69 east out of Florence, following the signs for Arezzo. The Mall and its car park are off to the right as you enter the village of Leccio. If coming from the south, you'll see it signposted. It's about a 40-minute drive from Florence (depending on traffic).

SCUOLA DEL CUOIO Map pp248-9 Leather
☎ 055 24 45 33; www.leatherschool.it;
Piazza di Santa Croce 16; ⏰ 9.30am-6pm Mon-Sat,
10am-6pm Sun; 🚍 C
If you're lucky you will see apprentices beavering away at some hide here. It is also not a bad place to get some measure of the quality-price ratio, and the products are good (and only sold here). The Franciscans decided to set up and house the school in 1950, at a time when the lads of Santa Croce were hungry for any work they could get. Access is via the Basilica di Santa Croce, or through an entrance behind the basilica at Via di San Giuseppe 5/r.

OLTRARNO
Wandering around on the south bank of the river, you can't help but be charmed by the small boutiques and, particularly around Borgo San Frediano, the craftsmen's

workshops. In these modest and seemingly half-hidden spots you can come across anything from fine gold jewellery to top-quality handcrafted shoes.

ALESSANDRO DARI Map pp248-9 Jewellery
☎ 055 24 47 47; Via San Niccolò 115/r; 🚌 12, 13, 23 & C

This master craftsman turns out remarkable castellated rings and some (at times) rather over-the-top pieces of jewellery that not everyone would dare to don. However, the quality of the handiwork is high.

FRANCESCO DA FIRENZE
Map pp248-9 Shoes
☎ 055 21 24 28; Via di Santo Spirito 62/r; 🚌 D

If only every shoemaker made shoes this way. Handstitched leather is the key to this tiny family business. You should expect to pay a fair amount for your footwear here, but the investment will pay off as your shoes and sandals will be made to your specifications.

LA BOTTEGA DI LEONARDO
Map pp244-5 Crafts
☎ 055 21 75 05; Via de' Guicciardini 45/r; 🚌 D

This compact shop sells odds and ends aimed at the passing tourist trade, but the kids might be interested in the Leokits – unique wooden models of some of Leonardo da Vinci's wacky inventions.

MADOVA Map pp244-5 Gloves
☎ 055 239 65 26; www.madova.com; Via de' Guicciardini 1/r; 🚌 D

Dreaming of an elegant pair of leather gloves? Well, this place has been putting style on customers' hands since 1919. The gloves come in all sorts of colours and styles, are lined with anything from cashmere to silk, and are priced from €40 to €250.

MARSILI'S Map pp244-5 Chess Sets
☎ 055 264 54 88; Borgo San Jacopo 23/b; 🚌 D

Toss out your old magnetic chess set and indulge in a luxury game with characters from the Crusades for pieces, or perhaps Florentine mercenaries are more your thing? Or jump to the 21st century for modern metallic pieces and other imaginative options.

STEFANO BEMER Map pp248-9 Shoes
☎ 055 22 25 58; www.stefanobemer.it; Borgo San Frediano 143/r; 🚌 6 & D

Want handmade shoes to fit you fit like a glove? This could be the place if you have €1000 or so for the job. They will make a model of your feet (the *forma*) and then choose the materials to create a shoe to your taste and specifications. It all takes quite a while – you mustn't rush a craftsman!

STILE BIOLOGICO Map pp244-5 Clothes
☎ 055 277 62 75; www.organic-wear.it; Via dello Sprone 25/r; 🚌 C &D

The sprouts of a new fashion for the 21st century, where classy organic-food lovers will feel at home, have blossomed in this Florence store. Cotton, linen, wool and other natural materials are all guaranteed organically produced. In other words, the white, cream and beige threads that dominate have been untouched by pesticides. Buy right-on clothes with right-on attitude.

BEYOND CENTRAL FLORENCE

Beyond what were once the walls that held in the medieval city of Florence, now stretches the contemporary city's urban sprawl – a world of modern supermarkets and convenience stores. As a rule you will have little need or wish to reach out here for your shopping needs, but one or two options might grab your attention.

SPAZIO MULTICULTURALE
Map pp248-9 Ethnic Market
Lungarno G Pecori Giraldi; 🚌 8, 12, 14, 31, 32, 33 & 80

Set up in an attempt to clear central Florence of some of its many street vendors, and put a lid on the conflict that had arisen between them, the police and local residents, this ethnic market on the banks of the Arno is now the place to come for an orderly browse of all those African carvings, North African fabrics and similar objects you might find in your local *souq*.

Sleeping

Sleeping

Accommodation Styles

The city has hundreds of hotels in all categories and teems with alternatives, including hostels and private rooms. There are about 170 one- and two-star hotels in Florence, and countless smaller operations, so even in peak season it is generally possible to find a *camera* (room).

Azienda di Promozione Turistica (APT; www.firenzeturismo.it;) has branches in **Central Florence** (Map pp244–5; ☎ 055 29 08 32; Via Cavour 1/r; ☒ 8.30am-6.30pm Mon-Sat, 8.30am-1.30pm Sun & holidays) and **Amerigo Vespucci airport** (Map p238; ☎ 055 31 58 74; Via del Termine II; ☒ 7.30am-11.30pm). It has a list of houses and apartments offering B&B accommodation, an option rapidly growing in popularity. In general these places only offer a handful of rooms; they can, however, be a homelier and cheaper alternative to hotels. There's also **Bed & Breakfast Italia** (www.bbitalia.it), a nationwide network that has more than 50 listings for Florence; prices range from €45 for a single to €120 for a double. Look also at the **Associazione Bed & Breakfast Affittacamere** (AB&BA; ☎ 055 654 08 60; www.abbafirenze.it). Another option is the *affittacamere* (room rental), basically the same deal in private houses but without breakfast.

You'll find all sorts of *albergo* (hotel), from straightforward midrange places to carefully crafted boutique numbers, centuries-old mansions and a sprinkling of unashamedly modern design digs. Some in the Oltrarno area have more the air of country villas. There's more of the latter around Fiesole and beyond the city limits.

A *pensione* is generally a simpler, family-run establishment. The growing number of B&Bs is hard to distinguish from the average *pensione* as they are also generally family operations. Officially, to be considered a hotel or *pensione* and so star rated, a place must have more than seven rooms. Thus there are many tiny B&Bs that are good but have no star rating.

Hotels and *pensioni* are concentrated in three areas: near Stazione di Santa Maria Novella, near Piazza di Santa Maria Novella and in the old city between the Duomo and the Arno. Budget travellers have the choice of several youth hostels.

If you head out into the country you will also encounter *agriturismo* (country homestays), in which you stay on rural properties that may or may not still function as farms.

Many hotels boast parking but few actually offer it onsite. More often than not they have a discount deal with a nearby garage, but it can still be a costly addition – €20 to €35 per day.

Check-in & Check-out Times

Hotels do not hold rooms indefinitely. Always confirm your arrival, especially if it's going to be late in the afternoon or evening. Generally there is no problem if you have paid a deposit or left a credit card number. While you can check in at any time of the morning, you may not get access to your room until after noon, when it has been vacated and cleaned.

Check-out time is generally noon, although some places can be a little draconian and set a leaving time of 11am, or even 10am (rare)! Technically, if you overstay you can be charged for another night.

Price Ranges

Even in the low season, you're unlikely to pay less than €45/70 for a *singola/doppia* (single/double) without private bathroom. In the high season, only a handful of cheapies offer such prices. Expect to pay €80 to €130 for a good budget double in high season, sometimes with bathroom (which often means shower, washbasin and toilet). For good midrange places you can be looking at €150/200 for a *singola/doppia*. We have included some 'cheap sleeps' in this chapter, by which we mean places where you pay less than €70/100 for a single/double in high season.

Many places, especially at the lower end, offer triples and quads that work out cheaper per head if there are more of you than fits the standard *singola/doppia* arrangement. A *doppia* usually means two single beds. If you want a cosy bed for two, ask for a *matrimoniale*.

Lone travellers are penalised; most hotels have few, if any, single rooms, and such rooms are often rather poky. Alternatively, you may be offered a double at two-thirds to three-quarters of the price two people would pay.

Breakfast is often included, whether you want it or not. It can range from a simple continental affair to a varied buffet in the better hotels.

Some hotels post the same prices year-round, while others drop them when business slows. High season for those hotels that lift their prices starts in Easter and fizzles out by mid-October (many dip in the hot months of July and, especially, August, as much as halving rack rates).

The prices in this chapter are a high-season guide. Rooms come with private bathroom (which often means a shower and not a full bathtub) unless otherwise stated.

Reservations

Book ahead in high season (Easter to mid-July, September to October, Christmas and New Year periods). Weekends (especially Friday and Saturday nights) are the toughest. The hottest months (mid-July to the end of August) tend to go quieter because the Italian tourist quotient heads for the beaches and hills rather than sweltering in places like Florence, making reservations less important.

Longer-Term Rentals

To rent an apartment in Florence, save your pennies and, if you can, start looking before you arrive. Although locals are renting out more and more apartments to short-term guests (weekly), it can still be a tricky business. If you are staying long-term and looking for a normal rental contract, a one-room studio with kitchenette in the city centre will generally cost around €600 to €800 a month. You are unlikely to find a room in a shared student household for less than €250 a month.

Florence & Abroad (Map pp242–3; ☎ 055 48 70 04; www.florenceandabroad.com; Via San Zanobi 58) specialises in short- and medium-term rental accommodation for those with a liberal budget. **In Florence** (www.inflorence.co.uk) has small flats starting at around €1000 a month. **Rental In Florence** (www.rental-in-florence.com) has a greater range of flats on offer, but they tend to be more than €600 a week.

If you decide while in Florence that you want to stay, look for rental ads in advert rags such as *La Pulce* (three times per week) and the weekly *Il Mercato della Toscana*. You'll find few ads for shared accommodation, though.

For shared housing, check out schools frequented by foreigners where you can put up your own ad or hopefully find some likely candidates to share with. Other places to look for ads include English bookshops, Internet cafés, laundrettes and faculty buildings of the Università degli Studi di Firenze (Map pp242–3).

Those planning to stay for a week or more either in Florence or the surrounding countryside could consider renting an apartment or villa.

HOTEL ASSOCIATIONS

The following organisations can book you into member hotels. They usually offer a fair range of possibilities, but rarely drop below two stars.

- **Florence Promhotels** (☎ 055 55 39 41, 800 86 60 22; www.promhotels.it) With this service you can book a wide range of hotels online, customising your choice by checking off special requirements.
- **Gente di Toscana** (☎ 0575 52 92 75; www.genteditoscana.it) A comprehensive listing of B&Bs in Tuscany.
- **Inphonline** (☎ 800 00 87 77; www.initalia.it; 9am-7pm Mon-Sat) This phone and online booking service operates countrywide and is free. You can book hotels, rent cars and organise congresses.
- **Top Quark** (☎ 055 33 40 41, 800 60 88 22; www.familyhotels.com) This website has about 60 Florentine hotels in all categories.

Cuendet (☎ 0577 57 63 30, 800 370 477; www.cuendet.com; Strada di Strove 17, 53035 Monteriggioni, Siena) is a major Italian company with villas in Tuscany (as well as other parts of Italy and other Mediterranean destinations). Prices for an apartment or small villa for four to six people range from US$500 per week in winter up to US$1500 per week in August.

The US-based **Rentvillas.Com** (http://rentvillas.com) offers 900 holiday properties in Tuscany (about 70 in Florence itself). Australian-based **Cottages & Castles** (☎ 03-9853 1142; www.cottagesandcastles.com.au; 11 Laver St, Kew 3101, Victoria, Australia) has a range of holiday villas in Tuscany.

Other dealers abound on the Internet. **Wotspot** (www.wotspot.com) has apartments in Florence for around US$900 to US$1500 per week, sleeping two to six people. **Euroflats** (www .ccrsrl.com) has a dozen flats that sleep up to eight from €790 to €2160 per week. **Guest in Italy** (www.guestinitaly.com) has apartments ranging from €62 to more than €2000 a night (the latter for Medici family apartments); it also has B&Bs. **Interhome** (www.interhome.co.uk) has plenty of apartments and houses in and around Florence. **Carefree Italy** (www.carefree-italy .com) deals more in country houses and villas.

With all of these you must add booking and cleaning fees. People with pets in tow should make sure they are allowed before committing.

PIAZZA DEL DUOMO & AROUND

Perhaps surprisingly, the number of hotels in the immediate vicinity of the city's principal monument and symbol is rather low. And of those only a few recommend themselves.

TOP FIVE HOTELS WITH VIEWS
- Albergo Torre di Bellosguardo (p182)
- Villa San Michele (p184)
- Albergo La Scaletta (p181)
- Hotel Park Palace (p181)
- Hotel San Giovanni (opposite)

HOTEL BRUNELLESCHI Map pp244-5   Hotel
☎ 055 2 73 70; www.hotelbrunelleschi.it; Piazza Santa Elisabetta 3; s/d €245/360; 🖥 A; 🅿 €30
Bright, modern rooms have been tacked onto a medieval tower a stone's throw from the Duomo. In Roman times the spot was occupied by baths – you can see vestiges of them in the basement of the tower, now given over to the hotel bar and conference rooms (wifi equipped). The best rooms (on the upper floors) have views of Brunelleschi's nearby cathedral cupola. Hang out on the roof terrace.

HOTEL HELVETIA & BRISTOL
Map pp244-5   Hotel
☎ 055 2 66 51; www.royaldemeure.com; Via dei Pescioni 2; s/d to €285/530; 🚋 6 & A; 🅿 €30-35
Travel back in time to a moment of plush, self-indulgent luxury. Classic rooms bulge with art, silk drapes, lace and brocade. Antique furnishings and Carrara marble bathrooms with Jacuzzi help you pamper yourself while in Florence. Guests who've savoured the hotel's charm include Bertrand Russell, Pirandello and Stravinsky.

HOTEL SAVOY Map pp244-5   Designer Hotel
☎ 055 2 73 51; www.roccofortehotels.com; Piazza della Repubblica 7; s/d €340/517; 🖥 A; 🅿.
This stylish jewel in the Rocco Forte chain offers spacious living in rooms that have a fresh, contemporary feel. Some come with small balconies and big views and all have parquet floors or warm carpet. Bathrooms sparkle with marble and mosaics. If you aren't on your knees after a day of sightseeing, the hotel's fitness centre offers exercise with views.

PALAZZO RUSPOLI
Map pp244-5   Boutique Hotel
☎ 055 267 05 63; www.palazzo-ruspoli.it; Via de' Martelli 5; s/d €200/220;
🚋 1, 6, 7, 10, 11, 14, 17, 23 & A
Behind the magnificent façade of this Renaissance mansion lurk 20 charming rooms, decorated in a rather fulsome antique style, with polished timber floors, high ceilings and drapery cascading down over the bedheads. Some offer splendid views of the Duomo, almost close enough to touch it.

RELAIS IL CAMPANILE Map pp244-5   B&B
☎ 055 21 16 88; www.relaiscampanile.it;
Via Ricasoli 10; s/d €85/115;
🚌 1, 6, 7, 10, 11, 14, 17, 23 & A

Terracotta floors contrast with the clean lines of the room furnishings, wrought-iron bed heads, glass-topped bedside tables and dark timber wardrobes. The singles are small.

CHEAP SLEEPS
HOTEL SAN GIOVANNI
Map pp244-5   Pensione
☎ 055 28 83 85; www.hotelsangiovanni.com;
Via de' Cerretani 2; d/tr €96/120, s/d/tr without bathroom €55/75/97; 🚌 1, 6, 7, 10, 11, 14, 17, 23 & A

Although the stairwell up to the 2nd floor isn't promising, the charming and often spacious rooms in this Italian-Australian run hotel are worth seeking out. The hotel was once part of the bishop's private residence (see the traces of fresco in several rooms). Eight of the nine rooms have views of the cathedral and Baptistery.

PIAZZA DELLA SIGNORIA & AROUND

Some of Florence's most challenging innovations in the hotel business are taking place around here. Newer hotels, like those run by Ferragamo near the River Arno,

have a desire to shed the burden of history and present a fresh, modern concept in hospitality.

Those who don't want a modern setting needn't despair, as they are still catered to by the majority – you'll find wonderful places at varying prices, offering all the atmosphere and history you can handle.

DAVANZATI HOTEL Map pp244-5   Hotel
☎ 055 28 66 66; www.hoteldavanzati.it;
Via Porta Rossa 5; s/d €110/230; 🚌 A; 🅿 €26

The remnants of frescoes start in the stairwell on your way upstairs to the hotel. The hotel has 19 mostly spacious rooms (the singles less so) that are modern and clean with a splash of charm. Terracotta floors lend warmth and each of the rooms is slightly different. Staff are particularly helpful.

GALLERY HOTEL ART
Map pp244-5   Designer Hotel
☎ 055 2 72 63; www.lungarnohotels.com;
Vicolo dell'Oro 5; d from €352; 🚌 B; 🅿 €32

Ferragamo runs this edgy 21st-century designer hotel, a departure from the standard Florentine excursion into antique nostalgia. It caters to a very particular taste, with minimalist décor, a sushi-ish fusion fashion bar and clean-lined rooms. And just to rub in the counter-Renaissance point, you can admire contemporary art along the corridors and in the rooms.

The expanse of Hotel Savoy (opposite)

HOTEL CONTINENTALE

Map pp244-5   Designer Hotel

☎ 055 2 72 62; www.lungarnohotels.com;
Vicolo dell'Oro 6r; s/d from €275/480; 🚇 B; 🅿 €32
Another in the growing chain of Ferragamo
anti-antique hotels, this place right opposite the Gallery Hotel Art shrieks ultra-
new 21st-century pad with its trendy Sky
Lounge for drinking in cocktails with sunset
views. Modular rooms with CD player (DVD
on request), contemporary art and pink
chairs are comfortable and cool.

IN PIAZZA DELLA SIGNORIA

Map pp244-5   B&B

☎ 055 239 95 46; www.inpiazzadellasignoria.it;
Via dei Magazzini 2; s/d €210/260; 🚇 A
A 15th-century mansion turned into a
seriously upmarket B&B with just 10 rooms
over two floors, all decked out with antique
furniture and bathrooms that invite long,
contemplative showers. The rooms are all
individually decorated and named after
Tuscan characters. Elegant writing tables go
side by side with flat-screen TVs.

PENDINI Map pp244-5   Pensione

☎ 055 21 11 70; www.florenceitaly.net;
Via degli Strozzi 2; s/d to €110/150; 🚇 A; 🅿 €25
Pendini's rooms, on the 4th floor, have
seen guests come and go since 1879. They
are furnished with antiques and in some
cases are jumbled with tea tables and other
furniture. Reproduction prints add gaiety
and some rooms look out over Piazza della
Repubblica.

RELAIS UFFIZI Map pp244-5   Boutique Hotel

☎ 055 267 62 39; www.relaisuffizi.it;
Chiasso del Buco 16; s/d €120/180; 🚇 B; 🅿 €30
Right in the heart of the action, this stylish
kip is hidden away down an alley in a 16th-
century building, a hop from Piazza della
Signoria. From its breakfast room there are
unparalleled views of the square; it's tempting to just sit there and watch life seethe
below. Bedrooms are mostly generous,
some with four-poster beds and all tastefully furnished.

SOGGIORNO ANTICA TORRE

Map pp244-5   B&B

☎ 055 21 64 02; www.anticatorre.com; Piazza
della Signoria 3; s/d €100/140; 🚇 B; 🅿 €26
Right on the square, this guesthouse oozes
hundreds of years of history. Oak floors,
original ceilings and antique furniture contrast against the décor in each individual
room. Room names reflect dominating colours. The ivory room is the simplest, while
the gold room is a small suite.

TORRE GUELFA Map pp244-5   Hotel

☎ 055 239 63 38; www.hoteltorreguelfa.com;
Borgo SS Apostoli 8; s/d €140/260; 🚇 B
People have been coming and going in
this building for a good seven centuries.
Next to it rises one of the few medieval
towers to survive in Florence, incorporated
in the hotel. The building is filled with
plants and most of the attractive rooms
have four-poster beds. At the top of the
tower the owners have set up a terrace.
There are few better places in Florence for
a sunset drink.

CHEAP SLEEPS

IL PORCELLINO TOURIST HOUSE

Map pp244-5   B&B

☎ 055 28 26 86; www.hotelporcellino.com; Piazza
Mercato Nuovo 4; s/d €68/93; 🚇 B; 🅿 €26
Right over the bustling Mercato Nuovo, this
welcoming guesthouse offers six spotless,
comfortable rooms with parquet floors
and classic, simple furnishings. It closes for
August (everyone needs a holiday!).

SANTA MARIA NOVELLA & AROUND

The streets around the train station are lined
with cheap hotels and *pensioni,* so you can
usually quickly unload your bags and get a
kip within a short time of leaving your train.
Via della Scala (Map pp242–3), which runs
northwest off the piazza, is particularly laden,
although some of the rougher places do at
least a part-time gig as unofficial brothels.

TOP FIVE FOR LUXURY

- **Grand Hotel** (opposite)
- **Hotel Savoy** (p174)
- **Palazzo Magnani Feroni** (p182)
- **Hotel Helvetia & Bristol** (p174)
- **Grand Hotel Minerva** (opposite)

Via Fiume, on the northeastern side of the train station, is equally stacked with hotels but is rather a different story and could be termed the 'upmarket' hotel flank of the station.

The area covered in this section is considerably greater, stretching east to Via Cavour and along Via de' Tornabuoni to the Arno river.

CASA HOWARD Map pp242-3   Boutique Hotel
☎ 055 21 65 60; www.casahoward.it; Via della Scala 18; s/d €150/220; 🚍 11, 36, 37 & A

With six rooms, this is a delicious retreat near the train station. Building on a successful business started in Rome, the owners have created a set of unique and different rooms. Starting with the paintwork, ranging from lime green to russet red, each room boasts an unpredictable mix of styles and furnishings. You might have an old-style bath, a fireplace, and antique furniture.

GRAND HOTEL Map pp248-9   Hotel
☎ 055 2 71 61; www.starwood.com; Piazza d'Ognissanti 1; s/d to €735/1100; 🚍 A & B

The most expensive hotels in town (run by the same people) are this and the Hotel Excelsior, facing each other in self-assured style across Piazza d'Ognissanti. In the Grand Hotel, marble bathrooms, regal furnishings and river views characterise the best rooms. A stroll around the glorious ground floor, with its bars and restaurant, is overwhelming. The Hotel Excelsior (☎ 055 2 71 51) is listed on the same website and offers similar prices.

GRAND HOTEL BAGLIONI
Map pp244-5   Hotel
☎ 055 2 35 80; www.hotel-florencia.hotel baglioni.it; Piazza dell'Unità Italiana 6; s/d from €186/258; 🚍 1, 7, 10, 11, 14, 17, 22, 23, 36, 37 & A; ℗ €35-40

Timber beam ceilings, parquet floors and dark wood furnishings lend the rooms here a particular warmth in spite of the place's size (193 rooms), while the public areas in *pietra serena* (grey 'tranquil stone') have a softly grander tone. The rooftop terrace restaurant (the Terrazza Brunelleschi) and garden offer stirring views over the city.

GRAND HOTEL MINERVA
Map pp242-3   Hotel
☎ 055 2 72 30; www.grandhotelminerva.com; Piazza di Santa Maria Novella 16; s/d €270/420; 🚍 1, 7, 10, 11, 14, 17, 22, 23, 36, 37 & A

Rooms in this high-end hotel are light and bright, with cream colours dominating the décor. Family suites (€600) are attractive, mostly split level and with room for four people. Many of the rooms have views across to Basilica di Santa Maria Novella. The rooftop pool is ideal for a break from all those monuments.

HOTEL DÉSIRÉE Map pp242-3   Hotel
☎ 055 238 23 82; www.desireehotel.com; Via Fiume 20; s/d €82/135; 🚍 4, 7, 12, 13, 14, 25, 28, 31, 32 & 33; ℗ €20

This personable hotel offers fine rooms, many overlooking a tranquil, leafy courtyard out the back. The spick-and-span, high-ceilinged rooms have mosaic floors, iron or hand-painted timber bedheads and their own bathrooms. The same people run Hotel Cellini upstairs, where the rooms have balconies and the views, if anything, are better.

HOTEL TORNABUONI BEACCI
Map pp244-5   Hotel
☎ 055 21 26 45; www.tornabuonihotels.com; Via de' Tornabuoni 3; s/d €180/260; 🚍 6, 11, 36, 37 & A

Ignore all the designer frippery around you and head to the 15th-century Palazzo Minerbetti-Strozzi. The Minerbetti were descended from English refugees of the Becket family who wound up in Florence after the assassination of Thomas à Becket in Canterbury Cathedral in 1170. Faded elegance greets you in the period-furnished rooms of various centuries, kept in perfect order by the Bechi family. Enjoy breakfast on the rooftop terrace.

JK PLACE Map pp244-5   Boutique Hotel
☎ 055 264 51 81; www.jkplace.com; Piazza di Santa Maria Novella 7; s/d €315/350; 🚍 1, 7, 10, 11, 14, 17, 22, 23, 36, 37 & A

Architect Michele Bonan has made a name for himself in the designer hotel construction business in Florence. Here and at Ferragamo's Continentale (see opposite), he is the guiding hand behind this super-

Sleeping

SANTA MARIA NOVELLA & AROUND

chic option. Rooms welcome with warm colours (olive greens and ochre-rose), more reminiscent of an English country home than the fiery Mediterranean. The hotel is full of engaging touches like a glassed-over internal courtyard and a roof terrace.

PENSIONE LE CASCINE

Map pp244-5   Pensione

☎ 055 21 10 66; www.hotellecascine.it/; Largo Fratelli Alinari 15; s/d €120/170; 🚌 4, 7, 12, 13, 14, 25, 28, 31, 32 & 33; Ⓟ €12

Near Stazione di Santa Maria Novella, this three-star hotel is one of the better choices in an area with many hotels. Its rooms are attractively furnished and some have balconies. The better rooms are spacious, with divan and generous bathrooms.

CHEAP SLEEPS

HOTEL ABACO Map pp244-5   Pensione

☎ 055 238 19 19; www.abaco-hotel.it; Via dei Banchi 1; d with/without bathroom €90/75; 🚌 1, 4, 6, 7, 10, 11, 12, 13, 14, 22, 23, 25, 36 & 37; Ⓟ €24

This friendly hotel has nine charming baroque rooms with heavy drapes and chunky mirror frames. Antiques rule, as do deep-sea blue to rose-red colour schemes. Ceiling fans go some way to keeping you cooler in summer. There are no singles.

HOTEL CESTELLI Map pp244-5   Pensione

☎ 055 21 42 13; www.hotelcestelli.it; Borgo SS Apostoli 25; d €85-100, s/d without bathroom €50/80; 🚌 B

You enter a bright foyer capped by a grand stained-glass window. Of the eight rooms, all varying in size and quality, the best is the large No 5, with its own divan and window onto the narrow street below. All the rooms are pleasant, although the singles are a tad cramped.

HOTEL SCOTI Map pp244-5   Pensione

☎ 055 29 21 28; www.hotelscoti.com; Via de' Tornabuoni 7; s/d €70/95; 🚌 6, 11, 22, 36, 37 & A

This hotel on Florence's posh shopping strip is a wonderful haven. Grand rooms sprinkled with antiques form part of a grand apartment in a 15th-century mansion. The frescoed sitting room, complete with chandelier, is conducive to lazy chats.

MARY'S HOUSE Map pp242-3   Pensione

☎ 055 29 06 85; www.maryshouse.it; Via della Scala 43; s/d/tr without bathroom €40/60/90; 🚌 11, 36,37 & A

This is a straight down-the-line option: Mary's House is a family-run business with simple, clean rooms. Showers are communal but everything is kept shipshape, making this a decent budget option near the train station.

Hotel Botticelli (opposite)

SAN LORENZO

Animated by the bustle of the Mercato Centrale (Map pp242–3), the leather street stalls and the inevitable attraction of the Cappelle Medicee, this area has an in-the-thick-of-things feel about it, more animated than the awe-inspiring tourist hotspots of Piazza del Duomo and Piazza della Signoria.

HOTEL ACCADEMIA Map pp244-5   Hotel
☎ 055 29 34 51; www.hotel-florencia.accademia hotel.net; Via Faenza 7; s/d/tr incl breakfast €85/150/190; 🚍 1, 6, 7, 10, 11 & 17; 🅿 €25
The hotel is in an 18th-century mansion with impressive stained-glass doors, carved wooden ceilings and a cheerful little courtyard. Bedrooms are pleasant and parquet-floored, with bright sparkling bathrooms attached.

HOTEL BELLETTINI Map pp244-5   Hotel
☎ 055 21 35 61; www.hotelbellettini.com; Via de' Conti 7; s/d/tr/q €100/140/180/225, without bathroom s/d/tr €80/105/140; 🚍 1, 6, 7, 10, 11 & 17
This delightful, cosy hotel has about 30 well-furnished rooms – try for one with a view of the Basilica di San Lorenzo. It also has a couple of triples and quads and some slightly cheaper rooms without bathroom. The hotel has a slightly pricier annexe nearby.

HOTEL BOTTICELLI
Map pp242-3   Boutique Hotel
☎ 055 29 09 05; www.hotelbotticelli.it; Via Taddea 8; s/d €140/225; 🚍 1, 6, 7, 10, 11 & 17; 🅿 €21
This charming, bijou hotel near the San Lorenzo market is an attractive deal. The common areas are capped by impressive vaulting and the little rooftop terrace is an enticing place to relax over a drink and enjoy the views. Rooms are elegantly appointed, with timber furnishings and clean, spacious lines.

HOTEL CASCI Map pp244-5   Hotel
☎ 055 21 16 86; www.hotelcasci.com; Via Cavour 13; s/d/tr/q to €110/150/190/230; 🚍 1, 6, 7, 10, 11 & 17; 🅿 €23-27
This friendly family hotel with its attractive olive-green décor offers you the chance to stay in a 15th-century mansion on one of the city's main streets. Look up at the fresco as you scoff down your buffet breakfast, which includes fresh espresso coffee.

HOTEL IL GUELFO BIANCO
Map pp242-3   Hotel
☎ 055 28 83 30; www.ilguelfobianco.it; Via Cavour 57/r; s €135, d from €180; 🚍 1, 6, 7, 10, 11 & 17; 🅿 €24-30
Rooms are a curious mix in this central hotel. Bare-brick vaulting and similarly exposed walls set the tone. Juxtaposed with grand old ceramic heating of bygone days are works of contemporary art to lend a modern splash to some rooms. Others have classic ceiling frescoes. A handful of much-coveted rooms have private terraces.

CHEAP SLEEPS
B&B SAN LORENZO Map pp244-5   B&B
☎ 055 21 10 51; www.bandbsanlorenzo.com; Piazza San Lorenzo 7; s/d €80/110; 🚍 1, 6, 7, 10, 11, 14, 17, 23 & A
Right next to the church of the same name, this friendly little spot offers four scintillating rooms (each jollied up in different pastel shades, with punchy, modern art on the walls, parquet floors, timber beds and flowers). Sunlight flows through the windows of this friendly home away from home.

SAN MARCO

A sleepier quarter than most of the rest of central Florence, the San Marco area is not big on accommodation quantity but offers a handful of excellent choices to suit a range of budgets and tastes.

ANTICA DIMORA Map pp242-3   Hotel
☎ 055 462 72 96; www.anticadimorafirenze.it; Via San Gallo 72; s €90-110, d €130-145; 🚍 1, 6, 7, 10, 11 & 17
With just six individually decorated rooms (four with four-poster beds), this is a charming option in a quiet corner of the old centre. Some of the rooms boast high timber ceilings and all have warm, elegant furnishings and time-warp black-and-white prints of Florence of a bygone era.

HOTEL LE DUE FONTANE
Map pp242-3   Hotel
☎ 055 21 01 85; www.leduefontane.it; Piazza della SS Annunziata 14; s/d €126/182; 🚍 6, 31, 32 & C; 🅿 €10
This fine old building with well-presented rooms, each of them quite different in

terms of size and presentation, is right on one of Florence's finest squares. Doubles overlooking it are spacious, with parquet floors and dark-shaded bedclothes. Such rooms can be a good or bad idea, depending on how early you hope to fall asleep.

HOTEL LOGGIATO DEI SERVITI

Map pp242-3   Hotel

☎ 055 28 95 92; www.loggiatodeiservitihotel.it; Piazza della SS Annunziata 3; s/d €140/205; 🚌 6, 31, 32 & C

Centuries ago visiting prelates lodged here when in Florence. The building was designed by Antonio da Sangallo to reflect the look of Brunelleschi's Spedale across the square and was raised in 1517. It has operated as a hotel since 1924 and now has 29 varied rooms, including several small suites.

HOTEL MONNA LISA

Map pp242-3   Boutique Hotel

☎ 055 247 97 51; www.monnalisa.it; Borgo Pinti 27; s/d/tr from €180/290/415; 🚌 14 & 23; 🅿 €15

From the outside, this Renaissance *palazzo* seems to bristle, jealously guarding its Mediterranean garden and centuries-old rooms. Owned by relatives of the 19th-century sculptor Giovanni Dupré, some of whose works are scattered about the place among priceless family heirlooms, the hotel is a gentle haven.

HOTEL REGENCY Map pp242-3   Hotel

☎ 055 24 52 47; www.hotel-regency.it; Piazza Massimo d'Azeglio 3; s/d €363/445; 🚌 6, 31 & 32; 🅿 €30

Facing a leafy park, this hotel is a quiet, understated place with 49 modern, well-appointed if smallish rooms. It has an almost Anglo-Saxon sobriety about it and the park location, just beyond the reach of the tourist hordes, is a plus. Rooms are classically decorated without the antique fussiness that dominates in some older hotels.

RESIDENZA IL VILLINO

Map pp242-3   Boutique Hotel

☎ 055 200 11 16; www.ilvillino.it; Via della Pergola 53; s/d €100/135; 🚌 C

Tastefully modernised, the nine welcoming rooms in this late-19th-century residence are bound to have you feeling at home.

Heavy timber ceilings and dark wood furniture contrast with the crisp white décor. Out back is a peaceful garden for breakfast.

CHEAP SLEEPS
RESIDENZA JOHANNA I

Map pp242-3   Pensione

☎ 055 48 19 86; www.johanna.it; Via Bonifacio Lupi 14; s/d €60/95; 🚌 1, 4, 7, 12, 20, 25 & 33

You're unlikely to spend your money much better on a Florentine bed. Set in a 19th-century building (also home to the Swedish consulate) fronted by a courtyard in a quiet residential street, this small hotel is run with enthusiasm and care. Rooms are comfortable and furnished as you would expect in a hotel of greater standing. If you have no luck here, ask about its nearby neighbours, the Residenze Johlea I & II (see below).

RESIDENZE JOHLEA I & II

Map pp242-3   Pensione

☎ 055 463 32 92; www.johlea.it; Via San Gallo 76 & 80; s €70, d €95-105; 🚌 1, 6, 7, 10, 11 & 17

With a total of 13 rooms between them, these spots (run by the Johanna squad) offer tasteful, impeccable, individually decorated rooms with dinky mini-fridges. For extra space, ask for the suite in No 76 (€115). Johlea 1, which is at No 80 and acts as reception for both, has a gorgeous roof terrace.

SANTA CROCE

Better as a hunting ground when your tummy's rumbling, this area offers thin pickings when it comes to hotels. A few good lower budget options are worth considering though.

ALBERGO BAVARIA Map pp244-5   Pensione

☎ 055 234 03 13; www.hotelbavariafirenze.it; Borgo degli Albizi 26; d/tr/q €98/113/128, s/d without bathroom €50/70; 🚌 A

This hotel is housed in the fine Palazzo di Ramirez di Montalvo, and built around a peaceful courtyard by Ammannati. Rooms are furnished with fine antique pieces. With its warm ochre colours, low wooden ceilings and flexible pricing, it makes an excellent choice in its category.

TOP FIVE HOTELS WITH CHARM
- Hotel Monna Lisa (opposite)
- Residenza Il Villino (opposite)
- Hotel Botticelli (p179)
- Palazzo Ruspoli (p174)
- Antica Dimora (p179)

HOTEL DANTE Map pp248-9   Pensione
☎ 055 24 17 72; www.hotel-dante.it;
Via S Cristofano 2; s/d €88/120; 🚌 C; 🅿 €10-15
Tucked away in a quiet street right by the
Basilica di Santa Croce, the rooms here are
fine without being spectacular. Indeed the
decoration is a little chintzy. All have smallish bathrooms but the real distinguishing
feature is that half the rooms have kitchen
facilities.

CHEAP SLEEPS
HOTEL DALÍ Map pp248-9   Pensione
☎ 055 234 07 06; www.hoteldali.com;
Via dell'Oriuolo 17; d€75, s/d without bathroom
€40/60; 🚌 14 & 23; 🅿
A friendly, helpful young couple run this
spruce, simple and warmly recommended
hotel. Try for a room looking over the
serene inner courtyard. One room can
accommodate up to six so bring the gang.
There's also free parking, rare as icebergs in
Florence.

HOTEL WANDA Map pp248-9   Pensione
☎ 055 234 44 84; www.hotelwanda.it;
Via Ghibellina 51; d/tr €119/140, s/d/tr without
bathroom €70/88/119; 🚌 14
A somewhat higgledy-piggledy spot close
to Piazza di Santa Croce, this hotel has large
rooms, many with ceiling frescoes (some
people insist on Room 13, lined with centuries-old mirrors...).

OLTRARNO
Who needs to be in the thick of things on
the north side of the Arno when you could
thrive in the atmosphere of the Oltrarno, a
mere bridge or two away from the centre?
With laneways and green hills, it's a serene
destination. Some hotels on the south bank
offer a near country air and several budget
hostels also offer their services.

ALBERGO LA SCALETTA
Map pp244-5   Pensione
☎ 055 28 30 28; www.hotellascaletta.it;
Via de' Guicciardini 13; s/d €90/140; 🚌 D
Climb to the top floor to reach this charming hotel. Its best aspect is the breathtaking
views over the city from the roof terrace.
Rooms are straightforward enough, white-
washed clean with parquet floors and
minimal furnishings. They branch off long,
rambling corridors that wind over three
levels.

CASA GUIDI Map pp248-9   Residence
Piazza San Felice 8; 6-person apt per week from
€2000; 🚌 11, 36, 37 & D
Perhaps you have poetic leanings? Why
not take up residence where the Brown-
ings did? The place is full of Browning
mementos – you'll see they paid up to 25
guineas a week in rent. To rent a room,
contact the Landmark Trust (☎ 01628-825925;
www.landmarktrust.org.uk; Shottesbrooke,
Maidenhead, Berkshire SL6 3SW, UK), which
restores and conserves architectural mar-
vels in the UK and abroad.

HOTEL PARK PALACE
Map pp240-1   Villa Hotel
☎ 055 22 24 31; www.parkpalace.com; Piazzale
Galileo 5; s/d €200/250; 🚌 12 & 13
You wanted rooms with a view? All 26 of
them have one here. Spacious and simply
furnished, with an old-world comfort, the
lodgings' best quality is the choice of views,

Grand Hotel (p177)

often surprisingly bucolic. Even if you do peel yourself away from the view from your room, you probably won't make it past the pool, gardens or comfy lounge.

HOTEL SILLA Map pp248-9   Hotel
☎ 055 234 28 88; www.hotelsilla.it; Via dei Renai 5; s/d/tr €125/170/220; 🚌 12, 13, 23 & D; 🅿 €16
Meander into the tranquil Florentine courtyard and you know you are home. The mansion has served as private residence, temporary Allied HQ in late 1944 and convent. It opened as a hotel in 1964 and is set in one of the prettiest corners of the city; it's a brief walk across Ponte alle Grazie from central Florence.

HOTEL VILLA LIBERTY
Map pp240-1   Villa Hotel
☎ 055 681 05 81; www.hotelvillaliberty.com; Viale Michelangelo 40; s/d/tr €129/169/229; 🚌 12 & 13; 🅿
In a leafy location, this agreeable Art Nouveau *palazzo* offers spacious, charming rooms with high (in some cases frescoed) ceilings and period furniture. Many look onto the gardens. The place has its own restaurant and bar if a walk into town seems like too much effort. In summer, take the buffet breakfast in the peaceful garden.

PALAZZO MAGNANI FERONI
Map pp248-9   Residence
☎ 055 239 95 44; www.florencepalace.it; Borgo San Frediano 5; ste €320-750; 🚌 6 & D; 🅿
You will feel like the guest of some 18th-century Florentine toff. Twelve suites, all the size of decent flats, are richly furnished. The beds are bigger than some peoples' bedrooms and the building retains its salons, billiard room and libraries. Wander up to the rooftop terrace for the views or have a workout in the gym.

PENSIONE BANDINI Map pp248-9   Pensione
☎ 055 21 53 08; pensionebandini@tiscali.it; Piazza Santo Spirito 9; d with/without bathroom €135/112; 🚌 D
This rattling old *pensione* overlooks the hippest square in Florence from the 3rd floor. You can hang about the loggia (porch) overlooking the square or wander around admiring all the trinkets accumulated over the decades. The views from the grand log-

TOP FIVE HOTEL ROOF TERRACES
- **Grand Hotel Baglioni** (p177)
- **Torre Guelfa** (p176)
- **Hotel Continentale** (p176)
- **Grand Hotel Minerva** (p177)
- **JK Place** (p177)

gia running the length of Palazzo Guadagni compensate for any lack in the mod-cons department. Zeffirelli shot some scenes of *Tea with Mussolini* here.

RESIDENZA SERRISTORI PALACE
Map pp248-9   Apartments
☎ 055 200 16 23; www.serristorripalace.com; Lungarno Serristori 13; 2/4/6-person apt from €190/210/295; 🚌 12, 13, 23 & D
An attractive and tastefully renovated 19th-century villa, this residence offers large, fully equipped apartments for up to six people. Most offer river views.

CHEAP SLEEPS
OSTELLO SANTA MONACA
Map pp248-9   Youth Hostel
☎ 055 26 83 38; www.ostello.it; Via Santa Monaca 6; dm €17; 🚌 D
Friendly and run by a cooperative, this hostel doesn't do meals but guests get a special deal at a nearby restaurant. Accommodation is in single-sex dorms. There's a laundrette and a guests' kitchen (you'll need your own utensils). Sheet rental is included in the price.

BEYOND CENTRAL FLORENCE
If you need a break from the crowds, head for the hills of Fiesole and around. The fresh air is revitalising.

ALBERGO TORRE DI BELLOSGUARDO
Map pp240-1   Villa Hotel
☎ 055 229 81 45; www.torrebellosguardo.com; Via Roti Michelozzi 2; s/d €160/290; 🅿
Long appreciated as a bucolic escape from the simmering heat of summertime Florence, the Bellosguardo hill offers enchant-

ing views and enticing accommodation in what started life as a small castle in the 14th century. Heavy timber four-poster beds stand in grandiose rooms. The strategically placed pool is the best spot to drink in the views. If you don't have your own wheels, you can only get here by taxi.

FATTORIA DI MAIANO

Map p239   Agriturismo
☎ 055 59 96 00; www.fattoriadimaiano.com; Via Benedetto da Maiano 11, Fiesole; s/d per week €726-2025; Ⓟ
A functioning organic farm whose main product is the top-class Laudemio extra-virgin olive oil, the Fattoria is also home to a magnificent 15th-century villa that offers beautiful, rustic holiday apartments (sleeping two to seven). The villa, used for some scenes in *Room with a View* and *Tea with Mussolini*, makes the perfect set for a romantic Florence getaway. Minimum stay is three days in low season. There is no bus to the farm. Catch a taxi or take your own wheels.

LE CANNELLE BED & BREAKFAST

Map p239   B&B
☎ 055 597 83 36; www.lecannelle.com; Via Gramsci 52-56, Fiesole; s/d €80/114; closed mid-Jan–Feb; 🚌 7
It's hard to miss the rose-coloured façade of this delightful B&B, tucked away about 100m east of Piazza Mino da Fiesole, in the heart of the old hill town overlooking Florence. There's a variety of pleasant, mostly spacious rooms (five in all) with ceramic floors and grand timber beds.

PENSIONE BENCISTÀ Map p239   Villa Hotel
☎ 055 5 91 63; www.bencista.com; Via Benedetto da Maiano 4, Fiesole; s/d €85/150; 🚌 10; Ⓟ
About 1km short of Fiesole proper when coming from central Florence, aptly named Bencistà (One is Well Here) is one of the cheaper villa alternatives in the northern hills. The panoramic views alone make it a great place to stay. Rooms are spacious and have gracious timber furnishings.

VILLA POGGIO SAN FELICE

Map p238   Villa Hotel
☎ 055 22 00 16; http://poggiosanfelice.hotel -firenze.net; Via San Matteo in Arcetri 24; s/d €150/200; Ⓟ
This family escape lies just 5km south of Porta Romana amid the vineyards. Take up residence in one of the five huge guest rooms for your Tuscan country holiday, with Florence just up the road. Can't be bothered with the big city today? Well, flop down by the pool. The rooms are all different, ranging from one with two single four-posters to a romantic double with a huge French bed and lovely views over the terrace. There is no public transport but the villa offers a private shuttle.

www.lonelyplanet.com

Sleeping

BEYOND CENTRAL FLORENCE

Hotel Silla (opposite)

183

VILLA SAN MICHELE Map p239   Villa Hotel

☎ 055 567 82 00; www.villasanmichele.com; Via Doccia 4, Fiesole; s/d from €630/810; Ⓟ

A former 15th-century Franciscan monastery, this landmark has become one of the classiest hotel escapes in Florence. Well, around Florence. Sip a cocktail and contemplate the city and the Arno across the cypress tops from this privileged location just outside Fiesole. A grand variety of rooms and suites spreads out across the luxuriant gardens (some junior suites are right by the pool). The villa has a private shuttle service.

CHEAP SLEEPS
OSTELLO EUROPA VILLA CAMERATA

Map pp240-1   Youth Hostel

☎ 055 60 14 51; www.ostellionline.org; Viale Augusto Righi 2-4; dm/d/tr incl breakfast €17/46/57; 🚌 17, 17B & 17C; Ⓟ

This HI hostel, set in a 17th-century villa, is considered one of the most beautiful in Europe. Only members are accepted. Dinner costs €9, and there is a bar. You can get the bus from Piazza del Duomo or Stazione di Santa Maria Novella – make sure it's going in the direction of Verga.

Excursions

Excursions

Florence is just the tip of the iceberg. Around it swirls one of Europe's best publicised regions, a charming chessboard of magical medieval hill towns, Renaissance cities, vine-strewn countryside, mountain ranges and seaside. There is a reason why all those expatriates are so busy making a quick euro from their respective tall tales of life under a Tuscan sun.

A rich, roughly triangular area, occupying the central-western half of the Italian peninsula, Tuscany covers 22,992 sq km. It is bound to the north by the Apennines, which separate it from northern Italy and the Po valley. To the west it faces the Ligurian Sea, while to the east stretch the neighbouring hill regions of Umbria and Le Marche. To the south lies Lazio, sliced in two by the road to Rome.

All that apparent heavenly bucolic charm belies a long and violent past. Florence's rise as the senior medieval city of Tuscany and eventually its capital did not go uncontested. Rivals engaged in frequent and bloody tugs-of-war for local supremacy and in the process became splendidly independent centres. None resisted Florence's growing hegemony with greater tenacity than Siena. Pisa had an illustrious but brief career as a maritime power but succumbed to Florence in the 15th century. To the north of Pisa, nearby Lucca managed to remain surprisingly aloof and independent until 1799, long after Florence had ceased to be a major player in the European league of nations.

The Tuscan countryside is littered with lesser known, but equally striking cities and towns. Each has its own story, from the merchant centre of Prato to the medieval Manhattan that is San Gimignano. Sandwiched between eternal rivals Florence and Siena undulates the fabled Chianti wine country (impertinently dubbed, with a bit of a Britannic smirk, Chiantishire).

What we explore in this chapter can be done easily in day trips from Florence. It will likely whet your appetite for more, so grab Lonely Planet's *Tuscany & Umbria*.

FLORENCE'S MEDIEVAL RIVALS

If Florence is the birthplace of the Renaissance and cradle to its creators, Siena (p188) is its proud Gothic counterpoint. Perched high like an eagle's eyrie in rugged terrain to the south of Florence, the city's subjugation to its Renaissance rival may not have been beneficial for the Sienese, but it was a godsend for posterity. Its relegation to a second-tier town put a brake on commercial development and helped preserve the purity of its Gothic lines. To the northwest, two other medieval city-states faced vastly different circumstances. Pisa (p195) bloomed early and is home to some of the most spectacular Romanesque monuments in Tuscany, not to mention a grandly botched job – the Leaning Tower. Controlled by Pisa for a short while, the nearby walled city of Lucca (p195) is another rich Romanesque treasure chest.

The rolling fields of Chianti (p192)

TUSCAN TOWNS

The diversity of Tuscany's towns was born from the fractiousness of the Middle Ages. With the unity imposed by ancient Rome a distant memory, these settlements re-emerged from the bog of the Dark Ages with an understandable diffidence towards the rest of the world. Feudal warlords ruled them with an iron fist and jealously defended their independence. Even today they stubbornly retain their own character. Textile centre **Prato** (p198) and **Pistoia** (p198) each boast grand cathedral squares. **Montelupo** (p198) is known for its ceramics and the pretty hamlet of **Vinci** (p198) gave its name to one of the greatest figures of the Renaissance.

WINE COUNTRY

The rolling hills of Tuscany's classic wine area, **Chianti country** (p192), beckon just south of Florence. Walkers and energetic cyclists (those hills certainly work out previously unperceived muscles) love to stride out or pedal frantically here. Picturesque villages like **Greve** (p192), **Radda** (p192) and **Castellina** (p192) pop out from the hills, each with their own delightful flavour. Along back roads you will come across castles and country manors. The impressive walls of **Monteriggioni** (p192) will draw you into this quiet, half-abandoned village near Siena, while the spindly medieval towers of **San Gimignano** (p192) – beyond the Chianti but justly known for its own wines – make it a must on any Tuscan village circuit.

SIENA

According to legend, Siena was originated by the sons of one of Rome's mythical founding twins, Remus. The story runs that Senius and Aschius, fearing Remus' brother, Romulus, would kill them, fled here. Thumbing their noses at their tormentor, they stole a statue of a she-wolf feeding Romulus and Remus from the temple of Apollo before hitting the road. That image became as much a symbol of Siena as of Rome and can be seen all over the city today. On a more prosaic note, Siena may have been of Etruscan origin, although a proper town only emerged when, in the 1st century BC, the Romans established a military colony called Sena Julia.

In the 12th century AD, Siena's wealth, size and power grew with its involvement in trade (textiles, wine, saffron, spices and wax) and banking. Siena prospered under the rule of the Consiglio dei Nove (Council of Nine), a group dominated by the upper middle class. Many of the buildings (such as the cathedral) in the Sienese Gothic style, which give the city its unique appearance, were constructed under the council's direction. The Sienese school of painting also had its beginnings at this time with Guido da Siena, peaking in the early 14th century with the work of Duccio di Buoninsegna, Simone Martini, and Pietro and Ambrogio Lorenzetti.

Plague in 1348 and foreign rule signalled decline, but the real blow came when Florence's Cosimo I de' Medici, under the banner of Holy Roman Emperor Charles V, conquered Siena in 1555. The Sienese have never quite forgotten (or forgiven) that humiliation.

Today, Siena has at once the purposeful feel of a prosperous provincial centre, and the sense of having stood still in time. Fuelled by the twin turbines of tourism and banking, Siena's wealth also comes from a busy university life. Students from far and wide pump youthful vigour into a town strongly attached to its medieval traditions – best expressed in the madness of its chaotic twice-yearly Il Palio horse race. Horses may be allowed into the old centre but wheeled beasts are distinctly unwelcome; in 1966, the city became the first in Europe to close the doors of its ancient centre to virtually all motor vehicles.

By bus from Florence you will arrive at **Piazza Gramsci**, from where it is a short walk to Piazza San Domenico, with panoramic views of the city. Launching long shadows across the square is the Gothic **Chiesa di San Domenico**, begun in the 13th century. St Catherine of Siena, one of Italy's most revered saints, took her vows in the church's Cappella delle Volte. The Middle Ages were a weird old time and in the **Cappella di Santa Caterina** the saint's head is contained in a tabernacle on the altar. She died in Rome, where most of the rest of her body lies in repose, but in line with the practice of collecting relics of saintly stiffs, her head was returned to Siena. In a small window box to the right of the chapel are her desiccated thumb and the nasty-looking whip with which she flogged herself for the good of the faithfuls' souls.

Suitably chastened, walk east along Via della Sapienza and turn right down Costa di Sant'Antonio. On your right is the **Casa di Santa Caterina**, where the saint was born. The rooms are decorated with frescoes and paintings by Sienese artists, including Sodoma.

Back on Via della Sapienza, continue east and turn right into Banchi di Sopra to reach **Il Campo**. The magnificent, sloping, shell-shaped and café-lined square has been the city's civic centre since it was laid out by the Consiglio dei Nove in the mid-14th century. The square's paving is divided into nine sectors, representing the council members. In the upper part is the 15th-century **Fonte Gaia** (Gay Fountain), once the city centre's principal public source of water. The fountain's Renaissance panels are reproductions – the originals, by Jacopo della Quercia, are in the Gothic **Palazzo Pubblico** at the piazza's lowest point. Also known as the Palazzo Comunale (town hall), the palace houses the **Museo Civico**, fundamentally a series of rooms with frescoes by artists of the Sienese school. Of particular note is Simone Martini's *Maestà* (Majesty) in the Sala del Mappamondo (Map Room).

TRANSPORT

Distance from Florence 68km

Direction South

Bus Regular SITA and Tra-in buses from Florence (€6.50, 1¼ hours) run at least every hour (direct), arriving in Siena's Piazza Gramsci. More frequent services involve a change of bus at Poggibonsi.

Car Take the SS2, a fast *superstrada* (expressway) connecting Florence and Siena, or the SS222 (Strada Chiantigiana) through the Chianti hills.

Train Siena is not on a major railway line. Services from Florence (€5.50, 1¾ hours) are irregular and involve getting a local bus up to the centre of own – take the bus.

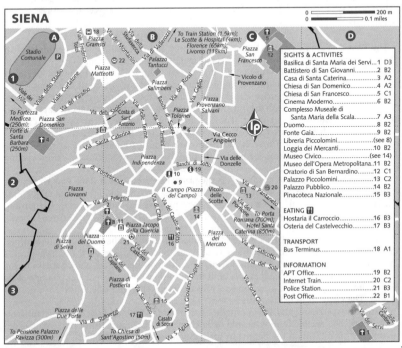

SIGHTS & ACTIVITIES
Basilica di Santa Maria dei Servi...1 D3
Battistero di San Giovanni............2 B2
Casa di Santa Caterina.................3 A2
Chiesa di San Domenico..............4 A2
Chiesa di San Francesco................5 C1
Cinema Moderno.........................6 B2
Complesso Museale di
  Santa Maria della Scala..............7 A3
Duomo.......................................8 B2
Fonte Gaia...................................9 B2
Libreria Piccolomini.................(see 8)
Loggia dei Mercanti...................10 B2
Museo Civico..........................(see 14)
Museo dell'Opera Metropolitana..11 B2
Oratorio di San Bernardino........12 C1
Palazzo Piccolomini...................13 C2
Palazzo Pubblico.......................14 B2
Pinacoteca Nazionale................15 B3

EATING
Hostaria il Carroccio..................16 B3
Osteria del Castelvecchio...........17 B3

TRANSPORT
Bus Terminus.............................18 A1

INFORMATION
APT Office..................................19 B2
Internet Train.............................20 C2
Police Station.............................21 B3
Post Office..................................22 B1

Excursions **SIENA**

189

IL PALIO

The thunder of hooves reverberates around Il Campo as 10 horsemen charge with all their skill around one of the world's oldest impromptu race courses. Just about anything goes as they spur their mounts round three times in a burst of colour and dust, watched by throngs of locals and outsiders. Some jockeys come a cropper, tempers flare and the crowds cheer and jeer in what must be one of the world's longest minutes. This is Il Palio (the Trophy), Siena's annual horse race, run twice every summer in honour of the Virgin Mary. Held on or around 2 July and 16 August, the wild charge is preceded and succeeded by flashes of medieval pageantry and much eating, drinking and celebrating.

Ten of Siena's 17 *contrade* (town districts) compete for the coveted *palio* (a silk banner). Each of the *contrade* has its own traditions, symbol and colours, and its own church and *palio* museum – needless to say, rivalry is keen.

On festival days Il Campo becomes a racetrack, with a ring of packed dirt around its perimeter serving as the course. From about 5pm representatives of each *contrada* parade in historical costume, bearing their individual banners.

The race is run at 7.45pm in July and 7pm in August. Jockeys are as often as not from outside town – Sardinians, known for their horsemanship, frequently saddle up. They can be the target of wild admiration or dark opprobrium, especially if there are suspicions that any have been bribed to throw the race.

A horse that loses its rider is still eligible to win and, since many riders fall each year, the horses are the focus of the event. There is one rule: riders are not to interfere with the reins of other horses.

Book well in advance if you want to stay in Siena around these times, and join the crowds in the centre of Il Campo at least four hours before the start. Once officials judge the area is full, barriers come down and no more people are allowed in. Once inside you cannot leave until it's all over. You are not allowed to enter with backpacks or any cumbersome objects. A camera and bottle of water are about the limit. If you want comfort, try for a seat on the provisional benches installed around the houses facing Il Campo. A spot can cost from €50 to in excess of €300. You can try dealing directly with building owners or see what tickets the tourist office has. It is also possible to get your name on a list with the tourist office in advance.

The race is televised live and can be seen online at www.paliodisiena.net (in Italian). You will find links to the 17 *contrade* here too. On the page of the Contrada del Bruco, for instance, you'll see a list of all the winners since 1644.

If you happen to be in town in the few days immediately preceding the race, you may see the jockeys and horses practising in Il Campo. Between May and October, **Cinema Moderno** (☎ 0577 37 85 68; Piazza Tolomei; adult/under 12yr/student €5/free/2.50; ⏱ 9.30am-6pm, Mon-Sat) runs a nail-biting 20-minute film about Siena and Il Palio.

The Palazzo Pubblico's graceful 102m bell tower, the **Torre del Mangia**, was completed in 1344. The views from the top are as spectacular now as they were then.

The **Duomo** (Cathedral), begun in 1196 and largely completed by 1215, is one of Italy's most splendid Gothic churches. Giovanni Pisano began the magnificent façade of white, green and red polychrome marble that was completed towards the end of the 14th century. The interior bristles with art but the most precious feature is the inlaid marble floor, decorated with 56 panels depicting historical and biblical subjects. The so-called crypt is adorned with 13th-century frescoes of episodes ranging from the flight from Egypt to scenes from the life and death of Christ. It was rediscovered during maintenance works in 1999. Thought to have been an area for medieval pilgrims to prepare spiritually before visiting the cathedral, it had been buried and forgotten for 700 years.

Through a door from the north aisle is the **Libreria Piccolomini**, which Pope Pius III (consecrated in 1503) built to house the books of his uncle, Enea Silvio Piccolomini (Pope Pius II). The walls of the small hall are covered by an impressive series of frescoes by Bernardino Pinturicchio. The sculptural group in the centre of the hall, the *Tre Grazie* (Three Graces), is a 3rd-century-AD Roman copy of an earlier Hellenistic work.

The art in the **Museo dell'Opera Metropolitana**, adjacent to the cathedral, formerly adorned the latter. The museo includes statuary that once stood inside and on the exterior of the cathedral, works by Duccio di Buoninsegna and, perhaps best of all, allows access to the *facciatone* (the big façade), all that was built in the 14th century of what was planned as an extraordinary expansion of the church, a project cut short largely due to the 1348 bout of plague. The views from here are the best in Siena.

Behind the cathedral and down a flight of stairs is the **Battistero di San Giovanni** (Baptistery of St John). The marble font by Jacopo della Quercia is decorated with bronze panels depicting the life of St John the Baptist by artists including Lorenzo Ghiberti and Donatello.

On the southwest side of Piazza del Duomo, the **Complesso Museale di Santa Maria della Scala** (the former pilgrims' hospice) boasts vivid frescoes by Domenico di Bartolo in the main ward, and a striking collection of Roman and Etruscan artefacts.

Take a short walk south of the cathedral and you'll run into yet more art in the 15th-century Palazzo Buonsignori, home to the **Pinacoteca Nazionale** (National Gallery) and masterpieces by Sienese artists. Look for Duccio di Buoninsegna's *Madonna dei Francescani* (Our Lady of the Franciscans), the *Madonna col Bambino* (Our Lady and Christ Child) by Simone Martini and a series of yet more Madonnas by Ambrogio Lorenzetti.

Also worth a peek when open are the **Oratorio di San Bernardino**, part of the Chiesa di San Francesco complex, and the **Chiesa di Sant'Agostino**. The former houses a modest museum of religious artworks.

From the Loggia dei Mercanti, north of Il Campo, take Banchi di Sotto east to the **Palazzo Piccolomini**. Siena's finest Renaissance palace, it houses the city's archives and a small museum. Further east are the 13th-century **Basilica di Santa Maria dei Servi**, with a fresco by Pietro Lorenzetti, and the 14th-century **Porta Romana** city gate.

Information

APT office (☎ 0577 28 05 51; www.terresiena.it; Piazza del Campo 56; ☽ 9am-7pm)

Combined Tickets You can make savings on individual admission costs by opting for one of several combined tickets (no child reductions): Museo Civico and Torre del Mangia €10 (valid one day); Museo Civico, Complesso Museale di Santa Maria della Scala and Centro d'Arte Contemporaneo €10 (valid two days); Duomo, crypt, Battistero, Museo dell'Opera Metropolitana and Oratorio di San Bernardino €10; Museo Civico, Complesso Museale di Santa Maria della Scala, Centro d'Arte Contemporaneo, Museo dell'Opera Metropolitana, Battistero di San Giovanni and Libreria Piccolomini €13 (valid seven days November–mid-March); Museo Civico, Complesso Museale di Santa Maria della Scala, Centro d'Arte Contemporaneo, Museo dell'Opera Metropolitana, Battistero di San Giovanni, Libreria Piccolomini, Oratorio di San Bernardino and Museo Diocesano €16 (valid seven days mid-March–October).

Hospital (☎ 0577 58 51 11; Viale Bracci) Just north of Siena at Le Scotte.

Internet Train (☎ 0577 24 74 60; Via di Pantaneto 54; per hr €4.30; ☽ 10am-10pm Mon-Fri, 3-10pm Sun)

Post office (Piazza Matteotti 1; ☽ 8.15am-7pm Mon-Sat)

Police station (questura; ☎ 0577 20 11 11; Via del Castoro 6)

Sights

Battistero di San Giovanni (www.operaduomo.siena.it; Piazza San Giovanni; admission €3; ☽ 9am-8pm Jun-Aug, 9.30am-7pm Mar-May & Sep-Oct, 10am-1pm & 2-5pm Nov-Feb)

Casa di Santa Caterina (☎ 0577 28 08 01; www .caterinati.org; Costa di Sant'Antonio 6; admission free; ☽ 9am-12.30pm & 3-6pm)

Chiesa di Sant'Agostino (Prato di Sant'Agostino; admission €2; ☽ 10.30am-1.30pm & 3-5.30pm mid-Mar–Oct)

Chiesa di San Domenico (Piazza San Domenico; admission free; ☽ 7.30am 1pm & 3-6.30pm)

Complesso Museale di Santa Maria della Scala (☎ 0577 22 48 11; www.santamaria.comune.siena.it; Piazza del Duomo 2; adult/under 11yr/student €6/free/3.50; ☽ 10am-6.30pm mid-Mar–Oct, 10.30am-4.30pm Nov–mid-Mar)

Duomo (Cathedral; ☎ 0577 4 73 21; www.operaduomo .siena.it; Piazza del Duomo; admission with Libreria Piccolomini €3; ☽ 10.30am-8pm Mon-Sat, 1.30-6.30pm Sun & holidays Jun-Aug, 10.30am-7.30pm Mon-Sat, 1.30-5.30pm Sun Mar-May; 10.30am-7.30pm daily Sep-Oct, 10.30am-6.30pm Mon-Sat, 1.30-5.30pm Sun Nov-Feb) The price goes up to €6 when the marble floor is revealed, between 10.30am and 7.30pm, late August to October. Crypt admission is €6, and it is open 9.30am to 8pm, June–August, and 9.30am til 7pm March–May and September–October.

Libreria Piccolomini (see Duomo)

Museo Civico (☎ 0577 29 22 63; www.comune.siena .it/museocivico; Palazzo Pubblico, Il Campo; admission adult/under 11yr/11-18yr €7/free/4.50; ☽ 10am-7pm mid-Mar–Oct, 10am-5.30pm Nov–mid-Mar)

Museo dell'Opera Metropolitana (☎ 0577 28 30 48; www.operaduomo.siena.it; Piazza del Duomo 8; admission €6; ☽ 9.30am-8pm Jun-Aug, 9.30am-7pm Mar-May & Sep-Oct, 9am-1.30pm Nov-Feb)

Oratorio di San Bernardino (☎ 0577 28 30 48; www .operaduomo.siena.it; Piazza San Francesco 10; admission €3; ☽ 10.30am-1.30pm & 3-5.30pm mid-Mar–Oct)

Palazzo Piccolomini (Banchi di Sotto; admission free; ☽ museum 9am-1pm Mon-Sat)

Pinacoteca Nazionale (☎ 0577 28 11 61; Via San Pietro 29; adult/child €4/free; ☽ 8.30am-1.30pm Mon, 8.15am-7.50pm Tue-Sat, 8.15am-1.15pm Sun)

Torre del Mangia (Palazzo Pubblico; admission €6; ☽ 10am-7pm mid-Mar–Oct, 10am-4pm Nov–mid-Mar)

Eating

Hostaria Il Carroccio (☎ 0577 4 11 65; Via del Casato di Sotto 32; meal €30-35; ☺ Thu-Mon & Tue lunch) This place, off Il Campo, has excellent pasta. Try the *pici* (a kind of thick spaghetti) or the *pappardelle al cinghiale* (broad ribbon pasta and wild boar), a Tuscan classic.

Osteria del Castelvecchio (☎ 0577 4 95 86, Via Castelvecchio 65; meal €25-30; ☺ Mon-Sat) Located beneath cool brick vaults, in an ancient mansion a stone's throw from the cathedral, the Old Castle is far from old hat. Delicious vegetarian dishes (like *la carabaccia* – a kind of onion soup that they say was first slurped in Renaissance times) feature on the ever-changing menu, so meat-loathers can safely accompany their carnivore friends. Try the *risotto con zucchine, menta e basilico* (courgette, mint and basil risotto).

Sleeping

Hotel Santa Caterina (☎ 0577 22 11 05; www.hscsiena.it; Via Piccolomini 7; s/d with breakfast up to €98/144; **P** €12) An elegantly renovated 18th-century villa, just outside the Porta Romana, this hotel is a tranquil haven. Rooms are tastefully furnished, the breakfast room is light and airy and there's a lovely garden with open views to the hills.

Pensione Palazzo Ravizza (☎ 0577 28 04 62; www .palazzoravizza.it; Pian dei Mantellini 34; s/d €130/160; **P**) This delightful Renaissance *palazzo*, which became a guesthouse in the 1920s, offers rooms with frescoed ceilings and antique furniture. The *pensione's* deluxe rooms and suites are more expensive but considerably more spacious. Many of the rooms have views over the garden.

IL CHIANTI & AROUND

For centuries the medieval communes of Florence and Siena quarrelled nastily over how much of the hills and valleys between them belonged to each. The final division split the area into Il Chianti Fiorentino and Il Chianti Senese. As you explore this rich wine country, you begin to understand what all the fuss was about. Rolling hills and vineyards are interspersed by warm-coloured villages, distinguished country manors and a smattering of *pievi* (Romanesque country churches).

Possibly the country's best-marketed (although not always best-quality) wine comes from here. Who hasn't heard of chianti? Chianti Classico is the best-known generic label, sold under the Gallo Nero (Black Cockerel) symbol, whose reds must be at least 75% made from Sangiovese, the local grape. The rest of Il Chianti is split into a further six classified wine-growing regions: Colli Fiorentini, Colli Senesi, Colline Pisane, Colli Aretini, Montalbano and Rufina, all with their distinct characteristics. As well as these wines, look out for *vin santo*, a sweet, aged dessert wine akin to sherry, produced by many wineries and often enjoyed with *cantucci* biscuits. You can get hold of maps marking wineries if you wish to do a little DIY wine touring, but be aware that few put on free tastings. A good starting place is the Strade del Vino (Wine Roads) website for the area (www.stradadelvino-chianticollifiorentini .com). It details itineraries and lists wine-makers (who participate to a greater or lesser degree).

About 20km south of Florence, on the picturesque Strada Chiantigiana (SS222) that links Florence with Siena, is **Greve in Chianti**, the first well-located base for exploring the region. Piazza Matteotti, the unusual triangular square at the centre of the town, is presided over by a statue of Giovanni da

The prolific vines of Il Chianti (left)

TRANSPORT

Distance from Florence Barberino Val d'Elsa 29.5km; Castellina in Chianti 39km; Certaldo 44.5km; Gaiole in Chianti 60km; Greve in Chianti 20km; Montefioralle 22km; Monteriggioni 53km; Radda in Chianti 50km; San Casciano in Val di Pesa 16.5km; San Gimignano 57.5km.

Direction South

Bus Unfortunately buses can be a slow way of getting around. SITA's regular buses run to Greve (€2.90) but take an hour. Only two buses run to Radda (€3.50, one hour). Only one leaves at 1.35pm for Gaiole (€4, one hour) via Castellina (€3.50, 40 minutes), which are better linked by bus with Siena (four or five a day). For Monteriggioni the only option is to get a SITA bus from Siena to Poggibonsi, and ask to be let off at or near the village en route; getting back is more hit and miss. Up to 15 buses a day run to San Gimignano from Florence (€5.90, 1¼ hours), but you must change at Poggibonsi.

Car Take the SS222 (Strada Chiantigiana) through the Chianti hills to tour Greve, Castellina, Radda and Gaiole. Otherwise follow the minor road that shadows the SS2 *superstrada* (motorway) between Florence and Siena. The more ambitious, wanting to reach San Gimignano along one of these routes, will have no choice but to do so by car.

Train Regular trains run from Florence to Certaldo (€3.70, one hour).

Verrazzano, a local hero who discovered New York harbour. He is commemorated in the New World by the Verrazano Narrows Bridge (the good captain's name lost a 'z' somewhere in the mid-Atlantic), linking Staten Island to Brooklyn.

Montefioralle, 2km west of Greve, is an ancient castle-village. It's worth the uphill walk, particularly to see its Santo Stefano church, which contains precious medieval paintings.

Castellina in Chianti, 19km south of Greve, was long a frontier town between forever-warring Florence and Siena. Wander into this wine town along Via delle Volte, a medieval street crowded in by shops and houses that together form a long vaulted tunnel.

Just 11km east of Castellina, **Radda in Chianti** has retained much of its traditional charm. Its nucleus is Piazza Ferrucci, where the 16th-century **Palazzo del Podestà**, its façade emblazoned with escutcheons of towns and governing *podestas*, faces the village church. From here you can push on 10km east for **Gaiole in Chianti**, a pleasant village surrounded by low hills. Just west of the village centre, set in woodland, is the early-12th-century Romanesque *pieve* of Santa Maria a Spaltenna and a small hill fortress. Two kilometres to the south is the bite-sized **Castello di Metelo**, where you can taste and buy wine. From here you can head south about 20km to Siena along the SS408.

Alternatively, back at Castellina, follow a narrow country road to the southwest for 14km, to arrive before the walls of the captivating medieval stronghold of **Monteriggioni**, just off the SS2 and about 12km short of Siena. The walls date back to the 13th century and, although some of the towers still stand only because of later surgical intervention, the place transports you to another age.

Another possible route south from Florence starts from the **Certosa di Galluzzo** (p109). Take the SS2 *superstrada* (motorway) that connects Florence with Siena, or the more tortuous and windy road that runs roughly parallel to it. Follow the latter to **Tavernuzze**, south of which there is a US WWII cemetery, and on to **San Casciano Val di Pesa**, an important wine centre. The town came under Florentine control in the 13th century and was later equipped with a defensive wall, parts of which remain. Continue south via Tavarnelle Val di Pesa to the medieval *borgo* (village) of **Barberino Val d'Elsa**, worth a stop for a brief stroll along the main street.

Just south out of Barberino, a minor road meanders west for about 15km to reach pretty hill-top **Certaldo**. The upper town (Certaldo Alto) is particularly captivating in the glow of the dying day's sun. It has Etruscan origins, while the lower town in the valley sprang up in the 13th century – by which time both had been absorbed into the Florentine republic.

The **Casa del Boccaccio**, where writer Giovanni Boccaccio (see p34) supposedly died and was buried in 1375, is on the upper town's main drag. It is a largely reconstructed version of his house, which was severely damaged in WWII. The library has some precious copies of Boccaccio's *Decameron*. Several doors up, the **Chiesa di SS Jacopo e Filippo** houses a cenotaph to the writer. The whole walled *borgo* of the upper town is dominated by the stout **Palazzo Pretorio** (aka Palazzo del Vicario), whose 14th-century façade is richly decorated with the coats of arms of those who ruled the town through the centuries. Frescoed halls lead off the Renaissance courtyard into an Escher-like construction. Within the labyrinth, one of the main halls is home to a modest collection of Etruscan and Roman odds and sods.

From Certaldo it's 13 winding kilometres south to **San Gimignano**, a quintessential symbol of Tuscany. As though cooked up by Monty Python, 13 uneven and somewhat wobbly-looking towers poke up from this 'medieval Manhattan' (once upon a time there were 72!), still proudly symbolising the wealth and power of their one-time owners. Such towers, as numerous as the noble families who could afford to build them, once bristled all over medieval Tuscan towns. As power in Florence and other major centres became concentrated in the hands of the emerging wealthy merchant class, noble families were increasingly obliged, at the city councils' demand, to dismantle these impressive and provocative structures.

Piazza della Cisterna is lined with houses and towers dating from the 13th and 14th centuries. In the adjoining Piazza del Duomo stands the Romanesque cathedral, or **Collegiata**. Among the frescoes inside are beautiful works by Domenico Ghirlandaio in the **Cappella di Santa Fina**. Across the square, the **Museo d'Arte Sacra** is crammed with religious art culled, in the main, from the town's churches.

The **Palazzo del Popolo**, left of the cathedral, still operates as the town hall. From the internal courtyard, climb the stairs to the **Museo Civico**, which features paintings from the Sienese and Florentine schools of the 12th to 15th centuries. Then, gird your loins to climb some more, up inside the palazzo's **Torre Grossa** (Big Tower) for an appreciation of a medieval watchman's views over town and country.

The **Museo Archeologico** contains a modest archaeological collection and, more interestingly, the **Speziera di Santa Fina**, a reconstructed 16th-century pharmacy and herb garden. Holed up inside the remains of the city fortress you will find the **Museo del Vino**, where a sommelier will take your tastebuds on a tour of local wines – sadly, though, there are no free tipples.

Information

Castellina in Chianti tourist office (☎ 0577 74 13 92; Via Ferruccio 40; ☻ 10am-1pm & 2-6pm Mar-Nov, 10am-1pm & 2-5pm Mon-Sat Dec & Feb, closed Jan)

Certaldo tourist office (☎ 0571 65 67 21; Viale Fabiani 5; ☻ 9.30am-12.30pm & 3.30-6.30pm Mon-Thu, 9am-12.30pm & 3.30-7pm Fri-Sun)

Chianti Slow Travel (☎ 055 854 62 99; www .chiantislowtravel.it, in Italian; Piazza Ferrante Mori 1, Greve in Chianti; ☻ 9am-1pm & 2.30-6pm Mon-Sat) Operates as a tourist office when the main one is closed. It also books accommodation and wine tours. Hours can be irregular.

Gaiole in Chianti tourist office (☎ 0577 74 94 11; Via Galileo Galilei 1; ☻ 10am-6pm Apr-Oct)

Greve in Chianti tourist office (☎ 055 854 62 87; Via Giuseppe da Verrazzano 59; ☻ 9.30am-1pm & 2.30-7pm Mon-Sat Mar-Oct) About 500m short of town when coming in along the SS222 from Florence.

Radda in Chianti tourist office ☎ 0577 73 84 94; proradda@chiantinet.it; Piazza Castello 6; ☻ 10am-1pm & 3-7pm Mon-Sat, 10.30am-12.30pm Sun Mar-Oct, 10.30am-12.30pm & 3.30-6.30pm Mon-Sat Nov-Feb)

San Gimignano tourist office (☎ 0577 94 00 08; www .sangimignano.com; Piazza del Duomo 1; ☻ 9am-1pm & 3-7pm Mar-Oct, 9am-1pm & 2-6pm Nov-Feb)

Sights

Casa del Boccaccio (☎ 0571 66 42 08; Via Boccaccio, Certaldo; admission €3.10; ☻ 10am-7pm Wed-Mon, 10am-4.30pm Tue Apr-Sep; 10.30am-4.30pm Wed-Mon Oct-Mar)

Collegiata (Piazza del Duomo, San Gimignano; adult/child €3.50/1.50, or combined ticket with Museo d'Arte Sacra adult/child €5.50/2.50; ☻ 9.30am-7.30pm Mon-Fri, 9.30am-5.30pm Sat, 12.30-5pm Sun Apr-Oct; 9.30am-5pm Mon-Sat, 12.30-5pm Sun Nov–mid-Jan & Mar)

Museo Archeologico (☎ 0577 94 03 48; Via Folgore da San Gimignano 11, San Gimignano; adult/child €3.50/2.50, or combined ticket with Museo Civico & Palazzo Pretorio adult/child €7.50/5.50; ☻ 11am-6pm Mar-Oct, 11am-6pm Sat-Thu Nov–mid-Jan, 11am-6pm Fri-Mon mid-Jan–Feb)

Museo Civico (☎ 0577 94 00 08; Palazzo del Popolo, San Gimignano; adult/child €5/4, or combined ticket with Museo Archeologico & Palazzo Pretorio adult/child €7.50/5.50; ☻ 9.30am-7.20pm Mar-Oct, 10am-5.50pm Nov-Feb)

Museo d'Arte Sacra (☎ 0577 94 03 16; Piazza Pecori 1, San Gimignano; adult/child €3/1.50, or combined ticket with Collegiata adult/child €5.50/2.50; 9.30am-7.30pm Apr-Oct, San Gimignano, 9.30am-5pm Nov–mid-Jan & Mar)

Museo del Vino (Rocca di Montestaffoli, San Gimignano; admission free; 11am-7pm Thu-Mon, 3-7pm Wed Mar-Oct)

Palazzo del Popolo (see Museo Civico)

Palazzo Pretorio (☎ 0571 66 12 19; Certaldo; admission adult/senior & under 15yr €3/1.50, or combined ticket with Museo Archeologico & Museo Civico adult/child €7.50/5.50; 10am-7pm Apr-Oct, 10.30am-4.30pm Tue-Sun Nov-Mar)

Eating

Mangiango Mangiando (☎ 055 854 63 72; Piazza Matteotti 80, Greve in Chianti; meal €25; Tue -Sun) A series of hearty meat dishes leads the way in this age-old dining room. Pasta dishes done with wild boar can be alternated with succulent steak or *faraona ripiena* (stuffed pheasant).

Osteria del Carcere (☎ 0577 94 19 05; Via del Castello 13, San Gimignano; meal €30-35; lunch & dinner Fri-Tue & dinner only Thu) Smack in the middle of the business, this place has nothing prison-like about it. Sit at the bar or head upstairs for light meals (tempting cheese and sausage platters). Otherwise, some hot dishes (Tuscan classics like *pappa al pomodoro*) make this a good lunch stop.

Sleeping

Albergo del Chianti (☎ 055 85 37 63; www.alber-godelchianti.it; Piazza Matteotti 86, Greve in Chianti; s/d €83/95) Overlooking Greve's central square, this venerable 11th-century inn offers the luxury of a small pool and gardens.

Castello di Tornano (☎ 0577 74 60 67; www.castel-loditornano.it; d €200-465; P) About 5km south of Gaiole in Chianti, and just left off the winding SS408 road to Siena (along about 1.5km of dirt track), is this medieval Tuscan escape in the heart of wine country. Choose from a selection of lavishly decorated rooms in the mansion or tower. Taste the wine, relax by the pool or go horse-riding.

Hotel La Cisterna (☎ 0577 94 03 28; www.hotel-cisterna.it; Piazza della Cisterna 24, San Gimignano; s/d €75/122) Spotless rooms with all modern comforts exude the charm of a hotel that has been in business for a century.

Villa Vignamaggio (☎ 055 854 66 53; www.vig-namaggio.com; Via Petriolo 5; d €150-450; P) This exquisite 15th-century manor house and winery, 5km south of Greve, is thought to be the place where Leonardo da Vinci painted the *Mona Lisa*. It was also used as a location in Kenneth Branagh's film *Much Ado About Nothing*. Take the SS222 south of Greve for 2km, then turn left and follow the signs for Lamole.

PISA & LUCCA

Known today for an architectural project gone awry, Pisa of the Leaning Tower was Rome's main naval base during the Punic Wars and a big medieval player in the rough and tumble of Mediterranean empire-building. Nearby Lucca, another Roman town founded by the Ligurians, fell under Pisan control in 1314, but later regained independence – which, despite Florence's best efforts, it clung to until 1799.

Pisa's heyday began late in the 9th century, when it became an independent maritime republic and a rival of Genoa and Venice. The good times rolled on into the 13th century, and some of the city's finest buildings date from this period. Eclipsed by its seafaring rivals, Pisa fell to Florence in 1406. The Medicis at least did the Pisans the favour of reestablishing the city's university. One of its most illustrious lecturers would later be Galileo Galilei, Pisa's favourite son.

The Pisans can justly claim that the **Campo dei Miracoli** is one of the most beautiful squares in the world. Set astride its immaculate lawns is an awe-inspiring display of Romanesque splendour – the cathedral, the baptistery and the Leaning Tower. You can plunge into this miraculous location online too, at http://piazza.opapisa.it.

TRANSPORT

Distance from Florence Lucca 71km; Pisa 79km.

Direction West

Bus Lazzi operates buses to Lucca from Florence (€4.70, 1½ hours). The train is cheaper and faster to Pisa.

Car For Pisa take the SS67 *superstrada* (motorway), which is not a toll road. The A11 toll road from Florence skirts around the south of Lucca. The two cities are 22km apart.

Train Regular trains run from Florence to Pisa (€5; up to one hour 20 minutes) and Lucca (€4.60, 1¼ to 1½ hours). Regular trains also connect Pisa and Lucca (€2.10, 15 to 25 minutes).

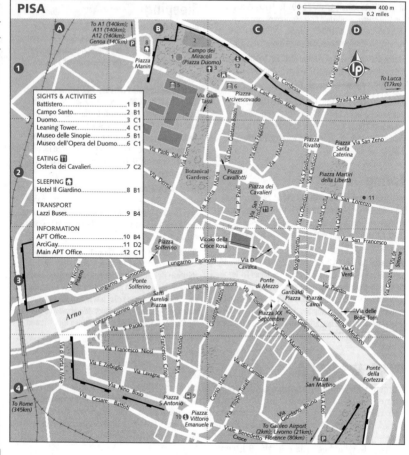

PISA

0				400 m
0				0.2 miles

To A1 (140km); A11 (140km); A12 (140km); Genoa (140km)

Piazza Manin

Campo dei Miracoli (Piazza Duomo)

To Lucca (17km)

Via Contessa

Strada Statale

SIGHTS & ACTIVITIES 🏛

Battistero..............................1 B1
Campo Santo.........................2 B1
Duomo.................................3 C1
Leaning Tower.......................4 C1
Museo delle Sinopie................5 B1
Museo dell'Opera del Duomo....6 C1

EATING 🍴

Osteria dei Cavalieri................7 C2

SLEEPING 🛏

Hotel Il Giardino....................8 B1

TRANSPORT

Lazzi Buses...........................9 B4

INFORMATION

APT Office............................10 B4
ArciGay...............................11 D2
Main APT Office....................12 C1

Via Galli-Tassi

Piazza Arcivescovado

Piazza Cant Pietro Maffi

Via Paolo Savi

Via Roma

Via Don Gaetano Bosco

Via della Faggiola

Via Martiri

Via Fratoleschi

Via T Carducci

Piazza Rivalto

Piazza Santa Caterina

Piazza Via San Zeno

Botanical Gardens

Piazza Cavallotti

Piazza dei Cavalieri

Via Santa Maria

Via P Paoli

Via San Frediano

Piazza Martiri della Libertà

Via C Oberdan

Via Santa Cecilia

Via San Lorenzo

Via S Cateri

Via Derna

Via San Francesco

Borgo Stretto

Via Calfini

Via Giovanni

Via de Simone

Piazza Solferino

Vicolo della Croce Rosa

Lungarno Pacinotti

Via D Cavalca

Via G Verdi

Via Palestro

Via Nicola Pisano

Lungarno R Simonelli

Ponte Solferino

Arno

Lungarno Sonnino Scalei

Saffi Aurelio Piazza

Lungarno Gambacorti

Via P Toselli

Ponte di Mezzo

Garibaldi Piazza

Lungarno Galilei Galilei

Piazza Cairoli

Lungarno Mediceo

Via delle Belle Torri

Via S Paolo

Via S Antonio

Via Giuseppe Mazzini

Piazza XX Septembre

Via San Martino

Ponte della Fortezza

Via di Porta a Mare

Via Francesco Niosi

Via Francesco Crispi

Via E Zerboglio

Via Lavagna

Via del Carmine

Corso Italia

Piazza San Martino

To Rome (345km)

Via Nino Bixio

Via Cesare Battisti

Piazza S Antonio

Via Filippo Turati

Via Giordano Bruno

Via A Ceci

Piazza Vittorio Emanuele II

To Galileo Airport (2km); Livorno (21km); Florence (80km)

Viale Benedetto Croce

The majesty of Pisa's **Duomo** (Cathedral) made it a model for Romanesque churches all over Tuscany. Begun in 1064, it is covered inside and out with the alternating bands of dark green and cream marble characteristic of the Pisan-Romanesque style. Enjoy the depth of detail that Giovanni Pisano imparted to the vibrant early-14th-century marble pulpit in the north aisle.

The **Leaning Tower** (Torre Pendente) is a monumental cock-up. The Duomo's bell tower (Campanile), started in 1173 but built on shaky ground, was always unstable. When it was closed to the public in 1990, it was 4.47m out of plumb and many thought it was going to fall. Engineers wrapped cables around the third storey in 1998 and attached them to A-frames. This stabilised the tower while workers removed portions of soil on the north side to create a counter subsidence. The famous lean, now 4.1m off the perpendicular, has been reduced and experts reckon the tower is safe for another 300 years.

The unusual round **Battistero** (Baptistery) took centuries to complete, which accounts for the architectural mix. The lower level of arcades is in the Pisan-Romanesque style, while the pinnacled upper section and dome are Gothic. The acoustics beneath the dome are like crystal.

Located behind the white wall to the north of the Duomo, the **Campo Santo** (Cemetery) is said to contain soil shipped from Calvary during the Crusades. They say the holy dirt reduces cadavers to skeletons in days! Frescoes, saved from Allied artillery bombardment around the cloisters in WWII, are gathered in a special room. The **Museo delle Sinopie** houses some reddish-brown sketches, originally drawn on to walls as the basis for frescoes, which were discovered in the cemetery after WWII. The *sinopie* have been restored and provide a fascinating insight into the process of creating a fresco.

The **Museo dell'Opera del Duomo**, near the Leaning Tower, features artworks from the tower, cathedral and baptistery, including an ivory *Madonna col Bambino* (Madonna and Child) by Giovanni Pisano. In summer (June to August) you can stroll along a stretch of old **city walls** here.

The Romanesque **Cattedrale** (Cathedral) of Lucca, 22km north of Pisa, dates from the 11th century and is every bit a rival to its Pisan counterpart. The exquisite façade, in the Lucca-Pisan style, was designed to accommodate the pre-existing bell tower. In the centre of the old town, the **Chiesa di San Michele in Foro** is another dazzling Romanesque church, started in the 11th century. The wedding-cake façade is topped by a figure of the Archangel Michael slaying a dragon. The **Chiesa di San Frediano** is also a must-see with its stunning exterior mosaic.

Lucca's busiest street, **Via Fillungo,** threads its way through the medieval heart of the old city and is lined with fascinating, centuries-old buildings. The **Torre delle Ore** (City Clock Tower) is about halfway along; puff your way up its 207 steps and enjoy the reward of a fish-eye lens–style view over the city. You can do it all again in the **Torre Giunigi**, part of the mansion of the same name. Just east of Torre delle Ore, the houses of **Piazza Anfiteatro** look out on to what was the Roman-era amphitheatre.

Take time out from the monuments to amble or cycle (you can rent bicycles at the main tourist office for €11 a day, as well as several other places around town) the 3km rim of the city's magnificently intact walls.

Information

Lucca main tourist office (☎ 0583 58 31 50; www.lucca
.turismo.toscana.it; Piazzale Verdi; 🕐 9am-7pm Easter-
Oct, 9am-5.30pm Nov-Easter)

APT main office (☎ 050 56 04 64; www.pisa.turismo
.toscana.it; Piazza del Duomo 1; 🕐 9am-6pm Mon-Sat,
10.30am-4.30pm Sun) This is where to buy tickets to visit
the Leaning Tower (see right).

APT office (☎ 050 4 22 91; Piazza Vittorio Emanuele 16;
🕐 9am-7pm Mon-Sat, 9.30am-3.30pm Sun)

Sights

Battistero (☎ 050 56 05 47; Campo dei Miracoli, Pisa;
adult/under 8yr €5/free; 🕐 8am-8pm Apr-Sep, 9am-7pm
Oct, 9am-6pm Mar, 10am-5pm Nov-Feb) You can also get
a combined ticket for the Battistero, Campo Santo, Duomo
(outside of winter), Museo dell'Opera del Duomo and
Museo delle Sinopie for €8.50; alternatively, admission is
€6 to just two of these monuments.

Campo Santo (☎ 050 56 05 47; www.duomo.pisa.it;
Campo dei Miracoli, Pisa; admission €5, or combined tickets
– see Battistero; 🕐 8am-8pm Apr-Sep, 9am-7pm Oct,
9am-6pm Mar, 10am-5pm Nov-Feb)

Cattedrale (Cathedral; Piazza San Martino, Lucca; admission
free; 🕐 9.30am-6.45pm Apr-Sep, 9.30am-4.45pm Oct-Mar)

Chiesa di San Michele in Foro (Piazza San Michele, Lucca;
admission free; 🕐 9am-noon & 3-6pm Apr-Sep, 9am-
noon & 3-5pm Oct-Mar)

City Walls (Pisa; admission €2; 🕐 11am-2pm & 3-6pm
Jun-Aug)

Duomo (☎ 050 56 05 47; www.duomo.pisa.it; Campo dei
Miracoli, Pisa; admission €2 or with combined ticket – see
Battistero, free Nov-Feb; 🕐 10am-8pm Mon-Sat, 1-8pm
Sun & holidays Apr-Sep, 10am-7pm Mon-Sat, 1-7pm Sun
Oct, 10am-6pm Mon-Sat, 1-6pm Sun Mar, 10am-1pm &
3-5pm Mon-Sat, 1-5pm Sun Nov-Feb)

Leaning Tower (☎ 050 56 05 47; www.duomo.pisa
.it; Campo dei Miracoli, Pisa; admission €15; 🕐 8.30am-
8.30pm Apr-Sep, 9am-7pm Oct, 9am-6pm Mar, 9.30am-
5pm Nov-Feb) You must book a place, either on the website
(€2 more) or in person, to be sure of a visit as numbers
allowed up are limited. You can also buy tickets at the Main
APT Office. Children can not visit for safety reasons.

Museo dell'Opera del Duomo (☎ 050 56 05 47; www
.duomo.pisa.it; Campo dei Miracoli, Pisa; admission €5, or
with combined ticket – see Battistero; 🕐 8am-8pm Apr-
Sep, 9am-7pm Oct, 9am-6pm Mar, 10am-5pm Nov-Feb)

Museo delle Sinopie (☎ 050 56 05 47; www.duomo
.pisa.it; Piazza Arcivescovado 8, Pisa; admission €5 or with
combined ticket – see Battistero; 🕐 8am-8pm Apr-Sep,
9am-7pm Oct, 9am-6pm Mar, 10am-5pm Nov-Feb)

Torre delle Ore (☎ 0583 31 68 46; Via Fillungo; admission €3.50 or with Torre Giunigi €5; 🕐 10am-7pm May-
Sep, 10am-6pm Mar-Apr, 9am-5.30pm Oct-Feb)

Torre Guinigi (☎ 0583 31 68 46; Via Sant Andrea,
Lucca; admission €3.50 or with Torre delle Ore €5;
🕐 9am-8pm Mar-Sep, 10am-6pm Oct, 9am-5.30pm
Nov-Feb)

Excursions

PISA & LUCCA

Eating

Osteria dei Cavalieri (☎ 050 58 08 58; Via San Frediano 16, Pisa; meal €30-35; ☻ Mon-Fri & Sat evening) In one of Pisa's most delightful restaurants, you can opt for a single dish (*piatto unico*) or choose from a mouth-watering menu. Fresh pasta first courses might come with rabbit or duck sauces.

Ristorante Buca di Sant'Antonio (☎ 0583 5 58 81; Via della Cervia 3, Lucca; meal from €35; ☻ Tue-Sat & Sun lunch) In business since the late 18th century, this stylish restaurant is a favourite with locals and it's always busy. The menu includes such treats as guinea fowl and spit-roast kid meat.

Sleeping

Hotel Il Giardino (☎ 050 56 21 01; www.hotelilgiardino .pisa.it; Piazza Manin 1, Pisa; s/d €70/90; **P**) You'll find sparkling, well-maintained rooms and friendly staff here. Enjoy breakfast on the tranquil terrace with the city walls and Battistero dome in view.

Piccolo Hotel Puccini (☎ 0583 5 54 21; www.hotel -puccini.com; Via di Poggio 9, Lucca; s/d €60/85) Smart, friendly, centrally located and within spitting distance of Piazza San Michele, Hotel Puccini offers high-ceilinged rooms with dark timber furnishings, soft colour schemes and a window onto the town centre.

PRATO, PISTOIA & AROUND

A 100km western circuit from Florence would see you exploring the industrious towns of Prato and Pistoia, followed by Leonardo da Vinci's birthplace and finally the ceramics centre of Montelupo. It is done easily enough by car, but can be a little more difficult by public transport as the links with Vinci are poor.

The textile town of **Prato**, 18.5km northwest of Florence, was founded by the Ligurians, taken by the Etruscans and finally absorbed into the Roman federation. By the 11th century Prato was an important centre for wool production and soon fell into Florence's orbit. Today, although capital of a separate province, it is close to being engulfed by Florence's suburban sprawl.

Prato's grand Palazzo Duomo is fronted by the 12th-century **Cattedrale di Santo Stefano**. The rather simple Pisan-Romanesque façade features a lunette by Andrea della Robbia, but the most extraordinary element is the **Pulpito della Sacra Cintola** jutting over the piazza on the right-hand side of the main entrance. The pulpit, created by Donatello, was expressly added so that the *sacra cintola* (sacred girdle) could be displayed to the people five times a year (Easter, 1 May, 15 August, 8 September and 25 December). It is said that the Virgin Mary gave the girdle (or belt) to St Thomas, and it later found its way to Prato from Jerusalem after the Second Crusade. Mind you, at least one other such girdle has been declared the real thing in the Syrian city of Homs. The original pulpit is housed in the **Museo dell'Opera del Duomo**, accessed through the church's charming cloister.

The **Museo di Pittura Murale**, reached through the cloister of the Gothic **Chiesa di San Domenico**, houses a collection of largely Tuscan paintings. Stars include Filippo Lippi, Paolo Uccello

Pisa's leaning tower (p196), soundly guaranteed for another 300 years

and Bernardo Daddi, with his polyptych of the miracle of the Virgin's girdle (it's a bit of a theme here). Enjoy too the 14th- to 17th-century frescoes and graffiti.

Prato's castle, the **Castello dell'Imperatore**, was built in the 13th century by the Holy Roman Emperor Frederick II. It's an impressive example of military architecture but rather bare inside.

Finally, the **Museo del Tessuto**, dedicated exclusively to textiles, is the only such museum in Italy and has more than 5000 samples, dating from the 3rd century to the present day.

Lying at the foot of the Apennines, and barely an energetic spit from Prato, **Pistoia** has grown beyond its well-preserved medieval ramparts and is today a centre for train manufacture.

Piazza del Duomo is the focal point of Pistoia's sightseeing wealth. The façade of the **Cattedrale di San Zeno** is Pisan-Romanesque, and boasts a lunette by Andrea della Robbia. Inside, in the **Cappella di San Jacopo**, is the

TRANSPORT

Distance from Florence Montelupo 23.5km; Pistoia 37km; Prato 18.5km; Vinci 61km (via Pistoia).
Direction West
Bus Regular Copit buses connect Vinci with Empoli (€2.50, 25 minutes), itself served by trains from Florence via Montelupo.
Car The best way to do this circuit, especially if you want to complete it in a day, is by car (otherwise all the destinations except Vinci are easily reached by train). Take the A11 west out of Florence for both Prato and Pistoia. From Pistoia the minor SP13 route winds up into the Monte Albano hill country on its way south to Vinci (24km) – car is the only way to do this stretch. From there you can drop south to Empoli and turn east on the SS67 for Florence via Montelupo.
Train Regular trains run from Florence to Prato (€1.60, 15 to 25 minutes), Pistoia (€2.60, 30 to 45 minutes) and Montelupo (€2.10, 30 minutes).

remarkable silver **Dossale di San Jacopo**, or Altarpiece of St James. It was begun in the 13th century, with artisans adding to it over the ensuing two centuries, until Brunelleschi contributed the final touch – the two half-figures on the left side.

Across the south end of the square, the **Battistero di San Giovanni** (Baptistery of St John), elegantly banded in green and white marble, was started in 1337 to a design by Andrea Pisano.

Dominating the eastern flank of Piazza del Duomo is the Gothic Palazzo del Comune, which houses the **Museo Civico** and its collection of Tuscan art from the 13th to 19th centuries.

The portico of the nearby **Ospedale del Ceppo** will stop even the more monument-weary in their tracks. The unique terracotta frieze by Giovanni della Robbia is a pageant of gay colour and depicts the Seven Works of Mercy, while the five medallions represent the Virtues.

A small country road (SP13) leads south out of Pistoia towards Empoli. After a long series of winding curves through the Monte Albano hills (a beautiful drive) and just 1.5km short of **Vinci**, you come across a sign pointing left (east) to the bare **Casa di Leonardo** in a place called

DETOUR: BATHING IN MONTECATINI

Those in need of a long, healthy spa bath could clip along to Montecatini, 15km down the A11 from Pistoia. Known to the Romans (who had a penchant for hot baths) and for a while owned by the all-grasping Medici, the hot springs of Montecatini Terme came into their own in the mid-18th century under the Hapsburg Grand Duke of Tuscany, Pietro Leopoldo. They caught on in the late 19th and early 20th centuries, fuelling a construction boom in elegant digs.

Nine separate thermal bath installations operate, mostly from May to October (only the Hotel Excelsior's facilities open year-round). Water bubbles up from a depth of 80m, collecting minerals and salts along the way. This water is used for medical and aesthetic treatments, ranging from hydrotherapy to cleansing douches, as well as mud therapy and massages. An afternoon at the baths costs €6, while an all-out body and facial with mud followed by bath costs around €110.

When you've had enough, take the funicular up to pretty Montecatini Alto, whose central square is graced with cafés that have long attracted lovers of the water who are equally partial to an energising post-relaxation tipple. Contact the **APT office** (☎ 0572 77 22 44; Viale Verdi 66; 🕑 9am-12.30pm & 3-6pm Mon-Sat, 9am-noon Sun) or the **Terme di Montecatini information office** (☎ 800 13 25 38, 0572 77 81; www.termemontecatini.it; Viale Verdi 41; 🕑 8am-1pm & 3.30-6.30pm Mon-Fri, 8am-1pm Sat & Sun).

Anchiano. Here it is believed Leonardo da Vinci was born, the bastard child of a Florentine solicitor, Piero.

Back down on the SP13, you are just short of Vinci itself. The town is dominated by the **Castello dei Guidi**, named after the feudal family that lorded it over this town and surrounds until Florence took control in the 13th century. Inside the castle nowadays is the **Museo Leonardiano**, which contains an intriguing set of over 50 models based on Leonardo's far-sighted designs (there are now similar museums in Florence itself; see p91 and p95).

From Vinci, head south to Empoli, where you can pick up a train for Florence. En route you could call into **Montelupo**, a market town on the confluence of the Arno and Pesa, and a celebrated centre of Tuscan ceramic production since medieval times. There are no shortage of shops here to browse or bequeath money to. In the third week of every month a pottery market is held, while in the last week of June the town hosts an international ceramics fair.

Information

Ospedale del Ceppo (Hospital; Piazza Giovanni XXIII, Pistoia)

Pistoia tourist office (☎ 0573 2 16 22; www.pistoia .turismo.toscana.it; Piazza del Duomo 4; ☒ 9am-1pm & 3-6pm Mon-Sat)

Prato tourist office (☎ 0574 2 41 12; www.prato.turismo .toscana.it; Piazza Santa Maria delle Carceri 15; ☒ 9am-1.30pm & 2-6.30pm Mon-Fri, 9am-1.30pm & 2-6pm Sat)

Sights

Battistero di San Giovanni (Piazza del Duomo, Pistoia; admission free; ☒ 9am-12.30pm & 3-6pm Tue-Sun)

Cappella di San Jacopo (Piazza del Duomo, Pistoia; adult/child €2/50c; ☒ 10am-noon & 3.30-5pm)

Casa di Leonardo (☎ 0571 5 60 55; Anchiano; admission free; ☒ 9.30am-7pm Apr-Sep, 9.30am-6pm Oct-Mar)

Castello dell'Imperatore (☎ 0574 3 82 07; Piazza Santa Maria delle Carceri, Prato; admission €3; ☒ 9am-1pm & 4-7pm Wed-Mon Apr-Sep, 9am-1pm Wed-Mon Oct-Mar) You can also buy a combined ticket for entry to the Castello dell'Imperatore, Museo dell'Opera del Duomo and Museo di Pittura Murale for €5.

Cattedrale di Santo Stefano (Piazza del Duomo, Prato; ☒ 7.30am-12.30pm & 4-7.30pm Jul-Sep, 7am-12.30pm & 3-6.30pm Mon-Sat, 7am-12.30pm & 3-8pm Sun & holidays)

Cattedrale di San Zeno (☎ 0573 2 50 95; Piazza del Duomo, Pistoia; ☒ 8.30am-12.30pm & 3.30-7pm)

Museo Civico (☎ 0573 37 12 96; Piazza del Duomo 1, Pistoia; adult/child €3.10/1.60; ☒ 10am-6pm Tue-Sat, 10am-12.30pm Sun & holidays)

Museo dell'Opera del Duomo (☎ 0574 2 93 39; Piazza del Duomo 49, Prato; admission €3, or combined ticket – see Castello dell'Imperatore; ☒ 9.30am-12.30pm & 3-6.30pm Mon & Wed-Sat, 9.30am-12.30pm Sun)

Museo del Tessuto (☎ 0574 61 15 03; Via Santa Chiara 24, Prato; adult/senior & under 14yr €4/2, free Sun; ☒ 10am-6pm Mon-Fri, 10am-2pm Sat, 4-7pm Sun)

Museo di Pittura Murale (☎ 0574 44 05 01; Piazza San Domenico, Prato; admission €3, or combined ticket – see Castello dell'Imperatore; ☒ 10am-6pm Mon & Wed-Sat, 10am-1pm Sun)

Museo Leonardiano (☎ 0571 5 60 55; Via della Torre, Vinci; adult/child/student €5/2/3.50; ☒ 9.30am-7pm, ticket counter closes at 6pm)

Eating

Osteria Cibbé (☎ 0574 60 75 09; Piazza Mercatale 49, Prato; meal €25; ☒ Mon-Sat) This *osteria* shelters beneath ancient vaults and offers traditional local cuisine. The *zucchine ripiene* (courgettes stuffed with meat) are memorable, as is the *minestra di riso e lampredotto* (broth with rice and veal tripe).

Osteria Baldovino (☎ 0573 2 15 91; Piazza San Leonardo 5, Pistoia; meal €25-30; ☒ Mon-Sat dinner only) Tucked away in a quiet central square, Baldovino offers carefully prepared local cooking, with some twists like the *tortelloni ripieni di bacallà* (a plump pasta with cod filling). Wine labels can be counted in their hundreds.

Sleeping

Hotel Flora (☎ 0574 3 35 21; www.hotelflora.info; Via B Cairoli 31, Prato; s/d €95/150; P €10) This attractive three-star place is in a 19th-century palazzo in the town centre. The 29 bedrooms, with parquet floors, are crisply decorated and quiet.

Hotel Leon Bianco (☎ 0573 2 66 75; Via Panciatichi 2, Pistoia; www.hotelleonbianco.it; s/d €65/95; P €5) A friendly, family-owned hotel, by far the most venerable in town, this has operated as an inn since the 15th century.

Directory ■

Directory

The information in this chapter is divided into two parts, Transport and Practicalities. Within each section information is presented in alphabetical order.

TRANSPORT

AIR

Flying to Florence for most people actually means flying into Pisa's Galileo Galilei airport, which is 80 minutes away by train. Pisa is a central Italian hub and flights arrive from many European centres (see opposite). A handful of European and domestic flights serve Florence's smaller Amerigo Vespucci airport (which, in spite of its size, handles 1.7 million passengers a year). You could also fly into Bologna and then grab a train south. For most intercontinental air travel you will have to change flights at least once, in Rome, Milan or at another European hub.

Within Europe and especially from the UK, you should check the low-budget airlines. They work on a first-come, first-serve basis: the earlier you book, the less you pay. These no-frills airlines skip extras such as in-flight meals (although you can buy snacks). From the UK, Ryanair serves Pisa and EasyJet flies to Bologna.

Within Italy, air travel tends to be expensive. In the northern cities (eg from Rome, Milan and Venice) it makes more sense to go by train, as the time saving by air is rarely that great and the economic savings by train are considerable. Alitalia and Meridiana are the main domestic airlines serving Florence, Pisa and Bologna.

Most airlines, especially the budget ones, encourage you to book on their websites. General sites to search for competitive fares include www.planesimple.co.uk, www.opodo.com and www.expedia.com.

Airlines

Most airlines don't have shopfront offices in Florence, so you'll need to either go online, call the following numbers or try a travel agent.

AerLingus (EI; ☎ 0818 365000 in Ireland, ☎ 02 43 45 83 11 in Italy; www.aerlingus.com) Direct flights from Dublin to Bologna.

Air Dolomiti (EN; ☎ 01805 838 426 in Germany, ☎ 199 400 044 in Italy; www.airdolomiti.it) Flights to Pisa and Bologna from Munich.

Air One (AP; ☎ 199 207 080; www.flyairone.it) Flights to Pisa and Bologna from other Italian cities.

Alitalia (AZ; Map pp244–5; ☎ 848 865 641/2/3, 055 2 78 81; Vicolo dell'Oro 1; www.alitalia.it) The national airline, with flights to Florence from various Italian and European centres.

Basiq Air/Transavia (HV; ☎ 0900 0737 in Holland, ☎ 02 6968 2615 in Italy; www.basiqair.com) Low-cost flights from Amsterdam to Pisa.

British Airways (BA; ☎ 0870 850 9850 in the UK, ☎ 199 712 266 in Italy; www.britishairways.com) Flights from the UK to Bologna and Pisa.

Central Wings (CO; ☎ 801 454545 in Poland; www.centralwings.com) Low-cost flights from Warsaw to Bologna.

DBA (DI; ☎ 01805 359 322 in Germany; www.flydba.com) Low-cost flights from Berlin (Tegel & Tempelhof), Cologne, Düsseldorf, Hamburg and Munich to Florence.

Denim Airways (3D; ☎ 01805 336462 in Germany, ☎ 055 306 16 23 in Italy; www.denimairways.com) Flights from Zurich to Florence and Bologna.

EasyJet (U2; ☎ 0871 244 2366 in the UK, ☎ 848 887 766 in Italy; www.easyjet.com) Flies to Bologna from London Stansted, and to Pisa from Berlin, Bristol and Paris (Orly).

Flybaboo (BBO; ☎ 0848 445 445 in Switzerland; www.babooairways.com) Flights from Geneva to Florence.

Germanwings (4U; ☎ 01805 955 855 in Germany, ☎ 199 404 747 in Italy; www15.germanwings.com) Flights between Cologne and Bologna.

Hapag Lloyd Express (X3; ☎ 01805 093 509 in Germany, ☎ 199 192 692 in Italy; http://book.hlx.com) Flights from Berlin and other German cities to Pisa.

Jet2 (LS; ☎ 0871 226 1737 in the UK, ☎ 199 309 240 in Italy; www.jet2.com) Budget flights from Manchester to Pisa.

Meridiana (IG; Map pp248–9; ☎ 199 111 333, 055 30 81 64; Lungarno Soderini 1; www.meridiana.it) Flights from Amsterdam, Barcelona, London Gatwick, Madrid, Sardinia

GETTING INTO TOWN

Bus

ATAF (☎ 800 42 45 00; www.ataf.net), Florence's local transport company, and **SITA** (☎ 800 37 37 60; www.sita on-line.it), a regional bus company, together operate the Volainbus shuttle bus service between Florence's airport and the SITA terminal in Via Santa Caterina da Siena, near the main train station. It costs €4, takes about 25 minutes and runs every half-hour from 5.30am to 8pm, and then hourly to 11pm.

The local bus 3 runs into central Pisa from Pisa airport for 80c. To Florence's Stazione di Santa Maria Novella, you can take the **Terravision** (www.terravision.it) bus. It runs 12 times daily (€7.50/13.50 one way/return) and takes 70 to 80 minutes. In Florence, tickets can be bought at the Agenzia 365 travel agency at the beginning of platform 5 of the train station. At the airport there is a special booth. You can also buy online in advance (which is slightly cheaper).

The **Aerobus** (☎ 051 29 02 90) service runs about every 15 minutes between Bologna's airport and central city train station (€4.50, 15 to 20 minutes). From there you can get a train to Florence (see below).

Taxi

A taxi from Florence's Amerigo Vespucci airport will cost around €12 to €15 and take about 20 minutes, depending on traffic, to reach the city centre.

From Pisa, a taxi to Florence would cost a fortune – in excess of €200. A taxi from Pisa airport into the centre of Pisa town is about €8 to €10.

From Bologna it would be prohibitively expensive to catch a taxi to Florence. From Bologna airport into Bologna city centre is approximately €12 to €16.

Train

From Pisa's airport there are 26 trains to Pisa Centrale (€1.10), from where you can get a host of trains to other destinations. There are also eight direct trains to Florence (€5, around 80 minutes), from 6.41am to 10.10pm.

Masses of trains run between Florence and Bologna, taking from one to 1½ hours. The first from Bologna leaves at 5.30am (a slow one with a change in Prato) and the last at 10.46pm. Tickets cost up to €13.17 depending on the type and speed of service.

and Sicily to Florence. Also flights to Bologna from Sardinia and Sicily.

MyAir (8I; ☎ 899 500 060; www.myair.com) An Italian budget airline with flights between Bologna and a series of domestic destinations, and Spain's Ibiza.

Norwegian (DY; ☎ 815 21 815 in Norway; www.norwegian.no) Low-cost flights from Oslo to Pisa.

Qantas Airways (QF; ☎ 13 13 13 in Australia, ☎ 06 5248 2725 in Italy; www.qantas.com.au) Flights from Australia to Italy in codeshare.

Ryanair (FR, ☎ 0871 246 0000 in the UK, ☎ 899 678 910, 050 50 37 70 in Italy; www.ryanair.com) Flights from London Stansted, Dublin, Glasgow, Liverpool, Barcelona (Girona), Brussels (Charleroi), Eindhoven (in Holland) Frankfurt (Hahn), Hamburg and Lübeck to Pisa.

SN Brussels Airlines (SN; ☎ 070 351111 in Belgium, ☎ 02 69 68 23 64 in Italy; www.flysn.com) Flights from Brussels to Florence and Bologna.

Snowflake (SK; ☎ 7010 2000 in Denmark; www.flysnowflake.com) This SAS subsidiary has flights from Copenhagen to Venice.

Sterling (NB; ☎ 7010 8484 in Denmark, ☎ 815 58 810 in Norway, ☎ 08 5876 9148 in Sweden, ☎ 02 69 63 35 95 in Italy; www.sterlingticket.com) Flights from Denmark, Norway and Sweden to Bologna.

Thomson Fly (TOM; ☎ 08701 900 737 in the UK; www.thomsonfly.com) Flights from Bournemouth, Coventry and Doncaster/Sheffield (UK) to Pisa.

Airports

Florence's **Amerigo Vespucci airport** (☎ 055 306 13 00, international flight info ☎ 055 306 17 02; www.aeroporto.firenze.it) is 5km northwest of the city centre at Via del Termine 11. The main building serves as the departures (partenze) hall, while arrivals (arrivi) is in a smaller building just to the rear of the building. In the latter you'll find a tourist office, a lost-luggage office, car-rental outlets and an ATM. There's a bank in the departures lounge. There is no left-luggage service at this airport.

Pisa's **Galileo Galilei airport** (☎ 050 84 93 00; www.pisa-airport.com) is the main gateway for passengers bound for Florence. The long, low terminal building is divided into arrivals on the left and departures on

Directory

TRANSPORT

the right. There is a tourist office in the arrivals section at the end of the hall. It handles left luggage (€6 per piece per day; 🕐 8am-8pm) and you can buy bus and train tickets too. There is a bank with an ATM roughly where the arrivals and departures sections intersect.

Bologna's **Guglielmo Marconi airport** (☎ 051 647 96 15; www.bologna-airport.it) has check-in desks on both the ground and 1st floors (departure gates are on the 1st floor). You'll find a general information desk on the ground floor, and several ATMs and bureaux de change scattered about across the two floors. There is no left-luggage service, but a lost-luggage service operates on the ground floor.

BICYCLE

Cycling is a good way to get around central Florence. It's not mandatory to wear a helmet, and many locals don't bother, but most outlets can provide one. The city runs a public bike-hire service, known as **Mille e Una Bici** ('A Thousand and One Bikes', which is something of an overstatement) with bikes available at eight points around the city (some handy ones have been mapped), including the main one just in front of the **train station** (🕐 7.30am-7pm Mon-Sat, 9am-7pm Sun, May-Sep). They cost up to €8 a day for nonresidents. Hours vary from one spot to the next, but many hire points do not operate on weekends. Other more regular rental options (which provide locks and, if you ask, helmets):

Alinari (Map pp242–3; ☎ 055 28 05 00; www.alinari rental.com; Via Guelfa 85/r; road bikes per hr/5hr/day/week €2.50/7/12/45; mountain bikes per hr/5hr/day/week €3/13/18/80; 🕐 daily Mar-Oct, Mon-Sat Nov-Feb)

Florence by Bike (Map pp242–3; ☎ 055 48 89 92; www.florencebybike.it; Via San Zanobi 91/r and Via San Zanobi 120-122/r; standard bicycles per day €13, mountain bikes per day €19, scooters per day from €31; 🕐 9am-1pm & 3.30-7.30pm Mon-Sat Nov-Feb; 9am-7.30pm Mon-Sun Mar-Oct)

BUS
Florence

ATAF (Azienda Trasporti Area Fiorentina; ☎ 800 42 45 00; www.ataf.net) buses serve the city centre, Fiesole and other areas in the city's outskirts.

USEFUL BUS ROUTES
Several main bus stops for most routes are around Stazione di Santa Maria Novella. Many routes stop operating by 9pm or so. The following lines offer a handful of runs until midnight or shortly after. Services are reduced on weekends and holidays. Some of the most useful routes operate from stops just outside the southeast exit of the station (Map pp242–3), including the following:

7 For Fiesole. Takes about 30 minutes.

13 Circular route to Piazzale Michelangelo via Ponte alle Grazie (on the way there) and Porta al Prato (on the way back). Takes about 30 minutes each way.

70 Night bus on a circular route for Campo Marte train station via the Duomo (on the way there) and Piazza dell'Indipendenza (on the way back). Operates nine runs from 12.40am to 5.35am.

A network of dinky and ecologically friendly (three of them are electric) minibuses *(bussini)*, which operates around the centre, can be handy for cross-town rides at the end of a long day's wandering. Only Linea D (which runs on a special diesel formula) operates from 7am to 9pm (every 10 to 15 minutes). The others run from about 8am to 8pm Monday to Saturday. You can get a map of the routes, published by ATAF, from tourist offices.

Linea A This route runs from the Stazione di Santa Maria Novella to Piazza della Repubblica via Via del Parione, Piazza d'Ognissanti and Piazza Santa Trinita, before going along Via Ghibellina and Piazza dei Ciompi to Piazza C Beccaria. From there it returns to the train station via Borgo degli Albizi, Via della Vigna Nuova and Piazza dell'Unità.

Linea B From Piazza Piave, this route runs to Piazza Santa Croce via Corso dei Tintori, thence to Piazza Signoria (for the Uffizi) and on to Ponte Amerigo Vespucci, which it crosses before following the river west to Ponte alla Vittoria. This it crosses and then turns east along Lungarno Vespucci and heads back to Piazza Piave along the riverside.

Linea C Starting at Piazza San Marco, this route passes along Via degli Alfani, Piazza Sant'Ambrogio, Via de' Pepi, Piazza Santa Croce and across Ponte alle Grazie to Piazza di Santa Maria Soprarno. It then recrosses Ponte alle Grazie and returns to Piazza San Marco via Via Verdi, Piazza dei Ciompi, Piazza Sant'Ambrogio and Via Colonna.

Linea D This route starts at the Stazione di Santa Maria Novella and weaves down to Ponte di Vespucci, from where it passes on along Borgo San Frediano, Lungarno Guicciardini, past Ponte Vecchio, down Via de' Bardi, and along the *lungarni* to Piazza Ferrucci. It then returns to Ponte Vecchio, turns down past Palazzo Pitti, up Via Sant'Agostino, through Piazza del Carmine and back across Ponte di Vespucci to the train station.

NIGHT BUSES

Of the four so-called night-bus routes, three operate only between 9pm and 1am. The only true night bus *(autobus notturno)* is bus 70 (see opposite).

TICKETS

Bus tickets should be bought at tobacconists or automated vending machines at major bus stops before you get on the bus, and must be validated in the machine as you enter. You can buy tickets and pick up a useful routes brochure at the **ATAF information office** (Map pp242–3) on Largo Fratelli Alinari, just outside the southeast exit of Stazione di Santa Maria Novella.

Tickets cost €1 for one hour and €1.80 for three hours. A 24-hour ticket costs €4.50 and a four-ticket set *(biglietto multiplo)* costs €3.90 (each ride valid for an hour). You are supposed to stamp these in the machine when you get on your first bus. There are tickets for any number of days up to one week (€16). If you are hanging around Florence longer, you might want to invest in a monthly ticket *(mensile)* at €31 (€20.70 for students).

A new chip-card ticket, the Carta Agile (€10/20 for 12/25 rides, each valid for an hour) is a further alternative.

The fine for being caught without a ticket on public transport is €40 – in addition to the price of the ticket.

Tuscany

Lazzi and SITA (see below) run buses to various destinations in Tuscany. Other companies also cover parts of the region, such as **CAP** (☎ 055 21 46 37; www.cap autolinee.it in Italian) and **COPIT** (☎ 800 27 78 25; www.copitspa.it in Italian), located next to one another at Largo Fratelli Alinari 9 and 11 respectively (Map pp242–3).

Long-Distance Buses

Buses leave from a variety of terminals scattered about Stazione di Santa Maria Novella. **Eurolines** (www.eurolines.com), in conjunction with local bus companies across Europe, is the main international carrier. Eurolines' website provides links to the sites

of all the national operators. In Florence, Eurolines tickets can be bought at **Lazzi** (Map pp242–3; ☎ 055 21 55 55; www.lazzi.it in Italian; Piazza Stazione 3), on the corner of Piazza Adua, or at the BOPA ticket agency in the train station (platform 5). Buses run several times a week from London, Paris, Barcelona and other European centres. Lazzi also has one or two daily services to various cities around the country, as far afield as the Veneto in the northeast and Sicily in the south. The same company, through its subsidiary **Sena** (☎ 800 93 09 60; www.sena .it), connects Siena with destinations all over Italy.

SITA (Map pp242–3; ☎ 800 37 37 60; www .sita-on-line.it in Italian; Via Santa Caterina da Siena 15) is just to the west of Stazione di Santa Maria Novella and also offers a handful of long-distance services, most to southern Italy and Sicily.

CAR & MOTORCYCLE
Driving to Florence

Florence is a 1235km drive from Berlin, 1555km from London, 1138km from Paris, 1665km from Madrid, 605km from Geneva, 296km from Milan and 267km from Rome.

The main points of entry to Italy are the Mont Blanc tunnel from France at Chamonix, which connects with the A5 for Turin and Milan; the Grand St Bernard tunnel from Switzerland, which also connects with the A5; and the Brenner Pass from Austria, which connects with the A22 to Bologna.

Florence is connected by the Autostrada del Sole (A1) to Bologna and Milan in the north, and Rome and Naples in the south. The Autostrada del Mare (A11) connects Florence with Prato, Lucca, Pisa and the coast, and a *superstrada* (expressway) joins the city to Siena. Exits from the *autostrade* (four- to six-lane motorways) into Florence are well signposted, and there are tourist offices on the A1 north and south of the city. From the north on the A1, exit at Firenze Nord and follow the bull's-eye *centro* signs; if approaching from Rome, exit at Firenze Sud.

Many of Italy's *autostrade* are toll roads and can be expensive. You sometimes have the choice of the toll road and a busy *strada statale* (main road; represented on maps as 'S' or 'SS'). These tend to pass through towns and can double your travel time. Smaller roads are known as *strade provinciali* (represented on maps as 'P' or 'SP').

Vehicles must be roadworthy, registered and insured (third party at least). Ask your insurer for a European Accident Statement form, which can simplify matters in the event of an accident. A European breakdown assistance policy, such as the AA Five Star Service or the RAC Eurocover Motoring Assistance in the UK, is a good investment.

You can pay for petrol with most credit cards in the majority of service stations. Those on the *autostrade* are open 24 hours per day. Otherwise, opening hours are generally around 7am to 12.30pm and 3.30pm to 7.30pm (7pm in winter). Most are closed on Sunday and public holidays; others close on Monday. Don't assume you can't get petrol if you pass a station that is closed. Quite a few have self-service pumps that accept banknotes.

Driving & Parking in Florence

Driving and/or parking in central Florence is virtually impossible for nonresidents. A system of cameras that photograph all vehicles entering the heart of the old city (resulting in a €50 fine for all those who do so without authorisation) and a tough line on parking in the wider central Florence area (within the series of boulevards, or *viali*, that surround the old centre as well as part of the Oltrarno between Ponte alle Grazie and Ponte Vespucci) mean you have to opt for private garages or blue parking zones beyond the centre.

The central area is a Zona, a Traffico Limitato (ZTL, Limited Traffic Zone), and is divided into five colour-coded areas for residents only. Nonresidents entering the centre in search of a hotel are exempt from the ZTL entry rules, as long they report their number plate and time of entry into the centre to their hotel desk. The hotel then sends a message to the authorities to avert a potential fine. If you drive in and don't wind up in a hotel, you will be fined.

The ZTL is active from 7.30pm to 7.30am daily, and again from 10pm to 2am, Thursday to Saturday between May and September. At other times nonresidents may enter. Motorbikes and scooters are exempt. 4WDs with tyres more than 70cm high or weighing more than 1800kg are not allowed in central Florence at all.

In any case, there is no nonresident daytime parking within the ZTL, so vehicles have to be parked in garages or blue zones beyond the centre. Fees can range as high as €50 a day. There are several car parks around the city-centre fringe. The cheapest options for a longer stay are those in Parterre and around Piazzale di Porta Romana in Oltrarno. Both cost €1.50 per hour or €15 for 24 hours.

You can try using the residents' parking zones (white lines) beyond the ZTL, but you risk being clamped, towed and paying a hefty fine to recover your vehicle. If you park in resident parking zones, keep an eye out for signs displaying a street-sweeping vehicle. The signs indicate the day of the week and time that cars must be moved to allow street sweepers through. This is usually between midnight and 6am; thus 'Sabato 0 a 6' indicates that from midnight on Friday until 6am on Saturday the street needs to be clear. Your car will definitely be towed if left in such a zone.

If your car is clamped or towed call the **Depositaria Comunale** (Car Pound; ☎ 055 78 38 82; Ponte a Greve, Lotto Zero).

Hire

Car-rental agencies are concentrated in the Borgo Ognissanti area. You will also find some motorbike and scooter outlets. Note that helmets are compulsory on all motorised two-wheel vehicles.

Alinari (see p204) Scooters and motorbikes are available from €28 (50cc) to €55 (125cc) per day. Motorbikes (500cc) cost up to €75 a day.

Avis (Map pp242–3; ☎ 055 21 36 29; www.avis.com; Borgo Ognissanti 128/r)

Europcar (Map pp248–9; ☎ 055 29 04 37; www.europcar.it; Borgo Ognissanti 53/r)

Florence by Bike (Map pp242–3; ☎ 055 48 89 92; www.florencebybike.it; Via San Zanobi 91/r & Via San Zanobi 120-122/r) Another outlet for rental scooters and motorbikes. Prices for a day's rental are €31 (50cc), €65 (125cc) and €95 (650cc).

Happy Rent (Map pp242–3; ☎ 055 239 96 96; www.happyrent.com; Borgo Ognissanti 153/r)

Hertz (Map pp242–3; ☎ 055 239 82 05; www.hertz.it; Via Maso Finiguerra 33/r)

Solo Giallo (Map pp242–3; ☎ 055 28 39 14; www.sologiallo.it; Borgo Ognissanti 96) These dinky, electrically powered, canary-yellow buggies (two to four people; €18 per hour, €72 per day, €110 per weekend) are allowed anywhere in the centre and have a range of about 100km. More than 100 charging points (free) are scattered around Florence. They are based inside Garage Europa.

Thrifty (Map pp242–3; ☎ 055 28 71 61; www.thrifty.it; Borgo Ognissanti 134/r)

TAXI

Taxis (☎ 055 42 42, 055 47 98, 055 44 99, 055 43 90) can be found outside Stazione di Santa Maria Novella and at other ranks around town. The flagfall is €2.54, on top of which you pay 82c per kilometre within the city limits (€1.47 per kilometre beyond). A cross-town ride will cost around €10, depending on traffic. Women travelling alone can (and should) ask for a discount from 9pm to 2am.

TRAIN

Train is the most convenient overland option for reaching Florence from other Italian cities or abroad. For information on travelling from the UK, contact the **Rail Europe Travel Centre** (☎ 08708 38 20 08; www.rail europe.co.uk; 178 Piccadilly, London W1V 0BA). For travel within Italy, you can get information at your nearest train station or travel agent. Alternatively, contact **Trenitalia** (☎ 892021; www.trenitalia.it).

A wide variety of trains run on the Italian rail network. They start with all-stops *locali,* and *regionali* – both slow local trains. *Interregionali* cover greater distances and don't necessarily stop at every station.

Intercity (IC) trains are fast services that operate between major cities. Eurocity (EC) trains are the international version. High-speed *pendolini* and other top-of-the-range services, which on high-speed track can zip along at more than 300km/h, are collectively known as Eurostar Italia (ES).

Apart from the standard division between 1st and 2nd class (*prima classe* and *seconda classe;* generally *locali* and *regionali* have 2nd-class seats only) you have to pay a supplement for taking a fast train (IC and up). You can pay the supplement separately from the ticket, so, if you have a 2nd-class return ticket from Florence to Milan, you might decide to avoid the supplement one way and take a slower train, but pay it on the way back to speed things up. You need to pay the supplement *before* boarding the train. If you know exactly which train you want, the supplement will be included in your ticket.

You can buy rail tickets (for major destinations on fast trains, at least) at the station (often crowded) and from most travel agents. If you choose to buy them at the station, there are automatic machines that accept credit cards and cash. You can also buy tickets on Trenitalia's website (www .trenitalia.it) or look for cheaper tickets at www.trenok.com. You can also book over the phone (☎ 892021). On the same number you can also book for ticketless travel on ES and IC trains. You must book a seat on all Eurostar Italia trains. On other services this is optional and generally unnecessary.

Validate your ticket in the orange machines on station platforms. Failure to do so will almost certainly result in embarrassment and a hefty on-the-spot fine when the ticket inspector comes around.

Florence Train Station

Florence is an important railway hub, and from the city's main train station, **Stazione di Santa Maria Novella** (Firenze SMN for short; Map pp242–3), you can get direct trains heading in most directions. Its line connects with Milan, Bologna, Venice and Rome. Trains also fan out to various parts of Tuscany, although buses can be more convenient for exploring the region.

The rail travel **information office** (☼ 7am-9pm), at the west end of the main vestibule has currency exchange bureaus, a bank (with ATM), phones and **left luggage** (*deposito;* Map pp242–3; €3.80 per item for first 5 hrs, then €0.60 per hr up until 12 hrs, & thereafter €0.20 per hr for total maximum of 5 days; ☼ 6am-midnight).

By 2009 a new station designed by Sir Norman Foster should be in operation for the high-speed train that will connect Naples with Turin, via Rome, Florence, Bologna and Milan. Located in the Belfiore area, it will be linked by tram to Stazione di Santa Maria Novella. The high-speed trains (Treni ad Alta Velocità, or TAV) will pass along 7km of underground track beneath the city.

TRAM

ATAF is building a hyper-modern 8km tramway between the Stazione di Santa Maria Novella and the southwest satellite suburb of Scandicci. It is due for completion by the end of 2007. Two further lines have also been approved, one linking the centre with the airport and another, the Fortezza da Basso, with Careggi.

TRAVEL AGENTS

Florence is not awash with good-value travel agents, but you could try the CTS (Centro Turistico Studentesco e Giovanile; Map pp244–5; ☎ 055 28 95 70; www.cts .it in Italian; Via dei Ginori 25/r), which is the main Italian student and youth travel organisation. The city also has a second CTS branch (Map pp240–1; ☎ 055 33 41 64; www .cts.it; Via Maragliano 86/i).

PRACTICALITIES
ACCOMMODATION

Sleeping options range from cheap and cheerful youth hostels to grand old hotels and leafy villas. See the Sleeping chapter (p172) for specific recommendations. The options are presented by district and in alphabetical order. The emphasis is on midrange accommodation but we have slipped in some of the city's great top-range hotels too. Each section ends with a Cheap Sleeps list for those travelling on a tighter budget.

BUSINESS
Opening Hours

In general, shops are open 9.30am to 1pm and 3.30pm to 7.30pm, Monday to Saturday. They may remain closed on Monday morning or Saturday afternoon, or both. Laws on opening hours are fairly flexible so shopkeepers have a large degree of discretion. Many skip the lunchtime break.

Big department stores, such as COIN and La Rinascente, and most supermarkets are open from around 9am to 7.30pm Monday to Saturday.

Banks open from 8.30am to 1.30pm and 3.30pm to 4.30pm Monday to Friday, but hours often vary. A few may open on Saturday morning.

Bars (in the traditional Italian coffee-and-sandwich sense) and cafés generally open from 7.30am to 8pm, although some

stay open after 8pm and turn into pub-style drinking and meeting places. Pubs and bars mostly shut by 1am, except on Friday and Saturday nights, when quite a few will kick on until 2 or 3am.

For lunch (pranzo), restaurants usually open from 12.30pm to 3pm, but many prefer taking orders after 2pm. At nights, opening hours for dinner (cena) vary, but people start sitting down to dine at around 8.30pm. It's difficult to find a place still serving after 10.30pm.

CHILDREN

Children may well weary of traipsing around worthy art galleries and grand churches. A few books could help you get the kids involved in the sightseeing, such as *Bambini alla Scoperta di Firenze* (literally 'Florence for Kids'), which uses an entertaining approach, with quizzes and other learning prompts. *Florence for Teens* has lots of bite-sized history lessons and pictures. *Florence: A Young Traveller's Guide* has many detailed illustrations of monuments and breezy text.

For more information on how to amuse the kids, see Lonely Planet's *Travel with Children*. The Palazzo Vecchio has some activities aimed specifically at children (see p76).

Baby-Sitting

Most of the medium- and upper-range hotels in Florence can organise a baby-sitting service.

CLIMATE

Florence's position in a river basin, walled in by hills to the south and the foothills of the Apennines to the north, largely determines its climate. In summer the city is a like a pressure cooker as heat and humidity soar.

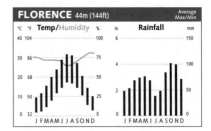

July is the worst month (closely followed by August) and there are dog days when there is not a whisper of air. The average highs hover around 31°C. Occasionally you can enjoy the temporary relief of a cracking thunderstorm.

Winter, on the other hand, is cool and often wet, although mercifully it doesn't last too long. Average temperatures in January range between 1°C and 10°C; snow is rare.

COURSES

Florence bursts with language schools. Most offer supplementary courses on Italian culture, art history, cooking, music and the like, although for these categories you will also find more specialised schools.

Florence's APT office also has lists of schools and courses, which it will mail out on request.

Non-EU citizens who want to study at a university or language school in Italy must have a study visa – obtained from your nearest Italian embassy or consulate.

Most schools will organise accommodation for students, on request and at added cost, either in private apartments or with Italian families.

A selection of course options follows.

Art & Design

Accademia Italiana (Map pp248–9; ☎ 055 28 46 16; www.accademiaitaliana.com; Piazza de' Pitti 15) This school offers a wide range of design programmes, including one-month courses and more rigorous semester-based courses in painting, graphic arts, glassware, furniture and fashion design and related fields.

Istituto per l'Arte e il Restauro (Map pp248–9; ☎ 055 24 60 01; www.spinelli.it; Palazzo Spinelli, Borgo Santa Croce 10) Here you can learn to restore anything from paintings to ceramics, interior and graphic design, gilding and marquetry. It has short courses and full academic programmes. A full-time four-week course costs €2000.

Università Internazionale dell'Arte (Map pp240–1; ☎ 055 57 02 16; www.uiafirenze.com; Villa Il Ventaglio, Via delle Forbici 24-26) Those contemplating serious art studies could look into courses offered by this institution. They range from museum studies through restoration, to specialist courses in such areas as African art history.

Cooking

Cordon Bleu (Map pp248–9; ☎ 055 234 54 68; www.cordonbleu-it.com; Via di Mezzo 55/r) This is the place

to go to learn some stylish cooking methods. Specialised courses range from haute cuisine to making gelato. Classes take from eight to 15 students. A basic eight-lesson cooking course costs €415.

Language

Centro Lingua Italiana Calvino (Map pp242–3; ☎ 055 28 80 81; www.clicschool.it; Viale Fratelli Rosselli 74) You have the option of standard and intensive courses here, the latter totalling 30 hours per week (€225). The main drawback is the unattractive location around the back end of Stazione di Santa Maria Novella.

Centro Lorenzo de' Medici (Map pp242–3; ☎ 055 28 73 60; www.lorenzodemedici.it; Via Faenza 43) This school is popular with American students. Four hours per day for a month costs €600. It offers many levels and a variety of courses in art, cooking, history and the like. You can also arrange individual tuition.

Istituto Europeo (Map pp244–5; ☎ 055 238 10 71; www.istitutoeuropeo.it; Piazzale delle Pallottole 1) One-week/four-week courses cost €220/440. It offers discount scholarships for students. And the school is a wifi zone!

Istituto di Lingua e Cultura Italiana per Stranieri Michelangelo (Map pp248–9; ☎ 055 24 09 75; www.michelangelo-edu.it; Via Ghibellina 88) Four-week course (80 hours) costs €540 in classes of not more than 12 people. The school will organise private one-on-one courses, starting at €728 a week (four hours a day).

Scuola Leonardo da Vinci (Map pp242–3; ☎ 055 26 11 81; www.scuolaleonardo.com; Via Bufalini 3) Four-week course (80 hours) costs €560. Courses offered range from two to 24 weeks, averaging four hours of class per day.

Società Dante Alighieri (Map pp242–3; ☎ 055 247 89 81; www.dantealighieri.it; Via Gino Capponi 4) The national cultural association, with branches worldwide, offers a broad range of courses. One month (80 hours) costs €480. The society is housed in the 16th-century former Oratorio di San Pierino, whose courtyard retains many frescoes from that time.

Performing Arts

Florence Dance Cultural Center (Map pp248–9; ☎ 055 28 92 76; www.florencedance.org; Borgo della Stella 23/r) Apart from being a hive of theatrical activity, this centre offers a range of courses in classical, jazz and modern dance.

Photography

Darkroom (Map pp248–9; ☎ 055 21 68 74; www.thedarkroom.it; Via del Leone 8/r) The Darkroom runs photography workshops in Italian and English, and also rents out darkrooms (per hour €7.50).

CUSTOMS

People entering Italy from outside the EU are allowed to bring in, duty-free, one bottle of spirits, one bottle of wine, 50mL of perfume and 200 cigarettes.

Duty-free allowances for travel between EU countries were abolished in 1999. For duty-paid items bought at normal shops in one EU country and taken into another, the allowances are 90L of wine, 10L of spirits, unlimited quantities of perfume and 800 cigarettes. People travelling between EU countries can also avoid paying VAT (value-added tax) by shopping in the duty-free shops at airports.

DISABLED TRAVELLERS

The Comune di Firenze (City Council) publishes a booklet, *Guida alle Strutture e ai Servizi della Città*, which lists hundreds of places – including churches, museums, banks, hotels and restaurants – with an accessibility rating and description. The booklet comes with a map of central Florence outlining accessible footpaths and crossings for those in wheelchairs. It is sometimes available at the tourist offices.

The council also runs a website, **Cittadini con Disabilità** (http://disabili.comune.fi.it, in Italian), which has links to such things as city itineraries thought out for the disabled. The site is largely addressed to local residents. Perhaps of more interest is the city council's NoBarriers page. From the council's Italian-language home page (www.comune.firenze.it), click on Servizi. Under I Luoghi you can click on NoBarriers. When the page comes up you can switch to other languages. Here you can get some idea of the degree of accessibility of anything from churches to chemists.

A still better source of practical information is Cornelia Danielson's *The Accessible Guide to Florence* (October 2004). Here you can find anything from accessible eateries to galleries that allow blind visitors to touch sculptures. Danielson also runs the Florence-based Barrier Free Travel Services (see right).

The majority of Florence's ATAF buses are equipped for wheelchair access. The problem is that uneven bus stops sometimes provide obstacles about which ATAF can do little.

Organisations

Accessible Travel & Leisure (☎ 01452 729739 in the UK; www.accessibletravel.co.uk; Avionics House, Naas Lane, Gloucester GL2 4SN) Claims to be the biggest UK travel agent catering for the disabled.

Barrier Free Travel Services (☎ 055 233 61 28; www .bftservices.it; Via Benedetto da Foiano 19) This is the most useful on-the-ground service for the disabled in Florence. It can help with travel and tours, procure wheelchairs and electric scooters, and organise entry to sights otherwise difficult to access.

DISCOUNT CARDS

An **ISIC** (International Student Identity Card; www.isic.org) can get you discounted admission prices at some sights, and help with cheap flights out of Italy. Similar cards are available to teachers (ITIC) and nonstudents (IYTC). The cards also carry a travel insurance component. They are issued by student unions, hostelling organisations and some youth travel agencies. In Florence they're only good for smallish discounts at a handful of minor museums, but can also be used at a range of accommodation venues, restaurants, bars, shops and vehicle rental outlets. Check out the full list on the website. Those under 26 should also have a look at the **Euro<26 card** (www .euro26.org).

ELECTRICITY

The electrical current in Florence is 220V, 50Hz, as throughout the rest of continental Europe. Some countries outside Europe (such as the USA and Canada) use 110V, 60Hz power, which means appliances from those countries might perform poorly. In this case, use a transformer. Plugs have two round pins, like in the rest of continental Europe.

EMBASSIES & CONSULATES

Most countries have an embassy in Rome; look them up under *Ambasciate* in the capital's Yellow Pages (*Pagine Gialle*). Various countries also maintain consulates in Florence, and include:

German Consulate (Map pp242–3; ☎ 055 29 47 22; Lungarno Amerigo Vespucci 30)

Swiss Consulate (Map pp240–1; ☎ 055 22 24 31; Piazzale Galileo 5)

UK Consulate (Map pp244–5; ☎ 055 28 41 33; Lungarno Corsini 2)

US Consulate (Map pp242–3; ☎ 055 26 69 51; Lungarno Amerigo Vespucci 38)

EMERGENCIES

Tourists who want to report thefts or obtain a residence permit will need to visit the **main police station** (Map pp242–3; ☎ 055 4 97 71; Via Zara 2). The rather self-important building is a late-18th-century curio, originally built as a hospital. The **police station** (Map pp248–9; ☎ 055 20 39 11; Via Pietrapiana 50/r; ☯ 8.30am-7.30pm Mon-Fri, 8.30am-1.30pm Sat) off Piazza dei Ciompi is especially used to dealing with tourists and their problems (petty theft etc).

Ambulance (ambulanza ☎ 118)

Fire Brigade (vigili del fuoco ☎ 115)

Highway Rescue (soccorso stradale ☎ 116)

Military Police (carabinieri ☎ 112)

Police (polizia ☎ 113)

GAY & LESBIAN TRAVELLERS

Homosexuality is legal in Italy and reasonably well tolerated in Florence, although open displays of gay affection are not always well received – a little discretion is advisable.

The city offers a handful of gay bars and clubs, but Florentine gays agree the options are limited – and they blame tourist literature and guidebooks for creating an unduly positive image of Florentine gay life! If you're looking to do some nighttime cruising, head for Le Cascine park, especially in the area around the Meccanò disco (see p152). Be aware that the activity comes with a degree of risk attached as gay bashing does sometimes occur.

ArciGay (www.arcigay.it), the national gay organisation, has general information on the gay and lesbian scene in Italy, while the companion website **Gay.It** (http://it.gay.com in Italian) provides listings for everything from bars and discos to gay beaches and beauty centres.

The Tuscan branch of **ArciGay** (Map p196; ☎ 050 55 56 18; www.arcigay.it/pisa in Italian; Via San Lorenzo 38) is based in Pisa.

In Florence, **Azione Gay e Lesbica Finisterrae** (Map pp240–1; ☎ 055 22 02 50; www.azionegayeles

bica.it in Italian; Via Pisana 32/r) welcomes newcomers to town and keeps tabs on what's going on in local gay circles.

Ireos (Map pp248–9; ☎ 055 21 69 07; www .ireos.org in Italian; Via de' Serragli 3/5; ☯ 5-8pm Mon-Fri) is a gay-lesbian association that organises cultural events and runs a medical and psychological counselling service. It is possible to organise HIV tests here.

At the **Libreria delle Donne** (☎ 055 234 78 10; http://associazioni.comune.fi.it/coop-erativadonne/libreria/home.htm in Italian; Via Fiesolana 2/b) women's bookshop and cooperative you can obtain information on the lesbian scene.

For written information, check out the annual *Chiquito Italian Gay Travel Guide* (€10), available in some bookshops.

HOLIDAYS

For Florentines, the main holiday periods remain summer (July and August), the Christmas–New Year period and Easter. August is a peculiar time as all Italy grinds to a halt, especially around Ferragosto (15 August), when just about everything closes. Travelling to and around Florence in this holiday period is far from ideal. For information on the city's colourful festivals and other events, see p9. National holidays:

New Year's Day (Anno Nuovo) 1 January

Epiphany (Befana) 6 January

Good Friday (Venerdì Santo) March/April

Easter Monday (Pasquetta/Lunedì dell'Angelo) March/April

Liberation Day (Giorno della Liberazione) April 25 – marks the Allied Victory in Italy, the end of the German presence and of Mussolini in 1945.

Labour Day (Giorno del Lavoro) 1 May

Republic Day (Festa della Repubblica) 2 June

Feast of the Assumption (Ferragosto) 15 August

All Saints' Day (Ognissanti) 1 November

Feast of the Immaculate Conception (Immaculata Concezione) 8 December

Christmas Day (Natale) 25 December

Boxing Day (Festa di Santo Stefano) 26 December

INTERNET ACCESS

If travelling with a portable computer, make sure you have a universal AC adaptor, a two-pin plug adaptor for Europe, and a reputable 'global' modem. Italian telephone sockets are mostly the US RJ-11 type (if you find yourself confronted with the old-style Italian three-prong socket, most electrical stores can sell you an adaptor). Some of the better hotels are set up with wifi or standard Internet connections. If you need more detailed information on travelling with a portable computer, contact www .teleadapt.com.

Major Internet Service Providers (ISPs) like **CompuServe** (www.compuserve.com) have dial-in nodes in Italy; download a list of the dial-in numbers before you leave home.

Some Italian servers can provide short-term accounts for local Internet access. **Agora** (☎ 800 304 999; www.agoratelema tica.it) is one of them. Several Italian ISPs offer free Internet connections: check out the websites (in Italian only) of **Tiscali** (www. tiscali.it), **Kataweb** (www.kataweb.it) and **Libero** (www.libero.it).

If you intend to rely on Internet cafés, you'll need to carry three pieces of information: your incoming (POP or IMAP) mail server name, your account name and your password.

Internet Cafés

Florence is awash with Internet centres. Some offer student rates and also have deals on cards for several hours' use at reduced rates. A handful of options follow:

Il Cairo Phone Center (Map pp248–9; ☎ 055 263 83 36; Via de' Macci 90/r; per hr from €2.10, per 5hr €10; ✆ 9.30am-1am) A friendly, Egyptian-run Internet and cheap phone shop.

Internet Train (www.internettrain.it; per hr online €4.30) Via dell'Oriuolo 40/r (Map pp248–9; ☎ 055 234 53 22; ✆ 10am-10.30pm Mon-Thu, 10am-8pm Fri-Sat, 3-7pm Sun); Via Guelfa 54-56/r (Map pp247–3; ☎ 055 264 51 46; ✆ 9am-11pm Mon-Fri, 10am-8pm Sat, noon-9pm Sun); Via de' Benci 36/r (Map pp248–9; ☎ 055 263 85 55; ✆ 9.30am-1am Mon-Fri, 10am-1am Sat, noon-1am Sun); Borgo San Jacopo 30/r (Map pp244–5; ☎ 055 265 79 35; ✆ 11am-11pm Mon-Fri, noon-8pm Sat-Sun); Via Porta Rossa 38/r (Map pp244–5; ☎ 055 274 10 37; ✆ 9.30am-midnight Mon-Sat, 10am-midnight Sun); Borgo de la Croce 33/r (Map pp248–9; ☎ 055 234 78 52; ✆ 10am-midnight Mon-Sat, 11am-midnight Sun); Stazione di Santa Maria Novella (☎ 055 239 97 20; ✆ 10am-8.30pm Mon, 9am-8.30pm Tue-Fri, 11am-8.30pm Sat-Sun) This chain has 13 branches around town, and its services include mobile-phone rental, VOIPTel (free calls computer to computer),

Fedex express courier, fax, scanning, printing, film processing and CD writing. You can hook your laptop up to the Web here too. A handy one is in the subterranean pedestrian passage beneath Stazione di Santa Maria Novella.

Netgate (Map pp248–9; ☎ 055 234 79 67; www .thenetgate.it; Via Sant'Egidio 14/r; per hr/5hr €2.50/7.50; ✆ 9am-11.30pm) Has a few other smaller branches and some terminals set up in many shops, hotels and cafés.

Webpuccino (Map pp244–5; ☎ 055 277 64 69; www .webpuccino.it; Via de' Conti 22/r; per hr €4; ✆ 10am-10pm Mon-Sat, noon-9pm Sun) Offers mobile phone rental, digital photo printing and CD burning. You can surf on your own laptop (€10 to set up and €2.90 per hour).

LAUNDRY

There are no shortage of self-service laundrettes around central Florence. You generally pay €3.50 for a wash load of around 7kg, and the same again to dry. Most are open seven days, around 9am to 10pm. Several have been marked on the maps.

LEGAL MATTERS

The biggest news in 2005 was the application of a new law in Florence (and some other Italian cities) imposing fines on those caught buying fake products from street vendors. Fines can run into thousands of euros, making the real Gucci bag look cheap compared with the fake if you're caught red-handed!

Another municipal initiative is the rule banning people from lying down or picnicking in the immediate vicinity of the Duomo.

Drivers should note that heavy on-the-spot fines are imposed for speeding. The blood-alcohol limit is 0.05%. Dipped headlights must be used day and night on highways. Helmets are compulsory for riders and passengers on motorbikes and scooters. If you have to exit from your vehicle on a highway, you are obliged to wear a reflector jacket.

Since early 2005 smoking in all closed public spaces (from bars to elevators, offices to trains) has been banned.

LOST PROPERTY

The city council and the local police, or *vigili urbani*, operate the **lost-property office** (*ufficio oggetti trovati*; Map pp240–1; ☎ 055 328 39 42/43; Via Circondaria 19; ✆ 9am-noon Mon, Wed & Fri, 9am-noon & 2.30-4.30pm Tue & Thu), located northwest of the city centre.

MAPS

The free map of Florence distributed by the tourist office is not overly helpful and a sensible investment would be *Florence,* a map produced by the Touring Club Italiano (TCI), who also publish a map of the city centre.

MEDICAL SERVICES

EU citizens (and those of Switzerland, Norway and Iceland) are entitled to the same free health services in public hospitals as Italians, but will need to present a European Health Insurance Card (EHIC; formerly the E111).

Australia has a reciprocal arrangement with Italy that entitles Australian citizens to free public health care – carry your Medicare card.

Citizens of New Zealand, the USA, Canada and other countries have to pay for all services. Most travel insurance policies include medical cover. In an emergency, head for the *pronto soccorso* unit of any hospital.

For minor health problems you can try your local pharmacy *(farmacia),* where pharmaceuticals tend to be sold more freely without prescription than in places such as the USA, Australia or the UK (see p214).

If your country has a consulate in Florence, staff there should be able to refer you to a doctor who speaks your language. The APT has lists of doctors and dentists of various nationalities. If you have a specific health complaint, obtain the necessary information and referrals for treatment before leaving home.

The following medical services may be of use to travellers:

Centro MTS (Malattie a Trasmissione Sessuale; Map pp242–3; ☎ 055 275 86 28; Piazza Brunelleschi 4 or Via della Pergola 64; ☼ 8am-noon Mon-Fri) Anonymous walk-in service for AIDS tests at the rear end of the Ospedale di Santa Maria Nuova.

Guardia Medica (☎ 055 233 94 56 for central Florence; ☼ 8pm-8am Mon-Fri, 10am on Sat to 8am Mon) A night-time call-out service with doctors (locums).

Misericordia di Firenze (Map pp244–5; ☎ 055 21 22 22; Vicolo degli Adimari 1; ☼ medical attention for tourists

2-6pm Mon-Fri) You will be charged for this service. It also runs ambulances from here as well as charitable operations for the town's poorer folk.

Ospedali Riuniti di Careggi (Map p238; ☎ 055 427 71 11; Viale Morgagni 85) The city's main hospital, but a long way from the centre.

Ospedale di Santa Maria Nuova (Map pp242–3; ☎ 055 2 75 81; Piazza di Santa Maria Nuova 1) Just east of the Duomo. In an emergency go to the *pronto soccorso.*

Tourist Medical Service (Map pp242–3; ☎ 055 47 54 11; Via Lorenzo Il Magnifico 59; ☼ 24hrs) No appointment is required. Doctors speak English, French and German.

METRIC SYSTEM

Italy uses the metric system. Basic terms for weight include *un etto* (100g) and *un chilo* (1kg). Like other continental Europeans, the Italians indicate decimals with commas and thousands with points.

MONEY

As in 11 other EU nations, Italy's currency is the euro. See p16 for a discussion of the economy and costs.

Changing Money

You can exchange money in banks, at post offices or in currency exchange booths (bureaux de change). Banks are the most reliable option and tend to offer the best rates. You should look around and ask about commissions, which can fluctuate considerably. There are plenty of banks throughout the city centre. Check commissions at bureaux de change, which can be as high as 10%.

American Express (Map pp244–5; ☎ 055 5 09 81; Via Dante Alighieri 22/r; ☼ 9am-5.30pm Mon-Fri, 9am-12.30pm Sat)

Travelex (Map pp244–5; ☎ 055 28 97 81; Lungarno degli Acciaiuoli 6/r; ☼ 9am-6pm Mon-Sat, 9.30am-5pm Sun)

Credit/Debit Cards

Major cards such as Visa, MasterCard, Maestro and Cirrus are accepted throughout Italy. They can be used in many hotels, restaurants and shops. Cards can also be used in ATMs displaying the appropriate sign, if you have a PIN. If you have no PIN, some (but by no means all) banks will allow you to obtain cash advances over the counter (a lengthy process). MasterCard and Visa are among the most widely recognised for such transactions. Check charges with your bank. Most banks now build a fee of around 2.75% into every foreign transaction. In addition, ATM withdrawals attract a further fee, usually around 1.5%.

If your card is lost, stolen or swallowed by an ATM, you can call toll-free to have an immediate stop put on its use. For MasterCard the number in Italy is ☎ 800 870 866, for Visa it's ☎ 800 819 014. For Diners Club call either ☎ 06 357 53 33 (Rome) or a reverse charges number to the country of issue (☎ 702 797 55 32 in the USA).

Amex is also widely accepted (although not as commonly as Visa or MasterCard). The office in Venice (see p213) has an express cash machine for cardholders. If you lose your Amex card, call ☎ 800 864 046.

Travellers Cheques

These are a safe way of carrying your money because they can be replaced if lost or stolen. It is, however, generally more practical to use plastic. If you wish to use cheques, Travelex, Amex and Visa are widely accepted brands.

Keep your initial receipt, along with a record of your cheque numbers and the ones you have used, separate from the cheques themselves. Take your passport when you go to cash travellers cheques. For lost or stolen cheques, call these toll-free numbers:

Amex (☎ 800 72 000)

MasterCard (☎ 800 870 866)

Travelex (☎ 800 335 511)

Visa (☎ 800 874 155)

NEWSPAPERS & MAGAZINES

A wide selection of national daily newspapers from around Europe (including the UK) are available at newsstands all over central Florence, and at strategic locations like the train and bus stations. The *International Herald Tribune*, *Time*, the *Economist*, *Der Spiegel* and a host of other international magazines are also available.

Italian Press

There is no 'national' paper as such, but rather several important dailies published out of major cities. These include Milan's **Corriere della Sera** (www.corriere.it in Italian) Turin's right-wing **La Stampa** (www.lastampa.it, in Italian) and Rome's centre-left **La Repubblica**. This trio forms the nucleus of a national press, publishing local editions throughout Italy.

The main local paper is the archly conservative **La Nazione** (www.lanazione.quotidiano.net, in Italian), poor on national and foreign news, but alright for a round-up of local happenings. The paper carries a fairly decent cinema and theatre listings section. Competition comes from the slightly racier **Il Corriere di Firenze**. You can get a Florence edition of **Il Giornale della Toscana** (www.giornaletoscana.it in Italian) and *La Repubblica* publishes a good Florence insert (www.firenze.repubblica.it in Italian), criticised by some, though, for being too much of a mouthpiece for the Democratici di Sinistra (DS; ex-Communist) party that has long-ruled Florence and much of Tuscany.

Useful Publications

For straight news in English, the free weekly *The Florentine* can't be beat. Pick it up in English-language bookstores and other selected locations (the paper itself carries a list).

Amid the landslide of printed information and disinformation available from the tourist offices is a handy booklet called *Florence – Concierge Information*. It is an advertising vehicle for local enterprises (shops, restaurants, shipping services and the like) aimed at visitors to Florence. *Firenze Spettacolo*, the city's definitive entertainment publication, is available monthly at newsstands. The quarterly English-language magazine *Vista*, sometimes available in better hotels and tourist offices, carries interesting articles about the city and Tuscany.

PHARMACIES

Some pharmacies open for extended hours (8am to 9pm); tourist offices can provide a list of these. Twenty-four-hour pharmacies include the following:

All'Insegna del Moro (Map pp244–5; ☎ 055 21 13 43; Piazza di San Giovanni 20/r)

Farmacia Comunale (Map pp242–3; ☎ 055 21 67 61; Stazione di Santa Maria Novella)

Molteni (Map pp244–5; ☎ 055 28 94 90; Via de' Cal-zaiuoli 7/r) One of the oldest pharmacies in the world, dating to the 13th century, although the furnishing is much more up to date – from the 19th century. They say Dante used to pop by here regularly.

POST

Le Poste (☎ 803160; www.poste.it), Italy's postal service, is notoriously slow, but it has improved over the past few years.

Stamps (*francobolli*) are available from post offices and authorised tobacconists (look for the official *tabacchi* sign: a big 'T', often white on black).

The **central post office** (Map pp244–5; Via Pellicceria; ⏰ 8.15am-7pm Mon-Sat) is off Piazza della Repubblica. Another big one is on the corner of **Via Giuseppe Verdi and Via Pietrapiana** (Map pp248–9; ⏰ 8.15-7pm Mon-Fri, 8.15am-12.30pm Sat).

Postal Rates

The cost of sending a letter by airmail (*via aerea*) depends on its weight and where it is being sent. For regular post, letters up to 20g cost 45c within Europe, 65c to Africa, Asia, the Americas and 70c to Australia and New Zealand. Postcards cost the same.

Few people use the regular post, preferring the slightly more expensive priority mail service (*posta prioritaria*), guaranteed to deliver letters sent to Europe within three days and to the rest of the world within four to eight days. Letters up to 20g sent *posta prioritaria* cost 62c within Europe, 80c to Africa, Asia, the Americas and €1 to Australia and New Zealand. Letters weighing 21g to 50g cost 85c/€1.45 (standard/priority) within Europe, €1/1.50 to Africa, Asia and the Americas, and €1.20/1.80 to Australia and New Zealand.

Sending Mail

Officially, letters sent *posta prioritaria* within Italy should arrive the following working day; those posted to destinations in Europe and the Mediterranean basin within three days; and those to the rest of the world in four to eight days.

Parcels (*pacchetti*) can be sent from any post office. You can purchase posting boxes or padded envelopes from most post offices. Parcels usually take longer to be delivered than letters and a different set of postal rates applies.

Receiving Mail

Poste restante is known as *fermo posta* in Italy. Letters marked thus will be held at the Fermo Posta counter in the main post office of the relevant town. You need to pick up your letters in person and present your passport as ID. The counter at Florence's central post office is through the entrance at Piazza de' Davanzati 4. Poste restante mail should be addressed as follows:

> John SMITH,
> Fermo Posta,
> Posta Centrale,
> 50100 Florence,
> Italy

Amex card or travellers-cheque holders can use the free client mail-holding service at the Florence office (see p213).

RADIO

There are three state-owned stations: RAI-1 (87.8MHz FM), RAI-2 (90.5MHz FM) and RAI-3 (98.4MHz FM). They offer a combination of classical and light music, with news broadcasts and discussion programmes. To listen to RAI programmes on the web go to www.international.rai .it/engl/radio.

Many of the local stations are a little bland. For a good mix of contemporary music you could try Controradio (93.6MHz FM), Nova Radio (101.5MHz FM) or Radio Deejay on 106.3MHz FM. For classical music, tune to FM Classics (105MHz FM).

You can pick up the BBC World Service on short wave at 6.195MHz, 7320 MHz, 9.410MHz, 12.095MHz and 15.485MHz, depending on where you are and the time of day. Voice of America can be found on short wave at 1593MHz, 9685MHz, 11,835MHz, 15,255MHz and 17,555MHz.

SAFETY

All in all Florence is a fairly secure city, but you need to keep an eye out for pick-pockets and bag-snatchers in the most heavily touristed parts of town, especially around the Duomo and the train station.

Prevention is better than cure. Only walk around with the amount of cash you intend to spend that day or evening. Hidden moneybelts or pouches are a good idea.

Never leave anything visible in your car and preferably leave nothing at all. Foreign and hire cars are especially vulnerable.

If anything does get lost or stolen, report it to the police and get a written statement from them if you intend to claim on insurance.

TAX & REFUNDS

A value-added tax (Imposta di Valore Aggiunto or IVA; VAT in English) of up to 20% is slapped onto just about everything in Italy.

Tourists who are resident outside the EU may claim a refund on this tax if they spend €155 or more in the same shop on the same day. The refund applies only to items purchased at retail outlets affiliated to the system – these shops display a 'tax-free for tourists' sign, or something similar. If you don't see a sign, ask the shopkeeper. You must fill out a form at the point of purchase and have it stamped and checked by Italian customs when you leave the country (you will need to show the receipt and purchases). At major airports and some border crossings, you can then get an immediate cash refund at specially marked booths; alternatively, return the form by mail to the vendor, who will make the refund, either by cheque or onto your credit card.

TELEPHONE

Most of the orange Telecom payphones now only accept phonecards (carte/schede telefoniche). Some card phones also accept special credit cards produced by Telecom – the formerly state-owned telecommunications company – and even commercial credit cards. A few send faxes (see right).

You will find Telecom phones in an unstaffed Telecom office (Map pp244–5; Via Cavour 21/r; ☺ 7am-11pm). You can buy phonecards (€2.50 and €5) at post offices, tobacconists and newsstands, and from vending machines in Telecom offices. Snap off the perforated corner before using it. Other Telecom phones have also been mapped (see Map pp242–3).

Calling Florence from Abroad

Dial the international access code (☎ 00 in most countries), followed by the code for Italy (☎ 39) and the full number, including the initial 0. To call the number ☎ 055 234 77 77 in Florence, for example, you need to dial the international access code, followed by ☎ 39 055 234 77 77.

Costs

A local call (comunicazione urbana) from a public phone costs 10c every minute and 12.5 seconds. For a long-distance call within Italy (comunicazione interurbana) you pay 10c when the call is answered and then 10c every 57 seconds.

A three-minute call from a payphone to most European countries and North America will cost about €2.10. To Australasia it would cost €2.80. Calling from a private phone is cheaper.

Domestic Calls

Area codes are an integral part of Italian telephone numbers. The codes all begin with 0 and consist of up to four digits. You must dial this whole number, even if calling from next door. Thus, any number you call in the Florence area will begin with 055.

Mobile phone numbers take a three-digit prefix such as 330, 335, 347 or 368. Freephone or toll-free numbers are called green numbers (numeri verdi) and start with 800. National rate (a call rate that applies across the country) numbers start with 848 or 199. There are also some six-digit national rate numbers (ie for rail and postal info).

For any national directory inquiries, call ☎ 12.

Fax

You can send faxes from post offices and some tobacconists, copy centres, Internet centres and stationers. Faxes can also be sent from some Telecom public phones. Expect to pay around €1.50 a page for faxes sent within Italy, and more for those going abroad. You can receive faxes at Internet Train (see p212) centres for 50c a page.

International Calls

Direct international calls can easily be made from public telephones by using a phonecard. Dial 00 to get out of Italy, then the relevant country and city codes, followed by the telephone number.

Useful country codes are: Australia 61, Canada and the USA 1, France 33, Germany 49, Ireland 353, New Zealand 64 and the UK 44. For international directory inquiries, call ☎4176.

To make a reverse-charge (collect) international call from a public telephone, dial ☎170. It is easier and often cheaper to use your country's Country Direct service. You dial the number and request a reverse-charge call through the operator in your country. Get a hold of the access numbers before you leave your home country.

International Phonecards & Call Centres

Some private companies distribute international phonecards offering cheaper rates on long-distance calls; keep an eye out at newspaper kiosks, tobacconists and the like. Another option is call centres like **Il Cairo Phone Center** (Map pp248–9; ☎ 055 263 83 36; Via de' Macci 90/r; ☿ 9.30am-1am). Or you could try out VOIPTel, a service offered by the Internet Train chain of Internet centres (see p212).

Mobile Phones

You can buy SIM cards in Italy for your own mobile phone from home (provided you have a GSM, dual- or tri-band cellular phone), as well as prepaid call time. This only works if your national phone hasn't been code blocked, which is usually the case, so find out before leaving home. You won't want to consider a full contract unless you plan to live in Italy for a good while. You need your passport to open any kind of mobile phone account, prepaid or otherwise.

Telecom Italia Mobile (TIM) and Vodaphone-Omnitel offer prepaid (*prepagato*) accounts for GSM phones (frequency 900 MHz). The card can cost as little as €10 (with €10 of calls loaded!) with Vodaphone. You can then top up in their shops or with cards from outlets like tobacconists and newsstands. TIM and Vodaphone-Omnitel retail outlets operate in virtually every Italian town. Rates vary according to an infinite variety of call plans.

Wind and 3 are two smaller mobile phone operators with consequently fewer outlets around the country.

US mobile phones generally work on a frequency of 1900 MHz so, for use in Italy, your US handset will have to be tri-band.

TELEVISION

The three state-run stations, RAI-1, RAI-2 and RAI-3, are run by Radio e Televisione Italiane. Historically, each has been in the hands of one of the main political groupings in the country, although in the past few years these affiliations have become less clear-cut. The appointment of station directors and senior staff is highly politicised.

Of the three, RAI-3 tends to have some of the more interesting programmes. Generally though, these stations and the private Canale 5, Italia 1, Rete 4 and La 7 tend to serve up a diet of indifferent news, tacky variety hours (with lots of near-naked tits and bums, appalling crooning and vaudeville humour) and game shows. Talk shows, some interesting but many nauseating, also abound. Several minor local stations also operate but are generally of minimal interest.

TIME

Italy (and hence Florence) is one hour ahead of GMT/UTC during winter, and two hours during the daylight-saving period, from the last Sunday in March to the last Sunday in October. Most other Western European countries are on the same time as Italy year-round, the major exceptions being the UK, Ireland and Portugal, which are one hour behind.

When it's noon in Florence, it's 3am in San Francisco, 6am in New York and Toronto, 11am in London, 9pm in Sydney and 11pm in Auckland. Note that in North America and Australasia, the changeover to/from daylight saving usually differs from the European date by a couple of weeks.

TIPPING

You are not expected to tip on top of restaurant service charges, but it is common to leave a small amount, say €1 a person. If there is no service charge, the customer might consider leaving a 10% tip. In bars, Italians often leave any small change as a tip, often only five or 10 cents. Tipping taxi drivers is not common practice, but you should tip the porter at higher-class hotels.

Bargaining is common in flea markets, but not in shops – although you might find that the proprietor is disposed to giving a discount if you are spending a reasonable amount of money. It's quite acceptable to ask if there is a special price for a room in a *pensione* or hotel if you plan to stay for more than a few days.

TOURIST INFORMATION
Tourist Offices Abroad

Information on Florence is available from the following branches of the Ente Nazionale Italiano per il Turismo (ENIT), the Italian State Tourism Board:

Australia (☎ 02-9262 1666; italia@italiantourism.com .au; Level 4, 46 Market St, Sydney NSW 2000)

Canada (☎ 416-925 4882; www.italiantourism.com; Suite 907, South Tower, 175 Bloor St East, Toronto M4W 3R8)

France (☎ 01 42 66 03 96; www.enit-france.com; 23 rue de la Paix, 75002 Paris)

Germany (☎ 030-247 83 98; www.enit.de; Kontorhaus Mitte, Friedrichstrasse 187, D-10117 Berlin)

Germany (☎ 089-531 317; Lenbachplatz 2, 80336 Munich)

Germany (☎ 069-259 126; Kaiserstrasse 65, 60329 Frankfurt am Main)

Netherlands (☎ 020-616 82 44; enitams@wirehub.nl; Stadhouderskade 2, 1054 ES Amsterdam)

Switzerland (☎ 043 466 40 40; info@enit.ch; Uraniastrasse 32, 8001 Zürich)

UK (☎ 020-7408 1254; italy@italiantouristboard.co.uk; 1 Princes St, London W1B 9AY)

USA (☎ 312-644 0996; www.italiantourism.com; 500 North Michigan Ave, Suite 2240, Chicago, IL 60611)

USA (☎ 310-820 1898; 12400 Wilshire Blvd, Suite 550, Los Angeles, CA 90025)

USA (☎ 212-245 4822; 630 Fifth Ave, Suite 1565, New York, NY 10111)

Tourist Offices in Florence

Main APT Office (Azienda di Promozione Turistica; Map pp244–5; ☎ 055 29 08 32; www.firenzeturismo.it; Via Cavour 1/r; ☼ 8.30am-6.30pm Mon-Sat, 8.30am-1.30pm Sun & holidays)

APT Office (Map p238; ☎ 055 31 58 74; Amerigo Vespucci airport, Via del Termine II; ☼ 7.30am-11.30pm)

Comune di Firenze tourist office Piazza della Stazione (Map pp248–9; www.comune.firenze.it; ☎ 055 21 22 45; Piazza della Stazione 4; ☼ 8.30am-7pm Mon-Sat & 8.30am-2pm Sun & holidays); Borgo Santa Croce (Map pp248–9; ☎ 055 234 04 44; Borgo Santa Croce 29/r; ☼ 9am-7pm Mon-Sat, 9am-2pm Sun & holidays Mar-Nov, 9am-5pm Mon-Sat, 9am-2pm Sun & holidays Dec-Feb) Florence's city council operates this information service from these two branches.

Tourist Helpline

The APT office located at Via Cavour 1/r also offers a special summer service known as **Sportello Tutela Diritti del Turista** (☎ 055 276 03 82) for tourists needing guidance on matters such as disputes over hotel bills.

Useful Websites

There is a plethora of websites dedicated to all things Florentine. Some of the more useful ones include:

ATAF (www.ataf.net) All you ever wanted to know about Florence's public transport system.

Comune di Firenze (www.comune.firenze.it) Florence's town council's official website, in Italian and English, with some interesting background information on the city and its events. You can also find useful items, such as the day's late-opening pharmacies.

Ente Nazionale Italiano per il Turismo (www.enit.it) The Italian national tourist body's website has information on everything from local tourist office addresses to town-by-town museum details, and has general introductions to Florentine food, art and history. Look for upcoming cultural events too.

Firenze.net (www.firenze.net) This site is full of useful listings, ranging from monuments to the latest events, from bars to B&Bs.

Florence 2000 (www.florence2000.it) An online hotel reservation site for Florence in English.

Florence For Fun (www.florenceforfun.org) A site aimed at international students in Florence, with some nightlife info and general travel stuff. The people who run it organise parties in some of the city's clubs, for students in town doing courses.

Florence Online (www.fol.it in Italian) A general city site with links to everything from accommodation to business services.

Michelangelo Buonarroti (www.michelangelo.com/buonarroti.html) For information on the life and works of one of the greatest figures of the Florentine Renaissance.

Niccolo Machiavelli (www.the-prince-by-machiavelli.com) Could be useful for budding tyrants. Here you can read the English translation of Machiavelli's controversial treatise on how to rule, *The Prince*, and commentaries on its interpretation.

Studentsville (www.studentsville.it) Site dedicated mainly to foreign students in town for a while.

Trenitalia (www.trenitalia.it) Plan rail journeys, check timetables and prices and book tickets on Italy's national railways site.

WeekendaFirenze (www.weekendafirenze.com) An interesting sight with some solid listings. Of particular note is the shopping section. You can also book tickets for major museums.

Welcome to Florence (www.firenzeturismo.it) The Florence APT tourist office site.

Welcome to Oltrarno (www.firenze-oltrarno.net) A cheerful site dedicated to the goings-on across the river, from where to dine to artisans' workshops.

VISAS

Italy is one of 15 member countries of the Schengen Convention, under which 13 EU member countries, plus Iceland and Norway, have abolished checks at common borders. The other members are Austria, Belgium, Denmark, Finland, France, Germany, Greece, Luxembourg, the Netherlands, Portugal, Spain and Sweden. Legal residents of one Schengen country do not require a visa for another Schengen country. Citizens of the remaining 12 EU countries are also exempt. Nationals of some other countries, including Australia, Brazil, Canada, Israel, Japan, New Zealand, Switzerland and the USA, do not require visas for tourist visits of up to 90 days.

All non-EU nationals entering Italy for any reason other than tourism (such as study or work) should contact an Italian consulate, as they may need a specific visa. They should also insist on having their passport stamped on entry as, without a stamp, they could encounter problems when trying to obtain a residence permit *(permesso di soggiorno)*.

If you are a citizen of a country not mentioned here, check with an Italian consulate whether you need a visa. The standard tourist visa issued by Italian consulates is the Schengen visa, valid for up to 90 days. A Schengen visa issued by one Schengen country is generally valid for travel in all other Schengen countries. However, individual member countries may impose additional restrictions on certain nationalities. These

visas are not renewable inside Italy. For more information and a list of countries whose citizens require a visa, check the Italian foreign ministry website (www.esteri.it).

Permits

EU citizens do not need permits to live, work or start a business in Italy. However, they are advised to register with a police station *(questura)* if they take up residence and apply for a residence permit *(permesso di soggiorno)*. That is the first step to acquiring an ID card *(carta d'identità)*. While you're at it, you'll need a tax file number *(codice fiscale)* if you wish to be paid for most work in Italy. Go to the **police station** *(questura*; Map pp242–3; ☎ 055 4 97 71; Via Zara 2) to obtain precise information on what is required. Study and work visas (all non-EU citizens require them) must be applied for in your country of residence.

WOMEN TRAVELLERS

Florence is not a dangerous city but women travelling alone may find that they are plagued by unwanted male attention. In bars and discos especially, the attention can be more intense than you'd like. If you do get talking, but start to wish you hadn't, a reference to your husband *(marito)*, boyfriend *(fidanzato)* or even children *(figli)* may put a brake on your interlocutor's ardour. The Tuscan tourist board publishes a brochure *Benvenute in Toscana/Tuscany Welcomes Women*, with a list of hotels around the region that supposedly pay particular attention to the travel needs of women travelling alone or with children; services can range from children's play areas to hotel deals with local hairdressers and beauty salons. The following contacts might also be of use.

Artemisia (Map pp240–1; ☎ 055 60 13 75; Via del Mezzetta 1 Interno) A help organisation for women and minors who have been the victims of physical and/or sexual assault. It can provide legal advice and counselling.

Libreria delle Donne (☎ 055 234 78 10; http://associazioni .comune.fi.it/cooperativadonne/libreria/home.htm in Italian; Via Fiesolana 2/b) Drop into this women's bookshop for information on local women's groups and lesbian issues.

WORK

It is illegal for non-EU citizens to work in Italy without a work permit *(permesso di lavoro)*, but trying to obtain one through your Italian consulate can be a pain. EU citizens are allowed to work in Italy, but they still need to obtain a residence permit (permesso di soggiorno) from a police station. Immigration laws require foreign workers to be 'legalised' through their employers. This applies even to cleaners and baby-sitters. The employers then pay pension and health insurance contributions. This doesn't mean that illegal work can't still be found.

Doing Business

People wishing to make the first moves towards expanding their business into Italy should contact their own country's trade department. The commercial department of the Italian embassy in your own country should also have information – at least on red tape. In Italy, the trade office of your embassy can provide tips and contacts.

For organising business conventions in Florence, getting temporary accommodation for clients, secretarial services and so on, contact the following.

The **Firenze Convention Bureau** (☎ 055 497 32 01; www.conventionbureau.it; Guardiola del Pratello Orsini 1, 50123 Florence) has many events organisers and support services (such as interpreters) listed on its website. The affiliated **Firenzefiera** (☎ 055 4 97 21; www.firenzefiera.it; Piazza Adua 1, 50123 Florence), runs the three main convention spaces available in the city: the **Fortezza da Basso**, a 16th-century fortress whose interior has been remodelled for congress space; the **Palazzo dei Congressi**, located in a 19th-century mansion and with a 1000-capacity auditorium, and **Palazzo degli Affari** (Map pp248–9; Piazza Adua 1, 50123 Florence), which has conference halls, seating for almost 2000 people, interpreting and translation services and a buffet area. Various trade fairs are held here throughout the year.

Employment Options

The best options are trying to find work in bars, restaurants and shops (such as leather outlets). Non-EU citizens, even if they have no kitchen experience and little Italian, can sometimes get 'cooking' work, which can be little more than assembling pre-prepared pizzas. But even qualified cooks could earn as little as €5 to €10 per hour, for long hours. We are talking about the tourist-trap restaurants here, that are quite happy to serve up deep-frozen, precooked stuff. What's worse, eating it or preparing it?

Another option is au pair work organised before you come to Italy. A useful guide is *The Au Pair and Nanny's Guide to Working Abroad* by Susan Griffith and Sharon Legg. Susan Griffith's *Work Your Way Around the World* is also worth looking at.

The easiest source of work for foreigners is teaching English (or another foreign language), but even with full qualifications, a non-EU citizen will find it difficult to secure a permanent position. Most of the larger, more reputable schools will hire only people with work or residence permits or both, but their attitude can become more flexible if they come across someone with good qualifications.

The **British Institute** (Map pp244–5; ☎ 055 26 77 81; www.britishinstitute.it; Piazza degli Strozzi 2) is the main UK centre for English teaching in Florence (you can also take Italian classes). The **British Institute library** (Map pp248–9) is at Lungarno Guicciardini 9.

University students or recent graduates might be able to arrange an internship with companies located in Florence. The **Association of International Students for Economics and Commerce** (www.aiesec.org), with branches throughout the world, helps member students find internships in related fields. For information on membership, check out the website.

Language

Language

It's true – anyone can speak another language. Don't worry if you haven't studied languages before or that you studied a language at school for years and can't remember any of it. It doesn't even matter if you failed English grammar. After all, that's never affected your ability to speak English! And this is the key to picking up a language in another country. You just need to start speaking.

Learn a few key phrases before you go. Write them on pieces of paper and stick them on the fridge, by the bed or even on the computer – anywhere that you'll see them often.

You'll find that locals appreciate travellers trying their language, no matter how muddled you may think you sound. So don't just stand there, say something! If you want to learn more Italian than we've included here, pick up a copy of Lonely Planet's comprehensive but user-friendly *Italian Phrasebook*.

SOCIAL
Meeting People
Hello.
Buongiorno.
Goodbye.
Arrivederci.
Please.
Per favore.
Thank you (very much).
(Mille) Grazie.
Yes/No.
Sì/No.
Do you speak English?
Parla inglese?
Do you understand (me)?
(Mi) Capisce?
Yes, I understand.
Sì, capisco.
No, I don't understand.
No, non capisco.

Could you please ...?
Potrebbe ...?
repeat that	ripeterlo
speak more slowly	parlare più lentamente
write it down	scriverlo

Going Out
What's on ...?
Che c'è in programma ...?
locally	in zona
this weekend	questo fine settimana
today	oggi
tonight	stasera

Where are the ...?
Dove sono ...?
clubs	dei club
gay venues	dei locali gay
places to eat	posti dove mangiare
pubs	dei pub

Is there a local entertainment guide?
C'è una guida agli spettacoli in questa città?

PRACTICAL
Question Words
Who?	Chi?
What?	Che?
When?	Quando?
Where?	Dove?
How?	Come?

Numbers & Amounts
1	uno
2	due
3	tre
4	quattro
5	cinque
6	sei
7	sette
8	otto
9	nove
10	dieci
11	undici
12	dodici
13	tredici
14	quattordici
15	quindici
16	sedici

17	diciasette
18	diciotto
19	dicianove
20	venti
21	ventuno
22	ventidue
30	trenta
40	quaranta
50	cinquanta
60	sessanta
70	settanta
80	ottanta
90	novanta
100	cento
1000	mille
2000	duemila

Days

Monday	lunedì
Tuesday	martedì
Wednesday	mercoledì
Thursday	giovedì
Friday	venerdì
Saturday	sabato
Sunday	domenica

Banking

I'd like to ...
Vorrei ...

cash a cheque	riscuotere un assegno
change money	cambiare denaro
change some	cambiare degli assegni
travellers cheques	di viaggio

Where's the nearest ...?
Dov'è il ... più vicino?

| automatic teller machine | bancomat |
| foreign exchange office | cambio |

Post

Where is the post office?
Dov'è la posta?

I want to send a ...
Voglio spedire ...

fax	un fax
parcel	un pachetto
postcard	una cartolina

I want to buy ...
Voglio comprare ...

an aerogram	un aerogramma
an envelope	una busta
a postage stamp	un francobollo

Phone & Mobile Phones

I want to buy a phone card.
Voglio comprare una scheda telefonica.
I want to make ...
Voglio fare ...

| a call (to ...) | una chiamata (a ...) |
| reverse-charge/ collect call | una chiamata a carico del destinatario |

Where can I find a/an ...?
Dove si trova ...
I'd like a/an ...
Vorrei ...

adaptor plug	un addattatore
charger for my phone	un caricabatterie
mobile/cell phone for hire	un cellulare da noleggiare
prepaid mobile/ cell phone	un cellulare prepagato
SIM card for your network	un SIM card per vostra rete telefonica

Internet

Where's the local Internet café?
Dove si trova l'Internet point?

I'd like to ...
Vorrei ...

| check my email | controllare le mie email |
| get online | collegarmi a Internet |

Transport

What time does the ... leave?
A che ora parte ...?

bus	l'autobus
plane	l'aereo
train	il treno

What time's the ... bus/vaporetto?
A che ora passa ... autobus/batello?

first	il primo
last	l'ultimo
next	il prossimo

Are you free? (taxi)
È libero questo taxi?
Please put the meter on.
Usa il tassametro, per favore.
How much is it to ...?
Quant'è per ...?
Please take me to (this address).
Mi porti a (questo indirizzo), per favore.

FOOD

breakfast	prima colazione
lunch	pranzo
dinner	cena
snack	spuntino/merenda
eat	mangiare
drink	bere

Can you recommend a ...
Potrebbe consigliare un ...?

bar/pub	bar/pub
café	bar
restaurant	ristorante

Is service/cover charge included in the bill?
Il servizio/coperto è compreso nel conto?

For more detailed information on food and dining out, see the Eating chapter, pp00–00.

EMERGENCIES

It's an emergency!
È un'emergenza!
Could you please help me/us?
Mi/Ci può aiutare, per favore?

Call the police/a doctor/an ambulance!
Chiami la polizia/un medico/un'ambulanza!
Where's the police station?
Dov'è la questura?

HEALTH

Where's the nearest ...?
Dov'è ...più vicino?

chemist (night)	la farmacia (di turno)
dentist	il dentista
doctor	il medico
hospital	l'ospedale

I need a doctor (who speaks English).
Ho bisogno di un medico (che parli inglese).

Symptoms

I have (a) ...
Ho ...

diarrhoea	la diarrea
fever	la febbre
headache	mal di testa
pain	un dolore

Glossary

abbonamento mensile – monthly pass for public transport

ACI – Automobile Club Italiano (Italian Automobile Association)

affittacamere – rooms for rent in private houses

albergo (s), **alberghi** (pl) – hotel (up to five stars)

alimentari – grocery shop

amaro – Italian liqueur (literally: 'bitter')

ambasciata – embassy

APT – Azienda di Promozione Turistica (provincial tourist office)

autostazione – bus station/terminal

autostrada (s), **autostrade** (pl) – motorway, highway

bagagli smarriti – lost luggage

baldacchino – canopy of fabric or stone over an altar, shrine or throne in a Christian church

benzina – petrol

biblioteca (s), **biblioteche** (pl) – library

biglietteria – box or ticket office

biglietto – ticket

birreria – brewery or pub

borgo (s), **borghi** (pl) – walled village

bottega – shop

bussino – electric minibus network that operates around the centre of Florence

calcio – football (soccer)

campanile – a bell tower, usually free standing

cappella – chapel

carabinieri – police with military and civil duties

carnevale – carnival period between Epiphany and Lent

carta d'identità – identity card

cartoleria – stationery shop

casa – house, home

castello – castle

cattedrale – cathedral

cenacolo – refectory (or Last Supper scene)

centro – city centre

centro storico – historic centre, old city

chiesa (s), **chiese** (pl) – church

chilo – kilogram

chiostro – cloister; covered walkway, usually enclosed by columns, around a quadrangle

ciborio – goblet-shaped lidded vessel used to hold consecrated hosts for Holy Communion

cimitero – cemetery

collina – hill (colle in place names)

colonna – column

comune – equivalent to a municipality or county; town or city council; historically, a commune (self-governing town or city)

corso – main street

CTS – Centro Turistico Studentesco e Giovanile (Centre for Student and Youth Tourists)

cupola – dome

deposito bagagli – left luggage
digestivo – after-dinner liqueur
duomo – see **cattedrale**

ENIT – Ente Nazionale Italiano per il Turismo (Italian State Tourist Office)
enoteca – specialist wine shop/bar
ES – Eurostar Italia; very fast train
(un) etto – 100 grams

fermoposta – poste restante
ferragosto – Feast of the Assumption; more often refers to the major August (summer) holiday period
ferrovia – train station
festa – feast day; holiday
fiaschetteria – snack bar, serving alcohol
fiume – river
fornaio – bakery
fortezza – fort
francobolli – stamps
FS – Ferrovie dello Stato; Italian State Railway

gabinetto – toilet, WC
gelateria – ice-cream parlour
guardia di finanza – fiscal/finance police

IAT – Informazioni e Assistenza ai Turisti (local tourist office)
IVA – Imposta di Valore Aggiunto (value-added tax)

largo – (small) square
lavanderia – laundrette
libreria – bookshop
locanda – inn, small hotel
loggia – covered area on the side of a building, porch
lungarni – roads that follow the course of the river Arno

marche da bollo – tax stamps for official payments
mercato – market
merceria – haberdashery shop
mescita di vini – wine outlet
mezza porzione – half or child's portion
motorino – moped
municipio – town hall
(le) mura – city wall
musei statali – state museums

numero verde – toll-free number

oggetti smarriti – lost property
orto botanico – botanic gardens
ospedale – hospital
ostello – hostel
osteria (s), **osterie** (pl) – traditional bar/restaurant

palazzo, palazzi (pl) – mansion, palace, large building of any type (including an apartment block)
panetteria – bakery
passeggiata – traditional evening stroll
pasticceria – cake/pastry shop

pellicola – roll of film
pensione – small hotel
permesso di lavoro – work permit
permesso di soggiorno – permit to stay in Italy for a nominated period
piazza, piazze (pl) – square
piazzale – (large) open square
pietà – literally pity or compassion; sculpture, drawing or painting of the dead Christ supported by the Madonna
pinacoteca – art gallery
piscina – pool
ponte – bridge
porta – city gate
posta – post office
posta prioritaria – priority mail
prepagato – prepaid (eg, mobile phone account)
pronto soccorso – first aid; (riparto di) pronto soccorso is a casualty/emergency ward

questura – police station

regioni – administrative regions in Italy, such as Tuscany
ricevuta – receipt
Risorgimento – late-19th-century movement led by Garibaldi and others to create a united, independent Italian state
robbiane – terracotta medallions; architectural feature

sala – room in a museum or a gallery
salumeria – delicatessen
scala – staircase
scala mobile – escalator, moving staircase
sedia a rotelle – wheelchair
seggiolone – child's high chair
senza piombo – unleaded (petrol)
servizio – service charge in restaurants
sindaco – mayor
stazione – station
stazione di servizio – petrol or service station
supplemento – supplement, payable on a fast train

tabaccheria, tabaccaio – tobacconist's shop, tobacconist
tavola calda – (literally 'hot table') self-serve buffet
teatro – theatre
terme – baths, hot springs
tondo – circular painting/portrait
torre – tower
trattoria/e – cheap restaurant/s

ufficio postale – post office
ufficio stranieri – foreigners' bureau (in police station)

via – street, road
via aerea – air mail
vicolo – alley, alleyway
vigili urbani – municipal police
vinaio – wine bar or shop

Behind the Scenes

THE LONELY PLANET STORY

The story begins with a classic travel adventure: Tony and Maureen Wheeler's 1972 journey across Europe and Asia to Australia. There was no useful information about the overland trail then, so Tony and Maureen published the first Lonely Planet guidebook to meet a growing need.

From a kitchen table, Lonely Planet has grown to become the largest independent travel publisher in the world, with offices in Melbourne (Australia), Oakland (USA) and London (UK). Today Lonely Planet guidebooks cover the globe. There is an ever-growing list of books and information in a variety of media. Some things haven't changed. The main aim is still to make it possible for adventurous travellers to get out there – to explore and better understand the world.

At Lonely Planet we believe travellers can make a positive contribution to the countries they visit – if they respect their host communities and spend their money wisely. Every year 5% of company profit is donated to charities around the world.

THIS BOOK

This fourth edition of *Florence* was written by Damien Simonis, as were the previous three. The guide was commissioned in Lonely Planet's London office and produced by:

Commissioning Editor Michala Green, Tasmin McNaughton

Coordinating Editors Katrina Webb, Sarah Hassall

Coordinating Cartographer Jacqueline Nguyen

Coordinating Layout Designer Gary Newman

Managing Cartographers Corrinne Waddell, Mark Griffiths

Assisting Editors Pat Kinsella, Nancy Ianni

Cover Designer Pepi Bluck

Indexer Kate Evans

Project Manager Rachel Imeson

Language Content Coordinator Quentin Frayne

Thanks to Stephanie Pearson, Nicola Williams, Sally Darmody, Celia Wood

Cover photographs Damien Simonis, José F Poblete

Internal photographs by Juliet Coombe except for the following: p2 (#3,5), p 8, p12, p15, p20, p24, p29, p33, p52, p55, p66, p70, p83 (#1,4), p85 (#3,4), p86 (#1,2,3,4), p87 (#1), p88 (#1,2), p89 (#1), p90 (#3), p92, p96, p140, p144, p153, p154, p164, p192 Martin Hughes/Lonely Planet Images; p198 Philip and Karen Smith/Lonely Planet Images; p83 (#3), p85 (#1) Dallas Stribley/Lonely Planet Images; p84 (#1) Michelle Lewis/Lonely Planet Images; p87 (#3) Bethune Carmichael/Lonely Planet Images; p2 (#1), p87 (#2), p90 (#4) Damien Simonis/Lonely Planet Images; p85 (#2) Greg Elms/Lonely Planet Images

All images are copyright of the photographer unless otherwise indicated. Many of the images in this guide are available for licensing from Lonely Planet Images: www.lonelyplanetimages.com.

THANKS
DAMIEN SIMONIS

To those who helped me return immediately to life on the Arno, *grazie di cuore*! They include: Monica Fontani and Matteo Benvenuti, Luisa De Salvo, Fabiana Boccuni, Michela d'Ippolito and Barbara Dall'Acqua (all of whom shared excursions into the Florentine night with me); Fabrizio Gesi (that was quite a night out in the hills around town!); Alessandro Parini and Dr Luca Bardi (who welcomed me into

SEND US YOUR FEEDBACK

We love to hear from travellers – your comments keep us on our toes and help make our books better. Our well-travelled team reads every word on what you loved or loathed about this book. Although we cannot reply individually to postal submissions, we always guarantee that your feedback goes straight to the appropriate authors, in time for the next edition. Each person who sends us information is thanked in the next edition – and the most useful submissions are rewarded with a free book.

To send us your updates – and find out about Lonely Planet events, newsletters and travel news – visit our award-winning website: www.lonelyplanet.com/feedback.

Note: We may edit, reproduce and incorporate your comments in Lonely Planet products such as guidebooks, websites and digital products, so let us know if you don't want your comments reproduced or your name acknowledged. For a copy of our privacy policy visit www.lonelyplanet.com/privacy.

their country home); Martino Bruni, Alessandro Finardi and family (for helping with the flat, laughs at lunch and dinner at home); Lucia Montigiani and William fforde (for the wonderful dinner in the hills of the Oltrarno); Massimo Vanni (local journalist and font of Florentine knowledge); Cristiana Vannini (for revealing a secret of the Brindellone!). Miguel Ángel Aquiso popped down for a quick trip to traipse around Fiesole with me – *gracias por tu compañia*!

A big *grazie mille* goes to colleague Miles Roddis, who was in Tuscany ahead of me and dropped me some time-saving tips. Thanks also to APT staff for help with tricky questions.

Finally, thanks and more to Janique LeBlanc, who accompanied me part of the way and shared the early broiling days of this return to the Renaissance treasure chest.

OUR READERS

Many thanks to the travellers who used the last edition and wrote to us with helpful hints, useful advice and interesting anecdotes:

Chris Bachovchin, Steve Bailey, Sarah Balck, Svea Breckberg, Valerie Bridgeman, Michael Buckley, Pam Cheadle, Simon Cope, Martin Corroy, Ryan Devries, Susan Duca, Claire Featherstone, Marjolein Fredrix, Cindy Gregory, Michael Guerin, Frederik Helbo, Benjamin Hetzel, Holly Hooper, Katie Koprinik, Anne McDonnell, Barbara Merlo, Noelle Myers, Jiun Hao Neoh, James Perry-Keene, Norman Rosen, Karl Ruppenthal, Emily Sachs, Arthur Schwartz, Anne Sear, May Sharman, Edith Springveld, Andrew Stephenson, Betsy Thayer, Jeanette Thompson, Ian Ward-Brown

Notes

Notes

Index

See also separate indexes for Eating (p234), Shopping (p235) and Sleeping (p235).

000 map pages
000 photographs

MAP LEGEND

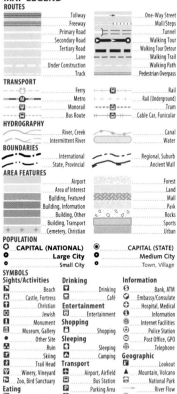

ROUTES

............Tollway
............Freeway
............Primary Road
............Secondary Road
............Tertiary Road
............Lane
............Under Construction
............Track

............One-Way Street
............Mall/Steps
............Tunnel
............Walking Tour
............Walking Tour Detour
............Walking Trail
............Walking Path
............Pedestrian Overpass

TRANSPORT

............Ferry
............Metro
............Monorail
............Bus Route

............Rail
............Rail (Underground)
............Tram
............Cable Car, Funicular

HYDROGRAPHY

............River, Creek
............Intermittent River

............Canal
............Water

BOUNDARIES

............International
............State, Provincial

............Regional, Suburb
............Ancient Wall

AREA FEATURES

............Airport
............Area of Interest
............Building, Featured
............Building, Information
............Building, Other
............Building, Transport
............Cemetery, Christian

............Forest
............Land
............Mall
............Park
............Rocks
............Sports
............Urban

POPULATION

○ **CAPITAL (NATIONAL)**
● **Large City**
● Small City

◉ CAPITAL (STATE)
● Medium City
● Town, Village

SYMBOLS

Sights/Activities
⬛ ....Beach
🏰 ....Castle, Fortress
✝ ....Christian
✡ ....Jewish
❚ ....Monument
🏛 ....Museum, Gallery
● ....Other Site
⬛ ....Ruin
⬛ ....Skiing
⬛ ....Trail Head
⬛ ....Winery, Vineyard
⬛ ....Zoo, Bird Sanctuary

Eating
🍴 ....Eating

Drinking
🍷 ....Drinking
☕ ....Café

Entertainment
🎭 ....Entertainment

Shopping
🛍 ....Shopping

Sleeping
🛏 ....Sleeping
⛺ ....Camping

Transport
✈ ....Airport, Airfield
🚌 ....Bus Station
🅿 ....Parking Area
🚕 ....Taxi Rank

Information
💲 ....Bank, ATM
◎ ....Embassy/Consulate
✚ ....Hospital, Medical
ℹ ....Information
@ ....Internet Facilities
⊛ ....Police Station
✉ ....Post Office, GPO
☎ ....Telephone

Geographic
⬛ ....Lookout
▲ ....Mountain, Volcano
⬛ ....National Park
→ ....River Flow
🚫 ....Waterfall

Maps

0   2 km
0   1 mile

SIGHTS	
& ACTIVITIES	(pp60–112) (pp155–6)
Certosa di Galluzzo	1 C4
Poggio Imperiale	2 D4
Villa Careggi	3 D1
Villa Medica di Castello	4 C1
Villa Medica La Petraia	5 C1
EATING	(pp126–42)
Da Stefano	6 C4
La Capponcina	7 E2
ENTERTAINMENT	(pp150–4)
Teatro della Limonaia	8 C1
Tenax	9 B2
SLEEPING	(pp172–84)
Villa Poggio San Felice	10 D4
INFORMATION	
APT Office	11 B1
Ospedali Riuniti di Careggi	(see 3)

Settignano

To Arezzo (49km)

Fiesole

See Fiesole Map (p239)

Via Gabriele D'Annunzio

Via Fra Giovanni Angelico
Via Giuseppe Mantellini

Via A Gramsci

Via Faentina

Via Bolognese

Via di Maiano

Via del Salviatino

Via San Domenico

Via Aretina

To Rome (240km)

Stazione Campo di Marte

FLORENCE (FIRENZE)

Arno

Stazione di Santa Maria Novella

See Florence Map (pp240–1)

Giardini di Boboli (Boboli Gardens)

Via San Matteo in Arcetri

Stazione Porta al Prato

Via Della Panche

Via Reginaldo Giuliani

Castello

Stazione di Rifredi

Via Undici Agosto

Le Cascine

Viale Francesco Redi

Belloguardo

Via Sense

Galluzzo

Isolotto

Amerigo Vespucci Airport

Stazione delle Cascine

Viale Francesco Baracca

Via Pistoiese

Via de' Cattani

Casellina

Via Pratese

To Pistoia (25km)

Autostrada Firenze-Mare

Via di Rimaggio

Via Inflora

Via Etruria

Scandicci

L'Olmo

To Poggio a Caiano (14km); Pisa (35km)

Autostrada del Sole

To Siena (62km)

FIESOLE

0 ————————— 200 m
0 ————————— 0.1 miles

Via Faentina

Via Giovanni Duprè

Via Riorbico

Via A Costa

Via G Bastianini

Via delle Mura Etrusche

Via Becherine

Via P Banchi

Via del Campo Sportivo

Zona Archeologica

Via Marini

Via D Cannelle

Via Portigiana

Via Gramsci

Via degli Angeli

S Girolamo

Via di Sant Francesco

Giardino di Sant Francesco

Piazza Mino da Fiesole

Vecchia Fiesolana

Via S Ansand

Via Bandini

Via Giuseppe Verdi

Via S Maria

Via Mangani

Via de Massimo

Via delle Querce

Fiesole

Via F Poeti

Via de Medici

Via de' F Colzi

Via Corsica

Via di Poggio Maiterini

Via A Mari

Via del Pelagaccio

Via Paramonda

Via S Apollinare

Via Belvedere

Via Fra Giovanni Angelico

Via Dei Ferruzzi

Via Montecceri

Via della Doccia

Via del Pelagaccio

Via Doccia

Via Giuseppe Mantellini

S Domenico

Via delle Fontanelle

Bel Riposo

Largo Leonardo da Vinci

Via Benedetto da Maiano

▲ Mt Ceceri (414m)

Poggio Sereno

Cave di Maiano

Via Benedetto da Maiano

Maiano

Via Cave di Maiano

To Florence (4km)

A **B** **C** **D**

1

Viale Alessandro Guidoni

To Amerigo Vespucci
Airport (3km)   Area Ex-FIAT

Ponte di Mezzo

Via di Novoli

Via Francesco Baracca

Ponte di Mezzo

Ponte
di Mezzo

Via di
Rifredi

Via Giovan Filippo Mariti

Piazza
Dalmazia

17

18

Rifredi

Il Poggetto

Via Morgagni

Via Filippo

Via Corsica

Via A Tavanti

Via
C Beslo

12

22

Via M Mercati

Piazza
P Leopoldo

Montughi

4

Via F Stibbert

Via Vittorio Emanuele II

2

Ponte di
S Donato

Ponte alle
Mosse

Torrente Mugnone

Via Luigi Boccherini

Via Francesco Vezzani

Via Maragliano

36

Lost Property Office
(Ufficio oggetti trovati)

Via Circondaria

Viale Francesco Redi

San Jacopino

Via dello Statuto

See San Marco & Nearby Quarters Map (pp242–3)

Torrente Mugnone

3

Via Pietro Toselli

Via del Ponte alle Mosse

Via Benedetto Marcello

Via delle Porte Nuove

Viale Belfiore

Viale Fratelli Rosselli

**Ippodromo
delle
Cascine**

Canale Macinante

3

Viale degli Olmi

Viale Abramo Lincoln

Stazione
Porta al Prato
(Ex-Stazione
Leopolda)

23

24

Piazzale
Porta al
Prato

6

Via Magenta

Via Filippo Strozzi

**Fortezza
da Basso**

Palazzo
dei
Congressi

Stazione
di Santa Maria
Novella

Viale Spartaco Lavagnini

Piazza della
Indipendenza

Piazza
San Marco

Piazza
del Mercato
Centrale

4

Via del Sansovino

Via Bronzino

Via Pisana

Monticelli

Piazza
P Uccello

Lungarno del Pignone

Via de' Vanni

28

25

Ponte della
Vittoria

Piazza
Gaddi

16

Pignone

Via del Ponte Sospeso

Piazza
Pier Vettori

37

Via di Monte Ulivelto

Viale
Raffaello
Sanzio

33

Corso Italia

Lungarno Amerigo Vespucci

15

27

Arno

Borgo Ognissanti

See Central Florence Map (pp244–5)

Piazza
dell'Unità
Italiana

Piazza di Santa
Maria Novella

Piazza delle
Repubblica

Piazza Carlo
Goldoni

Duomo

Borgo degli Albizi

5

Bellosguardo

Piazza di
Bellosguardo

Via di San Carlo

Via di Bellosguardo

11

19

Via B Cozzoli

Via J Giacomo
Zanella

Via dell'
Arcionella

14

13

35

Via Pisana

Via Ludovico

Ponte
Amerigo
Vespucci

Ponte alla
Carraia

San Frediano

Ponte
Santa Trinita

Ponte
Vecchio

**Santo
Spirito**

20

Via A Aleardi Ariosto

Via Domenico
Burchiello

Viale Francesco Petrarca

Piazza
Tasso

29

Giardino
Torrigiani

Giardino di Boboli
(Boboli Gardens)

Isolotto

San Niccolò

Forte di
Belvedere

6

Via Piana

Via Senese

Viale del Poggio imperiale

To Galluzzo
(2.5km)

Istituto
d'Arte

Viale Niccolò Machiavelli

Chiesa di San
Leonardo

Via di San Leonardo

30 **38**

Via della Torre
del Gallo

See Oltrarno Map (pp248–9)

Ponte alle
Mosse

0 ____ 600 m
0 ____ 0.4 miles

SIGHTS	(pp60–112)
& ACTIVITIES	(pp155–6)
Campo Sportivi ASSI	1 E6
Cenacolo di San Salvi	2 G4
Le Pavoniere Swimming Pool	3 A3
Museo Stibbert	4 D1
Nannini Swimming Pool	5 H5
Porta al Prato	6 C3
Società Canottieri Comunali	7 G5
Stadio Comunale Artemio Franchi	8 G3
Torre del Gallo	9 E6
Università Internazionale dell'Arte	10 F2

EATING	(pp126–42)
Ashoka	11 B4
Baroncini	12 C1
Fontanka	13 B4
Il Vico del Carmine	14 B4
Nanamuta	15 B4
Trattoria Vittoria	16 B4

DRINKING	(pp145–9)
Barcelò	17 C1
Café de Paris	18 C1
Universale	19 B4

ENTERTAINMENT	(pp150–4)
Arena Chiardiluna	20 B5
Arena di Marte	21 G3
Auditorium Flog	22 C1
Central Park	23 B3
Esterno Notte	(see 22)
Ex-Stazione Leopolda	24 B3
Meccanò	25 B4
Parco Sud	26 H5
Teatro Comunale	27 B4

SHOPPING	(pp158–70)
Mercato delle Cascine	28 B4

SLEEPING	(pp172–84)
Albergo Torre di Bellosguardo	29 B5
Hotel Park Palace	30 D6
Hotel Villa Liberty	31 F6
Ostello Europa Villa Camerata	32 H2

TRANSPORT	(pp202–8)
Mille e Una Bici	33 B4

INFORMATION	
Artemisia	34 H4
Azione Gay e Lesbica Finisterrae	35 C4
CTS	36 B2
Istituto Politecnico Internazionale della Moda	37 B4
Swiss Consulate	38 D6

241

SAN MARCO & NEARBY QUARTERS

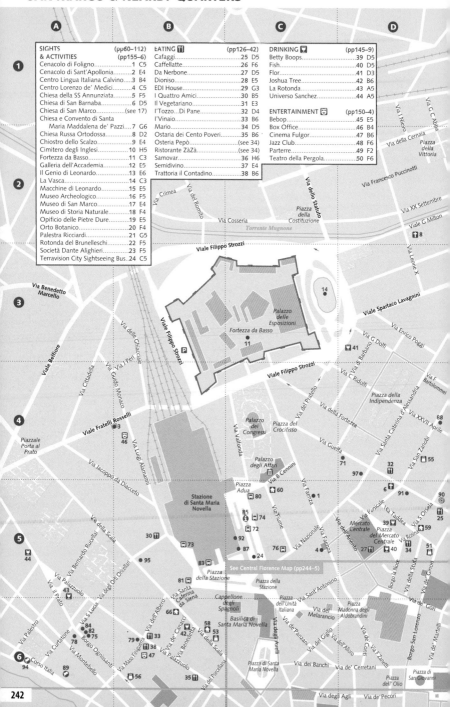

See Oltrarno Map (pp248–9)

243

See San Marco & Nearby
Quarters Map (pp242–3)

Via Ricasoli
Via dei Servi
Via Bufalini
Via dell' Oriuolo
Via del Proconsolo
Borgo degli Albizi
Via de' Pucci
Via de' Biffi
Via Ricasoli
Via de' Martelli
Via de' Conti
Via della Stufa
Via de' Ginori
Via del Canto de' Nelli
San Lorenzo Market
Borgo la Noce
Borgo San Lorenzo
Piazza San Lorenzo
Piazza del Mercato Centrale
Mercato Centrale
Via Sant' Antonino
Via Faenza
Via dell' Ariento
Via de' Cerretani
Via F. Zanetti
Via de' Conti
Via dell' Alloro
Piazza Madonna degli Aldobrandini
Via del Melarancio
Via del Giglio
Piazza dell'Unità Italiana
Via de' Panzani
Via dei Banchi
Largo Fratelli Alinari
Via degli Avelli
Piazza della Stazione
Stazione di Santa Maria Novella
Piazza della Stazione
Piazza di Santa Maria Novella
Via della Scala
Via del Moro
Via Palazzuolo
Via dei Fossi
Via della Spada
Via del Sole
Via delle Belle Donne
Via degli Agli
Via de' Rondinelli
Via de' Tosinghi
Via Roma
Via de' Calzaiuoli
Via de' Pecori
Via de' Vecchietti
Via dei Pescioni
Via de' Tornabuoni
Via degli Strozzi
Piazza della Repubblica
Via de' Brunelleschi
Via del Campidoglio
Piazza dell' Olio
Via de' Cerchi
Piazza dei Cavalieri
Via de' Medici
Via de' Speziali
Via del Corso
Via de' Donati
Piazza di San Donato
Via dello Studio
Via de' Bonizi
Via de' Banchi
Via dei Campanile
Piazza del Duomo
Piazza di San Giovanni
Misericordia di Firenze
Piazza del Adimari
Via degli Albenghi
Via dell' Oche
Via Santa Elisabetta
Piazza Santa Elisabetta
Via del Giglio
Via Santa Elisabetta
Via della Canonica
Piazza del Capitolo
Piazza di S. Benedetto
Piazza delle Pallottole
Chiesa di SS Michele e Gaetano
Piazza di Santa Maria Maggiore
Piazza degli Antinori
Piazza San Pancrazio
Palazzo Rucellai
Via del Parione

244

A   B   C   D

1

Via Melegnano
Borgo Ognissanti   149
161
Via Montebello
151   141
Lungarno Amerigo Vespucci
Piazza
d'Ognissanti
154   B.go Ognissanti
116
Lungarno di S Rosa
Via Sant' Onofrio

97
Via Porcellana
11
8
103
Piazza di
San Paolino
Ospedale di
San Giovanni di Dio
136
84

60
Via Palazzuolo
Piazza degli
Ottaviani
Piazza San
Pancrazio

Via delle Belle Donne
Via del Sole
Via della Spada
Via della Vigna Nuova
Via del Parione
Via Porta Rossa

Via degli Agli
Via de' Pecori
Via del Campidoglio
Piazza della
Repubblica
Via de' Sassetti
Via delle Terme
Borgo SS Apostoli

Via de' Tornabuoni
Via de' Pescioni
Via Roma
Via Speziali
Via Calimala
Via Pellicceria
Via Por Santa Maria

2

Via L. Bartolini
di Verzaia
Piazza
del Tiratoio
59
Via del Piaggione
163   93
13
Piazza di
Cestello
147   Piazza
de' Nerli
Borgo San Frediano
Via San Giovanni
Via dell'Orto
76

Lungarno Soderini
Arno
Ponte alla
Carraia

137
Piazza Carlo
Goldoni
Lungarno Corsini
Ponte
Santa Trinita
Lungarno Acciaiuoli
Ponte
Vecchio
Lungarno Archibusieri

San Frediano
177
85
Via del Drago d'Oro
Via del Leone
74 83
Piazza del
Carmine
P
Via Santa Monica
Piazza
Piattellina
113 20
157
4
162 Piazza
N Sauro
79
158
171   **Santo Spirito**
Via dello Santo Spirito
139
92
6   Piazza
Scarlatti
Piazza
de' Frescobaldi
Borgo San Jacopo
Lungarno Guicciardini
Borgo della Stella

3

165   58
Piazza
Torquato
Tasso
101
104
Via dell'Ardiglione
Via de' Serragli
Via S Agostino
Via della Chiesa
Via Minima
Via di Camaldoli

Piazza
Santo Spirito
90
106
159
Mercato
dell'Antiquariato
Via delle Caldaie
44
Via Mazzetta
Via de' Preto di S Martino
Via de' Velluti
Via Sguazza
5
10
Via Michelozzi
100
Sor de' Pitti
19
45
16
34
Piazza di
Santa Felicità
Corridoio
Vasariano
26
Piazza
dei Rossi
Costa di San Giorgio

4

Via Giano della Bella
Viale Francesco Petrarca
176
Via del Campuccio
Giardino
Torrigiani
Santa Maria
Via delle Caldaie
Via de' Serragli
Borgo Tegolaio
12
150
Piazza
San Felice
Via de' Guicciardini
Piazza
de' Pitti
Palazzo
Pitti
2 23
49
24   39

29

Via Forte di
San Giorgio
Forte di
Belvedere
21
Porta San
Giorgio
Vic della Cava

5

Via V Monti
Via Ugo Foscolo
Via del Ronco
Via della Meridiana
Via del Poggio Imperiale
Via de' Serragli
Piazza
della Calza
53
Piazzale
di Porta
Romana
P
Via Romana
Viale dei Cipressi
Giardino di Boboli
(Boboli Gardens)
Isolotto
Viale del Pellami
Fontana del
Forcone
35
Via di San Leonardo
Via Madonna della Pace
Via del Mascherino
Via del Bobolino
Via del Bobolino
Chiesa di San
Leonardo

6

66
Via Dante
Via Cantagalli
Via Senese
Via Michele di Lando
Viale Nicolò Machiavelli
Istituto
d'Arte
30

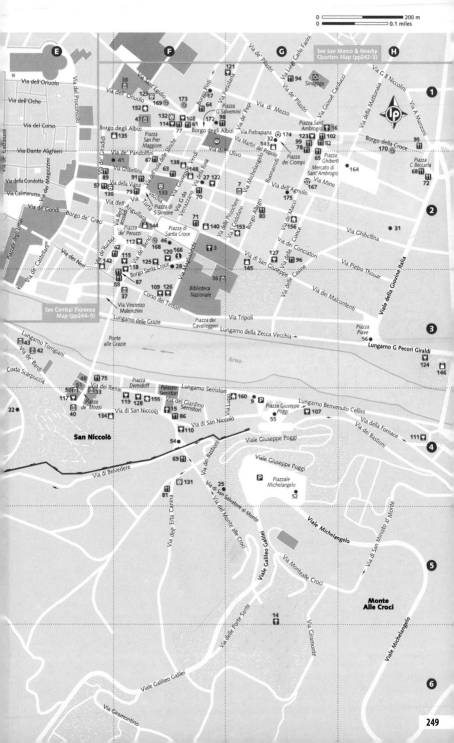

Via dell'Oriuolo
Via dell'Oche
Via del Corso
Via Sant'Egidio
Via dell'Oriuolo
Via dei Servi
Via de' Pilastri
Via Luigi Carlo Farini
Via G B Niccolini
Via della Mattonaia
Via A Manzoni
Via Giosuè Carducci

Via dei Lanzauoli
Via Dante Alighieri
Via dei Proconsolo
Borgo degli Albizi
Borgo Pinti
Via Fiesolana
Via de' Pepi
Via di Mezzo
Sinagoga
Piazza
G Salvemini
Piazza Sant'Ambrogio

38
129
152
47
173
169
114 132 108
77
64
97
94
16
123
99
78
102
82

Via della Condotta
Via Calimaruzza
Via de' Gondi
Borgo de' Greci
Via dei Magazzini
Via de' Giraldi
Via de' Pandolfini
Borgo degli Albizi
Via Pietrapiana
Piazza
San Pier
Maggiore
Via Martini del Popolo
Via dell'Olivo
Piazza
dei Ciompi
Mercato di
Sant'Ambrogio
Piazza
Ghiberti

135
41
67
138
174
32
143
65
164
95
68
72

Via Ghibellina
Via della Vigna
Via dell'Anguillara
Torta S Simone
Via Giuseppe Verdi
Via de' Isola delle Stinche
Via G da Verrazzano
Via de' Macci
Via dell'Agnolo
Via de' Conti
Via Pietro Thouar
Via Ghibellina

57
89
130
91
73
63
133
148
27
122
7
175
156
31

Piazza
de' Peruzzi
Piazza di
Santa Croce
Borgo Allegri
Via delle Pinzochere
Via Ghibellina
Via de' Ruzci
Via de' Benci
Via dell'Agnolo
Via de' Conciatori
Via dei Malcontenti
Viale della Giovine Italia

144
112
168
120 166
3
153
80
127
96
145

62
142
115
125
28
88
37
87
109 126
Biblioteca
Nazionale
36
Via San Giuseppe Casine

Borgo Santa Croce
Corso dei Tintori
Via Vincenzo
Malenchini
Lungarno delle Grazie
Piazza dei
Cavalleggeri
Via Tripoli
Lungarno della Zecca Vecchia
Piazza
Piave
56
Lungarno G Pecori Giraldi

Lungarno Torrigiani
Via de' Bardi
Costa Scarpuccia
Ponte
alle Grazie
Arno
124
146

50
51
117
40
48
33
75
Via dei Renai
119 128 155
134
Piazza
Demidoff
Piazza
de' Mozzi
Palazzo
Serristori
Lungarno Serristori
Via del Giardino
Serristori
15
86
Via Lungo
160
Piazza Giuseppe
Poggi
55
Lungarno Benvenuto Cellini
107
Via della Fornace
Via dei Bastioni
111

22
San Niccolò
Via di San Niccolò
110
54
69
131
81
25
Via di San Niccolò
Viale Giuseppe Poggi
Viale Giuseppe Poggi
Piazzale
Michelangelo
52
Via di San Salvatore al Monte
Via del Bastioni
Via di Belvedere
Via dell'Erta Canina
Via delle Porte Sante
Via del Monte alle Croci
Viale Michelangelo
Via di San Miniato al Monte
Viale Michelangelo

14
Monte
Alle Croci

Viale Galileo Galilei
Via Monteaalle Croci
Via Ciramonte
Viale Galileo Galilei
Via Giramontino

See Central Florence
Map (pp244-5)